RICHARD

The First Ward IV

His
Lips
Forgot
The
Taste
Of
Truth

❧❦❧

The First Ward IV
is dedicated to the memory of

my mother

Jeanne Schuteker Sullivan Schwartz

and my father

David J. Sullivan

whose ancestors live once more in the characters and events in this volume.

Other Books
by Richard Sullivan:

The First Ward I
The First Ward II: Fingy Conners & The New Century
The First Ward III: Murderers, Scoundrels and Ragamuffins
Driving & Discovering Hawaii: Oahu
Oahu Spectacular Beaches: Driving & Discovering Hawaii
Driving & Discovering Hawaii: Maui and Molokai
Reclaim Your Youth: Growing Younger After 40
Family Tree Secrets & Genealogy Search Tips

The First Ward IV: His Lips Forgot The Taste Of Truth
by
Richard Sullivan

First Edition
EntireBookCopyright©2019RichardSullivan

Montgomery Ewing Publishers
montgomeryewing@ymail.com

No part of this work or publication may be reproduced, stored or transmitted in any form or by any means whether digital or analog without prior permission of the publisher Montgomery Ewing Publishers LLC.
"Mutual Rowing Club" is a trademark of the Sullivan Family Trust.

ISBN-13: 978-1974190126

ISBN-10: 1974190129

Montgomery Ewing

ACKNOWLEGEMENTS

At the dawn of the 20th Century in the United States, the localized idioms, phrases and habits in use in both speaking and writing were quite unique. Varying from neighborhood to neighborhood and publication to publication, so distinctive are these from the homogenized mainstream language that we know today that any attempt to mimic this unexampled prose is destined to end in failure. As a writer I have tried, but found it impossible at times to successfully paraphrase or adapt early 1900s language into my own author's voice in a manner or style faithful to the colorful inimitable original. Therefore I acknowledge I have freely purloined phrases and entire sentences from unnamed published news writers of the day to whom I would gladly give credit had a byline appeared alongside their news story. Unfortunately this was rarely the case.

Transcriptions of actual news articles are sprinkled throughout every volume of The First Ward series including this one, *His Lips Forgot The Taste Of Truth*. Although ultimately a work of fiction, the copious use of actual historical figures, facts, and reported news events lies at the heart of my The First Ward series.

It is especially vexing to accept that so authoritarian a figure as Fingy Conners, who had his four-fingered hand in every pocket and his threatening fist in everyone's face, could have disappeared into the mists of time so unpunished, so richly rewarded for his chicanery. The characters in The First Ward are my ancestors, whether through blood or marriage, including the infamous Fingy. You can visit virtually the entire cast of characters at Holy Cross Cemetery in Lackawanna NY if so inclined.

I am indebted to my cousin Corky Connors whose stories, as told him by his grandfather Harry Bullen in the 1930s about events connected to Fingy Conners, contributed invaluably to this series. Equally valuable were the recollections of my brother Dennis C. Sullivan and my late cousin Mildred Driscoll.

A special appreciation goes to Mary Lou Woelfel who entrusted me with a handwritten history of life in Buffalo's Old First Ward as authored by her many family members, and to Joe Coutrara of Vincennes Street for sharing with me his remembrances of the Beaches and of the Mutual Rowing Club boathouse on South Street.

The First Ward series would not be possible without the accomplishments of Tom Tryniski <www.fultonhistory.com> and his online newspaper archive Fulton Postcards. On his own, with no funding from any outside source, Mr. Tryniski had as of 2019 archived 44 million newspaper pages from his home in Fulton NY, all searchable online. By contrast, The US Library of Congress has received $22 million in public funding as of 2015 to archive only a fraction of that number of news pages.

SPECIAL THANKS

to my friends, relatives and fans
for their various contributions and moral support:

Elizabeth Baker
Corky Connors
Dennis C. Sullivan
Donna Sullivan
Mildred Driscoll
Patricia Driscoll-Carveth
Jeannie Datz-Rice
Norman Carby
Steve Hoban
Steven Whelan
Sonja Stieglitz
Dorothy Wolf Nelson
Ken Baron

Most especially I wish to thank my sister

Barbara Sullivan

or her tireless promotion, support and encouragement.

The First Ward IV

AND SO, ON IT CONTINUES...IN THE FIRST WARD

The two-story brick structure at photo center is the Mutual Rowing Club.
Tents have been erected for a rowing regatta being held that day.
The house with the streaked roof to the extreme right is that of
Alderman John P. Sullivan.
The Barcolo factory is seen in the background.
The Buffalo River is at left.
This photo was taken from atop a hoist at the Buffalo Union Furnace.
Photo courtesy of Dorothy Wolf Nelson.

Buffalo Police Dept. Chief Mike Regan and Detective Jim Sullivan are drawn into a missing child case in neighboring Lackawanna due to the small town's limited resources and incompetent police chief. The boy's family go to extraordinary lengths in their search, hounding the clueless Lackawanna Chief to not allow the case to go unsolved. The scenario ends in horror and tragedy with the region in an uproar. Baffling missteps and stunning coincidences mark the sorry episode.

Unsuspected drunken serial killer *J. Frank Hickey* is arrested by Buffalo *Detective Jim Sullivan* in a brawl. While in jail Hickey brags about his committing a recent child murder, but the police higher-ups fail to take him seriously, releasing him to continue his attacks on children for another ten years. Regardless of his being blameless in the matter, Detective Sullivan is deemed in part responsible anyway for what ultimately transpires. Worn down by the incessant tragedies he's encountered as a police officer, Sullivan once again takes the helm at the Mutual Rowing Club as its president for a much-needed diversion.

As he becomes immortalized in popular culture, *Fingy Conners'* living legend of cruelty grows. His lies go too far for once, costing him his political career. Truth be told, Conners doesn't need political office in order to bulldoze over people or create chaos.

David J. Nugent, rescued from imminent penitentiary incarceration by his mentor and wife Minnie's uncle Fingy Conners, fails to recognize his good fortune, steamrolling over his family regardless. Fingy betrays his niece *Minnie Hayes-Nugent* ordering her to do the unthinkable, leading to her three sons ending up hospitalized.

Hannah Sullivan's friend *Ruth McGowan* is tracked down by the brutal prostitute mother who threw her out into the streets as a young girl, and is dragged into court for failing to provide the woman shelter and financial support in her old age.

Alderman John J. Kennedy is elected Treasurer of New York State despite knowing nothing at all about New York State's finances—or even the basics of its banking system. Once he's exposed, Fingy Conners throws him under the bus.

Alderman John P. Sullivan is forced out of city government after twenty-five years, but not before he and his cronies feverishly line their pockets. Hannah and Jim Sullivan's eldest son Jim Jr. accepts a marriage of convenience. His reward is a runaway bride.

The worldwide Spanish Flu epidemic of 1918 wreaks havoc. Emergency measures are quickly put into place, but regardless the disease's swift spread takes a terrible toll on the city. The Sullivan family loses a beloved son.

William J. "Fingy" Conners

The Principal Characters

Fingy Conners
Millionaire labor contractor, thug, shipping magnate, newspaper publisher, Chairman of the Democratic Party of New York State, murderer.

Minnie-Hayes-Nugent
Fingy Conners' orphaned niece

David J. Nugent
Minnie's husband, Fingy Conners' top henchman & Hannah Nugent Sullivan's brother

Brothers
John P. Sullivan, Alderman
and
Jim Sullivan, Detective-Sergeant, BPD

Hannah Nugent Sullivan
Wife of Detective Jim Sullivan and sister of David J. Nugent

Jim Jr., Nellie and David Nugent Sullivan
Hannah and Detective Jim Sullivan's children,

Ruth McGowan
Hannah Sullivan's best friend and neighbor

John J. Kennedy
Former Alderman; State Treasurer of New York

Michael Regan
Buffalo Chief of Police

J. Frank Hickey
Serial killer

The Joseph Family:
George & Nezla
Nora, Edward and Joey

Conners-Nugent-Sullivan Tree

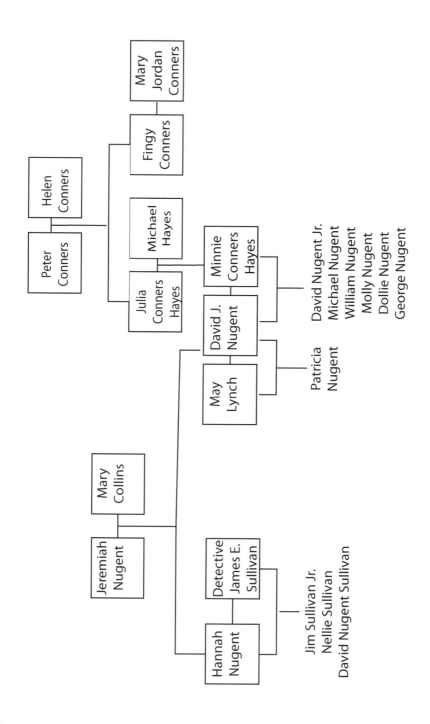

MICHAEL KRUCK

The Newsboy

On the afternoon of December 19th, 1902, J. Frank Hickey celebrated his successful escape from the clutches of the New York City police to the safe haven and anonymity of Buffalo 400 miles west by getting himself dead drunk. As he threw back, he pictured in his mind the pretty little boy lying dead in the snow, and he smiled.

He was seated at a table in a Seneca Street saloon near the boarding house wherein he had just taken a room. He brooded beneath the boughs of holly, drinking liberally. He sampled the complimentary crackers from the small bowl set before him, breaking off chunks using the one and only tooth remaining from his uppers.

The saloon proprietor was in a cheery holiday mood. This irritated Hickey no end. The saloonkeep hummed along with the music as he installed colorful strings of pear-shaped carbon filament Santa Claus Electric Candles around the periphery of the mirror behind the bar. More of the same awaited their edging around the street-facing windows, a junction box at the ready to connect the multiple light strings.

The wooden boxes that had held the lights rested empty on the adjoining table within Hickey's reach. The colorful end label portrayed three small children dressed in sailor outfits decorating a perfect Christmas tree. The depiction of the boy especially caught Hickey's eye. He found the young man's image arousing.

The saloon's proprietor busied himself to the accompaniment of Edison cylinders playing on an Edison phonograph; Joy To The World by the Edison Concert Band and Silent Night by the Edison Quartet. Hickey judged the scene contrived and depressing. Despite the irritating manufactured holiday joy he recollected with amusement the previous week and all that he had accomplished.

On December 10th previous, as daylight waned, Hickey had assumed a similar posture in one of New York City's finer saloons. The resort was located in the mid eighties—86th Street to be exact. Hickey was an educated man with a talent for highly technical things. In addition to collecting a fine mechanical engineer inspector's salary, he profited an additional $200 a week from graft. He did not hesitate to spend every penny.

I

It was not at all unusual for him to fritter away $100 in a single night in some oak-paneled, crystal-chandeliered establishment favored by Manhattan's upper classes. He won favor buying drinks for the house and entertaining fellow tipplers with his many stories. $100 at that time could have paid a full month's rent on a fine apartment right off New York's 5th Avenue. However, Hickey chose to live in a furnished room in some unexceptional boardinghouse. His passions required his remaining anonymous, unencumbered by worldly possessions, thus allowing him to move freely and often and on a moment's notice. Customarily as he drank, these passions ignited predictably, most notably his mania for squeezing the life out of little children—little male children.

Frank Hickey had been married at one time. His wife abandoned him for reasons left entirely unexplained by him. On the other hand he freely boasted of having sired a beloved son currently on the cusp of young manhood, a boy about whom he was exceedingly proud despite having abandoned him since the age of three. He bragged about him continually. Perhaps whenever Hickey happened to be in the midst of murdering a child it failed to enter his head how he himself might feel if his own cherished son suffered the great misfortune of encountering a demon much like himself. But then again, that's precisely why society classifies as monsters such low forms of human life as J. Frank Hickey.

Eleven year old French immigrant Michel Ricac Kruck customarily sold newspapers alongside his twelve-year-old brother Jule on the street for two hours each day after school, but on this particular afternoon he went out alone. He left his parents' apartment on the second floor of the dumbbell tenement house at 771 Columbus Avenue near Ninety-eighth street at four-forty-five in the afternoon. As he passed his father Henri's tailor shop at Ninety-eighth and Eighth, he poked his head inside to greet his Papa.

"*Je vais retourner...* uh, I'll be home by eight-thirty, Papa—as usual," the little boy chirped.

His father insisted the family all speak English, even amongst themselves at home. He was concerned about failing to assimilate. Upon arrival in New York, Henri immediately became Henry, Jule became Jimmy, and Michel became Michael. Henry worked diligently to lose as best he could his charming French accent. He had not yet fully realized what an asset such an affectation would prove in his particular profession.

The elder Kruck, busy with a customer, smiled and silently nodded his response to his son and sweetly waved him off. Michael continued happily on his way. He had taken 40 cents with him to purchase his supply of papers and for making change for his customers. It was his custom to buy his papers at Columbus and Eighty-first, after which he went to his beat at Eighty-sixth and 8th Avenue across from the entrance to Central Park. Contrary to his known habit, it seems he did not arrive at his established spot until shortly after eight o'clock, much later than usual. The punched streetcar transfer found later in his pocket attested to this unusual variance. He had retreated from his normal routine to buy a special Christmas present for his mother for which he'd been saving for six months, a gold crucifix on a neck chain.

J. Frank Hickey was the sort of drunk who showed little outward sign of inebriation even as his brain lost all reason. Shortly after 8 o'clock he exited the saloon in which he had spent the previous three hours guzzling. Kicking scampering rats out of his path he headed toward Central Park West. There on the corner, hoping to get rid of the last of his papers so he might go home for supper, stood Hickey's favorite prey, a newsboy, stomping his little feet against the freezing cold. The anticipation of the look on his mother's face come Christmas morning was more than enough to keep the little boy warm.

Newsboys were counted among some of America's most vulnerable citizens, some being as young as age six. The erroneous belief was widely held that mostly, newsboys were orphans. The majority of them in fact had families, and homes, and parents with bank accounts. There was a not-uncommon class of parent who demanded their boy go out on the street, rain or shine, and earn his keep. A fixed amount was expected to be brought home nightly. If the established goal was not met, a boy might receive a sound beating. This was not the case with Michael and Jimmy Kruck; the brothers gladly handed over twenty-five cents or more daily to their worry-prone but exceedingly kind mother Rosa.

In the big cities, ragamuffin newsboys could be found late at night still circulating in the saloons or plying the center aisle aboard streetcars hawking their papers. These children frequented some of the country's most dangerous and illicit resorts, often to their woeful disadvantage. In dark saloons they were all too often in peril of being overwhelmed by some drunken pervert, raped or beaten solely for the assaulter's intoxicated amusement. They had no defender to look out for them.

As traffic hurried by Hickey inched his way closer to the small-for-his-age Michael Kruck. No one paid any attention. Christmas shoppers intent on their main objective were out in droves. Streetcars rumbled and clanged beneath sparking overhead wires. Drivers of slip-sliding horse carriages jostled for right-of-way on the icy cobbles. Police officers busily entered and exited the adjacent Arsenal Police Station. These policemen did not deter Hickey in the slightest from his intended plan. Far from it. Their threatening presence provided the game a titillating measure of excitement. Brazen acts carried out amid public view produced in Hickey an electric charge.

Hickey said hello to Michael Kruck. He bought one of his papers with a dime and refused the change. Michael smiled broadly at his generosity. His mother would be very happy. The two chatted, the boy agreeing with whatever it was Hickey had to propose. No one but Michael and Hickey would ever know what that was exactly.

In previous encounters such as this Hickey had offered to buy all of a newsie's papers if only the boy would just unbutton his fly for him for five minutes. It was not known if Michael Kruck may have been propositioned in this particular manner, for when he was discovered shortly thereafter all of his clothing was entirely intact. But he did for whatever reason agree to accompany Hickey across the street and into the relative seclusion of Central Park.

The street lighting was exceptionally bright, what with a hard layer of reflective snow pack covering the ground. Finding an appropriately darkened spot might entail walking a few hundred yards into the park at the very least. Hickey's exhibitionist character however did not obligate this precaution. And so just yards from the entrance of the busy Arsenal Police Station, with its continual flow of police officers coming and going, within a minor depression visible from the sidewalk along Central Park West to anyone who cared to know what was going on there, the little newsboy bent to place his canvas newspaper sack down onto the snow.

The child momentarily distracted, Hickey took his chance. He encircled his victim's neck, squeezing and throttling the little fellow brutally, quelling the boy's ability to scream. Shocked, Michael tried his best to fight, but the experienced, practiced, iron-gripped Hickey knew precisely how to control the now-familiar exercise.

As the boy began to slip from consciousness, Hickey, savage beast that he was, chomped hard onto Michael's innocent face like a dog crazed by hydrophobia, sinking his single evil yellowed upper tooth deeply into the flesh of the boy's right cheek. He held his prey like that, embedded and immobilized. He became aroused by the taste of his captive's blood. Panting with delirious excitement he ingested the anguished tears that poured copiously from the dying boy's woebegone eyes. Hickey's hands, even as strong and experienced as they were, grew tired and aching, but he held fast until the boy became dead weight.

The killer sought assurance that the child was good and dead before he dared disengage his fatal grip. As he ultimately did so, his hands at long-last relaxed. He extracted his fang from Michael's innocent trusting face and allowed the boy to slump to the ground onto the hard-trampled snow.

Hickey stood above him admiring his handiwork for some long moments as he luxuriated in the primitive tastes yet glazing his mouth.

He bent over to rearrange the body so that it might appear the newsboy was merely asleep. He grasped the sack with its bundle of newspapers, lifted the child's head, and arranged the canvas bag under it as if it were a pillow.

"Sleep well, my little one," he murmured.

At that same moment he spotted a policeman approaching on the bridle path. The copper was not looking in his direction. The murderer skittered in the direction opposite. Rather than keep running, as both logic and instinct might demand, he calmly hid himself in the snow-covered shrubbery. From that point of vantage he commenced observing the entire investigation with great exhilaration.

As Patrolman Bernard Koerstiger drew closer he noticed something odd. There appeared to be a dark figure lying on the snow. At first he assumed a drunk had passed out.

"Hope the poor bugger ain't already froze to death," he worried aloud to himself. But as he reached the collapsed form he realized that it was a little boy. Aggressive rats squealed and scattered as he swatted them away.

"Getcher fuckin' damn selfs outa here, yous devils!" he hollered.

He crouched down to check for signs of life. A silk kerchief was tied loosely around the boy's neck. Koerstiger had to move it to access Michael's carotid artery. He discerned no pulse, yet the child was quite warm. Spotting fellow policeman William Parker at a distance, Koerstiger called out to him. Parker came running. Examining the boy for himself and feeling his warmth, Parker ran back to the station to call for an ambulance. Dr. Van Ingan, who responded, pronounced the boy dead, but stated that the end had come just a few short minutes before.

The path alongside where Michael was found was frequented often by the workmen in the workshops at the Reservoir Station. The shallow excavation in which Michael lay was just a few yards off the pathway. Koerstiger had already begun to categorize in his head those workmen whom he had previously presumed suspicious.

More policemen arrived on the scene. They searched the ground in the area and the approaches for any clue. The ground, frozen hard with icy snow, imprinted no footsteps or other indication or clue, no sign of who had been there, nor even any suggestion that a scuffle might have taken place. They observed bruises on the boy's throat and a laceration on his cheek. There were no other obvious marks of violence nor any indication that his clothing had been disarranged or undone.

Defying all common sense the police determined then and there that the boy had died of natural causes.

Hickey bristled with excitement as some of the officers came within yards of his hiding place in their search. He held his breath until they retreated. The boy's body was removed. Ultimately the cops gave up their scant investigation and vacated the area. Determining that it was safe to emerge, Hickey gathered himself and casually strolled away, smug in his cleverness at having avoided detection yet again.

※※※

Michael Kruck usually returned home from his newsboy duties by nine o'clock at the latest. That particular evening he did not. By nine thirty his mother became worried. She sent Michael's brother Jimmy out to look for him.

Jimmy could find no trace.

At midnight, Michael's father returned home to the family apartment from his shop. Jimmy was still out looking. Henry showed concern upon learning that Michael had not yet returned, but was not unduly worried. He calmed his Rosa.

"He's with Jimmy. They'll be home soon enough, *cherie*," he stated confidently. "Come, let's go to bed."

Now worried about both sons, Rosa managed to fall asleep despite her concerns as the result of an exhausting day of doing the family laundry.

Jimmy returned home alone sometime later. He felt relief finding the apartment quiet save for his father's snoring. Everyone was sound asleep. He naturally assumed Michael had returned home while he had been out looking for him. He felt his way past lines of laundry hanging to dry and into the darkened bedroom where his parents and two sisters lay slumbering in the dark. He took to his straw mattress on the floor and went out like a light.

At five o'clock the following morning Rosa awoke with a start as if having received a voltaic jolt. She jumped out of bed to discover Jimmy asleep. Michael was nowhere to be found.

"Jule! Jule! Wake up!" She shook him from a deep slumber. *"Où se trouve Michel? Où est-il?"*

Groggily, Jimmy looked around, confused. Michael's mattress was vacant.

"I thought he was here, *maman*. I thought he came home while I was out looking for him. When I came home everyone was sound asleep, so I assumed he was here!" he exclaimed guiltily.

The commotion woke the rest of the family.

"Henri! Wake up! Michel is not yet home!" she exclaimed in a panic.

Without a word Henry shot from the bed trying to disguise his alarm from the children. He dressed in a flash and immediately left to visit the close-by West 100th Street police station to report his son's disappearance. He quickly returned home to find his wife distraught over a story in the morning newspaper about the discovery of a boy answering Michael's description found murdered in Central Park near 85th Street. They were well aware that this was Michael's customary territory. Together the panic-stricken parents hastened to the Arsenal Station. From there they were taken to the Morgue, where in hysterics, they identified their little boy's body. They were horrified at the bite wound on his sweet face and the bruises around his neck.

"*Mon enfant a été assassiné!* My boy he is murdered!" Rosa Kruck shrieked.

The police disagreed.

The cops still maintained that Michael had died of natural causes. They insisted to the Krucks in their all-knowing and infuriatingly condescending manner that the boy had "expired from cold and exhaustion," despite the fact that the police officers stated they had found Michael's skin warm to the touch.

Upon hearing this preposterous theory after seeing with their own eyes the vicious and obviously human bite mark on Michael's ghostly face and the dark bruises on his neck, the appalled parents concluded the police were incompetent, if not downright criminal in their stupidity. Isolated and alone in their shock and disbelief, they returned home to grieve and question and fume and await the release of their little boy's body for burial.

Dr. E.T. Higgins completed the autopsy at five-thirty o'clock that same afternoon. While not in as good a physical condition as a child of more prosperous parents might be, he concluded Michael had not been ill-nourished despite finding his stomach empty. All his organs were in a healthy condition.

Coroner Higgins' statement concluded, "The child died of asphyxia due to violence. In other words to strangulation. It was the result from all appearances of a leather thong or cord or whip drawn around the throat. The marks indicate that it must have been a knotty piece, for the black indentations are not fingerprints. There was a most peculiar bruise on the boy's right cheek. I cannot explain it—it is one of the most puzzling wounds I have ever seen. It is somewhat like a laceration and there is the suggestion in its nature of the possibility that it was caused by a bite of one of the incisor teeth of a man or perhaps an animal. It was an ante-mortem wound and I cannot understand it. Microscopic examination will be made."

Initially insisting that a knotted cord was used to strangle Michael, the coroner soon enough changed his mind about the nature of the bruises. Photographs were taken of the "ape-like" manual contusions on Michael's neck and shoulder, inflicted by someone's right hand. Fingerprints were detected therein and were preserved photographically as per the new Scotland Yard method.

An expensive cigar stub found at the scene of the newsboy's murder was soon hailed as a monumental clue. "Find the owner of the cigar and you will find the murderer!" declared one New York yellow sheet. In fact, the bridle path was trafficked daily and heavily by many a well-to-do man, and for its entire length it was littered with hundreds of such stubs.

On the morning following little Michael Kruck's murder, J. Frank Hickey, a native of Lowell, Massachusetts, hastily boarded a train for the familiar territory of Boston in order to cool his heels and think. Two days later, having collected himself, he returned to New York and his lucrative engineering inspector's job. He visited the library daily to study all the newspapers reporting the details of Michael Kruck's murder investigation to learn exactly what might be known, and to delight in the loathsome effect his savage act had inflicted upon the boy's distraught family. He noted that they were set to bury him at the Washington Jewish Cemetery in Brooklyn.

Hickey, as a result of his ongoing perverted obsession, cared not to spend a significant amount of time in any given place. His training and experience allowed for him to procure well-paid employment wherever he might end up—this having proved an ideal circumstance for a habitual murderer of children. Uninterested in amassing any worldly goods other than what might fit inside a valise, Hickey's fleeing to a new place impetuously presented no obstacles. The ease with which he was able to secure employment combined with the specialized jobs' high salaries instilled in him a take-it or leave-it attitude toward whatever position in whatever city he held at any given time. Hickey's twisted pleasures took all precedence.

Soon enough he read in the *Evening Telegram* that the police had found important clues at the scene of the murder. This news gave him pause. In his mind he went over every detail he could recall of his debauch, but in the end was forced to concede that his state of inebriation at the time of the murder might be responsible for lapses in memory. When on the following day the *Telegram* announced that the police had zeroed in on a suspect and that an arrest was imminent, Hickey quickly packed up and fled to Grand Central Station. There he hopped aboard the New York Central for Buffalo. Upon arrival he rented a room on Seneca Street. True to his patterns he spent significant time in saloons in that area, and also true to his patterns, he took to drunkenly bragging to his saloon mates, much to his own detriment.

※※※

Police Detectives Jim Sullivan and Jerry Lynch found themselves on Seneca Street at about three o'clock in the afternoon inspecting pawnshops for suspect merchandise. Three men's cashmere overcoats had been shoplifted from the big Kleinhans store on Lafayette Square. The detectives were keen on locating these. Upon exiting one Shylock's emporium, they witnessed a commotion spilling out onto the street at Langley's Saloon next door. A drunken brawl was taking place. In their attempt to break it up the officers were interfered with by a small bookish man wearing spectacles who, in an officious manner, questioned their authority. The little man, although not involved in the brawl, soon became combative with the detectives. He appeared extremely inebriated. They placed him under arrest along with the others and took the trio to Headquarters. The prisoner gave his name as J. Frank Hickey of Boston Massachusetts.

Hickey was placed in a cell in the third floor "freezer" with one of the other combatants. The third brawler was secured in the adjoining cell, solo. Both brawlers' manners were by this time subdued, whereas Hickey see-sawed unpredictably between mania and delirium. As the deranged prisoner ranted and railed to his semiconscious cell mate he recited the name of Michael Kruck and declared himself the murderer of the little New York City newsboy. This murder had been headline news in the previous week's *Buffalo Courier*.

The guard on duty instantly called down to Chief of Detectives Patrick Cusak who dispatched Detectives Sullivan and Lynch back up to the third floor.

"That drunk yous put in the freezer is sayin' he murdered a newsie—go on up there 'n' try an' get him to talk," ordered Cusak.

Sullivan and Lynch seated themselves outside the cell and attempted to engage Hickey in conversation. He would only repeat what he had previously stated and nothing more, that he had killed the newsboy Michael Kruck. Then he fell fast asleep.

The detectives were well aware of the Kruck case.

"I'll call," stated Jim Sullivan.

"You go right ahead there, Sully," acquiesced Lynch. Jerry handed over a small leather covered notebook wherein he had scribbled Hickey's details. He idled nearby as Sullivan placed a call to the New York City police.

NYPD Inspector James McCafferty took the call. His ears pricked up when he heard the newsboy's name. It was the break McCafferty had been waiting for. The Inspector instantly dispatched Detective Sergeant Arthur Carey to Buffalo with instructions that he remain in the suspect's cell until a complete history of his doings at the time of the Kruck boy's murder could be obtained from him.

The following morning, refreshed and sober, Hickey was no longer in a chatty mood. As Sullivan and Lynch questioned him once more, he denied having said anything. He claimed that he had earned a reputation as someone who spouted nonsense when drunk. He went so far as to say when inebriated he recited details from stories from the newspapers by habit, and since he had recently read about the murder of the newsboy, that might well explain it.

When Detective Carey arrived in Buffalo he was escorted to Hickey's jail cell post haste. Hickey kept his mouth shut except to vehemently deny he knew anything whatsoever about the Kruck case, despite his previous admission to Sullivan and Lynch. As the hours ticked by, Carey never ceased haranguing Hickey, but the prisoner just as stubbornly protected his vile secret.

Hickey was released the following day after paying a fine. Detective Carey's hopes were crushed. There was no evidence on which to hold Hickey other than a drunken rant. Carey brooded all the way back to New York, worrying that McCafferty, with whom he had recently been at odds, might use his failure to get anything useful out of Hickey detrimentally against him.

From jail Hickey returned to his rooms at 437 Seneca Street to plan his next move. He sat in the window pleasuring himself, his eyes following with excitement the progress of a handsome Italian newsboy with the words *Buffalo Express* emblazoned on his canvas sack making his way from saloon to saloon, peddling his papers.

Next door at that very moment at N° 435 Seneca, Nezla Joseph, an immigrant from Syria, announced to her husband George that she was expecting a baby, their third.

"I can feel it in my bones, dear husband. He is a boy. You will have another son."

HIS LIPS FORGOT THE TASTE OF TRUTH

JNO. J. KENNEDY, Buffalo.

O'Doul's Cafe

Alderman John J. Kennedy had been prone to bouts of depression ever since boyhood. Popular, affable and universally well-liked, weeks could go by when he commiserated with others hardly at all, including members of his own family. There were instances he'd beg off his turn to speak at Common Council meetings despite heading the body as its President. Other times he remained away from his saloon, his home, and city hall for days at a stretch, even while serving as acting Mayor of the city. Nobody could find him and no one knew the whereabouts of his retreats or hideouts, except perhaps his tight-lipped confidant, Alderman John P. Sullivan.

JP had known Kennedy his entire life. As teenagers he had envied the older boy for his handsome looks and sensitive spirit.

"If only he possessed the proper sort of stone-cold heart to accompany that remarkable face, there's no telling what heights he might achieve," Sullivan liked to joke.

Kennedy was tethered to Fingy Conners as securely as a newborn to its mother's teat, despite their at-times mutual disdain for one another.

It was during Kennedy's bouts with darkness that JP would cunningly seek some advantage. Contrarily it was during such episodes that Kennedy would predictably grow more talkative than usual with JP. He would sometimes reveal, along with useful political strategies, precious tidbits of the complicated history between himself and Fingy Conners, things he might otherwise never have divulged.

So it was no coincidence when JP ran into his depressed colleague in a corridor at Buffalo city hall. It had been clear to JP that Kennedy was again in the midst of one of his somber moods. JP took the initiative.

"Some days I just can't tolerate all this damned blusterin' and malarkey in the Council chamber, Kize, and today's one of them. How's about you and me we run away for an hour, friend? Let me buy you a nice lunch over at O'Doul's."

While under the spell of his moody periods Kennedy was understood to recoil from social interactions. Sullivan was equally known for his ability to lighten even the heaviest situation and for being a skilled, sincere and good-natured charmer. Even though O'Doul's luncheonette faced busy Shelton Square across from the Guaranty Building's Turkish Baths, which were well patronized by the finer denizens of the city hall, none of the politicians frequented that particular café. O'Doul's was a place where Kennedy knew he could count on avoiding acquaintances. He would be relieved there from having to put on a social face. JP Sullivan knew well how to read people, especially his friends, and he offered Kennedy exactly what he needed at that particular moment.

"Let's get outa here, Kize. Let's find us a dark corner and enjoy a fine Cuban and a few beers. We'd both do well to extricate ourselves from the clutches of these vultures for an interval."

As they made their way past the terracotta-cladded Louis Sullivan Guaranty Building, JP upheld the entire conversation, keeping it light. He again referred to the famed architect as his cousin, although there was never any proof offered of such a blood relation. JP would seize any opportunity to promote himself, stretching the truth or even lying outright if it suited him. He had met Louis Sullivan once during an aldermen's trip to Chicago, and impressed with the architect's fame and his extraordinarily handsome looks, "adopted" his family namesake right there on the spot.

O'Doul's was buzzing. One or two customers gave the well-dressed men a brief once-over upon entering but nobody bothered them. JP ordered two hot dogs with sauerkraut and warm German potato salad. Kennedy chose a ham sandwich with a double portion of Swiss cheese and asked that the mustard pot be brought to the table and left. When his plate was set down in front of him, Kennedy took the large pickle, dipped it deep into the pot, stirred it around, took a generous bite, wiped the yellow from his moustache with his napkin, then repeated the ceremony.

Halfway through his consuming the pickle, something caught his eye. He put the pickle aside, picked up the mustard pot, stuck his index finger into it and swirled it around until he'd fished out a huge ugly black fly, long dead. Reaching beneath the table he deposited it there atop an inconspicuous ledge where already resided lumps of ancient chewing gum, childrens' rejected vegetables and other hoary relics that no one in the midst of enjoying his lunch wishes to picture. Then, without cleaning his finger he picked up the pickle and resumed dipping.

The two old comrades talked. JP sustained the bulk of the conversation, praising his two eldest sons, expressing concern about spoiled daughter Mazie's newly running wild, and ruminating about certain neighbors. Cagily, he avoided talk of work entirely.

Kennedy in turn resorted to long ago memories of what, filtered through the mists of time, he now recalled as having been simpler days, although some might argue. He recounted boyhood adventures on the Great Lakes when as mere children he and Fingy Conners ran off together to the working life aboard Great Lakes passenger steamers. JP provided Kize his full attention, smiling at his stories, Kennedy brightening considerably as he told them. His doldrums began to lift a little.

Kize Kennedy had never discussed the infamous meat cleaver incident that provided Fingy Conners his nickname. He had chopped off Conners' thumb on a brazen adolescent dare. JP had long awaited an opportunity to steer Kennedy in that direction and take advantage of his vulnerability to finally hear the tale straight from the horse's mouth, but something else nearly as satisfying came up instead.

"Me and Fingy didn't just decide on a lark one day to run off and have us a grand adventure on the lakes, JP. My mother had at that time recently died of the cancer. She suffered somethin' awful whilst my father turned his back on us and drank away his troubles and temper and all his wages. He'd abandon his work on the docks at ten o'clock in the morning to drown himself in brew at some Ganson Street saloon, then soon enough get himself fired for never returnin' to the job."

"Didn't your father work for his brother?" asked JP.

"Not…well, yes—but at that time my mother was sick he had long since been banished from my uncle's grain contracting business, as well as his life. So Pa drifted from one job to the next after that. We had no money, no food, no coal in winter, and I was left to care for my poor Ma all by myself. My Pa told stories of bein' bitterly wronged by his brother that I believed at the time. He forbade me from having any contact with him or my cousins, so I hardly knew them back then. He forbade me to go to them and ask for help, even when my Ma was in a terrible state, sufferin' so. With me own stomach growlin' empty 'n' hollow I walked the rails at dawn in the dead of winter, scourin' the snow for dropped coal so's to try and keep my Ma warm, prayin' to God the coppers didn't catch me up and cart me off to jail, for as you know, scavenging for coal in train yards was a criminal offense. And that was tough for a twelve year old, JP. To feel alone and so helpless, unable to make my one and only dear sweet mother…"

He stopped there for a moment to prevent the tears from flowing, taking a big gulp of his beer. He'd barely gnawed at the sandwich but had entirely devoured the pickle.

When recomposed he continued his story.

"My mother was dead but a few days when me and Fingy set to goin' wild, gettin' into all sorts of trouble, stealin', settin' things afire, gettin' into brawls. I was completely alone then, with him my only friend, so we was both very accommodatin' when either of us would proffer some novel stunt.

"He was always at odds with his Ma and Pa, Fingy was, stealin' candy from his mother's little store to sell to other kids at school, sufferin' the whippins of his father whenever old man Conners caught him doin' somethin' worse even than the previous time, receivin' the threats of the other parents in the neighborhood after Fingy had beat up their son or mishandled their daughter. Fingy and his father were a match to a striker, so much so that whenever they came together there was a burst of flame. And I may use those words as a metaphor, JP, but one of the interests that most fascinated Fingy was fire buggin', as you well know yourself."

JP nodded in agreement.

"And he lied about everything—to his parents, the neighbors, to the other kids—even *me*. Sometimes with him I didn't know up from down or right from left. He lied so often and so relentlessly that somewheres along the way I swear his lips forgot the taste of truth."

Kennedy paused in silent thought. Not wishing to stem the flow of his seldom-disclosing friend, JP stoked the furnace, so to speak.

"You know, Kize, I'm not sure I ever told you this before, but one night when I was nine or ten my brothers and me woke to fire bells," began JP, "and we looked out our window to see the roof of the Union Ironworks office across the street all ablaze. Fingy was standing on the planks right there below our house, dancing around, celebrating the fruits of his mischief. Then in the middle of the night, Patrolman Whelan—you remember old Whelan, don't you, Kize?"

"Yeah. That old bastard!"

"Well, Whelan come poundin' on our front door. He said that Fingy had been caught and that Fingy claimed I was helping him set the fires—that and the others previous including his Pa's saloon. That I was in fact the one who planned them all. So my poor mother and my brother Jim had to accompany me down to the precinct at 2 o'clock in the morning where the coppers proceeded to threaten to throw me into the workhouse. I was shittin' me trousers, I'll tell you that much. My mother was outraged and threatened the coppers up and down to within an inch of their lives because they had no proof, none at all—just Fingy's lies and accusations. She stormed 'round the station like a tornado, screaming, menacing. You should have seen her!"

Kennedy began to laugh. "*Your mother!*" he exclaimed, shaking his head in wonderment. "Now *there* was a force of nature if I never seen one!"

"Yeah! Wasn't she, then?" JP agreed. "Anyways, them cops were roundly scared of that woman! There they were, all vinegar and false bluster, accusing me. Indeed they had no proof because I had nothing to do with it, so when the sky brightened they gladly sent us on our way to put an end to Ma's hysterical terrorizing. Then, as we passed by the Conners' house, she banged on the door where old Pete Conners had just finished beating the shit out of Fingy for whatever he'd been up to in those wee hours. Ma read old Pete the riot act. She told him that she'd drown Fingy in the river with her own bare hands if the old man didn't put a stop to him one way or the other."

Kennedy nodded agreeably, never having heard this story which so neatly juxtaposed with his own.

"Yeah," Kennedy recalled. "One night we were up on the roof of his father's boarding house." Kennedy paused to take a bite off a second pickle. "And he wanted to show me how he learnt to build a bomb with a beer bottle filled with kerosene and stoppered with a rag. As he was demonstratin' he carelessly dropped it and the roof set afire. Whoosh! Just like that. We ran off like bats outa hell but not before old man Conners seen us. The neighbors and fire volunteers were able to save the saloon. Mr. Conners damn near beat the life out of Fingy once he hunted him down, but instead of Fingy learnin' his lesson from it, he took to buildin' even bigger bombs! We'd set them off at the Union Ironworks to test them out, 'cause we figgered nobody would take suspicion of a fire thereabouts—you understand, because it was a *furnace*—they'd figure it was just sparks from the furnace what caused it.

"One night after takin' another good beatin' from his old man, Fingy and me, we made some bombs and instead of settin' them off down by the edge of the river like usual, he tossed one atop his father's boardin' house, again out of pure spite. Fingy was heated with him for everything and nothing, and then we ran down South Street and bombed the Union Ironworks roof as well. It made for a real ruckus in the ward that night, the firemen runnin' ragged, back and forth, and I was sure Fingy would get near killed by his Pa, and then we'd *both* get our arses thrown into the workhouse.

"Don't you see, JP? Fingy blamed you just so's to keep me out of it. Old Pete Conners knew Fingy would soon be arrested and sent off to the Boys Industrial School in Rochester, if not Auburn Prison, and told him it was either jail for him or he had best pack up and leave home before the coppers arrived to the door. It was old man Conners who sent him down to the docks to rid himself, to get Fingy out from the family and out from the cops. We didn't just go off to sea on some notion,

JP. It was either that or jail for Fingy, and I guess for me too, considering how riled up and feeling sorry for myself I was. I didn't have nobody at all no more. My Pa was a good for nothin' toper. He wouldn't o' even took notice had I ended up dead like Ma done. So I joined in with Fingy on the ship."

JP worked diligently on his second frankfurter as he listened intently.

"The next day we met down at the docks and asked around and we got hired on the big steamer *Niagara* for little more than food and a swing bunk. So no matter where the boat docked thereafter we had practically no money, and we had to mind our P's and Q's real good so as not to get thrown off and left behind in Duluth or some other godforsaken place. But Fingy, right away he figured ways to get money for us, mostly from bamboozlin' passengers, or rollin' drunks outside waterfront saloons whenever the ship docked anyplace. We lived that life on the lakes until we got weary enough to try somethin' else."

JP nodded and smiled, hoping to coax Kennedy further, but that right there ended Kize's recollecting. Kennedy thereafter picked at his meal in silence. He never asked JP about Annie or the kids or made small talk. He had abruptly retreated back into his dark mood. As the two finished their lunch, JP, an inveterate cheapskate, dawdled, hoping Kennedy would volunteer to at least pay for his half. He did not.

"So," JP said, "Fingy claimed it was me helping him set all those fires, when it was you? What a nightmare I was being set up for! I might have ended up at that Boys Industrial School because of him..."

JP paused. Kennedy remained silent.

Then JP couldn't help but add "...and because of you too."

"Let's get outa here," said Kennedy rising noisily from his chair. JP paid the server grudgingly. The two grabbed toothpicks from the jar on the counter and exited the luncheonette into the smoky sunlight to the clanging of streetcars and the rantings of the preacher shouting from the horse-drawn Gospel Wagon that was a Shelton Square fixture. Out front Kennedy bid his goodbyes, then turned and walked toward Main Street, leaving JP to return by himself in the opposite direction to city hall pondering a decades-old troublesome riddle now newly solved. Looking over his shoulder, JP noticed that Kennedy had stopped to study the window of the Columbia Phonograph Company store across from the Ellicott Square. As JP continued on his way, Kennedy entered the shop.

"I've come to pick up a recording arm I brought in to be repaired last week. The name's Kennedy."

"Yes, of course, Alderman Kennedy, sir. I know who you are," said the clerk.

"And give me half a dozen Edison Gold cylinders too while you're at it.

Years earlier JP had introduced Kennedy to the benefits of rehearsing his important speeches on the Edison cylinders. But on his own Kennedy had discovered the novelty of recording his thoughts in the form of an audible personal journal in his own voice, something he believed everyone would soon emulate.

"The practice of writing in a paper journal is dead," he told his wife, confidently. "Foil technology will soon enough make writing paper obsolete."

THE FIRST WARD IV

Addiction

Hannah Sullivan hovered on the little porch at Ruth McGowan's front door on South Street determined that this time she was going to wait it out.

She had visited the previous day and the day before that. She had knocked and knocked but Ruth never came to the door. Hannah suspected she was in there, hiding, although she could just as well have been out holiday shopping, but for what or for whom Hannah couldn't imagine. Ruth had no family except her estranged mother and God knows she'd sooner deliver a bullet to the old bitch than a wrapped gift.

When Ruth's eyes met Fingy Conners' that time at the Alderman's Thanksgiving Day dinner there had been sparks, but not of the romantic variety. His Honor had showed up uninvited at the Alderman's door crassly interrupting the family's holiday celebration. Ruth's facial expression at seeing him was one of shock and dismay. She felt as if all the blood had suddenly drained from her brain. There was no doubt that Fingy had recognized her as well. Ruth's orange frizzy hair was a most unforgettable feature. Witnessing the tension between them, Hannah instantly put two and two together based on Ruth's stories about growing up in a Michigan Street brothel under the heavy hand of her prostitute mother. Hannah had faithfully shared Ruth's stories with not a soul.

Ten minutes passed. Still no one came to Ruth's door. The day was sunny and unseasonably warm. With no cleansing wind to speak of, the Union Furnace's choking smoke settled heavily over the neighborhood. Silica particles sparkled in the dim sunshine like glitter from the heavens as they drifted and fell. The line of massive hoists that swung menacingly five stories overhead the Sullivan brothers' homes on Hamburg street squealed and clanged as they transferred endless tons of iron product to and from waiting Great Lakes freighters and open-hatched whalebacks.

Hannah lingered. No sound came from inside Ruth's house. River traffic was unusually sparse. Street traffic was as per usual. A massive ship noisily unloaded grain into the Electric Elevator on the other side of the river amid laborers' shouts. A couple of the Mutual Rowing Club's sculls skimmed over the still waters, members taking advantage of the balmy weather for some rare winter training.

A few more minutes ticked by. Placing her mouth close to the door jamb, Hannah called softly as she rested her forehead against the portal.

"Ruth? Are you in there, dear? It's me, Hannah. Ruth...*please.*"

A gaggle of young First Ward girls fresh off their shift from the nearby Barcolo factory walked by and recognized her. They all waved to each other and called out their hellos.

Hannah tried knocking again.

"Ruth, I'm concerned, that's all. I just want to make sure you're all right."

As she lingered there a Pierce Arrow delivery truck owned by the Sullivan Ice Company made its way down South Street stopping in front of almost every house. Each had placed their ice card in their front windows, rotating it so that the amount of ice they wanted that particular day appeared at the top of the outward-facing card: 20 lbs., 30 lbs., 40 lbs., or 50 lbs. She didn't recognize the delivery men. They were not Joe and Jerry, the regulars. They passed right by Ruth's house. They looked but didn't wave to Hannah. It was only then that Hannah noticed there was no ice card displayed in Ruth's window. This is when she knew something was surely wrong.

Hannah peered intently through the lace curtains covering the door glass and knocked once again, more insistent this time. The gossamer curtains made it difficult to see in. At long last she discerned an interior door slowly open. A disheveled figure shuffled out, taking a good half minute to reach the door. The latch lifted with a click. The door opened by itself, just a crack.

"Are you all right, Ruth?" asked Hannah through the opening. "Let me in. Please."

Ruth's distinctive orange hair was wildly disheveled. She turned away, leaving the door ajar, shuffled over to the sofa and plopped down with a grunt. Hannah gently pushed the door open. Ruth did not look up. She stared downward, seemingly fixated on the stagnant air floating above the small Turkish carpet at her feet.

Various unpleasant smells invaded Hannah's nostrils. She flinched a little. She entered and closed the door behind her and stood for a few beats assessing her friend.

"Have you been feeling ill, Ruth?" Hanna gently asked.

Ruth remained intently transfixed on nothing. She half-raised her hand in response, indicating something halfway between I don't know and I don't care.

Hannah looked about the room. A record lay on the Victrola's felt pad, the arm still resting on the disc as if it had been left to play until the wind-up device ran out of energy.

"Can I get you some water, Ruth?"

Ruth mumbled trance-like. Hannah's apprehension escalated. She walked into the kitchen. It was a mess. Spoilt milk perfumed the air. She opened the ice box. The overpowering stench of rotten chicken shocked her nostrils. The drip pan was full, overflowing onto the floor, the ice having long since melted. She opened the faucet to rinse a dirty glass. Rusty water sputtered out, indicating it hadn't been opened in quite some time. She abandoned the task and returned to the parlor. Ruth was deeply quiet. She breathed slowly, seeming strangely at peace.

"Wouldn't you like to walk home with me and have a nice bowl of stew, Ruth? I..."

Hannah noticed among the objects disarranged on the little table next to Ruth's resting place a small bottle almost emptied. She picked it up. The label read "N.Y.Q. & C. Works Ltd., New York. Sulfate of Morphine."

After slipping and falling on the ice the previous winter, Ruth had been suffering with severe recurrent headaches. At the hospital her skull had been X-rayed. The doctors discovered a network of long-healed cracks. Ruth confessed to the physicians that as a child her vicious mother habitually struck her on the head with a metal hairbrush. The doctors could not imagine that she survived such damage seemingly intact. They considered among themselves after leaving her bedside the emotional damage from the ongoing assaults that had undoubtedly been visited upon her. They fully understood when Ruth described the incessant pain torturing her ever since her slip and fall, and sought to bring the poor woman whatever relief they might.

They prescribed her small doses of morphine.

They cautioned her on the medicine's use. They pointed out the skull and crossbones on the label.

"It's there for a reason, ma'am," they told her. "Take too much, and you'll die, Mrs. McGowan. Take it too often and you may develop a hopeless addiction."

She assured them there was no need for worry. That she had seen with her own eyes the terrible results of morphine addiction. She did not volunteer that it was about her own mother she was speaking.

Upon their having administered a dose to her, Ruth felt better immediately and unwisely demanded she be released from the hospital right then and there. As with any serious head injury, the doctors were concerned that she might die in her sleep. They encouraged her to remain hospitalized for two more days propped upright and prevented from sleeping. She refused. Not until Hannah spoke up and promised the physicians that she would nurse Ruth at her own home did they reluctantly agree to let her go.

"These doctors, they might not be able to cure any diseases," chuckled Ruth at the time, "but they certainly do know how to relieve the pain."

Hannah looked around the parlor afraid of what else she might discover. Ruth sat motionless.

"If you won't come home with me, Ruth, then let me look around in your pantry for something for you to eat."

Hannah reentered the kitchen. She located a rusting can of Van Camp's Pork and Beans, an unopened box of Huntley & Palmer's Christmas Biscuits, and a half box of Shredded Wheat. Under the sink was the garbage pail, unlidded. She looked inside. There she found two more empty brown morphine vials.

"Dear Lord," she sighed. "Help us."

His Lips Forgot The Taste Of Truth

Author Edward Sheldon

February 11, 1910
The Boss

Certain men capture the imaginations of the public through their leading lives that are equal parts extraordinary and unbelievable. Men who rise to unprecedented heights through unusual achievements are customarily accorded legendary status in the press as well as in the eyes of both critics and defenders alike. Among such rarefied storied individuals were two newspaper publisher-politicians and cohorts, William Randolph "Randy" Hearst and William James "Fingy" Conners.

Conners was a nefarious multi-millionaire labor contractor, violent street thug and crippler of men, a brewery owner, newspaper publisher, urban railway director, street paver, director in three banks, saloon boss, kingmaker, con artist, and unelected politician. Ironically, like most people in Fingy Conners' life, the relationship between him and William Randolph Hearst vacillated wildly over the decades of their acquaintance, from that of closest of associates to mortal enemies and back again.

Both men's stories set flowing the creative juices of writers mining for inspiration from which to ground their next great popular work. Fingy Conners' improbable story sat topmost on the pile. Author and playwrite Edward Sheldon—handsome, Harvard educated, young and newly successful, wielded the shovel.

The celebrated author of the sensational and controversial hit Broadway play "The Nigger," the story of a mulatto man who could pass for white marrying a woman who was purely Caucasian, had put him squarely on the map after his initial work, "Salvation Nell" was an instant success.

Sheldon's eagerly awaited follow-up to "The Nigger" was the story of a Buffalo man whose accomplishments were improbable even in his own time, whose name was linked with abject cruelty, unspeakably violent actions, powerful and prestigious political office, and enormous ill-gotten wealth.

"The Boss" had been inspired by Will Irwin's profile of William J. "Fingy" Conners published in *Collier's* Magazine. The article had caught the attention of Sheldon's older brother who convinced Edward of its value as a stage play. Ed Sheldon traveled to Buffalo to learn more about his newest obsession. Fingy

Conners intrigued the author as no character before him ever had.

From his suite at the Iroquois Hotel, Edward Sheldon reached out to those local lights who had been identified by name in the *Collier's* article.

Seduced by the offer of a gourmet lunch with a New York celebrity, Alderman John P. Sullivan, who had greatly enjoyed a performance of Salvation Nell while visiting New York the year previous, agreed to meet with Sheldon. JP regaled Sheldon with wild anecdotes about Fingy Conners and other essential names. Sheldon confided in JP that he wished also to meet with Police Chief Regan, who at first demurred. But upon JP's coaxing and Sheldon's invitation for Regan and his wife Ellen to travel to New York and see "The Nigger," the police chief changed his mind.

Regan during their meeting relayed to Sheldon his objection to that play's title which as a police officer he found inciting. Sheldon explained, "I surely meant in no way to cast any reflection on the Negro, Chief Regan. Quite the contrary, I wanted to get into the title of the play the attitude of the white race to the black. When the play is seen I am sure that the development of the character will show you how ironical the title is meant to be."

Sheldon asked for both Sullivan's and Regan's help in securing a meeting with Archbishop James E. Quigley, the central opponent in Fingy Conners' scheme against his grain shovelers in their labor strike of 1899. Quigley had adamantly refused him. The impenetrable Quigley had been Archbishop of Buffalo during that uprising, but had since moved on to become Archbishop of Chicago. Quigley was keen to leave the Fingy Conners chapter of his life far and permanently behind him, what with its unrelenting battles and threats of personal violence.

It was believed that Fingy, having suffered his greatest defeat ever at the hands of Quigley upon his loss in the grain scoopers strike, lobbied to install Quigley as Archbishop of Chicago to get him out of Buffalo, out of the equation, and out of his hair. It was rumored he'd made a surreptitious donation of one million dollars to the Church in Rome to bring the prelate's Chicago appointment about.

Through Sheldon's meetings with those whose names he was provided, he was informed of the peril of revealing certain details pertaining to Conners about which he was made privy off the record. He was after all a playwrite and not a social reformer as such, a peaceful man from a cultured Chicago real estate family, a man whose main goal in life was personal serenity. Certain things Sheldon learned about he knew would make for the most sensational and titillating of content, but he was pragmatic enough to edit his choices judiciously. Sheldon had learned that the unreformed street thug Conners' two favorite tools of persuasion historically were his fists and a box of matches. That Conners' sister had died in a mysterious fire; that his stepmother and father too died mysteriously, all three within one year; that the entirety of their properties and life insurances were appropriated by Fingy despite his dead sister being survived by a living child, Minnie Hayes, and Fingy having two additional adult siblings.

The saloon inherited from his father Fingy cultivated as a meeting spot for political activists possessing dark motives. His inherited money bought him influence and the wherewithal to bribe important city officials. Soon enough he had cornered the waterfront labor market and bought for himself the entirety of the Buffalo Police Department, including current Police Chief Michael Regan, half the city's elected officials, and all the local judges.

Fingy Conners thrived on chaos even whilst scheming fresh turmoil. He was a master puppeteer. In the infamous 1899 Grain Scoopers Strike, he had mightily battled the Archbishop Quigley who had stepped in to represent the laborers of Conners' workers' uprising. Fingy Conners' fierce public warring with waterfront Aldermen John P. Sullivan and John J. "Kize" Kennedy were the stuff of local myth and lore.

Edward Sheldon took the story of Fingy Conners, assigned the players new names with a wink and a nod, and titled both his novel and his stage play "The Boss." In these works Fingy Conners was renamed "Michael Regan" after the police chief. Bishop Quigley was renamed "Bishop Sullivan" after the alderman. Sheldon's story was that of a charitable young girl from a wealthy family, a thinly disguised representation of the Kennedy clan, who, in exchange for Fingy's agreement to keep from ruining her family, agreed to unite with him in an unconsummated marriage. It was promoted as both a love story and a tale of redemption.

The Boss became the best selling novel of 1910, helped along just a bit by the headlines of concurrent real life crises, primarily Fingy's searingly public humiliation suffered during his attempted ouster as Chairman of the Democratic Party of New York State. The following year The Boss was a hit Broadway play starring the celebrated actor Holbrook Blinn. In 1913 The Boss became a hit motion picture. Blinn reprised his stage role in the film as well, which went on to great success.

❧❦☙

Fingy Conners acknowledged to no one that he was the play's inspiration, despite the overwhelmingly obvious.

On the night of the Broadway premiere of The Boss, both the author and protagonist were absent.

Author Sheldon had been out on a party the previous night and well into the following day celebrating with friends and his family members whom he had brought in from Chicago for the event. By dinnertime Sheldon was exhausted, experiencing, unbeknownst to him then, the initial effects of the disease that would eventually rob him of both his sight and his motor skills and reduce him to a confined bedridden state. He took to his bed in his suite at the Hotel Royalton, his residence at the time, and slept the sleep of the dead.

Many luminaries however did attend the premiere of *The Boss*, including Mayor of New York William Jay Gaynor, a close Tammany cohort of Fingy Conners. Gaynor was lured by the "rumor" that the play portrayed his controversial associate. Other prominent curious politicians were in attendance also. It was said that Sheldon grinned widely the next morning upon reading in the *Evening World* that the Mayor had "betrayed no sign that he had even a bowing acquaintance with such a type" as the Fingy Conners character.

Sheldon however was far more interested in the reaction of one other famous attendee that evening, Henry James, author of many best selling novels, including "Daisy Miller" and "The Bostonians." Celebrated author James—playwrite and literary critic—was enjoying his last visit to America before returning to England to legally become a British citizen, and soon enough thereafter pass away. James confided privately to his companion Mrs. Cadwalader Jones, a very close friend of Sheldon's, that he had disliked the play immensely and the audience even more so. However he wrote a charming letter to Sheldon expressing his opinions in a graceful obliquity about which Sheldon did not take offense. Indeed, Edward Sheldon treasured James' letter until his own dying day.

Some critics had their reservations about *The Boss* but none denied the play's power and authority. Just as had Sheldon's two previous works, *The Boss* gave rise to earnest social conversation which, even more than favorable reviews by critics, drove customers to the box office. The Boss not only made Edward Sheldon famous, but wealthy in his own right apart even from his family's real estate fortune.

❧❦❧

"But darling, we *must* go and catch the play next week when we are in New York!" exclaimed wife Mary.

"Not a chance. Anyways it even ain't about me. That Sheldon fella already said so," insisted Fingy.

Mary laughed loud and long.

"Oh dear me, Jim, really? Everyone who's anyone knows full well it's *all* about you! There is no doubt in anyone's mind as to that! The author of course is going to deny it, that's what they do, his sort. It's a transparently disguised representation of you. Most likely he just wants to not ruffle your feathers—or get himself *sued*," she giggled.

"Damn it, I said no, Mary!"

"Well then, I'll just go with one of the ladies from the Club."

"You'll do no such thing."

"Oh darling, please stop being so obtuse. You've made yourself famous, and intentionally so! You have to expect consequences such as this. Come on, we'll even put you in disguise if that'll make you feel better. It'll be fun. I know you well, my darling, and I know you're just dying inside to be a fly on the wall in that theater."

"I ain't. That book is garbage!"

"Oh, come now! I thought it was quite sweet. They say in the end you capture everyone's heart. Holbrook Blinn, darling! Holbrook Blinn is playing you! What a thrill! He has gotten absolutely marvelous reviews in the role. You cannot tell me that you are not dying to see how the famed thespian Holbrook Blinn play-acts at being yourself on a Broadway stage!"

Fingy went silent. Not silent boiling mad, as was his custom, but rather silent in his swirling contemplation. At that point Mary knew she had turned the corner. Now all she had to do was back away slowly and change the subject, leaving him alone to mull it over on his own.

"The shirtmaker delivered your new order today, dear, and I had Bridget iron the blue striped number and the white Egyptian cotton for you to choose from to wear to your meeting tonight."

❦

As Mary put the finishing touches on his "disguise" at the Hotel Astor the following weekend, Fingy grew increasingly agitated.

"Somebody's gonna recognize me. Then what?"

"Nobody will recognize you dear, I promise. With these spectacles and false moustache, you are transformed. Now relax. I know you'll be happy that we came."

"I gotta go sit on the crapper," was his reply.

Fingy closed the door over but made no effort to disguise the noises. Mary moved away from the door. Raising her voice to be heard above his grunting exertions, she said, "Here, let me read you a lovely review from *Collier's*."

"I ain't got nuttin t' do with *Collier's*. Not after wot they wrote about me. I'll get that Collier bastard yet. Just yous wait."

"It's titled, 'A Portrait.' Are you listening, dear?"

"Do I got a choice?'"

She read the piece aloud:

A Portrait

PLAYS ABOUT POLITICS in America so far have failed to create any other personage so actual and so impressive as EDWARD SHELDON'S adaption of FINGY CONNERS in "The Boss." The mastery of suspense, of effective situation, and of what is sometimes known in theatrical parlance as "the punch," combine, with a ready and successful supply of comedy to make "The Boss" sure to have the marked popularity of "Salvation Nell" and "The Nigger." What gives it special value, apart from popular success, is the firm and highly intelligent picture of the typical American boss, with his arrogance, his tradition of generosity and warmth to individual supporters, his shrewdness, his ignorance, his violence and cunning. Mr. SHELDON shows his protagonist rescued at the end by a woman's influence, his own misfortunes, and his own qualities, but he paints him without compromise, with the brush of a master.

"There! You see? No one is making fun of you. Audiences and critics both love the play. I'm so terribly excited!"

"Yeah, yeah. Not so sure we shoulda ate supper beforehand. Don't want me steak risin' up in me throat if I get mad watchin' 'em makin' me look bad."

The toilet flushed powerfully, then the door opened.

"Dear, please wash your hands, will you? And don't splash your suit."

Fingy obediently turned and perfunctorily dabbed at his fingers under the faucet a bit, then wiped them on a pristine white bath towel which he then tossed into the bathtub.

"Don't ferget t' call the maid fer more towels, Mary."

"Yes, darling."

She stood holding his topcoat open for him to slide his arms into, then straightened his collar. He pressed firmly on the fake moustache to make sure it was well affixed, then handed Mary her bejeweled bag. Mary took one last look at herself in the mirror, and together they stepped out. Minutes later they arrived at the Astor Theater.

As the play progressed Fingy squirmed in his chair.

"They're makin' me out t' be a fool!" he whispered a bit too loud, drawing unwanted attention. People turned in their seats. He sunk lower in his chair wishing to disappear. Then one actor in particular caught his eye.

"Hey, don't I know that guy there? I know that fella from somewheres."

An actor playing a small part, that of a patrolman, found himself the object of Fingy's attention.

"I think I know him!"

"Shh!" scolded Mary.

"Don't I know that fella? Where the hell do I know him from?"

"Darling, please!"

It stuck in his craw. There was barely enough light coming from the stage to illuminate his program. He opened it and scanned the list of players. He took off his spectacles and squinted. At the very bottom he read:

Another Police Officer................................Mr. H.C. Weir

"Weir? It's that same fella wot interviewed me fer that magazine, Human Life! That's his name, right? Yeah, Weir. That's it. Wot's he doin' up there play actin'?"

"Shh! Please, Jim!"

Hugh C. Weir had indeed previously interviewed Fingy Conners for *Human Life* magazine. He also wrote books and plays and screenplays for the new motion picture industry. He also dabbled in acting, and having interviewed Edward Sheldon for a recent magazine piece, also for *Human Life*, boldly leveraged information in exchange for a part in his newest play. Fairly or not, he won the role, ironically in a play based on the odious object of one of his more troubling interviews, a man with whom he had spent considerable unpleasant time three years previous. Certainly he'd supplied the playwrite with personal observances, anecdotes and habits of the protagonist that had been incorporated into the play.

Weir had written about Holbrook Blinn as well, and Blinn, upon learning of Weir's association with the very man he was portraying on stage, pumped him for anecdotes and for tips on how to most effectively portray Fingy Conners.

By play's end Fingy's nerves had calmed. He was relieved that in the finale, despite some rocky passages early on, his character was provided a sympathetic arc.

As was his habit he insisted they remain in their seats until the majority of people had exited, after which the couple rose and made their way to the lobby.

'Well, if it ain't Jim Conners! Fancy meeting you here!" the man shouted ruefully. It was his political nemesis and the current target of Fingy's nasty character assassination, political boss Charles Murphy, the last person on earth he would ever have wanted to encounter in this particular situation.

"Just couldn't help yourself, eh, Conners? Had to sneak in to see for yourself how they depicted you on the stage! I knew it. I told Chalmers there was no chance of your keeping away, and now here you are, caught in the act, so to speak. Ha! You see Conners, that's your weakness—pretending not to care about what others think about you when any fool can see by the way you conduct yourself that you do indeed care. In fact you care too much. You're always lecturing others against showing their weakness, yet here you stand, taking time out in the midst of the fight for your very political life, showing yours. And for what? For vanity's sake, that's what!"

Murphy laughed uproariously. People stared.

"Got to say though, you do look rather more distinguished with a moustache. Too bad a lack of the proper hormones prevents you from growing the actual stuff." Murphy smirked, turned on his heel, and scuttled away. Mary nearly wrenched her arm trying to hold Fingy back.

"Lemme go Mary! Me bunches o' fives is just itchin' t' let 'im have it!"

"Not here, Jim!" she scolded. "You'll have plenty of opportunities amidst the more sequestered shadowy venues that Albany offers. Let Charlie Murphy squirm for a while, worrying around which corner you await him—and when."

HIS LIPS FORGOT THE TASTE OF TRUTH

Holbrook Blinn stars as Fingy Conners in "The Boss."

Fingy Conners as Chairman of the Democratic Party of New York State.

February 22, 1910
Humiliation

Almost two weeks later, on February 22nd, Fingy Conners found himself sequestered at the Waldorf Hotel in Manhattan frantically marshaling his forces to fight the movement to oust him from his leadership as Chairman of the Democratic Party of New York State.

For months the fight had already raged in Buffalo to remove him from the leadership of the Erie County Democratic organization. A secret meeting was held on the 28th of January in Buffalo which included all the top political names including Aldermen John P. Sullivan and John J. "Kize" Kennedy. A manifesto was drawn up calling for Conners' ouster.

Even his closest friends and supporters had by this time given up the ghost: Conners' political career was ruined, they all agreed, and entirely by his own hand, or more accurately put, his big mouth. He had gone much too far this time in his ceaseless pursuit of extending the tentacles of his dominance beyond all previous limits. His formerly formidable support network was now in disarray.

The day before as he prepared to leave Buffalo, Fingy's wife pulled him aside as his valises were being loaded into his depot-bound Pierce-Arrow. She well knew the pivotal seriousness of the situation. Mary Jordan Conners feared how it might impact all her plans, her hard-won social elevation, the seductive oath he had once made to her, if Fingy was indeed deposed.

"Remember, Jim, what you promised me all those many years ago when you dropped down on one knee and proposed marriage. 'Stick with me, Mary,' you pledged, 'and you and me and our children will be living in the White House.' Well, the clock is ticking, husband. I've been packed and ready for ages now—and very patient I might add. Now's the time—the time to fight like you've never fought before.

"Remember too, Mr. Chairman," she stated tersely, "I would much rather be the widow of a brave man than the wife of a coward."

He stopped and stared at her for a moment not knowing whether to sock her or kiss her. She stared right back with a fierce determination in her eyes.

※※※

In New York Fingy responded to his adversaries in the tried and true manner that had always served the raging bully well: he threatened careers and lives.

Mary's parting words had energized him. He had taken on publisher William Randolph Hearst's campaign for Governor of New York back in 1906 knowing Hearst's ultimate goal was the White House. He saw Hearst as his ticket in back then—that is, until Hearst allowed his mammoth ego to run away with him, taking his chances for New York's governorship with it.

Fingy observed Hearst's mistakes and learned valuable lessons he might apply to his own aspirations. He must not flounder. He must not lose sight of the ultimate goal. He must not repeat Hearst's blunders. Fingy Conners could not afford any backward slide if he was to realize his dream of attaining the presidency of the United States, and so he shifted into high gear. He had brainstormed in his hotel room the night he arrived. There he decided on a strategy to make Tammany the enemy, to destroy its ruling members and use their cold dead cadavers to step him upward. He thought he might reinvent himself as the people's hero, the enemy of evil and corruption and money in politics, for no one knew more about the connection between evil and corruption and money than he.

Fingy Conners screamed wild forebodings and ranted preposterously for the sole benefit of those of weaker backbone and of newsmen covering the imbroglio, knowing his apocalyptic messages concerning certain individuals would be spread far and wide. He had volumes to say about what he intended to do to Tammany and to the "gang" if they dared persist in their "outrageous attempt" to oust him. An explosion of threats and castigations spewed forth like an upset bottle of seltzer water. He made outrageous public statements against his former friends. He privately called in various uncooperative upstate party members to read them the riot act and make none-too-vague accusations against them of a decidedly perverted sexual nature based, he claimed, on the reported findings by his team of professional private detectives.

There was no team of detectives. At least not yet.

Much to his bafflement his ominous threatenings failed to impact as they always had before. United in their new found common disgust for the man they had once blindly followed, his former allies refused to lie down and roll over any longer. For the first time ever they were standing straight-spined against the psychotic despot and his unhinged lying and terrorizing.

"Yous owe everything wot ye got from me, yous dirty bastards, and now yer welchin'!" he accused.

Fingy's intrusion at dinner at the Sullivan household the previous Thanksgiving Day, whereby he uncharacteristically begged the Alderman for his help, had gobsmacked all those who had witnessed it. Fingy had never been known to reveal any vulnerability—not ever—to any individual, even friend-since-childhood JP Sullivan. Blurting out his fears within earshot of the entire family as he did was unheard of. Like blood in the water, JP right then and there smelled that the end was nigh for Fingy's political ambitions. Politics might be a crazy cutthroat business, but Fingy Conners' methods and aspirations reached far beyond the pale. The ease with which the Buffalo Police Dept., the city fathers, local judges and religious leaders all kowtowed obediently to his every whim in his home city had deluded Conners into believing that what he had engineered locally he could machinate nationwide as well.

Loyal democracy-loving Americans would tolerate neither an authoritarian nor a dictator, and ultimately it turned out that neither would the members of the Democratic Committee of New York State.

Having planned for himself a seat in some President or other's White House Cabinet before assuming his rightful place in the Oval Office himself, and completely self-assured without question that he would succeed in bringing that objective about no matter what, the realization that all his longtime allies whom he claimed to have wooed and nurtured, rather than threaten and manipulate, had conspired to do away with him and destroy his dream—well, it was all too impossible for Conners' out of control narcissism to accept.

The Alderman had sent Fingy on his way that Thanksgiving with an ambiguous pledge of support. Under any other circumstances Fingy would find such an easily obtained pledge patronizing, but in the frenzy and desperation of his mental state at the time he believed his habitual collaborator would rally to his aid as he had numerous times historically to their mutual benefit. However, JP discerned no benefit for himself, political or otherwise, in helping Fingy Conners this time around.

JP Sullivan had risen to the pinnacle of local political power in Buffalo and Erie County. As a delegate many times over at the National Conventions, he had the ear of every Democrat at the State Capitol in Albany and had friends and allies and admirers spread nationwide. However, he was getting weary. He no longer entertained the higher political ambitions he once did. Despite his influence, JP Sullivan did not rally any of these friendly forces on Fingy Conners' behalf. Rather, he sat and watched, not unlike a patient vulture on some convenient branch calmly awaiting the imminent collapse of a mortally wounded prey.

Fingy had shown up on the Alderman's porch that Thanksgiving only out of despair upon realizing he was being conspired against by those he'd believed had long been his loyal, if not true, political friends. As would be natural, Conners, now newly untrusting of men with whom his history was brief in comparison, again reassessed his lifelong kinship with John P. Sullivan. The two were enemies and combatants more often than friends or allies, but throughout their entire lives they had been there for each other during weighty times. They had united time and again when mutual interests, political and financial, made an alliance, a partnership, beneficial to both. Beneath the many layers of discordance between the two lay a mutually shared history from boyhood. As schoolboys Fingy abused and denigrated the younger JP even as the latter admired him and sought his approval despite these offenses. Profoundly betrayed by those he had trusted most, Fingy's disturbing upbringing had from his earliest years molded a confused and mercurial personality. Before anyone might seize upon any opportunity to betray him, he preemptively drove away those who initially exhibited any possibility of becoming a trusted friend. Everyone except the doggedly persistent and nonthreatening optimist, JP Sullivan.

JP grew up understanding the demons that plagued Fingy Conners even as those same demons were unleashed by Conners at times against him and his family. Fingy successfully exhausted everyone with whom he came in contact, and now after nearly 50 years of enduring his shenanigans, the Alderman was depleted, worn out. He thought it high time Fingy Conners suffered the well-earned consequences of his bulldozing iron-fisted malevolence. And so, in spite of his inference of assistance made with a sympathetic smile that day, JP in fact did nothing whatsoever. Neither did he help nor did he overtly hinder Fingy Conners.

Publisher-politician William Randolph Hearst on the other hand presented quite a different matter, as too did Tammany boss Charles Murphy, both of whom in the past had been Fingy's closest allies. No one really knows which of the two fanned the flames hotter as they worked together in conspiracy to take down Conners. But Hearst certainly had the more effective delivery vehicle. Across the nation in his great newspapers spanning from Boston to San Francisco, Hearst published a detailed biography of Fingy Conners that resurrected some of his most egregious sins. Woven together like hemp in a hangman's noose, these incidents' cumulative effect on the nation's public was gasp-inducing.

This "biography" described the penultimate event in millionaire labor contractor

Fingy Conners' adult life as his defeat in the great Grain Scoopers Strike of 1899 in which his vast work force finally rebelled after nearly twenty years of virtual indentured servitude.

❦❦❦

In 1880 a typical wage of a dockworker in Buffalo was $19 cash a week. Nearly twenty years later under Fingy Conners' despotic control of the workforce, the cash wage had been reduced almost by half. To add injury to insult, 25% of that which was paid as "wages" was in the form of brass checks redeemable solely for alcohol at Fingy's saloons. In April of 1899 he further slashed the cash wage from $10 a week to $9, striking the match that lit the bomb that exploded into the Great Scoopers Strike which effectively paralyzed the entirety of Great Lakes shipping for weeks, costing the US economy tens of millions.

Fingy fancied himself a great benefactor for generously supplying the gift of poverty wage employment to thousands. Notoriously thin-skinned to an unnerving degree, during the strike he adopted the role of persecuted victim to the hilt.

Never mind the number of wives and children of workers, and workers themselves, who had sickened and died directly due to the drastically reduced wages or the resultant alcoholism-induced illnesses, poverty and domestic violence borne of Conners' methods. His diabolical saloon boss brass-check system which rewarded jobs first to those who spent the greatest part of their cash wage above and beyond even their brass checks in his various saloons was at the root of his Catholic Church-condemned evil.

Losing the Scoopers Strike was a threshold event in Conners' life, his first major defeat since his early 1880s political loss to incumbent Jack White in the electoral race for Alderman of Buffalo's First Ward. Still young at that early juncture, he had yet to fully master the art of rigging elections. Immediately following the 1899 scoopers victory, labor contractor Conners' freight handlers, emboldened by the scoopers victory, next rose up in opposition to him. In the nearly two decades between these two losses he had experienced nothing but success. He had become a multi-millionaire and accumulated a vast amount of power locally, entirely controlling the economic fortunes of the First Ward and the majority of its inhabitants.

The loss of the Scoopers Strike so unbalanced him that his violent behavior, almost always obscured previously by filtering his murderous retaliations though layers of lieutenants, street thugs and hired goons, now became at times quite open. Instituting plans to abandon Buffalo for Montreal to relocate all his businesses in Canada, he no doubt felt liberated to allow his personal demons a freer reign during his assumed final days in the city.

Unlike his previous atrocities carried out undercover, his 1899 crimes were committed in broad daylight before the eyes of scores of witnesses and reported in great detail in the city's rival newspapers. Buffalo's citizens, all aware of two decades' worth of rumors and legends told of Fingy Conners, now had dastardly examples documented in black and white, and their eyes ate up every word.

Conners' political enemies in Albany fed these stories to the nation's newspapers as they set in motion the apparatus to topple him from his pedestal. The message was that of a violent, authoritarian, vindictive, reprehensible, bare-faced dangerously emotional liar occupying a high government position the equal of which had never before been seen in America.

A headline trumpeted in Hearst's *San Francisco Call:*

> Following Are the Accounts of Crimes Personally Committed by the Reckless Man Currently Holding the office of Chairman of the Democratic Party of New York State."

❦

At about 10 o'clock a.m. on June 12, 1899, a few weeks after the Scoopers Strike ended in defeat for Conners, Gus Wahl, president of the freight handlers union, was walking down Buffalo's Ohio Street past Joseph "Sloak" Slattery's saloon-hotel. Slattery was widely known to be Fingy Conners' closest friend since boyhood. It was Fingy who had purchased the saloon as a gift for his friend. As Wahl walked by, Slattery bounded from his tavern and used profane and obscene language in a loud tone of voice as he pummeled Wahl to the ground. Slattery pulled a revolver and held it to Wahl's head, threatening to blow his brains out. All of this was done in the immediate presence of a Buffalo policeman, Patrick Bresnahan. Wahl demanded Bresnahan arrest Slattery, but instead the patrolman shoved Slattery back inside the shelter of his saloon, refusing to arrest him and telling Wahl instead to go get a warrant.

Ninety minutes later the same Patrolman Bresnahan was requested by Mike Winsierski, inspector for the freight handlers union, for a police escort past the same Slattery's saloon. Winsierski was in the company of two associates.

The *Buffalo Evening News* reported Winsierski's account:

> I was walking up Ohio Street toward Chicago Street last Monday morning in company of two other men. I feared then an effort might be made to assault me, so I asked a policeman who was standing nearby

to protect me, but he did not think there would be any need of it. We approached the saloon of "Sloak" Slattery, almost opposite the New York Central Freight House. Almost as we reached Slattery's place I noticed William J. Conners, the contractor, driving down Ohio Street in a buggy. Mr. Conners usually carries a cane with a crook. When he saw me he leaped from his buggy, came up to me, put the crook around my neck and roughly pulled me down to the sidewalk and shouted, "What do you want here, you (expletive) Polish son of a (expletive)?"

"I want the rights of the union," I answered."

"We'll give you all you want," Conners sneered, adding, "there won't be a single (expletive) Polack left living on these streets by tonight!"

Then a man named Dick Nugent who was standing next to Slattery's hotel punched me and two or three other Conners associates jumped upon me as well and they all beat me. My body still is sore from the blows. My eye is blackened and swelled from the blows. I expected the patrolmen who were near the place would arrest some of the men who assaulted me but they did not. Then I met Timothy P. Donovan, the inspector appointed by Bishop Quigley, and told him about it. The next day, Tuesday, Mr. Donovan and myself went to the Police Court to swear out warrants for the arrest of some of them, including Mr. Conners.

When I asked Judge King to issue a warrant for the arrest of Mr. Conners he refused to do so, saying after I had told him the circumstances about Conners wrenching me by the neck with his cane and pulling me roughly to the hard pavement that he had not assaulted me. A warrant however was issued for Dick Nugent, but only after a public outcry after the account was published in Buffalo newspapers. Conners immediately bailed Nugent out. All of them should have been arrested.

The police court, led by Conners' puppet Judge King, ultimately refused to move on the crime, suspending investigation or trial against Dick Nugent while at the same time publicly denigrating Winsierski.

Seventh Precinct Captain John M. Lynch tried to turn a blind eye to the incident, as he had to so many others preceding, but the combined forces of Catholic Bishop James Quigley and the ragings of the *Buffalo Evening News* forced his hand.

Lynch suspended Patrolman Bresnahan and filed charges against him.

In Lynch's statement, headed "Conduct Unbecoming an Officer and Neglect of

Duty" it was stated in part, "when in front of said Slattery's saloon, William J. Conners got out of his buggy and met the said Winsierski and had some words with him, the said Conners using profane and obscene language, that said Conners did assault the said Winsierski by catching him around the neck with the crook of his cane and so holding him, and that while holding him, one Richard Nugent and several others came out of the said saloon and the said Nugent did assault the said Winsierski, striking him in the face and blackening his eyes, that the assault was committed within his sight and hearing and that the said Patrolman Bresnahan did fail and neglect to give said Winsierski the protection he asked for."

The *New York Herald* later wrote:

> It probably will be hard for those who do not know of Conners' antics personally to believe that a man who is now State Chairman could have taken personal part in dock scrimmages only seven years ago, but the police department records and the Police Board's records contain corroborated affidavits and corroborated sworn testimony bearing out the charge. All those records are public property. They were examined at police headquarters today by a HERALD correspondent.

In 1897 scores of freight handlers and scoopers were interviewed for the Tenth Annual Report of the Board of Mediation and Arbitration of New York State for the Board's investigation of Fingy's saloon boss system. Teetotaler workers complained bitterly at being paid partly in alcohol they had no use for at the saloon boss' taverns, then having to work twice as hard to make up for the drunks who were not physically capable of doing their job, but received preferential job treatment nonetheless, due to their spending almost their entire wages on saloon boss booze. When winter's ice called a halt to Great Lakes shipping, these same alcoholics entered hospitals or the city's poor houses to survive until the spring thaw once again opened shipping lanes.

The absolute societal and moral havoc dealt Conners' six thousand workers and their families by his saloon boss system had brutally catapulted the communities in which they lived into pandemonium and economic depression. The damage Conners inflicted extended far beyond the immediate victims and ward boundaries. It bled over into surrounding neighborhoods and indeed the entirety of the city's resources, social order and quality of life by way of increased crime, rampant domestic abuse borne of alcoholism and poverty, and the limited resources of the police and of the courts to deal with the chaotic result.

The intended effect of these published collections of irrefutable facts about Fingy Conners was an unassailable illustration borne of public records stretching back twenty years of his unfitness to serve, and thus helped put an end to his bullying political career.

The public, much to their credit, adjudging Conners' lack of ethics, blatant lies and unbridled vindictiveness as traits totally unsuitable for someone holding high political office, acted in accordance with the honorable ideals and morals instilled deeply within them as Americans.

However, no one had warned them that Fingy Conners did not have to hold any public office in order to continue carrying out his destructive agenda.

THE FIRST WARD IV

1910: Canal Street

From its very inception Buffalo's First Ward attracted like a magnet a howling den of hot-headed roughnecks and hooligans. The Sullivans and the Nugents and the Conners first arrived in the city in the latter 1840s when underfed cattle were commonly held inside the front gates of residents' ramshackle huts, and nests of prostitution thrived even in the shadow of schools and churches.

The harlot trade was the first profitable business established in Buffalo, it being in service to the blister-handed multitudes digging the Erie Canal. Whoredom flourished gloriously from 1820 onward, first to fulfill the lustful yearnings of the canal builders, then upon its completion to indulge the hordes of frontiersmen that had made their way down the shallow waterway from back east to pursue adventure in the young nation's most notorious hinterland.

Buffalo was the famed and storied Wild West where "anything goes," and indeed anything *did* go. The booming town boasted more saloons and whorehouses per capita than any other North American place.

George H. Sweet in his 1865 US Census enumeration conducted in the First Ward responded to the written questions posed him by the government body overseeing the national tally with these personal remarks at the close of his head count:

> Q: What changes in the condition of the people have you observed since 1860?
>
> A: A large increase in prostitution and a tendency of our judiciary not to protect respectable neighbourhoods from the curse of Houses of Prostitution together with our Police regulations which scatters them all over our ward instead of confining them to one locality = our Laws is defective = License them and confine them to one Locality and many valuable lives would be saved of the Virtuous and the lower classes would also be benefitted.
>
> Our city loses a number of thousands of inhabitants by the people living in summer season on canal boats and vessels with their whole families and are not Enumerated. Labourers does less work than

formerly with the increased wages and are more idle. Over Twenty Dwellings in my district are supported wholly or in part in the receipts of the proceeds of prostitution.

From the outset debauchery overflowed the First Ward northward into the waterfront Nineteenth, both wards divided and crisscrossed as they were by a web of canals and slips and basins that extended the Erie Canal's and the city's natural waterways' reach deep into neighborhood businesses requiring access to water delivery for the goods they produced. Most disreputable of the city's districts was Canal Street, known far and wide as "the wickedest street in the world." Born as Rock Street, then Cross Street, its name became Canal Street once the Erie Canal was finished and was up and running. A mishmash of brothels, saloons, concert halls and convenient boarding houses, the saloons on the east side of the street were of a most notorious variety, having been built with their rear ends extending out over the Erie Canal's waters and equipped with trap doors and chutes for the convenient jettisoning of dead bodies.

The business of Canal Street and those surrounding—Water, Peacock, Fly, and Maiden Lane, among others—was the business of men and the women who loved them: drinking, gambling, fistfighting and whore mongering.

A profusion of cockfighters and dogfighters abounded for bet makers, as well as betting contests of cats against rats, or rats against each other. No betting opportunity was overlooked including basement fistfight matches involving both men and women combatants. Gouging matches pitted those of lesser intelligence or desperate circumstance against rivals adopting elongated sharpened fingernails or cutting appendages attached to their fingertips with which to slice and rupture faces and take out eyeballs.

There was money aplenty. The commission of ordinary crimes, and often too the most heinous ones, were winked at by the authorities and passed unnoticed. Nary a day went by when as morning dawned a dead body was not seen floating in some canal or slip in the First Ward or the Canal Street District.

The sporting women of Canal Street were not only among the prettiest but were experts at separating men from their money. They wore good clothes and most of them sang well and drank wine. Out of Mother Carey's boardinghouse girls barely into their teens with no better prospects were sold as "cooks" and "companions" to lonely ships' captains.

Canal Street men were criminals of a superlative variety. They stooped to very few petty thefts, for in those days the robbing of a drunk or a sleeper was not necessary. There were crooks making their headquarters in the Canal Street district then that were experts at every line of graft known to the profession; bankbreakers and housebreakers, the holdup and confidence men, the pickpocket and all the others—they were all represented and they all had money. Among this population of grifters there were no poor ones.

The trade on the lakes was at its height at that time and many a hard-earned dollar was shaken down or stolen outright from the captains and sailors of the great boats of the Great Lakes. Murders were not of infrequent occurrence and fights and brawls ensued with the predictability of the setting sun. Many an officer of the law in the performance of his duties there endured ordeals that tried the men's souls. Yet in recounting their experiences they often spoke with something of respect about those crooks they hounded down and drove from their concert saloons and seedier haunts. They were thieves and murderers the lot of them, but they were also men with the bark on, brave men who knew not the meaning of the word fear, always ready for a fight, never surrendering without a struggle, and criminals that they were, no one could say they were cowards. Among those most captivated by the single-minded objectiveness of these determined men was the young and highly impressionable Fingy Conners.

※※※

"My nose's been broke so many times I lost count," said Detective Sergeant Jim Sullivan.

He was gathered with ten or twelve lads at the Mutual Rowing Club boathouse in the upstairs parlor seated at the elegant bar the club had salvaged from the burnt Richmond Hotel. Sullivan was halfway through a second much-needed schuper after a long day. Jim Ring was there, and Dave Regan, the police chief's son and star rower of the Mutuals. Dan Bouguard encouraged Sullivan's storytelling about the olden days, for the old guy had surely lived a life and relished the telling of its many sordid tales. Sullivan's practiced diction relaxed a bit as a result of being in the company of alcohol and familiar companions.

"One of them more notorious traps down Canal Street way was a prized package of entertainment run by the pugilist Jack Smith. It was on the corner of Peacock and Evans. There came the drunker of the visitors to the district on weekends to test their strength in liftin' iron weights an' prove their mettle in wrestlin' an' boxin'. A couple o' strongarm men acted as fells for the visitors. One of these strongarm men and weightlifters was a mammoth hulk of a man named Fred Logren. Logren had a sweetheart, an honest hard-workin' woman who was a singer. Logren used to call around after work an' walk her home. One night he called to find his sweetheart bein' roughed up by a drunken sailor.

"'Have a drink?' conspired the sailor when Logren walked in on him.

"'I'll have yer life!' Logren screamed, an' punched the sailor so hard he knocked him complete down a flight o' stairs, breakin' his neck. Me an' Denny Flynn was patrollin' that night an' we hustled up upon hearin' the row an' saw what happened. Logren didn't deny it, an' when we set to collarin' him his lady started in on us, pullin' an' scratchin' at us an' saying Logren saved her from gettin' raped —an' it really started lookin' ugly for us when a sympathetic crowd did start to form around. We had to take him in at that point an' thus started a terrific battle to wrestle Logren down an' get the bracelets on.

"Now this was a man who used to allow stones to be broke on his chest at street fairs, an' our job was to get him to the station house with all three of us still in one piece. I took an elbow to the nose when it was only just healin' up from a punch I got the month before, so I went down to the floor like a ton o' bricks—an' that's when the mob started movin' in on me to get their licks in.

"Denny pulled out his pistol an' shot the ceiling an' we heard a shriek come from up above. Seemed the bullet must've hit a girl upstairs. Half the mob turned their attentions away from me and thundered up the stairs to investigate. Denny took advantage of the ruckus and pulled me up off the floor bleedin', an' we started to drag Logren out but it was like tryin' to pull a ragin' bull down the street. He was cursin' that I was gettin' blood all over his new shirt and both Denny an' me took our share o' punches from 'im. We got 'im into the patrol wagon finally and took off.

"Later we found out nobody got hit by Flynn's bullet but it come close an' caused the lady to scream. Worse for her she was attached to a feeder at the time fillin' her veins with cocaine, so when Lynch an' Jackson showed up right then to investigate, they got her unhooked and brought her in to the station as well."

Just as Jim was winding up his story, Jim Jr. poked his head in the doorway.

"Pa, Sorry to interrupt, but Ma's got supper on the table. You comin'?"

"Yep. All right, here I come. See you later, fellas."

Jim rose a bit unsteadily and accompanied his eldest son out the door and around the corner.

"How's work?" the detective asked Junior.

"Fine. I'm up for a raise and the dry dock's expanding, so things are looking good." He hesitated a few seconds and then said, "Pa, I been thinking about asking Mary Ellen Diggins to marry me."

Oh, Jesus! the detective thought to himself, but he remained silent. Neither he nor any other family relation approved or understood the attraction. Nellie in fact couldn't be crueler about her brother's choice—that in spite of all evidence that the two girls were more like two peas in a pod than not.

Junior was better than this, Jim believed. The Diggins girl was haughty. She displayed a superior attitude. She lorded over people and sniffed at those not up to her high standards, and made no pretense at disguising her disapproval. She was highly judgmental of others and dismissed those out of hand who did not meet her lofty criteria. She shunned people for reasons apparent only to her.

"I know ye think you're gettin' older son. What are you now? Twenty-five? But you're still young with plenty of time to make your mark. Open your eyes! There are so many other girls all around you son, girls who'd be thrilled to have a husband with a booming career in the electrical field like you got, in a ward where so many men are satisfied with bein' just everyday laborers. I don't think you realize your true value around here."

Junior fell silent. He'd heard it all before.

His mother had recently called the Diggins girl "an iceberg" and questioned hurtfully why Junior would continue to tolerate her very chilly disregard for his own parents.

"More 'n' more marriages are fallin' apart these days Jimmy," Hannah had pleaded, "but your blood family is forever. I don't like that Diggins girl and she don't like us. There, I said it! And not just because she's so distant and rude to your father and me, and downright mean to your sister, but because she's so demanding of you. Can't you see that? And that poor sister of hers, Josephine! Why, Jo is more of a servant or a lady-in-waiting to her than she is family! Your father and I want to welcome a new daughter into this family who is just as welcoming to us—and your Mary Ellen certainly is not. She is complicated and has you distracted and forever walkin' on eggshells tryin' to please her. Pleasing someone should not be a demand."

"I just think it's about time, Ma. I want a family," he told her.

"Well, if she expects to start a family with you, Junior, you best tell her she needs to get right with the family you already got before you can even consider startin' a new one with her."

THE FIRST WARD IV

THE END

Fingy Flays Hearst
Doodle Dees Scored by New York Democratic Chairman
SPECIAL DISPATCH TO THE SAN FRANCISCO CALL

NEW YORK, Sept. 25. — "Fingy" Conners, chairman of the Democratic State Committee, says:

"Hearst nominated his editor for president, his lawyer for governor, and his valet for attorney general. The people ain't goin' to throw away votes on that party. What do they do? They take a piece of the Republican platform, chop a block off the Democratic platform and then they have a new platform.

"That's what this Independence party did. It's a one man platform; ours was written by the people and will win.

"Huh! The Hearst bunch makes me sick!"

As the planet's axis predictably shifted, so too did Fingy Conners'.

Benefiting mightily both politically and financially in his capacity as campaign manager for William Randolph Hearst in his run for Governor of New York State in 1906, Conners could not say enough good about Hearst back then. But things were different nowadays; Hearst and his allies were now making Fingy "sick."

Fingy's strategy, such as it was both in politics and in life, relied heavily on making enemies out of friends and political allies, mudslinging them mercilessly in the press or threatening personal violence against them when they displeased him, and then elevating them to ally status once more when convenient.

This cunningly disorienting and tumultuous back-and-forth was his tactic always. His method when things were not going his way was to create chaos, to instill fear, confusion, distraction and apprehension. Historically, this had worked effectively in his favor.

Buffalo Alderman John P. Sullivan, New York Tammany boss Charlie Murphy, newspaper publisher and perennial political candidate William Randolph Hearst —all these and more were on the outs as often as they were allied with Fingy

Conners. However, as the first decade of the century came to a close, the up and coming generation of politicians, which included the brilliant Franklin Delano Roosevelt, as well as quite a few of the Old Guard, were increasingly put off by Conners' machinations. In fact, Roosevelt delighted in regularly telling anecdotes defiling Fingy Conners at every opportunity, so generous was Conners in his own creation of them.

In an interview with reporters from the New York press, Conners had only most recently bragged that he would be the next Senator from New York State while at the same time expressing contempt for the average voter.

"Party principals!" he ranted. "Tush! Just make the people think you're going to win. What do the people care about platforms or principals? They just want to be on the winnin' side."

More youthful men had begun rising steadily within the ranks of New York State's Democratic Party. These men were not slavishly inured to Conners' Machiavellian ways, not cowed into total submission by the sheer force of his reputation as were their elders, not quite so terrified by the aging man's threats, pugilistic or otherwise. These newer younger men were increasingly in accordance with Tammany leader Charles F. Murphy, Conners' former closest political ally and now his most determined political enemy.

Their unified objective was to rid the party of the vicious thug who had slanderously accused Murphy of engaging in the auctioneering of judgeships. To Murphy, Conners' fabricated accusation, repeated over and again on a number of occasions despite having been disproved, was an example of the kind of out of control tyranny the Party might expect from Conners if he were not soon stopped, as he steamrolled over whomever got in his way on his quest for total domination. Conners and Murphy had formerly been so close for so long that Fingy on numerous occasions was quoted as stating, "There ain't nothin' can come between me and Charlie Murphy. They don't make nothin' thin as that."

Conners had boasted long and hard that he would fight to the death to retain his leadership of the Democratic Party. But on February 24th that boast, as the *New York Times* stated, "dwindled into nothingness. To the amazement of both his friends and his enemies, he permitted Charles F. Murphy to lead him meekly to the slaughter."

So desperate was he not to be fired for his lies, to finish out the last few weeks of his term as Chairman, that Fingy initially acquiesced to every demand made by his intended ousters.

Nothing could be more shameful to the entrenched self-described "winner" than a humiliation as monumental as a very public firing.

He'd retained his title thus far but at a political cost that shocked what few remaining allies he had. To a man they questioned why he was willing to sacrifice far more than the position was worth.

They were unable to comprehend that, to Conners, his pride trumped all.

In return for not being flagrantly and immediately terminated, as was his Party's original intent, Fingy agreed to disappear without a fuss once his incumbency expired come April 17th, a mere few weeks hence.

Even more mortifying, he was to stand before the entire committee in Albany and take back every word of his infamous *New York Herald* interview in which he accused Murphy of selling judgeships to the highest bidder despite presenting no evidence to that end. He would rescind this and all other provocative statements and reckless accusations he had made about Murphy. He would promise to aid his successor in the leadership changeover. Fingy Conners was forced to make the personally excruciating choice between saving face or saving his scalp.

Notoriously thin-skinned and insecure, the blustering bully initially chose saving face.

Conners had taken a count of supporters, which determined that he was a goner. Quizzically, rather than being rightly humbled by this, he was emboldened to double-down. Challenging the other side's demands, he sent word to Murphy's camp that he would not press his previously debunked charges against Murphy if Murphy would agree to allow Conners to finish out his term.

Upon hearing this from his messengers, Murphy burst out laughing.

"The sheer hubris of that asshole!" he roared.

Murphy's on-the-record response was a bit less crude, although swift and blunt: "Mr. Conners must be in his advanced dotage to suggest such a ludicrous thing."

Murphy knew full well that to allow such allegations to go rigorously unchallenged would be interpreted as tantamount to an admission of his guilt, therefore nothing less than an unmitigated retraction by Conners would satisfy him. Murphy placed all his money on Conners' having stated that the thing that would rankle with him most would be the failure of his many boasts claiming he would remain State Chairman until the end of his term. Murphy set out to call his bluff.

Faced with the reality of the situation, Conners was indeed, it turned out, willing to publicly retract his allegations if Murphy would allow him to serve out his term. Accepting at long last the inevitable truth, that no one at all was entirely in his corner any longer, Fingy Conners accepted Murphy's demand in order to save his office and avoid, by *his* barometer at least, the greater public shame. Thus, he set himself up to do something he had virtually never done during his entire lifetime. Such occasions could be counted on the remaining fingers of Conners left hand with a few digits left over: he agreed to swallow his pride and apologize for his lies in a statement made before the committee and the press.

Once Conners' pledge was made he predictably reversed himself, initiating an aggressive back and forth over the conditions of the repudiation. Conners' intent was to camouflage his retraction amid vague and nebulous terms in order to save his pride. Murphy, the victim of the false accusation, would accept nothing less than a full scale public self-humiliation from Conners.

❧❧

Late that afternoon in Albany at the Ten Eyck Hotel, Chairman Conners called the meeting to order. Originally it was scheduled for noon, but wrangling between Conners and Murphy delayed it. The opening gavel was sounded at 3 p.m. The meeting lasted all of 15 minutes.

Fingy's snarl-like smile turned to a scowl almost immediately. It was clear he did not relish the dose that had been prepared for him. He pounded the gavel calling the rowdy meeting to order so forcefully that the wooden hammer split in two. He ordered the roll call and then announced he had a statement to deliver.

Conners stood naked as never before.

His face alternated between crimson and dead pale as he struggled through the prepared statement, hanging his head at times in obvious and unprecedented shame. One could have heard a pin drop during his pauses. His former friends in the room were horrified. Even his opponents were stunned. This was not the Fingy Conners anyone knew. An admission of wrongdoing? A public apology? This was not their chief. Their disdain as embodied in downcast eyes and slow back-and-forth woeful head shaking made it universally clear that Conners' leadership was acceptable to them no longer.

He commenced his speech:

"Gentlemen. Before we proceed with any other business I wish to make a personal statement to the members of the committee."

He stopped, took a few large gulps from his glass of water, then proceeded nervously.

"I have been for several years now Chairman of the body, havin' been elected at the Buffalo convention in 1906, and served throughout that term, and again at the Carnegie Hall convention in April 1908, when I was elected, as I claim, for the term of two years. I expect and desire to serve out that term of office but I wish now to give you timely and ample notice of the fact that under no conceivable circumstances will I be a candidate for reelection to this office.

"With all due regard for the honor conferred by this distinction, the office of State Chairman of the party is a thankless and difficult job. I have given you the best that is in me for all the time that I have been at the head of this body and I believe that the party throughout the state is now in good fightin' condition for the comin' campaign.

"But as you all know, I got large business interests to attend to, and I have neglected them during the last four years. I got a large family and I need to give them more time and attention than I have been able to do."

Fingy paused to take another generous drink of water in preparation for the hard part. He cleared his throat, then steeled himself for the previously unimaginable.

"I must admit to havin' some infirmities of temper which lead me to say from time to time things in passion and heat which are unjustified in fact and not meant by me to be taken seriously. I have said some of these things lately, and I sincerely regret them. My accusation against Mr. Murphy—that he was auctioneerin' judgeships—ain't true and I hereby withdraw these statements and apologize to Mr. Murphy and to his family for the upset I caused."

As historically has been proven time and again in cases involving disorderly individuals who allow their deepest fears and insecurities to wildly skew their actions, unless they are categorically challenged, escalations in their unruly behaviors are inevitable. So it was with Fingy Conners.

Secure in his second term as State Chairman and mistakenly self-convinced of a third, Conners was hungry for more and greater power. He was overtaken by dreams and delusions of himself sitting at the right hand of one President or another, if not sitting in the Oval Office himself. Fingy Conners had exceeded all previous intimidations with the full intention of forcing out longtime Tammany boss Murphy at any cost, including committing slander.

Conners' monumental blunder was in underestimating Murphy's willingness to respond in kind to his unhinged lies. Similar examples littered Fingy's past in which he responded like an unjustly accused child, insulted and wounded, when victims of his cruelty had the gall to defend themselves by means of a counterattack.

A supreme narcissist, Conners believed that his savagery should by all rights go unchallenged, that resistance against his brutality in any form was disrespectful and inappropriate.

The overall opinion held by his cronies was that Conners had ended his political career in humiliation and capitulation, weaknesses that could be neither forgiven nor forgotten. What transpired in that meeting in the grand parlor of the Ten Eyck Hotel astounded everyone. All had fully expected and indeed eagerly looked forward to a knock-down, drag out, scratching and clawing contest between Conners and Murphy. Instead the whole thing deflated as quickly and as surely as a ruptured hot air balloon.

Immediately after delivering his remarks, Conners hurried from the meeting room. He returned upstairs to the Presidential suite where his bags awaited already packed, his bellboy at the ready. He splashed cold water on his face and partook of a swig of Canadian Club from his flask before combing his full head of hair in the mirror admiringly, then vaulted for the rail station. Waving his cane menacingly he refused to make any remarks to the herd of agitating news reporters awaiting him. He boarded the New York Central for Manhattan. He declined to speak to anyone at all. He lay down on the mohair settee in his first class compartment and took a long nap, the swaying of the car rocking him like a babe in his mother's arms.

In New York he caught the evening train for Florida, for he required a sojourn to his villa in Palm Beach. He longed for sun and fresh ocean air and to sit on the veranda with a cool drink and watch the promenade flow past his mansion at Ocean Boulevard and Australian Avenue. He craved the fawnings of his high society Florida friends known to reinvigorate his ego, the luxury of long dinners and a brandy at the Breakers Hotel to renew his spirit, the warm evening breeze and swaying coco palms to salve his humiliation, the sound of ocean waves to lull him to sleep at night. Most of all he lusted for the exotic techniques of his latest mistress, a girl of nineteen, assured that her enchantments would no doubt resuscitate from deep within him the energies of his achingly missed distant youth.

Mary Jordan Conners only learned of her husband's capitulation by reading about it in the newspapers the following morning. Afraid to face her, he was unwilling yet to endure her judgment over his derailing. He could not face her wrath with regards to the abrupt halt in his political momentum and what that ultimately meant regarding their shared dream of living in the White House. Thus, he chose not to return home. Florida would give him time to think and plan his comeback.

This told Mary Jordan Conners all she needed to know.

His Lips Forgot The Taste Of Truth

Samuel Clemens aka Mark Twain

In Artistic Disarray

Jim Sullivan stopped for a moment in front of his house at N⁰ 16 Hamburg Street before entering. The sleuth's well-oiled suspicions had been raised. A few doors up, in front of the house at N⁰ 24 that took in short-term boarders, he observed a woman with two children in the company of a man about whom, Jim surmised, the woman was much friendlier than any wife had a right to be toward a husband of such longstanding. He lingered there observing them for a minute or two before swinging open the gate. Zeke barked deeply from behind the closed front door. Jim opened it and the big black lab bounded out, jumping and running circles around him joyously, tail whipping as though he had not seen him in a year, when in fact it had only been a few hours.

"Go have your piss, Zeke," he laughed amid a frenzy of hugs and kisses.

Zeke wanted out of the closed gate. Jim backtracked a few steps and obliged. The dog inspected the full length of the fence bordering the sidewalk for freshly laid competitive scents with which to cover with his own.

Jim again was distracted by the amorous couple with the two children. The kids clung to their mother, not interacting at all with the man, almost as if he were a stranger to them. Jim kept one eye on Zeke, lest he look ready to wander off in search of female company. The neighborhood bitches were in heat. He admired the black lab's fierce determination to reclaim his fence. Once the barrier had been fully anointed end to end, with some encouragement Zeke galloped past Jim back into the house.

"Sit," Jim ordered after following his faithful friend and shutting the door behind them.

Zeke sat and offered his paws one by one for cleaning without being prodded, the ceremony being rote by this point. Jim bent down, back aching, to thoroughly wipe all four, then led his furry charge inside. The heavenly aroma of Hannah's beef stew beckoned.

"Hannah?" he called. "I'm home!"

No answer.

"Nellie? You home?"

Again, no answer. He entered the kitchen. There was a note propped against the sugar bowl on the oil cloth covering the kitchen table:

> Honey,
> I've gone to a meeting at Pet's about the church bazaar. There's stew on the stove. Heat it up for yourself. Don't dare give none to the dog! Nellie's teaching a music lesson at the Atwoods and won't be home until 7. Davey's next door with Annie.
> Love, H.

The stew was still acceptably warm. He scooped up a big bowl full and opened a bottle of Beck's. Zeke looked at him beseechingly.

"Don't you go tellin' your mother, now," Jim warned. Zeke's tail went wild with expectancy as Jim fixed him a dish. Jim placed the bowl of stew on the floor, the dog attacking it as soon as it touched the linoleum. Its contents disappeared completely within seconds.

A few minutes later a noisy commotion out front caught Jim's attention. Zeke at his heels, he walked over to the parlor window and looked out to witness a noisy parade coming down the street. As Jim stood there shoveling beef stew into his mouth he watched JP being surrounded by a small army of angry women, shouting. Jim chuckled. "Serves you right, brother," he confided to Zeke. "Serves the little bastard right and good, now don't it, good boy?"

Zeke barked in agreement.

The women were teachers infuriated by the city's stonewalling them as to a well-deserved long-overdue pay raise. JP publicly praised the enormous contributions of the city's teachers, but in practice their cause was of minor importance to him, since women, despite decades of suffragettes' efforts, did not yet have the vote. Many men in fact, mostly poorly paid laborers, demonstrated fiercely to the alderman against a pay raise for teachers clearly out of jealousy. The mere thought of a young unmarried female "with no family to support" getting paid significantly more than laboring family men while enjoying shorter working hours and a summer vacation rankled these workers no end.

JP patiently pointed out to the workers that there were many other jobs available to men that also paid more than laborers' jobs, because those jobs too required a diploma. He stopped short of reminding them that for most, dropping out of school had severely limited their employment choices and had thus sealed their fate, while those who stuck with it and got a diploma, such as had the lady teachers, enjoyed the spoils. JP knew full well that to these men it was neither a matter of logic or education, but a case of simple misogyny mingled with a large helping of sour grapes.

For the purpose of getting through to the city's recalcitrant aldermen it was agreed among the teachers that they should amass according to the wards in which they lived and march to the homes of their respective representative to exact a pledge from him through such demonstration of their determination.

As an influential leader in the Board of Aldermen, JP Sullivan was a prime target, but tracking down the infamously slippery representative was another matter.

Knowing a woman's voice would likely be a tipoff, the wards' teachers had a male ally call the Sullivan Ice Co. and ask to speak to JP about placing an order. Once established that Alderman Sullivan was present on site, the women closed in and the little army divided their ranks into two groups of about 20 each to watch over the only two streets from which he might escape. Once within their sights they ran to surround him and then accompanied him noisily to his home on Hamburg Street. At first he tried to put them off with some of his jocular remarks, to which one of the leaders shouted, "Oh, cut that out John P.! We mean business! Will you stand for a resolution of the kind we intend to have introduced? That's what we want to know!"

At their destination he stood on his porch steps and addressed the assembled. "Ladies, your earnestness has so impressed me that I promise you that I will vote as you desire me to vote."

The teachers were a bit shocked, then suspicious, as they had expected a knock-down drag-out battle. As they grew more contentious he assured them he was serious and that they had earned his support.

Jim watched as the female warriors departed skeptically and suspiciously as JP entered his house, wondering if his brother would indeed honor his word, for the Mayor had promised to veto the action. Time would tell.

Jim walked back into the kitchen. Zeke trailed after him.

The detective sat down at the table and continued his meal. He allowed the *New York Times* waiting there to remain folded. JP often picked up a copy for him from the daily delivery to the city hall, leaving it on his doorstep, but Jim had experienced just about his fill of life's tribulations that particular day. The *Times* could wait. His shift had been an unusually stressful one. After gobbling a few more thick spoonfuls he got up and opened the cupboard, rummaged around amidst the spice tins and flour and sugar canisters, and retrieved a bottle of Bayer aspirin. He popped two into his mouth, then sat and resumed eating.

He thought about the many incidents of the previous twelve hours. The image of the beautiful young girl, no older than daughter Nellie by his determination, lying there on the perforated copper table at the Morgue, white as a ghost, weighed heavily on his mood, as might be expected of any father having a precious daughter of his own.

He had been called to Mrs. Blanchette's Boarding House at 176 West Huron St. that morning. There the girl lay in her bed, beautiful and dead, blood staining the sheets, copious amounts of it appearing to have erupted from her vagina.

"Her name is Annie Cavanaugh," whimpered Mrs. Blanchette. "She told me she's from Canada."

Blanchette told Detective Sullivan that the girl had arrived on Monday; that she had stated she was from a well-to-do family but she had left home because she was dissatisfied with her lot. She had come to Buffalo so that she might make her living in the States. Blanchette gave her a sunny room on the second floor looking out over Huron Street.

"Come to think of it," Blanchette sniffled, "me and the other boarders thought she was acting queerly, though I did not suspect anything was wrong."

Annie Cavanaugh had left Mrs. Blanchette's house Tuesday evening and disappeared up the street on foot. When she returned a couple of hours later she looked weakened and complained she was not feeling well. A doctor visited her later on in her room.

"She went to bed and remained there all through yesterday fighting a fever," Blanchette said. "Last night she was even worse." The landlady told Jim she wanted to send for the doctor again, but the girl refused, arguing she thought she would be all right.

"I just need to sleep. I'll be all right in the morning," Miss Cavanaugh predicted.

Come morning she was worse still. Blanchette summoned the doctor. The girl lingered until about 9:30 and then she died.

It was not long after that when Jim was called to the scene to initiate an investigation. Coroner Danser too was summoned. He completed his examination, then removed the body to the morgue.

Jim asked Mrs. Blanchette who the doctor was who arrived to treat Miss Cavanaugh. She said it was Dr. J.G. Harper, whose house was right up the street. Jim left to pay the good doctor a visit. Harper claimed he was called to the boarding house and did not know the young lady, having never met her previously. Jim returned to Mrs. Blanchette's. He told Blanchette what the doctor had said.

"Oh, he knew her all right, Detective. In fact it was he who made the arrangements for the girl to stay here in the first place."

Blanchette then whispered something into Jim Sullivan's ear.

Jim returned to Headquarters where an order for Dr. Harper's arrest was made. Jim determined that Harper was paid the sum of $100 by Miss Cavanaugh to perform an illegal operation. She was pregnant and had crossed the border to relieve herself of her shame in a city where no one was acquainted with her. The identity of the father of the unborn child was found to be that of a Toronto man. A telegram was sent to the Canadian authorities in Toronto, Miss Cavanaugh's home. An arrest warrant was sworn on the young man.

Mrs. Blanchette was quite upset about the events. She cried profusely.

"She was quite an unusually good-looking girl," the landlady sniffled. "She was dressed so stylishly. She had all the attributes of refinement. What a shame!"

Jim had made a thorough examination of the dead girl's room. Her clothes were well made and of good material. On a small table was a pitcher full of flowers. Beside them was an empty box from Anderson's Florist Shoppe addressed to "Miss Lee," the name under which the room was rented. A purse was found, inside of which was a card with the name "H.C. Leacy, Cardinal." A volume of "Trilby" on which was printed the name of Dr. J.G. Harper with a rubber stamp marring its decorative frontispiece. A Roman Catholic medal inscribed with a French epitaph. One-half of a round trip ticket Toronto-Buffalo. An unopened bar of Cadbury's milk chocolate and a small sum of money were in one drawer, a wool shawl in another.

Mrs. Blanchette said that after having summoned the doctor that he came downstairs in a distressed state after visiting with Miss Cavanaugh and informed the landlady that the young woman upstairs was dead. He left the house in a hurry and did not return. She thought this quite cold and unfeeling. He had left it entirely up to her to figure out what to do about the distressing situation. No helpful counsel from the doctor had been forthcoming. She immediately notified the police of the affair, saying she thought there was something unsavory amiss.

Jim went and fetched Dr. Harper himself. He was in the midst of a physical examination of a wealthy Delaware Ave. man having a giant tumor growing atop his already ample stomach.

"And just what do you expect me to do?" hollered the exposed patient as the doctor was hauled out.

Jim saw no need to handcuff the physician, who accompanied him to Headquarters peacefully. Once there Jim led him into the office of Chief of Detectives Paddy Cusak. There the doctor broke down completely and sobbed like a heart-broken child.

"It was not an illegal operation!" he insisted. "The procedure was necessary to preserve the young lady's life!"

The police did not buy it.

"I'm ruined!" he cried. "My life is wrecked! For heaven's sake, keep this away from the newspapers!"

The prisoner gave every indication of being on the verge of convulsions. He trembled like a leaf. His mental agony was pitiful. Cusack ordered him to jail. He directed the attending officers to maintain a strict watch over him, fearing the doctor might attempt suicide if given even a ghost of a chance.

❦❦❦

Later that afternoon Jim was passing on lower Main Street lost in his daydream of reliving that morning's tragedy. "Four lives ruined," he mumbled out loud to himself. "Four! The girl, her beau, the unborn baby, and the doctor."

Abruptly his attention was attracted by a great outcry from Commercial Street. He ran in that direction in time to see a wild-eyed man running at full speed pursued by an excited crowd yelling for him to stop.

"Catch him! Stop him! He's murdered a man on Canal Street!" was the collective outcry.

Jim, still fleet of foot despite his advancing years, joined in the chase and was soon running with the leaders.

Thomas Reilly turned his head as he ran to glance over his shoulder. He was alarmed by the increasing number of pursuers, which now included the policeman. He tried increasing his speed but was tiring fast. He had run from Canal Street to Commercial, and when Detective Sullivan joined the crowd, Reilly turned into Lloyd Street and ran down that thoroughfare with the leaps of an alarmed deer. When he reached Water Street he began to realize he would soon be overtaken if he continued running in the street, so he dashed into an open stairwell. Detective Sullivan by that time was but a few yards behind the flagging escapee. When the panting fugitive shot up an open stairway, Jim Sullivan was hot on his tail.

Reilly climbed the stairs one flight after another until he reached the top floor four stories up. There he made his way through an open window to the roof of a neighboring building where he gave up and collapsed to the tar paper from fright and exhaustion. Jim followed and soon had him under arrest. He took him to Headquarters, Reilly protesting every step of the way.

Captain Taylor's men investigated. It developed that Reilly had been begging on

Canal Street when a gang of roughs who he had asked for money threw him to the ground and inflicted upon him a severe thrashing. As soon as Reilly could escape he started on a run, his assailants pursuing him. This race attracted hangers-on, and just as in the tale of Oliver Twist, mistaken cries of "Thief!" and "He's murdered a man!" were taken up by one after another of the pursuers along his route until the growing crowd was convinced they were chasing down a desperate escaped criminal.

Learning the details of this wasteful exercise caused Jim's spirit to plummet, the event coming as it did directly on the heels of Miss Cavanaugh's terrible tragedy. He felt a fool now, following the crowd's lead without questioning, endangering himself, endangering the poor man he'd pursued who himself had been the victim of a violent crime. It was days like this that made him question why he was ever a cop in the first place, why he was a cop still after almost thirty years of it.

Maybe it was time to retire.

"I'm too old for this shit!" he muttered angrily to himself for the umpteenth time. He had to drag himself home by sheer will, so depleted in spirit was he, so exhausted and aching his aging muscles.

As the two best pals slurped up the last of their beef stew, a few random large black letters printed on the folded *New York Times* across the table coalesced in his mind, beckoning Jim's attention. He opened the journal.

The terrible headline read "Mark Twain Is Dead at 74."

Jim's heart sank to the soles of his shoes.

He tried to read, but tears flooded his eyes. His old friend, his mentor, his teacher, was gone.

"And I forgot his birthday last November!" he chastised himself, taking out his handkerchief. Zeke, the tenderest of dogs, was alerted by his master's sniffling. He rose with some arthritic difficulty from his place on the floor and laid his chin atop Jim's knee, gazing up at him with sad soulful loving brown eyes.

"Aw Zeke..." Jim cried, voice cracking, "our Sam is dead."

He wiped his eyes so he might read the long report on Sam's last weeks of life as the Great One had see-sawed between illness and recovery. When Sam's daughter Jean died the previous Christmas Eve, discovered unresponsive in her bathtub at Stormfield, Jim had asked himself, as he mailed his condolences to his old friend, how much more tragedy could poor Sam possibly endure? He'd lost his entire family at this point, save for his daughter Clara. And now here, on the twenty-second of April, less than four months later, Jim had his answer: Sam could endure no more.

Through his tears he chuckled at one of the lines in Twain's obituary:

> "It is a legend that he was vastly proud of his famous mop of white hair, and used to spend the pains of a court lady in getting it to just the proper stage of artistic disarray."

"Artistic disarray!" Jim chuckled, wiping his eyes. He smiled, recalling his seventeen year old self leaning on his lawn rake, conversing with Samuel Clemens in his front yard on Delaware Avenue, Sam's fingers raking through the wild luxurious dark disheveled curly mane, of which the younger Sam he was well acquainted with and in admiration of, was so proud and so vain.

Jim finished his stew, cut himself a big slice of rye bread, retrieved a chunk of ice from the Jewett icebox and a clean dishrag in which to wrap it, and laid himself down on the parlor divan. His head and back were throbbing in tandem.

"You ain't supposed to be up here," he gently scolded Zeke, who had settled in next to him, head resting in the crook of Jim's arm. "Your mother's gonna kill us both."

Somehow massaging the dog's brow soothed his own. His imagination wandered back to the day when he first met Sam, downtown out front of the stationary store on Main Street when he had just turned seventeen.

Sam's carriage had glanced over his foot and Sam had insisted on giving Jim a ride home. Sam ultimately offered him weekend employment at his handsome house on Buffalo's street of millionaires, Delaware Avenue. For more than a year they'd talked and joked there between chores. Sam was at that time editor of the *Buffalo Express* newspaper, and through their conversations Jim learned the workings of writers and editors and was provided much useful minutiae by his employer.

"Did you know Buffalo has more millionaires per capita than any city in the entire world?" Sam stated, gesturing toward his neighbors. "It's true, although I'm not one of them..." he paused a moment, then added with a twinkle in his eye, "...yet!"

They both laughed.

All the while Sam's sickly wife Livy was concerned that Jim was taking advantage, stealing Sam's time and money when Jim should have rightly been busying himself raking, trimming and sweeping.

One day Sam leaned in close to Jim as Livy glowered disapprovingly from the front window at their carousing and said, "I do believe my dear Livy is a bit jealous of you, Jimmy!"

That little conspiracy warmed Jim's heart without end. Not too long after, upon suffering too great a number of personal setbacks, Sam packed up his wife and newborn baby and departed Buffalo in pursuit of more welcoming spaces. His unexpected departure left Jim—his home life at that time in utter turmoil, and Sam his sole respite—with a cavernous void to fill.

Jim drifted off to sleep on the divan for a little while, arm dangling, hand resting on Zeke now snoring protectively on the floor beside him. He awoke after a bit, parched, confused at first about where he was. He raised himself up creakily and shuffled to the kitchen for a drink of water. Just then, Hannah and Nellie both walked into the house at the same moment.

Nellie gave him an unenthusiastic peck on the cheek. "Hiya Poppa," she said.

"Hello dear husband," chirped Hannah. "How was your day?"

"Fine, Honey. Just fine," Jim smiled.

They sat in the kitchen, all three enjoying stew as Nellie animatedly recounted the day's trials at her job at the Larkin Soap factory's office building, a commodious modern spectacle designed by Chicago architect Frank Lloyd Wright.

"I forgot my shawl, and the heat was on the blink. My hands were so cold all day long I could barely operate my Underwood! Say Pa, did the police ever locate that Hungarian woman and two kids who ran away from her husband?" Nellie asked. "I read she took all that poor man's savings with her."

He startled to attention. "What woman was that?"

"That woman who was in the newspapers this morning. She took her two kids and all her husband's money and ran off with another Hungarian man. They been lookin' all over the place for her."

Jim did recall the story, but since it was a Fruitbelt occurrence rather than his own jurisdiction he failed to pay proper attention.

"I'll be right back," he excused himself.

Jim hurried down the stairs to the street, then walked up to N⁰ 24 and knocked.

"Mrs. Manahar, are you boarding a Hungarian couple here with two small children?"

"Why yes, Jim. Look. Here they come now."

Jim turned to see the group approaching the house. They spotted him at the same moment, turned on their heels suddenly and retraced their steps.

"Halt, there!" Jim hollered.

Within seconds he had the man in wrist cuffs. Quietly so as not to upset her children he leaned in and said to the woman, "And you! If them little ones weren't here with you right now lady, I'd be providin' you with some pretty bracelets of your own as well. Now you come with me. An' don't you dare be thinkin' 'bout givin' me no trouble—for their sake."

Cold Turkey

"Ruth, I can't help but think that your current malaise has something to do with your encountering Fingy Conners at my brother-in-law's house last Thanksgiving."
Ruth didn't answer.
"I saw the way you looked at him, with fear in your eyes," Hannah stated.
Again Ruth failed to respond.
"You told me what happened to you in that house, when you were just a girl, with that terrible man. Ruth, is Fingy Conners the terrible man who attacked you?"
She wouldn't say.
It turned out that Ruth had experienced a dependence on morphine previously. She was well aware of what lay ahead if she did not stop. She had promised herself on that Thanksgiving evening after returning home from the Alderman's dinner in a state of discombobulation after laying her unbelieving eyes on Fingy Conners that her indulgence would be just a one-time thing. Just to relieve the shock of coming face to face with that despicable man after all these many years.

The meager dosage she took for her headaches had surely been helping. She used the drug responsibly, cautiously. She diminished each successive dosage of her own free will so as to not again become seduced. But finding herself facing her long-ago abuser she was shocked by her own reaction. She had often thought about what she might do, how she might react, if again confronted with the noxious sneer so permanently a part of her memory of her nemesis' face. Her assessment assured her if such an occasion presented itself that she would act as if nothing at all had happened, that she would excuse herself from the situation and put her mind to better things, constructive things, creative things.

But that's not what happened.

The evil delivered to her at age 12 washed over her anew like a tidal wave, resurrecting shards of terror and hate and dread that she had invested so much time and effort in burying. Until recently she believed she had successfully accomplished this, that she had risen above, that she could at long last retire the shovel back on its nail and carry on with her life anew.

Annie Sullivan had surprisingly and generously welcomed Ruth into her and the alderman's home that Thanksgiving Day based on Hannah's admiration for the woman. Hannah was delighted, thinking they might all become good friends. But Annie's tolerance for such things as a person's weakness concerning alcohol or drugs was nil. Hannah guarded her friend's secret torment.

Each time the Alderman suffered one of his many life-threatening illnesses or injuries it was Annie who took control of dispensing her husband's medications, which included laudanum. She would have it no other way.

The Alderman tried assuring her he had no such addictive tendencies. The politician used as proof his example of attending banquets and celebrations on a weekly schedule where the alcohol flowed like water, yet he himself rarely had partaken of more than a drink or two. Regardless, Annie had seen JP's cronies in politics and certain members of the Mutual Rowing Club descend into the hell that alcohol created for the men and by association their suffering wives and children. In the waterfront First Ward, many a small family business included a "dash saloon" as Annie always referred to the phenomenon. The shoemaker's was a Shoemaker-saloon. The grocers a Grocery-Saloon. The barber shop a Barber-Saloon. Even the candy store wasn't entirely immune.

"I wouldn't be at all surprised to learn someone wanted to install a saloon in church!" sniffed Annie one day.

"Don't think for a moment it hasn't been suggested," laughed Hannah, "and considering Father Cornelius's religious devotion to the bottle, it's close to a miracle it hasn't happened as of yet."

Laboring men on the docks were known to interrupt their work on a whim and march off *en masse* to a saloon and get drunk, then return to work almost useless. That had always been the way on Buffalo's waterfront.

To take full advantage, saloons were opportunistically wedged between towering grain elevators, leaned buttress-like against warehouses, and were hung precariously on stilts off the sides of slips, especially along Ganson Street. Anywhere a saloon could fit, a saloon was fitted.

The alderman's wife was not about to let any such problem take hold in her home, to her family. Hannah thus decided that she'd keep Ruth's morphine problem to herself, knowing full well Annie's reaction would be damning.

Ruth had set Hannah down and grimly described in disturbing detail what suddenly stopping the drug had previously done to her.

"It's absolute hell on earth, Hannah. I wouldn't wish that kind of suffering on my worst enemy."

She paused a few beats, then added, "Well...maybe just *one* enemy."

His Lips Forgot The Taste Of Truth

Sculpture Court, Albright Art Gallery, circa 1910

NAKED

On Saturday mornings the Alderman and his eldest sons Thomas and Daniel traditionally enjoyed breakfast together before they left for the Sullivan Ice Company's giant ice house out on the beach near Stony Point.

That morning, Thomas had been uncharacteristically quiet until he abruptly spoke up.

"Pa, why are you trying to have the Sunday picture shows shut down?"

"Why, because it's the Sabbath, Thomas. And people should be doing more wholesome things on that day, such as going to church and spending time with their families."

"Pa, do you think of me as a child?" the twenty-three year-old challenged, locking his eyes to his father's.

"Uh...why no. No, Thomas. Not at all. You've grown to become a fine young man, just the way your mother and I raised you."

"Why are you trying to have the picture shows closed on Sundays?"

The alderman grew uncomfortable and silenced. Thomas waited attentively for his response.

"I just told you, Tom."

"I recall Pa, ten long years ago, when the religious bullies of this city tried to close the Pan American Exposition on Sundays. Your argument against that was that the very men who built the Exposition, the laborers, would never get to see it if it closed on Sundays. And now here we are ten progressive years into the future, and you're trying to bully the people of this city in the same way as those religious hypocrites did."

"Thomas, excuse me for becoming more aware as I get older of the value of spending time with one's family!"

"Is that it, Pa? Is that what you wanted to do when you were my age? Spend your Sundays with Peter Halloran?"

Halloran was the Alderman's cruel despised stepfather, a man who had once sunk a butcher knife into his mother's neck as he and his brothers watched horrified.

The alderman fell silent.

Son Daniel did not look up from his eggs. Unlike his older brother, Daniel was non-confrontational. He admired Thomas for his bravery for speaking up, for tackling thorny issues head-on. Daniel was a bit ashamed of himself for not being more like his older brother. Daniel was four inches taller than Thomas. Unlike Thomas, Daniel was built like a quarterback. He played basketball fiercely for the world champion Buffalo Germans team. He was as handsome as a Leyendecker illustration in an Arrow Collar advertisement. But despite having all the physical manifestations of an admired leader, he was not—at least, not yet.

"Those religious busybodies, they saw a drop in church attendance due to the exposition, and that meant less money in the collection basket, so their incentives were clear. What political favors could you possibly owe someone that you would try to force such a travesty upon every man, woman and child of this city, including your own?" Thomas accused.

"Thomas!" JP shouted.

"Alderman Sullivan!" Thomas shot back. "I work hard all week for you at this ice house, and half days on Saturdays too, and I will not be told what I can do on my one and only day off! Not by my father, not by my employer, not by the church—and certainly not by some politician!"

"Thomas, I am your father and you will not speak to me in that way."

"I just did, Pa," he stated strategically. "I. Just. *Did*."

❧❧

The Alderman was up to his old tricks. His insatiable appetite for publicity and attention had resulted in yet another even more outlandish crusade than the Sunday picture show debacle. Alderman John P. Sullivan of the First was now calling for the draping of all the Albright Art Museum's nude statues residing in its grand Sculpture Court.

Because he was a well-acknowledged jokester, keeping things lively in the Common Council whenever *ennui* and tedium threatened, and a very popular Master of Ceremonies assured to enliven any banquet or gathering over which he presided, everyone laughed at first. They believed he was joking absurdly. He was not.

To their credit the museum directors responded in a controlled and calmed manner, pointing out the obvious: that this was an art museum, filled with art, visited only by people who love art and were willing to pay good money to view art. An entrance fee was required. The kind of citizen who paid an admission charge to patronize prestigious fine arts museums like the Albright Art Gallery did not need some priggish politician legislating their morals for them. Behind his back, and more than a few right to his face, the entire city thought JP Sullivan a complete fool.

❧❦❧

Hannah was in high spirits. Her youngest and her last, David Nugent Sullivan, was making his Confirmation at age twelve. Davey's unplanned entry into this world had come on the heels of profound tragedy—the loss, one by one, of Hannah's four youngest children during a nightmarish interval encompassing a period of less than five years.

Little Davey's uncle and namesake, Hannah's brother David J. Nugent, had long been Fingy Conner's top lieutenant, henchman, terrorist, right-hand enforcer and murderer. Additionally, he was married to Fingy's niece Minnie Hayes, daughter of Julia, Fingy's sister who died in a highly suspicious house fire. The Nugents at this time lived in Milwaukee, not by choice, but out of having been banished there.

The unrepentant henchman had petitioned his sister for months prior to his nephew's anticipated religious ceremony. Despite his living with his own robust family in Wisconsin overseeing Fingy's operations at that end of the Great Lakes, he was quite enthused about carting the whole brood east to Buffalo to join in the Catholic solemnization. He missed Buffalo and all his Buffalo friends—especially one in particular. He took every excuse to return "home" for a visit. His request was to aid his big sister in throwing a grand party at the Mutuals' boathouse in honor of his namesake nephew—entirely at his expense. Detective Jim Sullivan was at first against the idea.

"Let's have a small party instead here at home Hannah, where we can best control the situation," the detective cautioned, suspicious of his brother-in-law's motives.

Years of sparring between Hannah and Jim over the undue influence each had individually allowed their own younger brother had driven a wedge of contention between them just as often as had brought them closer together in resolution. Ultimately they had decided it made sense for both to keep their respective brothers, the Alderman and the Henchman, both unapologetic trouble-makers, at affectionate arms' length while under a vigilant eye.

To include either brother in a family event or situation necessitated negotiation, a strategy that both agreed prudent. Hannah, historically unable to deny her brother basically anything he wished, insisted to him the party would best be held at the family home where she could better manage rather than in the daunting free-for-all environs of the Mutual Rowing Club's boathouse.

"But yous ain't got room there atcher little house to fit everybody in, Hannah!"

her brother protested.

"Who's *everybody*?" Hannah responded.

"You know...Davey's little friends, all our cousins, neighbors..."

His list went on and on, causing Hannah to begin feeling overwhelmed. After a week of his expensive long distance phone calls haranguing and upsetting her, she agreed at least to reconsider; it would be another challenge altogether to convince her husband. She did however think it unusual for her brother to be so insistent on this matter.

After thinking it through for a few days Hannah once more decided it would be best to provide a modest buffet for a small number of guests at her home. Opposingly, the penultimate decision was determined upon Uncle David's conspiring with his namesake nephew. Hannah's son looked up to his uncle as a dangerous hero of sorts, just as his uncle at the same age had looked up to Fingy Conners as being such. David J. Nugent conspired with his nephew to insist that his mentor and wife's uncle Fingy Conners be invited to the celebration, which by default, would have to include Fingy's socialite wife Mary.

Young Davey let his strong wishes be known to his mother.

"Over my dead body!" exclaimed Hannah to Jim as she furiously sliced bread with the same deadly determination as Marie Antoinette's executioner. "That man will not be welcome in my house, and most certainly neither will his awful wife after what she done to us! Anyway, there's no chance in heaven that haughty social climber would reduce herself to step foot here into the First Ward, much less visit our house."

"But we're not havin' the party here at the house, Ma," little Davey reasoned, "Remember?"

"Yes we are, Davey."

"But it's *my* Confirmation, Ma!" the youngster argued. "An' everybody I'm invitin' ain't gonna fit in our house!"

"And *I'm* the one payin' for it Davey—and you're right—there's just no room here for everybody you want to invite! So your guest list is just going to have to be shortened."

"Uncle Dave says *he's* payin' for it, Ma. You said so yourself. So why'd you tell Pa we can't have the party at the boathouse then? There's plenty of room over there! It ain't fair to say you're throwin' a party for me and then tell me I can't invite none o' my friends! Is it *my* party, or is it *your* party?"

"Don't you sass your mother like that, young man! Nobody said you can't invite your close friends, but you can't invite the whole ward obviously."

"I ain't invitin' the whole ward, Ma! Just the crick rats!"

The young man had determinedly dug in his heels.

"Stop it David! You're givin' me a sick headache. Go on now, let me think about it."

"Oh, thanks Ma!" Davey shouted victoriously. "It's gonna be the grandest Confirmation shindy ever, just you wait and see!"

❧❧❧

Hannah felt put over a barrel. She knocked on her friend Ruth's door on her way back from the bake shop. Ruth was still struggling, but to Hannah she seemed almost like her old self again.

"Why on earth would you ever invite that horrible man?" Ruth exclaimed in an understandably strident tone.

"Well," justified Hannah defeatedly, "my brother thinks we should. Fingy is his wife's uncle, after all. And his boss. And my brother's payin' for it all, lock, stock 'n' barrel. And he even got the nuns in on his side. I got stopped by two of 'em up on Elk Street talkin' to me about it!"

"What nuns?"

"Them Mercy nuns—the ones at St. Brigid's. You know my brother and them nuns! He worships them. Sister Patricia—even that awful Sister Mary Seraphim. He talks about 'em like they're saints on earth. Despite proof to the contrary!"

"Seraphim? Isn't that the nun they say beats the little children? Why have the parents allowed her to do that to their own children, for God's sake? Where are the priests in all this?"

Hannah only shrugged dismissively. "Well...as long as people believe they're the 'Brides of Christ' as they claim..."

"If that old bitch Seraphim fancies herself a Bride of Christ then I think it's about time Jesus started asking around for a good divorce lawyer," said Ruth.

Hannah laughed. "Ruth! You can't speak that way about the nuns! People just won't stand for it!"

"Oh my God. Hannah, darling..." Ruth sighed heavily with an expression of pity on her face. "*He* worships the nuns? Your brother? The man who shot innocent people for Fingy Conners and has had good family men beaten to within an inch of their lives—and Lord only knows what else?"

"There is no proof of that!" Hannah erupted.

"Dear sweet Hannah...it's right there in the newspapers," Ruth reminded her. "And don't think for a second those hypocrite nuns who love him so much don't read the newspapers."

Ruth had long been perplexed about why Hannah would ever have named her youngest son so pointedly after her violent, felonious, uncontrite brother. Ruth shook her head sadly over her friend's voluntary naiveté. She had heard multiple stories over the years of Nugent's ascribing to methods employed by Chinese highbinders on Conners' behalf, of their mutual enemies being discovered floating face down in the ward's canals and slips or stuffed into barrels. It was widely known that Nugent along with cohort Peter P. Dalton delivered gangs of imported Bowery thugs from the railway stations to local saloons under the cover of darkness to maim and murder their very own neighbors, fine upstanding men trying to organize against Fingy's dehumanized labor contracting methods so they might feed their babies more than bread and tainted municipal water.

She well knew the circumstances surrounding Nugent's leading the infamous invasion of the whaleback *Samuel Mather* just the other side of the Ohio St. bridge back in the Spring of '99. That crime, committed in front of more than three dozen witnesses and reported in newspapers nationwide, should have marked an abrupt and very public conclusion of Hannah's almost twenty years of trying to protect and defend her brother from both himself and the judgment of half the ward's population. She had up until the *Mather* event been able to deny and avert and deflect the rumors about Dave and his boss' known enemies ending up drowned or shot or bisected between the Erie Railroad tracks. But Hannah yet clung fiercely to the comforts provided by denial.

"And what if Fingy's wife decides to show up after all?" Ruth challenged. "You can't invite him and not her. In addition to that depraved monster, do you really want his terrible second wife in your home—*your very house!*—after all you and Jim went through with her trying to ruin your marriage? I imagine she would delight in finding plenty to ridicule and scoff at to all her uppity lady friends at their charity bazaars. Hannah, the boathouse would be a safer choice I believe. You surely do not want either of those two frightful people in your family home!"

"Oh my, you're so right," Hannah sighed. "I know Mary Conners would indeed be icy-blooded about her opinions of me."

"Those society ladies," Ruth agreed, "so bored and so rich, with all their alms-giving and book lending programs and such malarkey, convincing themselves that because they are doing a little good now and again that therefore they themselves are good people! They make me sick when I read about them in the Society columns. You wouldn't believe the lengths that truly awful people will go to convince themselves they're actually fine human beings despite abundant evidence to the contrary, Hannah. Mary Jordan Conners is a perfect example."

Ruth's warning caused Hannah to grudgingly finalize her choice of venue. She concluded the Mutuals boathouse would be more impervious in all respects. She gave in to having the party at the boathouse and she gave in to the idea of inviting Fingy Conners. What she didn't think about was the fact that Fingy, as the initial money man behind the rowing club at its founding, and its first vice president, might have entirely different ideas about how to conduct himself between the two venue choices. She didn't consider how Fingy might not feel the same propriety about minding his mouth and manners at his own clubhouse as he might seated in the Sullivan family parlor.

As could have been predicted, she would come to regret this oversight. The next day she told Ruth about her decision.

"I don't suppose you'd like to come join us?" Hannah asked.

"I...I couldn't stomach being in the same room..." said Ruth, hesitating a few beats, "but...well, thank you anyway, Hannah. Save me some ham, will you?" she smiled.

Hannah laughed. "I'll bring you a nice dish afterwards."

※※※

Two days prior to the celebration, David J. Nugent had arrived in Buffalo with his wife, Fingy's niece Minnie, and their six children in tow. The house at N⁰ 16 Hamburg was noisy and full, a mixed blessing. Hannah couldn't help but pause and think that this is how it might be all the time if only her four dead children had survived to marry and have families of their own. Between attending to company and arranging the party, she woke up the morning of the event wishing it were already over.

As all gathered in the upstairs parlor at the Mutuals boathouse, Hannah stressing over whether she had arranged for enough food, Fingy arrived a half hour late in the company of Hannah's Nugent cousins Dick and John, and her stepbrother Maurice Halleran, all members of Fingy's gang of street fighters. Thankfully though, the most vicious member of Fingy's circle, Mary Jordan Conners, was not with them.

"Mary ain't feelin' all that good t'day," Fingy announced, his apology transparent. Hannah was greatly relieved. She would not after all be forced to endure the woman's superior airs. At any rate Mary Jordan Conners had never visited the Mutual Rowing Club and most likely never would. It was far beneath her station.

Hannah observed something previously unconsidered by her. She regarded her brother Dave, her stepbrother Maurice and her Nugent cousins all conversing together and wondered how so many of her close family members had ended up cohorts in Fingy's tight little gang of thugs, so devoted to him, so willing to do wrong for him. Then she wondered why after all these years the profundity of this fact had never occurred to her before.

As all sat enjoying themselves in their little groups, Fingy began to proselytize. Confabulation and laughter quieted in direct relation to the raising of Fingy's voice. All eyes were now fixed upon him. Hannah had dreaded this might happen. This celebration was meant to be *her son's* special day.

She studied Fingy's face intently as he yattered on and on. It was, appropriate to his personality, bright pink and pig-like. His eyes were heavy-lidded and sleepy, arched over by perfectly shaped brows. Too perfect in fact, she thought. Was he taking a tweezers to them? He still retained his hair—she had to give him that. Her Jim had gone almost bald, as too had his brother JP. Fingy had a turkey neck and a mouth quite like that of a snapping turtle; prehensile, cruel and determined. The mammoth diamond in his tie pin, weighing at least four carats and foil-backed to further amplify its luminosity, sparkled in the dusty sunrays that angled in through the boathouse's parlor windows.

She waited patiently for him to stop, for someone else to speak, for lightning to strike or the world to end, anything at all to shut the man up. At long last, having heard her fill, and worried for the effect of his increasingly salty speech on all the children present, especially her impressionable Davey, Hannah finally interrupted. The room went silent.

"Mr. Conners, on this day at least, this parlor is an extension of my own home. This is my son's holy celebration, his special day on which he pledged his loyalty to the Holy Catholic Church. It is not a place from which to preach or boast or lord over others or to employ vulgar language. Neither is it a proper time or place to make one's self the center of attention."

You could have heard a pin drop.

Hannah's brother David stared daggers into her. His wife Minnie clutched Dave's arm securely as if half expecting him to launch out of his chair. The Nugent children, sadly accustomed to their father's violent temper and authoritarian manner, steeled themselves for yet another public humiliation. The Alderman uttered an almost inaudible "Uh-oh!" close to his wife Annie's ear. It was fully expected by all that fireworks would quickly detonate. After a few beats of silence, Fingy nodded for a few seconds as if considering the varied ways in which he might retaliate, then responded.

"Yer right Hannah," he conceded. "It *is* young David's day. Ain't that right Davey?"

Little David replied, "Sure is, Uncle Jim!" with a giant grin.

Fingy laughed and all joined in uncomfortably, not knowing really if his accommodation was genuine or some sly front to shroud what recrimination might yet be in store.

With the tension broken, bottles, glasses and cutlery once more began to clink. Previously expropriated conversations resumed.

The beer and whiskey had their expected effect. Tongues loosened. Vulgarisms surfaced here and there and parental protests against them lessened. All were relaxed. The Alderman, quite the jokester when sober but a tad acidic after a rare second drink, made an unflattering remark about the dress that Fingy's niece Minnie Nugent chose to wear. It was tight in the bodice, the focal point being her generous breasts. The alderman's public exposition embarrassed her. She turned red and bowed her head. David J. Nugent bristled.

Fingy took note and immediately attacked the alderman.

"I recall as a younger man yous having' quite different views on such things, JP," Fingy reprimanded. "And now here yous sit all high 'n' mighty after embarrassin' yourself by havin' yer name in all the papers callin' for the art museum to cover up all its naked statues!

"I heard ye say some stupid things in my day, Alderman, but don't that beat all? Ha! I tell ye, when I toured Europe last year 'n' met wit' the Kaiser, me 'n' Mary got t' visit three or four museums, includin' the Louvre in Paris France. And in Europe them people ain't only got naked statutes from Rome 'n' Greece all over their art museums, they got 'em sittin' right outside in the middle of their town squares too. It sure ain't harmed nobody over there none to see naked statues. You oughta be ashamed o' yourself talkin' like that, revealin' yourself a bald-faced hypocrite, t' bein' such a prude. T' think of yerself as somebody who's got the right t' make decisions like that fer the rest of us. Well ye ain't, JP. Ye ain't got no right t' tell people what they can and can't see at the *art museum*—of all places."

The Alderman took his well-deserved dressing down very poorly. He stood and grabbed Annie's arm as if to raise her to leave. Mortified, she refused to budge and yanked it away. The Alderman's sons and daughters too hung their heads, some smirking, equally embarrassed and relieved to have someone publicly counter the mortification of their father's overzealousness.

"Sit down, JP. I ain't done wich yous."

JP lingered.

"I said sit!" ordered Fingy.

The Alderman sunk back into his chair.

"I recall too how back in '01 when some of them Protestant church pastors were demandin' the Pan American Exposition close its gates on Sundays—and you went along with them damned fools at first.

"All them men from yer own ward and elsewheres wot worked six days a week buildin' that damn thing bein' told on their one 'n' only day off they were goin' to be deprived of enjoyin' the very exposition they raised from their own bleedin' hands? It was criminal what ye proposed, and as soon as people spoke up loudly against it you shriveled like a dried mushroom and pretended like you weren't no hypocrite 'n' never even bought into the scheme to begin with.

"I'll tell ye this much JP. At the office we get the wire service from all the newspapers from around the country, and Europe too, and that story about you wantin' to clothe the naked statues was picked up by sixty or seventy newspapers. All over the country yous just made yerself a fool laughin' stock.

"We're all Catholic here JP, but I don't see nobody here tellin' the rest how to live their lives, 'cept yous. As fer me, when I see men like yous, fearful 'n' full o' yerselfs and demandin' people do things yer way, as if yer some kind o' moral authority, treatin' people like they was children who ain't got a brain in their head t' think fer themselves, I don't see a strong man or a good man or an honorable man. Instead I just see a coward."

JP shot up again as if he were thinking about challenging Fingy to a heated hand-to-hand, despite his never engaging anyone in a fistfight in his entire life, which for a male having grown up in the First Ward was somewhat of a miracle. Always having had the gift of being able to talk his way out of trouble, JP was right then at a loss for words. No one came to his defense because sometimes, as in this instance, he was indefensible. His making himself a public figure meant his family were made public figures too, and not at all by any of their own choice or wish, but rather by cruel default, and often regretful of same due to their father's self-righteousness and inappropriate grandstanding.

"I'm findin' it 'specially interestin'," continued Fingy, "that at the Pan American Exposition that had more'n a hundred or so giant naked statues on pedestals and in the fountains, 'n' decoratin' the entrances of buildin's out there in full view of millions of men, women and impressionable little children walkin' past 'em all day durin' that whole year, that such a thing didn't seem to bother you one lick back then! How come? Now all of a sudden naked statues are the most important subject on yer mind? Sounds t' me that since yous ain't accomplishin' nuttin much honorable down there at the city hall, ye got t' invent somethin' stupid t' distract people from the fact yous been sittin' down on the job!'

JP threw down his napkin and stormed away toward the back and slammed the lavatory door behind him.

Fingy paid no mind. He continued addressing the other guests, chuckling.

"That's what politicians do. They invent red herrings like the naked statue nonsense to take your attention away from the fact they ain't accomplishin' nuttin like they promised they would, or worse, to distract yous from noticin' they're up to nothin' good at all."

JP's Annie just sat there dumbfounded, at first too astonished for words. No one had ever castigated JP publicly like that before.

But then Annie realized that behind Fingy's humiliation of the Alderman was the cold truth that JP had done nothing to aid Fingy in his time of trial. That Fingy was regretting his Thanksgiving Day visit during which, by basically begging for JP's help, he was revealing an unprecedented vulnerability, a show of weakness he was now lamenting, and trying to live down.

Annie, unable to hold it in any longer, shouted "How dare you of all people, Fingy Conners, to be sayin' such nasty things—and in front of me and all our children and family no less! You're a fine one to talk about others bein' up to no good, you hypocrite!"

Fingy laughed, dismissing her with a wave of his four-fingered hand. It was water off his back. Annie's eldest, Thomas, who secretly delighted in his father's comeuppance, gently took his mother's hand to calm her.

Fingy reached out and tousled little Davey's black hair. Davey grinned ear-to-ear, glowing in the attentions of the great Fingy Conners. Hannah didn't welcome Fingy showering his attentions on her malleable child, but having enjoyed every word of Fingy's dressing down her pompous brother-in-law, she felt a tad conflicted at that particular moment.

Jim through all of this was silent and detached, determined not to get involved, for he'd already done more than his fair share of policing that week.

Fingy fished into his coat pocket and pulled out a nubby Florida alligator skin wallet while holding fast to Davey's gaze. Although people carried on with one another, all kept one eye on Fingy. The thick fingers of his left hand fumbled amid the absence of a helpful thumb as he clumsily extricated a one hundred dollar bill from his thick collection of similars and stuffed it theatrically into Davey's breast pocket as if it were a kerchief.

"There ye go, Davey. Remember. Wishes don't bring riches. Rather, yous gotta be clever. I know ye'll be makin' somethin' of yourself someday. But fer now take yer girlfriend out fer dinner and cocktails someplace nice," he chuckled.

Davey's eyes widened at the unprecedented gesture. He choked out a stuttered thank you. "But I ain't got no girlfriend, Uncle Jim!"

"What? A fine lookin' laddie such as yerself, Davey Sullivan? Me, I won't be believin' a word of it—no, not fer a second! I'd think half the girls in the ward'd be chasin' yous down the middle o' the Erie rails just fer their chance t' be givin' yous a sweet kiss."

At that Davey and his mother both grew red, but for different reasons.

Little Davey sat on Fingy's left, his namesake Uncle Dave Nugent sat on Fingy's right, Dave's wife Minnie next to him, and the Nugent kids, David Jr., Molly, Michael, William, Dollie, and George, directly across the banquet table. All of the Nugent offspring were very subdued. From time to time one or the other shot a wary glance at their father. The eldest, David Jr., was 20; the youngest, George, 12. Throughout the dinner, Fingy spoke extensively with his nephew-in-law, saying very little to his niece Minnie and nothing at all to the Nugent children, his own grand-nephews and nieces.

When given the news two weeks previous of the impending trip to Buffalo, it was Molly Nugent who protested to her mother.

"None of *us* got no party for *our* Confirmation, Ma. And here the entire family's expected to pick up and head 600 miles away for the Confirmation party of a cousin we hardly even know? It's not fair! Why is that kid so important? More than us? Why can't we all just stay here in Milwaukee while our father goes to Buffalo by himself? I hate Buffalo!"

Minnie just shrugged. "Molly, you spent three months living with them during the time your father was on trial, so don't claim now that you hardly know little David. We're going, and that's that."

"But I really don't know him Ma! Me and him was only babies then. I don't even remember bein' there."

Her mother didn't admit that it was useless either to reason with her husband or try and explain his actions to her children. She had learned long ago that to get along with David J. Nugent meant to just go along.

The drinking, eating and conviviality continued. No one noticed exactly when it was that the Alderman skulked back in from his humiliation to rejoin the group, but even he by the end of the evening was smiling and laughing, although he avoided his friendly enemy Fingy Conners for the rest of the event. Getting up from the tables, groups broke off naturally. Women gathered with women, men with men, and the children persisted in exploring just how much trouble they could get away with in the fascinating environs of the Mutuals' clubhouse. As the children headed down the stairs, Jim warned "Don't none of yous so much as touch the sculls down there or you'll be gettin' the belt from me."

Fingy was at the head of the men's group. It was clear that some of those present grudgingly admired him for what he had won in life, even if it were directly due to the diminishment of, and in opposition to, their own fortunes and goals—after all, everyone in the ward was Fingy Conners' victim in some way or another. He viewed any and all as simply agents toward his own ends, as a tool to be used as needed, solely for his own enrichment.

He soon segued into a monologue of sorts, an interesting explanation of his life's philosophy, a speech that gave some of those present a few new ideas to mull over.

With the soggy stub of his Cuban cigar stuck between his lips, he expounded.

"As a newspaper man the most important t'ing I learnt ain't nobody can quote yous fer what yous never said. Keep yer opinions 'n' yer plans to yourself if ye wanna stay outa trouble. Power don't come from wot yous say, power comes from wot you don't say but rather have stewin' around inside o' yer own head. People are in jail today fer what they shouldn't 've said, when if they'd just kept their stupid traps shut the law wouldn't 've got nuttin' on 'em.

"People talk about revenge like it's a bad thing," he continued in an unusually tranquil voice. "Not only ain't revenge no bad thing, it's necessary if yer plannin' at all t' keep your place in this world, yer dignity, yer manhood. It's necessary if yer ever plannin' on gettin' ahead anytime soon. Yous t'ink I got where I am today by lettin' anybody walk one over on me? Not takin' yer revenge is the exak same t'ing as givin' 'em permission to take another swing atcha. It's exakly like yous sayin' 'yeah, go ahead, wrong me ag'in, see if I care.

"Lissen, 'cause I'm tellin' all o' yous this here straight: anybody out t' get yous is gotta be got in return, or better still, got before they can even get a first crack atcha. It's either gonna be them or it's gonna be yous. Revenge is a virtue. It's what real men do. I'll be damned t' figger why people don't rise up after somethin' terrible's been done to 'em, to their families. Why people go 'n' shoot their own outa anger rather than the ones what savaged them I'll never know. The dirty neighbor, dirty cop, dirty lawyer, dirty priest. Don't matter. Why so many just lie there and die without a fight. Yous better believe if'n the doc ever tells me I only got a coupla months yet to live, my list is comin' out from under me billfold flap, and I'm takin' more 'n just a few people wit' me. As many as I can. Don't t'ink I ain't already got it all planned out in my head. That I ain't already made me arrangements in the matter. There's gonna be a retribution. Yous kin count on it.

"There ye go. Free advice. I'll figger some way how's all o'yous can thank me later."

HIS LIPS FORGOT THE TASTE OF TRUTH

BUFFALO EVENING NEWS.

BUFFALO, N. Y., WEDNESDAY, JANUARY 17, 1900.

NUGENT'S SENTENCE IS FOR TWO YEARS.

Sent to Auburn Prison by Judge Emery This Afternoon--Appeal May Be Taken on Certificate of Reasonable Doubt.

David J. Nugent was arraigned for sentence before Judge Emery at 2:15 today. He was convicted in County Court in November last of assault, second degree, after a long and stubbornly fought trial, on an indictment charging him with assault, first degree, in shooting John Molk, an ore handler, in the hold of the wholeback Mather, in the riot on the docks in June last.

Judge Emery was on the bench at 2 o'clock, ready to take up the case, but Nugent and his counsel, William B. Hoyt, were late in arriving. District Attorney Penney appeared for the people. The court room was crowded with newspaper and curious spectators. None of Nugent's political friends were present when court opened.

Nugent was dressed in a neat suit of gray worsted, with a dressy brown overcoat and appeared perfectly cool.

Before the District Attorney could take his record, Attorney Hoyt raised his usual technical objections to the indictment of Nugent, the jurisdiction of the court, etc. He made a new point by claiming that the case was more properly under the jurisdiction of the United States Court. He made a motion that the taking of the record be arrested.

"I'll deny that motion," said the Judge.

The record was then taken. Nugent said he was 27 years old, married, a hotelkeeper by occupation, and lived at 486 South Park avenue. He said, in answer to question, he had never before been convicted of any crime.

"Have you any legal cause to show why the sentence of the Court shall not be pronounced on you?" asked the court

"I have none," replied Nugent. "Mr. Hoyt will take care of that part of it."

PLEA FOR CLEMENCY.

Mr. Hoyt then arose and made a strong plea for leniency. He referred to the guilty of a serious crime. Now some of the jurors have asked that you be fined only. I could sentence you to serve five years in prison, and to pay a fine of $1000 as well.

"It is unpleasant to sentence a man in any case. But the law directs what must be done in such a case. The verdict means that you went into the boat with a drawn revolver and shot into the hold upon a gang of poor, inoffensive and unarmed men. It is your good fortune that nobody was killed."

"Such crimes cannot be punished lightly or our laws and the authority of our courts would be defied at will, and render no protection to the community. It is most fortunate for every person that night on that boat, that no one was actually killed, when the charge would be more serious.

"Nevertheless, there is a possibility which the jury seem to have considered in recommending you to mercy, that you may have acted under great excitement, without understanding fully the effect or consequence of your acts.

"The court after much consideration has come to the conclusion to give you the benefit of the doubt in that respect, and also the doubt raised by previous good character, and not impose the extreme penalty of the law. In imposing the penalty which the court will pronounce, it is deemed by the court that due weight has been given to the recommendation of the jury at the time of the rendering of the verdict.

"It is proper for the jury to make that recommendation whenever deemed proper, and it is the duty of the court to heed the same, and the court believes that due consideration and due weight have been given to the recommendation of the jury for leniency.

NUGENT'S SENTENCE.

"The sentence of the Court in your case is that you be confined in the State's prison at Auburn at hard labor

DAVID NUGENT'S CONUNDRUM

That night David J. Nugent crept back into the house a little before 3 o'clock as the entire Sullivan household slept. He washed his genitals in the bathroom sink, then tiptoed up to the bed, creaking floorboards threatening to expose him. He slipped under the coverlet. Minnie never stirred. She pretended to be asleep.

The street light out on the corner of Hamburg and South streets illuminated cracks in the plaster ceiling above his head. He had forgotten about just how relentlessly noisy the Buffalo Union Furnace across the street was. He could clearly hear workers talking on the street below. The Regulator in the parlor chimed the hour. The gigantic iron hoists looming many stories above the vulnerable house creaked and swayed menacingly in the wind. He tossed and turned, reexamining his life.

He did not love his wife. Never did. His sons were an utter disappointment to him despite their heart-rending, desperate, unacknowledged attempts to please him daily. There was no pleasing David Nugent because his life had turned out not at all as he illogically wished or expected, and that had made him bitter. He never dreamed he'd be living in Milwaukee of all places, far away from all his Buffalo relatives, mates and old school chums. And May Lynch.

The family occupied a nice enough house on Milwaukee's South 28th Street, a duplex at N⁰ 722 1/2. It was not as nice as the single family houses across the street from it, not as nice as one he'd expected to own outright at this point in his life. And it was all due to his being banished there to head Fingy Conners' shipping operations. He lay staring at the ceiling, enveloped in the familiar warmth of his sister Hannah's comforting home, reliving key moments from his life.

He used to be a dandy. He loved tailored suits. He owned eight of them back in the day, when he was single and making his mark. He had a number of girls on a string all at one time, girls other than Fingy's niece. He was fucking all of them. He was thought of as a real catch back then, but he wasn't one to be tied down. He was handsome and it was widely remarked that he looked much younger than his years, even to this very day. He was still in fine physical form, playing handball with his Milwaukee mates three times a week. He was feared—and that made him feel like a big man. He had loved his bachelorhood and the money, respect, and local fame—but most especially the power that his association with Fingy Conners brought him—that is, until Fingy put the drop on him. He had to admit he was floored when it happened. Fingy ruled over everybody, but Dave Nugent never thought that he himself would number among them.

One day, right after Fingy had tied the knot with Mary Jordan, wife number two, he pulled Dave aside from a friendly poker game in Fingy's saloon and boardinghouse at 444 Ohio Street. At the time the place was named Nugent's Hotel. What further proof did anyone need that his association with Fingy Conners was above that of all others than having the boss put the Nugent name on his own business?

"Davey, come wit' me," Fingy beckoned.

They went next door into Fingy's contractor's office.

"So, didja enjoy yerself at me weddin'?" Fingy asked.

"Oh, yeah!" Dave had replied enthusiastically. "Never had French champagne before! That Miss Jordan is really somethin' special. Yous make a fine lookin' couple there."

"Yeah. Couldn't help but notice," connived Fingy, "what a grand time you was havin'—you 'n' Minnie. Seems t' me yous two've gotten real cozy. Which brings me t' the point of this here little chat. What're yer intentions regardin' me niece?"

"Uh...intentions? Whaddya mean?"

"Don't act no fuckin' wise guy, Dave. When are yous plannin' on askin' Minnie t' marry ye?"

"*Marry* me?" he yawped. "Nobody said nuttin 'bout *that!*"

"*I* just said it," Fingy stated with finality, seating himself behind his big desk.

"But, Boss! I ain't yet ready to marry nobody! Yous know that about me well as anybody."

"It's time yous settled down, Dave. Fun's over. Me niece needs a husband."

Pen in hand, Fingy occupied himself with paperwork as if to indicate the conversation had ended.

"But I'd make a right poor husband, Boss! We're just friends, me and Minnie. I got a lotta oats left to sow. I can't—"

"*Oats* yous say? Well then, I say it's about time t' bring in the crops, son. I been seein' wot's been goin' on wich yous. Yous two been sneakin' off together t' canoodle 'n' carry on a bit too often and a bit too long fer yous t' be 'just friends.' Ye don't play with the delicate affections of such a lovely lassie like her, Dave Nugent. Not such a girl as me own dead sister's only daughter at any rate. Instead yous'll be doin' right by her—the right thing by her, and the right thing by *me*. And whether ye appreciate it presently or not, ye'll be doin' right by yerself as well. Trust me."

"Oh, I don't know, Boss..."

"*I do*. Come to think of it, that's the exact phrase I expect t' soon enough be hearin' comin' outa both yer mouths—yers 'n' hers—'*I do*.' Now get outta here. Get over t' the house 'n' see her. Buy her some nice flowers. Roses. I'll figger some way how's ye can thank me later."

Right up until the wedding day Dave had racked his brain about how he could get out of it. But without Fingy his goose was cooked. Everything he was, everything he had, was because of Fingy. He justified the marriage in his head with the knowledge that he would continue to be provided for carnally by his other girls. Fingy certainly had *his* share of women during his first marriage and ever since. Every man of status had his mistresses and whores in addition to his wife. He was a man. He would adjust.

The morning of the wedding Dave was taken aback when only one fancy state carriage arrived, followed by a cabriolet. The coach was nearly collapsing under a smothering of a thousand white flowers; roses, carnations, lily-of-the-valley, calla lilies, huge Casablanca lilies. All pure white. It was obscene. Feeling nauseous anyway, their overpowering perfume made him gag. In the marriage carriage imperiously sat Fingy in his morning coat and top hat with wife Mary.

"C'mon yous two lovebirds, we're late. Get in. Them monsignors waitin' fer us at the church is costin' me a arm 'n' a leg wit' every minute that's tickin' by," Fingy coaxed.

A crowd had gathered. Neighbors poured out of their houses to witness the ostentatious spectacle. Minnie emerged with her bridesmaids looking spectacular in her beaded wedding gown. The bridesmaids climbed into the state carriage. While Dave stood at the cabriolet ready to help his bride up, suddenly Fingy jumped out, insinuated himself between the couple, and took command.

The two seats in the carriage faced each other. Fingy had Minnie seated next to him, with Mary facing them. Dave remained at the curb dumbfounded.

"C'mon Davey! Yous waitin' fer somebody t' light a roman candle under yer ass? Let's go," bellowed Fingy.

Dave climbed aboard dutifully, and blatantly cuckolded, resigned himself to sitting next to Mrs. Fingy.

"Almost breaks me proud heart to see ye lookin' so beautiful 'n' all growed up, Minnie. I'm proud as punch o' yous," Fingy complimented.

"Oh, Uncle! No matter how I tried I could never thank you enough for all you've done for me. You've been so generous, taking me into your home after Mama died, raising me just like I was your own blood daughter."

Fingy leaned in and whispered, "You *are* my blood! Remember, it was yous who saved me life that time, Minnie. An' I was near endin' it all after yer mother was killt," he lied. "I got so down in the dumps that it was only needin' t' take care o' yous that kept me from puttin' a gun in me mouth 'n' splatterin' me brains. Ain't nuttin I wouldn't do t' make me little girl happy. So are yous, Minnie? Are yous happy?"

"Oh yes, Uncle! Of course! But, oh—if only Mother could be here with us today! Don't you wish that too? She would be so emotional over everything you've done! I know she'd be kickin' up a ruckus to end all! I can guarantee it!"

Grinning uncomfortably at the memory of his sister Julia, Fingy deflected to Dave Nugent.

"An' yous, Dave. Yous always been jus' like a real son t' me—but now it's gonna be legal. I ain't gotta worry no more 'bout yous wanderin' off on yer own 'n' leavin' me."

Nugent forced an uneasy smile.

The carriage pulled up and stopped in front of the church. The guests awaiting them there cheered. Each taking an elbow, Fingy and David lifted Minnie down from the rig. Minnie gave Fingy a big hug. He looked at her with adoration.

Jim & Hannah Sullivan stood at the head of the welcoming crowd, Jim observing the public display sardonically .

Hannah reached out and hugged her brother. Softly the two confided.

"Oh, sis... I'm not feelin' so good right about now," he whispered in her ear.

"Well, I'm real proud o' ye anyways David. So buck up. This is a good thing for you. You need a family of your own. Settlin' down'll suit you good. You'll see."

Detective Jim shook Dave's hand a little too heartily. "Congratulations there Dave! Relieved to see I didn't need to put these on you after all." He pulled back his coat to reveal a set of handcuffs attached to his belt. "See you inside, pal."

The bridal party went ahead with Hannah happily trotting right behind, but Jim held her back.

He whispered, "Ye know what this means now don't ye, Hannah?"

She paused a moment. "What? I don't know what ..." she puzzled.

"It means yer now officially related to that murderin' asshole. You and Fingy Conners—you two are family now."

Jim chuckled at the irony after enduring years of Hannah's railing against the man. Fingy glanced back for a long moment at Hannah as if claiming her. Jim took notice. Hannah expelled an awkward pleasantry as she brushed by him in the vestibule.

The tears that Hannah Sullivan shed during the ceremony weren't entirely derived from happiness.

For a while after that things went all right for married man David J. Nugent. He did as he wanted, despite resenting having a wife waiting at home privileged with a direct line to his boss and mentor. Unlike most men he did not have the luxury of separating his work life from his family life, and felt all too often as if he were inching his way over thin ice. His frustration mounted as the months turned into years, which incited his fury, which made him an increasingly enthusiastic enforcer of Fingy's orders. He took his distemper out on the victims. He enjoyed the violence more than ever. He sought it out and craved even more, until that day a few weeks after the scoopers' strike had ended in favor of the thousands of dockworkers in Fingy's employ. The balance of power had shifted. The laborers no longer felt themselves entirely powerless or subservient. Some displayed their anger openly. Dave felt publicly disrespected for the first time since the beginning of his long association with Fingy Conners. He newly found himself gazing directly into the glarings of gangs of resentful men who had previously averted their eyes submissively and hung their heads as he passed.

Then dawned that regretful day in May that changed everything forever for Dave Nugent.

He and his lads—Fingy's half brothers William and Dennis Hurley, Hanna and David's stepbrother Maurice Halleran, their cousins Dick and Johnny Nugent, along with a dozen close associates—encountered an insolent gang of mostly Polish oremen on the Ohio Street bridge not paying them proper deference. Dave would later lie under oath that he heard one of them call him a scab. In truth it was he and the gang who had threatened the Poles. Rocks flew and shots were fired but no bullets found their mark.

Fuming, Dave's gang returned to Fingy's saloon, which was in sight of the bridge, to tell the Boss what happened in exaggerated terms. Although after the fact Fingy denied his involvement up and down, he did without a doubt encourage the gang to go out and teach the Poles a thing or two about respect and who was still the Boss of the First Ward. Dave's gang angrily stalked back across the Ohio Street bridge to where the Poles were working unloading the ore from the whaleback *Samuel Mather* tied up at the Minnesota Docks on the Buffalo River.

There the gang of seventeen sneaked aboard silently, approached the open holds down which defenseless men toiled loading ore buckets. The gang pulled their pistols. Going from one open hold to another, Nugent's gang fired a total of 200 rounds down upon the unarmed, unsuspecting laborers. The victims took refuge in dark corners or behind their raised shovels. Miraculously only three of the workmen took bullets. One man having a wife and five children took three and nearly died, but survived, although he was crippled for life.

The police very reluctantly arrested the entire gang later that day. Fingy arrived immediately to bail them all out. But ever since he had lost the strike even his toady police department had begun a slow retreat from their customary kowtowing. The newspapers, all except for Fingy's own *Courier* and *Enquirer*, reported the attack on the *Mather* in screaming front page headlines. Fingy's *Courier* newspaper on the other hand buried the story on page 5 adjacent to the center fold. Nowhere in the *Courier* story was there any mention of David J. Nugent. Dave and the rest were charged with simple assault.

The trial of gang leader David J. Nugent went on for weeks with dozens of character witnesses swearing to Dave Nugent's saintly nature. Newspapers remarked on his handsome youthful looks, his cool demeanor and stylish clothes, noting always that he was more finely dressed than even his attorneys.

Despite the outpouring of support, Dave was ultimately convicted and sentenced to two years in Auburn Prison. Fingy used every weapon in his and his attorneys' arsenal to challenge the ruling. His wily untiring legal team were able to delay and delay yet again as Dave remained free on bail as if his future freedom was but a given. Fingy's legal team employed its tactics to exhaustion and beyond.

Ultimately Fingy was advised by counsel that the peacocky, boastful, highly social Dave Nugent best be sent away for a time so as to keep him and his antics out of the public eye. This would make it easier for the attorneys to do their obfuscating, and for citizens' outrage to predictably amalgamate into the mists of time. Fingy appointed Dave Nugent superintendent of his Milwaukee operations. The family quickly packed up and left Buffalo.

Minnie was resentful having to leave friends and family and the protection of her uncle. The kids were angry that they had to abandon all that was familiar and comforting. To Dave the swaggering lifestyle that he had long enjoyed was unjustly snatched out from beneath him. He failed to see the bright side.

He did not seem to be at all aware that dumb good luck had generously smiled upon him yet again, saving him from prison, preserving the cohesiveness of his family, providing him with a very good living and a prestigious position from which to make graft, and especially, getting him out from under the ever-watchful eye of Fingy Conners. He was provided autonomy. His wife's direct line of communication with Fingy was severed, rendering her much easier to control. A new start in life was gifted him in a handsome cosmopolitan city fully capable of providing him and his family with everything they might ever need to enjoy a prosperous life and begin anew.

To complicate matters, atop all his previous resentments, there was his newest: May Lynch, a secretary with Fingy's Great Lakes Shipping. She had caught Dave's eye on a previous visit to Buffalo. She had at that time brazenly propositioned him. They'd slept together then, and now twice this week he had been able to arrange a tryst with her citing "getting together with old pals" as a reason to remove himself from the family hubbub at № 16 Hamburg Street. He never anticipated it, but he was falling in love, which made him resent his wife all the more.

No, David J. Nugent was not at all happy. His family was made to continually suffer his immature anger and bitter displeasure on every single day that followed his impulsive terrorist attack on the whaleback *Mather*.

Lying there in the dark, staring at the ceiling, seeing everything in his life as having gone wrong when in truth it had gone wonderfully, providentially and wholly undeservedly right, he missed his chance to yet again free himself from the cancer of self pity that had so diminished him, to make right all the wrongs that would eventually destroy any fragment of love his children might have had remaining for him.

❧❦❧

On the afternoon of Monday October 9, 1911, two employees of Alderman John P. Sullivan's icehouse had been drinking in a saloon on Seneca Street. Exiting through the rear, they observed a small man attempting to drag a protesting fifteen year old boy up the alley at the rear of № 209 Seneca where the boy lived. The workers intervened. They determined that the man was unknown to the boy and that the boy was being taken against his will.

The incident was remarkable in that the little man was manhandling the taller boy directly beneath the windows of the victim's own family's domicile as the boy yelled up to his parents for their help. The kidnapper was thoroughly undaunted by this. He in fact appeared energized with the sheer brass of undertaking such a galling public experiment.

It was all the more significant because the five foot five inch stranger, determined to retain his catch, shamelessly put up a physical fight when confronted by the two much larger men. The boy took advantage of the confrontation to break free and run inside his home as the would-be kidnapper aggressively asserted himself against the boy's rescuers. Then, breaking away as if repulsed by their touch, the kidnapper indignantly picked up his bowler, nonchalantly dusted it off, straightened his tie and strolled away at a normal pace as if nothing whatsoever had happened.

The two ice company employees just stood there, flabbergasted. They had never before encountered anyone quite like him.

His Lips Forgot The Taste Of Truth

OFFICE AND DRESSING ROOMS AT
NUGENT'S RUSSIAN & TURKISH BATHS
327 WASHINGTON STREET.

NUGENT'S RUSSIAN & TURKISH BATHS

When the Hearst Corporation established its Features Syndicate and put Moses Koenigsberg in charge, fear rippled up and down the spines of newsmen nationwide. Especially upset was *Buffalo Courier* and *Buffalo Enquirer* owner, Fingy Conners.

Non-Hearst newspapers were newly being offered access to the scores of highly popular Hearst features—for a price.

Competitors panicked at the idea that some local rival might heavily bid up one or another of the more coveted Hearst columns or features, thereby upsetting the delicate balance amongst cutthroat local adversaries.

Fingy had been unable to sleep, his stomach tightly tied in knots ever since Hearst's plan was revealed. Having mixed a spoonful of bicarbonate of soda into a glass of water, his face contorted with disgust as he gagged it down.

"Oof! Nasty stuff!" he growled.

Any threat that someone might better him automatically launched Fingy Conners into conniptions. William Randolph Hearst was advancing beyond his newspaper holdings in New York City, acquiring newspapers throughout New York State. It was rumored he was negotiating to buy the *Buffalo Express*, the only local daily of the current Buffalo seven with a lengthy record of having taken on Fingy Conners toe to toe from his earliest shenanigans beginning thirty years previous. If the rumor were true, the *Express*, with all of the popular Hearst features at its disposal, would become a deadly threat to Fingy's *Courier* and *Enquirer* newspapers.

The practical William Randolph Hearst had bought and paid for Fingy's favors previously, owing nothing further to the man. Fingy had been enriched handsomely for engineering Hearst's political campaign for Governor of New York State five years earlier, as publicly revealed in the national press by his now-enemy and recent ousterer from his leadership of the Democratic party of New York State, Charles F. Murphy.

Murphy claimed in a newspaper interview with the *San Francisco Call* that half a million dollars had changed hands from Hearst to Conners. Hearst's bill for services rendered had been paid in full. Hearst and Conners were no longer friends or comrades or business partners. There was no love lost between the two, and that was now proving a problem.

When Moses Koenigsberg arrived in Buffalo Fingy Conners went on high alert. Koenigsberg as a longtime member of Hearst's publishing organization was well aware of Conners and his frightful reputation. Koenigsberg wrote of Conners that "he had brought the wits of his early years through the burnishing process of the barroom. At the outset, Conners' knuckles advanced him faster than his finesse. After he took hold as boss there was never a dock-walloper or a bully on the Buffalo wharves who dared to 'pass up his score.' The few who tried to repudiate the account set out in chalk marks for settlement the next payday never created the attempt."

To avoid conflicts with non-Hearst newspapers in those geographical locations defined as competitive circulation areas, it was Hearst's policy to reserve for his own newspapers the exclusive use of his copyrighted elements. In an area of the country where Hearst had not established a publishing foothold, the State of Montana as an example, his policies as to what Hearst feature a local newspaper there could subscribe to were far more liberal. The barrier against Buffalo, 400 miles away from New York City, because it was geographically located in the state of New York, was even tighter than the fence Hearst had erected around Philadelphia, a city located barely more than a comparative stone's throw away from Hearst's New York City publications.

Koenigsberg's physical presence in Buffalo ultimately established to Conners that the Hearst agent was in town not to broker the purchase of a competing newspaper but rather to wage a bidding war for the Hearst features. On one hand he was relieved; on the other incensed that his local competitors were being provided an equal opportunity to acquire wildly popular Hearst features for their publications that Conners felt by all rights he should have been provided first dibs on.

Fingy fumed,"After all I done fer that silver spoon fucker—an' now he's treatin' me like I'm just another one o' the hoi-polloi."

Concerning his coast-to-coast canvassing, Koenigsberg liked to state with a smile, "The mixed feelings of those who receive me as a representative of the most menacing figure on their business horizon only adds spice to the work in hand." His canvass for Hearst Features reached virtually every city in the U.S. having greater than 75,000 population in or near which Hearst was not at that time already publishing a daily. Ultimately for Koenigsberg, this amounted to a quarter million miles of travel during his career, and he was quoted as stating that he loved every moment of it, almost.

It was pride, even more than profit, that was tied to the upper rungs of Conners' newspaper empire ladder. His admiration for Hearst's journalistic success bordered on the fanatic. Fingy's greatest aspiration was to duplicate in Buffalo, then elsewhere, a Hearst-like publishing triumph. All this should have smoothed out any possible wrinkle in Koenigsberg's first visit to the *Buffalo Courier* offices.

Instead it led to his hazing.

Koenigsberg paid his call to Conners after scheduling with a number of other Buffalo newspaper men first. The paranoid Conners refused to believe Koenigsberg's Buffalo visit was of his own volition, but rather had been personally engineered by Hearst to shake him down. Fingy interpreted Koenigsberg's refusal to provide him with the Hearst features he coveted the most as merely a bargaining ploy. These features were in fact forbidden to all Buffalo newspapers due to Hearst's geographical limitations policy.

In their meeting at the *Courier* offices their fruitless back and forth culminated in an invitation by Conners for Koenigsberg to take a breather at Fingy's expense and indulge in an extravagant hour or two of pampering at Nugent's Russian & Turkish Baths nearby on Washington Street, after which their amiable negotiation would resume.

"Thank you, no. I'm a bit wary of places like that," Koenigsberg chuckled. "You know..."

"Shit no, it ain't nothin' like wot yer thinkin', Koenigsberg—this ain't Greenwich Village after all! Only business and professional men allowed in there. It's the best in the city, newly relocated, with a big swimmin' tank, marble tubs, a steam room, an' only the finest clientele. I jus' attended the grand openin' there last month. The mayor, Police Chief Regan, State Treasurer Kennedy, judges an' police commissioners...everybody of importance was there. Yous should go. Relax a little. Ye never know who yous might run into. I'll make sure they take extra good care o' yous."

Taking the bait much to his later regret, Koenigsberg traipsed over to Washington Street and entered the establishment's Office and Dressing Rooms. Men in various stages of undress lounged around a large handsome oak-paneled Persian-carpeted parlor taking a break from the tank and dry heat and steam rooms. Koenigsberg stepped into a changing closet and removed his clothes, then handed them off to the attendant who then provided Koenigsberg with a beer, waiving the 25 cent charge.

"Compliments Mr. Conners, sir. Enjoy."

Wearing only a towel around his waist he was escorted across the parlor room to a barber's chair, one of three facing a line of large plate glass wall mirrors. There awaited a young man ready to provide a foot massage employing an array of aromatic oils and balms. Uneasy at first, Koenigsberg so quickly succumbed to the calming rub down that he almost fell asleep.

The amenity completed, he was then escorted to the steam room, after which he took a communal shower and then entered the swim tank for a float. Happily relaxed, his stomach grumbled for food. He returned to the oak-paneled kiosk where the awaiting manager apologized profusely for being able to neither locate Koenigsberg's clothes nor his hotel key nor his change purse at the moment.

Initially Koenigsberg thought it merely an oversight, but soon it became apparent to him that he was being held hostage. Having no friends in the city whose aid he could summon, and being naked and starving and without money, the staff at the Baths feigned concern and pretended being engaged in feverish activity on his behalf.

Fingy Conners' protégé, his nephew-in-law David J. Nugent, had put cousin John R. Nugent in charge of this enterprise, the business having been financially backed by Conners. The staff were under strict orders to keep Koenigsberg there by hiding his clothing and money. All day long Koenigsberg fumed and ranted to exhaustion. He was provided a place on the divan to sleep that night and yet, come morning, his belongings could still not be located and no outside contact was provided him. Koenigsberg later wrote about the escapade in his memoirs, calling his captors "bribed attachés under Conners' wicked supervision."

While Koenigsberg was being held captive, Conners had his attorneys draw up an elaborate contract. This document was brought to the baths for Koenigsberg to sign authorizing the subscription of a laundry list of Hearst features for Conners' *Courier* newspaper at what Conners pridefully regarded as the "enormous price" of $20,000 annually.

Koenigsberg sat there in his towel studying the document for a few brief moments, then put it aside.

"Without my spectacles I cannot read it," he dismissed.

"You don't need to read it. You don't need no spectacles to just sign your name," the stooge smirked. "Even a blind man could do it."

"Until all my possessions are laid out here right next to me I will not sign, due to all the insult I have already suffered," Koenigsberg insisted.

"Well, I don't think anyone will be able to locate your things until after you sign it," offered Conners' stooge.

"And how do I know you even have my things? That they were not stolen and removed from this establishment, or thrown away? I need to see them. Bring them here so I can see them, and if after a thorough accounting, if everything is intact, I'll then sign."

The stooge thought it over a bit, then excused himself to call the Boss to run it by him. A few minutes later he reappeared with an attendant carrying Koenigsberg's things, apologizing in an entirely insincere manner for their being misplaced, and laid them on an adjacent table. Koenigsberg put on his spectacles, counted the money in his change purse, and sorted through his clothing.

"C'mon, c'mon, I ain't got all day," the stooge complained.

Satisfied, Koenigsberg put pen to paper.

Although fully authorized in his capacity as the agent of Mr. Hearst to provide what Fingy demanded, Koenigsberg signed the document adding the disclaimer above his signature, "pending the approval of William Randolph Hearst."

Explaining to the contract bearer that it was merely a formality, it in fact voided the agreement altogether. After signing, Koenigsberg was provided his belongings and then allowed to remove himself, first to his hotel, and then within the hour quickly and gladly to the New York Central Terminal and out from Buffalo altogether.

The stunt, a variation on Fingy's scheme of keeping prospective business associates captive on his private yacht as it aimlessly sailed the Great Lakes until they agreed to terms favorable to himself, earned him a stinging rebuke by the Hearst Corporation. Consequently, no Hearst features were made available to Conners' newspapers until many years had passed and the details of an undisclosed agreement between Conners and the Hearst Corporation had been enjoined.

Joey Joseph

THE CANDY MAN

J. Frank Hickey was drinking.

He liked to claim he drank in order to block out cruel and incessant memories, despite historic proof that his drinking compelled him to engage in the very behaviors that incited the cruel memories to begin with.

At age sixteen Hickey had been employed as a clerk in a drugstore in Lowell Massachusetts. In September of 1883 a wandering druggist named Ed Morey, addicted to drink and having the annoying habit of visiting the store to beg for alcohol, stopped at the pharmacy once again. Having judged the man a pathetic nuisance, Hickey on that occasion gave him some whiskey that he had spiked with laudanum. The combination quickly propelled Morey into a state of delirium.

Mesmerized, Hickey paused in his work to observe.

As Morey convulsed on the floor the teenager felt no urgency to run and seek help. Rather, he clinically regarded the enthralling scene unfolding before his eyes, scrutinizing with fascination as his acquaintance slipped from life. He would claim sometime later that it happened entirely by accident. He would assert that he had once read somewhere that if one put laudanum in a drunkard's glass he would be cured of drink. This as it turned out was actually true, in the most final sense.

It did not necessarily follow that Hickey, having been brought up a strict Catholic, didn't suffer bouts of guilt from time to time about the incident. However, the bold act imbued Hickey with feelings of control and omnipotence the likes of which he had never before experienced, feelings that overrode whatever Catholic guilt he may have endured, feelings that overrode even the sexual debauchments visited upon him as a child by his own father.

He discovered that sending someone to their death was exhilarating.

He monitored rather academically as the man lay face up on the floor softly gurgling and spasming with eyes all abulge. Vomit overflowed his lips. Just as quickly the fluid was sucked back in and down the windpipe. He choked and struggled to breathe until he drowned in his own puke. Only after the man's thrashings had stilled for some long minutes and the rise and fall in his chest had ceased did Hickey remove the whiskey glass from the counter. He rinsed it thoroughly, dried it, and replaced it in a closed cupboard with similars. Looking around first to make sure he had missed nothing, he feigned an emergency, excitedly exited the store and ran down the street to the police station. There he breathlessly claimed that the man had stumbled into the shop in a drunken stupor speaking unintelligibly when suddenly he keeled over onto the floor.

Hickey was of the all-too-common sort for whom someone or something else was always to blame. Any and all disagreeable actions on his part had their root in something other than himself. The admirable trait of taking personal responsibility was just one of a wide assortment of laudables that had completely eluded him. His irresponsibility was not just a favored pursuit on those occasions when he was pressed by authorities to explain the reasons for his unfathomable actions, but was a wholly inbred habit rehearsed daily since his earliest childhood.

On October 12, 1911 Hickey was sent home from his employment at Lackawanna's Rogers-Brown Iron and Steel Company, located immediately south of the Buffalo city line, for having been drinking. He spent the rest of the morning into the early afternoon traveling from saloon to saloon along Ridge Road not far from the steel plant. There was no shortage of watering holes in Lackawanna.

An interesting feature of Hickey was that he could drink an amount that would cut a normal man off at the knees, or even land him in the hospital, yet Hickey gave little outward sign of being inebriated until which time he had approached his maximum capacity, which was beyond extraordinary.

He tried many times to quit the drink. Often too he had been a resident at his favorite sobering-up resort, the Keswick Colony for Inebriates located in Toms River N.J. So numerous were his residences at that facility that the proprietress had become a dear friend as well as his most ardent supporter. On each occasion of his being fully cured, Mother Rawes proudly watched from the porch as Hickey walked away cold sober after having taken yet another solemn oath to never again touch demon drink.

It was a little past noon on the Thursday following the thwarted kidnapping by Sullivan Ice Company employees of the boy on Seneca Street. Fred Fowler, a switchman on the Ridge Road streetcar line in Lackawanna, had been alerted about that odd incident and was asked by the police to maintain an observing eye.

Fowler during his back and forth noticed with suspicion the peculiar movements of a strange little pabulum of a man going from saloon to saloon in the neighborhood. On his run westward he noticed the man exiting Shanahan's. Then on his east run some time later he watched the same man approach Doyle's.

Hickey entered Doyle's Saloon and spent quite a bit of time there. He spoke to other customers and to the saloonkeeper. His particular attributes—being short in stature, bookish, educated, bright, free-spending—were such that those who encountered him that day remembered him. They recalled that he was frustrated by the lack of progress in obtaining a patent on a device that he had presented to his employers at the steel plant. The invention was designed to cover a railroad frog so as to eliminate the danger of catching the feet of switchmen. Hickey was certain a fortune could come his way if he could perfect and market his invention. He had sent a detailed drawing and description to his supervisor at Rogers-Brown, John Hoskyn, the man who had sent him home that day, but no response had as yet been forthcoming.

The saloonkeeper was impressed that after all he had consumed, the foppish little man was able to get up and walk out the door unassisted. Outside, Hickey arranged his muffler against the autumn chill. He observed two little boys sitting on the curb making mud bricks. He approached them.

"Either of you boys enjoy eating candy?" he smiled.

✥✥✥

Thirty-six year old Syrian immigrant Nezla Joseph of 108 Ridge Road was worried. Her little seven-year-old son Joey had run in from school a little after three o'clock, tossed his schoolbooks in the hallway, and called to his mother to say he was going out to play.

It was now dinner time and Joey had not yet returned to the family home situated above the family patriarch's men's clothing store.

She opened the windows and called.

"Joey! Joey, come home for supper! Joey!"

She waited there for him to appear as always, running toward home. But he did not.

She went downstairs to call again, first from the front yard and then the back. She listened and waited. Nothing. She poked her head into the storefront to ask her husband George if he had seen little Joey. He had not. She asked children playing nearby if they had seen him. They said they had not. She instructed her fourteen-year-old daughter Nora to keep an eye on the baby while she crossed Ridge Road to Frank's candy store at N⁰ 119, next door to Doyle's Saloon at N⁰ 121.

"Yes, he was here a while ago with his little friend," said the Syrian proprietor Tony Frank in his native language. "They bought lemon suckers. And peach pits."

"What little friend are you talking about?" Nezla asked.

"I don't know, Mrs. Joseph. I don't know the other boy's name."

"Where would he get money to buy candy? I didn't give him any money."

"He said a man waiting out front had given him some pennies."

"A man? What man?"

"I don't know. I didn't see any man there."

"Was the man a Syrian?"

"I don't know. I didn't see him. Sorry."

※※※

Young Gordon Pitton returned home.

"My word! Just look atcha!" scolded his mother. "Take them muddy shoes off yous outside right this minute, Gordie! I just mopped the floor! Where yous been anyways?"

"No place, Ma!' defended Gordon. "Me and Joey was just out playin', makin' mud bricks. A man got us some candy and then he took Joey away. Then another man told me it was time fer me to go home so's not to worry ye. So here I am."

"Well, ye best not've spoilt yer appetite. I don't break my back cookin' all day long fer nothin', ye know."

※※※

Nezla Joseph knocked on neighbors' doors. No one had seen Joey. She poked her head into Doyle's Saloon and asked the men drinking there if they had seen her little boy. No one had. She began to panic. In her heart she felt something was terribly wrong. Obedient Joey was not one to stray afar, having been forbidden to do so due to his being subject to fits. She asked her husband to close the shop and go find Joey. He tried to calm his wife even as tears welled in her eyes.

"Oh, don't worry, Nezla. He's just out playing somewhere," George justified. "He forgot the time, that's all. He'll be home soon."

Providing no comfort to his wife, his words rang hollow even to his own ear. Such behavior he knew was uncharacteristic of his son. Realizing this, he too soon became embroiled.

"I'll go out now and look for him," he announced suddenly as he locked the shop door. "Don't worry."

Dinner was left in the pot as ten year old Edward joined his father and mother in their search. All set out in different directions. Nezla and Eddie each knocked on neighbors' doors and interviewed pedestrians, calling for Joey as they went. As Nezla passed Doyle's Saloon a queer little man emerged from the narrow vacant lot next door to the saloon, rearranging himself. It was apparent he had just used the little outhouse patronized by Doyle's customers located at the rear.

"Have you see little boy? Syrian boy, seven years old?" she asked in heavily accented English. Desperation colored her voice. The man politely shook his head no, but said nothing. He then walked toward George Fowler's approaching Ridge Road streetcar. As he got on and took a seat the car passed by the increasingly frantic mother. He observed her erratic quest with some amusement. Fowler recognized him as the same man he had witnessed visiting one saloon after the other that day, including Doyle's. The man asked for a transfer as he deboarded at South Park.

George Joseph hunted up Ridge Road for his son in the opposite direction, toward the swamp. He scoured alleys, backyards and disreputable structures set well back from the well-traveled street. It was a chilly autumn evening, yet his forehead collected beads of sweat as he hastily traversed well-worn pathways through vacant lots. He examined piles of lumber and refuse and peeked into old barrels. He called hopefully as he went: "Joey! Where are you? Come home, now. It's supper time!"

As he reached its edge, his eyes swept over the eerie swamp while trying to expel ominous pictures from his imagination. Noting the sun about to dip below the horizon his imaginings ran increasingly wild. He returned home, thinking, hoping, that Joey will have returned to the house in his absence. He had not. Nezla was in a terrible state at this point. George immediately left once more to visit the Lackawanna police station located not far from the house. To their credit, the police immediately began a search. They worked steadfastly throughout the night. Lackawanna Police Chief Ray Gilson did not waste any time. The police search, which was carried forward until well past two o'clock in the morning, turned up nothing.

Geographically, the town of Lackawanna immediately abuts the southern boundary of its larger neighbor. Buffalo's police department had resources and experience the small Lackawanna force had not. Chief Gilson did not exhibit any of the maddening traits of some rival police departments that refused to cooperate with, or ask help from, other departments in neighboring districts. The first thing the following morning Chief Gilson put in a telephone call to Buffalo Police Chief Michael Regan to ask for his help. Then Gilson, Detective Thomas Daley and all the other members of the Steel City force, most of whom had small children of their own, threw themselves wholeheartedly into the search once again.

☙❧

Mrs. Pitton read the story in the following day's newspaper about the disappearance of her son's playmate Joey Joseph. She was very concerned, but not for the reasons one might expect. Her husband had recently received a job offer in Detroit, and the family was already packing up in anticipation. She was quite anxious for the change of scenery. She ordered Gordon to keep his mouth shut about Joey and the man who had taken them to buy candy. She didn't want their move to Detroit delayed by having to speak to the police, or worse, having to stick around for an investigation.

"Don't ye go talkin' to nobody 'bout this, ye hear me, Gordie? Nobody!"

"All right, Momma," he dutifully replied.

Obedient to a fault, Gordon Pitton never breathed a word.

The description given to police by Joey's parents revealed he was about four feet tall, stoutly built, with large black eyes, black hair and a dark complexion, with two front baby teeth missing. He was subject to convulsions.

During the first few days of his disappearance Joey was reported as having been seen in a dozen places or more. The nearby Goodyear slip was trawled, for it was hypothesized he had been seized with a paroxysm while playing there and had tumbled in. No body was located there. Every foot of Ingam's Swamp too was dragged after several residents suggested to Chief Gilson that Joey might have become lost there and drowned.

It was reported the boy was seen to follow a band of gypsies. Believing Joey might be with them, Chief Gilson and Detective Daley went in search of the Romanians at once. Little trouble was experienced in locating them. The boy was not in their camp. Every member of their group was accounted for, so the possibility that Joey was taken by one of them was disproved.

An unfortunate amount of importance was given over to the report of a sighting on the Abbott-South Park streetcar made by prominent Buffalo attorney J. Adam Weiss. Weiss said his attention was called to a certain boy due to the manner of unfamiliarity the man accompanying him exhibited towards the child. The boy seemed apprehensive, perhaps even frightened, Weiss claimed. Great weight was provided this clue due to the prominence of the witness, a man who, as he himself boasted, was trained to observe closely and to remember minute details clearly. The police did not realize that Weiss was of the sort who fancied himself essential and for whom injecting himself into this case provided him the attention he craved. Weiss' report proved a profound distraction and a misapplication of precious time and valuable resources. As a result already stretched-to-the-limit police manpower was directed primarily toward the alleged movements of Weiss' mystery duo to the point of which an artist's sketch was commissioned, printed and widely distributed.

So many unsubstantiated sightings came in during the first week that the police made the counterintuitive decision to disregard any additional sightings from that point forward.

Buffalo Police Chief Regan had flyers with Joey's photograph made up and sent to departments from San Francisco to Indianapolis to Boston and all points in between. He personally telephoned the chiefs of the police in departments all over the country. As the popular Vice President of the International Association of Chiefs of Police organization, Regan was on very friendly terms with most of his fellow chiefs nationwide. He implored their aid in locating Joey Joseph. They responded wholeheartedly. Regan assigned Buffalo Detectives Sullivan, Lynch and Holmlund to provide respectful discreet support to the Lackawanna Police upon request. During the first two weeks after Joey's disappearance, the Lackawanna Police requested assistance daily.

In addition to the obvious, the Lackawanna authorities questioned anybody and everybody. No one in the neighborhood was overlooked, from local residents to drunks in the saloons to streetcar conductors to delivery wagon drivers.

Buffalo Detective Sullivan suggested to Lackawanna Detective Daley that they board the streetcars to question the drivers. Daley had already questioned Fred Fowler, but was curious what Sullivan had in mind. As the car proceeded along its route, Sullivan stood very close to Conductor Fowler, bumping him as the car swayed and jolted. Sullivan called attention to various houses, stores and people along the way and each time asked Fowler to recall what he knew in general about each of those things. Sullivan probed aggressively for details. Fowler was clearly made uncomfortable by Sullivan's overbearing manner. The technique did prove somewhat fruitful in that Fowler said certain things that he had not recalled under Daley's questioning. The technique Sullivan described as the "skipping phonograph record," whereby the same question was asked time and again but in slightly different form, did indeed bring forth a different response. But Daley could plainly see Fowler felt under pressure, and he wondered to himself really how reliable this "new" information was. Any witness providing answers with the sole purpose of trying to appease the police while attempting at the same time to get rid of them did not strike Daley as a reliable approach.

As Daley observed, he concluded Sullivan's technique excessive, borne more from personal prejudices perhaps than solid police work. Lackawanna was a small town where the citizens and police knew each other by name, and therefore a less aggressive manner was utilized in investigations there. Daley adjudged Sullivan detrimentally hardened by his almost thirty years on the mean streets of the nation's eighth-largest city.

Fowler again told of the man he saw wandering from saloon to saloon the day Joey disappeared. He said the man's presence on his streetcar was uneventful. He had spoken to no one. As he stood to alight at the South Park stop, the man asked for a transfer. He smelled of alcohol but was steady on his feet. He did not seem uneasy or in any hurry. There was nothing about his manner that gave suspicion. Still, Fowler admitted he was suspicious of the man regardless. He provided a physical description to the detectives: bookish, wearing spectacles, shorter than average in stature, well dressed, meaty hands.

After grilling Fred Fowler the detectives alighted and boarded a car going the opposite direction, returning to the immediate area of the Joseph home. The two crossed Ridge Rd. and entered Tony Frank's candy store. It was the last place anyone had seen Joey. Tony Frank recollected to them that Joey had entered the store alone and that he had purchased lemon suckers for himself and a friend. He said Joey told him a man had given him the money. Frank said he never saw the man and thus could not describe him. Frank's manner was clearly evasive. He wanted the detectives gone. Sullivan nudged Daley to draw his attention to the gadget behind them in the corner.

"What's that?" Sullivan asked the candy store owner, although he knew full well what it was. He was pointing to a little cast iron machine with a glass front.

"It's a game of chance. For the children. They love it."

Having spent some recent time with Chief Regan, Daley had witnessed Buffalo's top copper railing against such machines. Regan had confiscated quite a few from Buffalo candy stores, stationary emporiums and ice cream parlors. "It's gamblin', pure and simple!" Regan had fumed. "We will not stand for these things teaching our children to gamble."

Detective Daley ordered Tony Frank, "Get rid of it, or we'll shut you down."

"But why?" questioned the proprietor. "The children can win a caramel. Or a stick of gum."

"How much does a caramel cost here in your store?" asked Detective Sullivan.

"Two for a penny," said Frank.

"Yes, two for a penny. And that machine costs a full penny to play. And most of the time the children win only a single caramel, isn't that correct?"

"Well, it's *fun*," he laughed. "The children love the game. They want to play it."

Such machines in most cases included an opening at the top for inserting a penny.

At the bottom of the machine inside the glass in plain view were a series of numbers. Small nails were arranged so that a penny can zigzag down from the opening in the top toward the numbers at the bottom where it lodges at one number.

A printed card on the machine lists the prizes given according to the number the penny strikes. Number one, for instance, gives the player a stick of chewing gum or a caramel candy for his penny. This number is the one where the penny generally stops. Number two will bring five cents worth of merchandise, and number ten will bring twenty-five cents worth.

The merchandise awarded in most stores was either cheap jewelry or candy. A child could invest over a hundred pennies before a high number like ten might be hit. A notice posted on the machine claims the machine is not a gambling apparatus but rather a device for the dispensing of merchandise.

"So," continued Sullivan, "the child plays a penny and perhaps wins one caramel for his penny when he could buy two caramels for the same penny. Correct?"

The proprietor shrugged. "Well, yes, but..."

"You heard me," interrupted Daley. "Get rid of it now, right this minute." The two detectives stood there and watched as Frank dislodged the machine from its position and carried it into the back room.

"If when I come back and see that machine displayed here again, it'll be the end o' yer doin' business here, Mr. Frank," warned Detective Daley. "I will shut your store down for good."

The detectives left the candy store and crossed Ridge Road to again question Joey's father. Entering Joseph's Men's Furnishings store they noticed that through the plate glass windows there was an unobstructed line of sight directly across the street to Frank's candy store and next door to it, Doyle's Saloon. Again they asked Mr. Joseph if he had seen anything or anyone suspicious, since his view was so clear. He could not help but feel as if the detectives were blaming him for the disappearance of his own precious son for not keeping a proper eye on him, for not witnessing Joey entering or leaving the candy store. Or perhaps it was just his own guilty conscience interpreting their line of questioning that way. He had berated himself ceaselessly from the afternoon Joey disappeared for never having noticed his son despite the boy playing only mere yards away.

A little boy matching Joey Joseph's description was reported abandoned by travelers at Little Falls N.Y., 200 miles from Lackawanna. After communicating with the Little Falls police, Chief Gilson and a very excited George Joseph boarded a train to make the long journey. On arrival they found that the boy was not only not Joey, but at barely five years of age, slight of build and with light skin and sandy hair, he didn't even remotely fit Joey's description. On the long journey home, George dreaded what effect this severe disappointment was bound to have on his fragile hopeful Nezla, awaiting her husband's return with bated breath.

His Lips Forgot The Taste Of Truth

THE FIRST WARD IV

POSTCARDS

On All Hallows Eve, nearly three weeks after Joey Joseph's disappearance, a postcard addressed to Lackawanna Police Chief Gilson arrived. It was postmarked Boston. It was not signed. It read:

> Joseph Josephs, will be found in bottom of water closet, with three seats, back of saloon near Doyles on Ridge road. A drunk crazed brain done the deed, and remorse and sorrow for the parents is bringing the results, which will soon come to the end. The demon whisky, will then have one more victim making four in all. Dig the closets with three seats.

Gilson sent two officers named Wiley and Jasper to follow the clues. He cautioned them not to inform anyone as to what they were investigating, especially Mr. and Mrs. Joseph if they happened to encounter them.
"Don't need to get them poor people all riled up again 'lessen we find somethin'," the dominating six-foot-six Lackawanna Chief instructed, recalling Little Falls.
The officers located the outhouse behind a fence in an overgrown lot to the rear of Doyle's saloon.
"Din't never knowed this was even back in here," said Wiley, kicking aside discarded debris.
"Me neither," agreed Jasper.
Jasper pulled at the rope attached to the rickety door. It wobbled as it opened. The hinges creaked. The smell was unmistakable.
"Don't think fer a fuckin' second that Gilson pickin' you and me to visit this here offensive place wasn't purposeful. He's gettin' back at me fer stayin' home when I got the influenza last month," complained Wiley.
"Well, two weeks was a long time, and there's only seven of us here, Wiley. The rest of us was all left with yer tasks to make up fer. What do ye figger he's gettin' back at me fer then, in that case?" asked Jasper.
"Oh Jeez! Goddamn it to hell! I just stepped in somebody's shit! Who takes a shit on the floor when the proper shit hole is only a foot away?" hollered Wiley.

"Some drunk who couldn't hold it in, maybe?" answered Jasper.

Wiley scraped his boot sole on the threshold. "God damn fuckin' stinkin' pigs..."

They peered warily downward past the rims of the seats into the blackness of the rank smelling offal below.

"Pee-yew! Don't see nuttin down there," said Wiley.

"Well o' course not. It's pitch black. We best go fetch us a lamp."

"I ain't traipsin' all the ways back to the precinct jus' to get no goddamned lamp, Jasper! If yous want a lamp, then yous go fetch it yerself."

Then it dawned on him. "Come to think of it, we best not use a lamp at all. It might ignite the gas that's got built up down there."

Jasper started to laugh.

"What's so funny Jasper?"

"Can't you just see it Wiley, if'n we dipped a lamp down there and the flame caused an explosion, leavin' me 'n' you covered head to toe in shit, landin' on our asses half a block away?"

The two stood there for a few long moments, peering down into it, laughing.

"Hey, I think I see somethin'," Jasper said.

"Where?" asked Wiley.

"Right there. Look. Oh...no. It's just a newspaper floatin' 'neath the offal. I'm goin' to look around outside to see if I can find a pole or a branch to stick down there and stir around."

"Are yous kiddin' me? This here's disgustin'. Okay, go right ahead there, Officer Do-Good, but I'm just about ready to lose my breakfast just standin' in here. I'm goin' out fer some breathin' air."

The two exited. Jasper began poking around the perimeter of the lot and at the back of Doyle's to locate a rod of some sort.

"Ain't nothin' round here like that, Jasper, okay? Let's just go. We got better things to do."

Jasper continued looking.

"Give it another minute, Wiley. We're already here, ain't we? Let's give it a go."

Jasper entered the back door of Doyle's. He was surprised at the number of drinking men present so early in the day.

"You the barkeep?" Jasper asked of the man wiping down the tables.

"Yep. Name's Goldsmith. What kin I do ye for?"

"You got a pole, Mr. Goldsmith, or a long stick, or a rake we can borrow for a few minutes?"

"Uh, well...let me think. No rake. How long a pole ye need? I got this here baseball bat behind the bar to keep the rowdies in check."

"Nah," Jasper answered. "It's got to be a long pole, the longer the better."

"Sorry," answered Goldsmith, then he resumed his cleaning.

Jasper and Wiley exited. Jasper lingered. Wiley was more than impatient. In their less than half-hearted endeavor they observed nothing reckoned suspicious. Neither the dull murky light, the pungent odor, nor the depth of the disgusting pool of sewage should have so easily dissuaded honorable men fancying themselves detectives.

Jasper finally gave in to Wiley's nagging, and they departed the property.

A landslide of misleading suggestions and clues, as well as more than a few outright crank messages, continued to inundate the town's little police department regarding the missing boy. Perhaps it was sheer fatigue combined with discombobulation from trying to discern the useful from the useless that explained a less than rigid enforcement of police investigative standards.

Whatever the case, such specific directions leading to a landmark as obscure as an outhouse, of all things, and detailed down to the number of seats it contained and the structure's being invisible to observers passing by on the street, therefore rendering it inconspicuous, should have raised any novice sleuth's hackles. The structure being known to few even in that very neighborhood, and with the clues concerning it originating from a source as far away as Boston, it was a mystery how such exacting instructions could have been so easily dismissed.

Discerning nothing awry in the officers' recounting their slap-dash examination, Chief Gilson challenged Wiley and Jasper's account of their search not in the least, but simply took their word for it. It was assumed by Gilson the postcard message was yet another hoax. The clueless Gilson did not bother to tell Buffalo Chief Regan about it, much less commiserate with him over the postcard's disturbing message. The missive was tossed into a drawer and forgotten.

On November 3rd George Joseph received a letter postmarked Boston. In it he was warned to cease his scrutiny of the case if he ever wished to see his son alive again. This provided George with hope that Joey was alive. Then, four weeks after Joey's disappearance, George received a postcard that said:

> Don't search any more for your boy. He has been choked to death.
> They have buried him where no one will find him.

George immediately took the horrible messages to Chief Gilson, who tried to calm him. Gilson assured him they were no more than a cruel prank. It didn't occur to Gilson to open his desk drawer to compare Mr. Joseph's two messages to the postcard he held there, to size up the handwriting on each for any similarities, or to find remarkable the fact they were all postmarked Boston.

His Lips Forgot The Taste Of Truth

Pawnshop: 136 Seneca St.

Pawnshop Law

Buffalo Police Chief Mike Regan and Detective Jim Sullivan had plenty of time to talk as they made their way out the Hamburg Turnpike to the suburb bearing the same name as the roadway.

"Remember how long it used take us to make this same route before we finally got this here automobile?" remarked Jim. "What a time saver!"

"Yep. Them horses got nothin' much to do these days," Regan said, "'cept to eat grass and enjoy their retirement. Oh. That reminds me. The *Express* telephoned yesterday and they want to interview Ed Stanton—so's to ask him what it's been like for him now that he's drivin' an auto rather than a team of horses like he done the last twenty five years. They want to write a big story about all his reminisces and such. It'll be good publicity for the Department."

Stanton was a founding member of the Mutual Rowing Club and had been a Buffalo police driver for close to three decades.

Jim went silent for a few beats.

"I'll bet Ed's poor horses don't know what to do with themselves no more. I'll bet they're missin' all the old excitement, the daily routine," he mused almost sadly.

"Well that there answers my question why yous ain't retired your tired old ass yet, Sully," Regan chuckled. "What's it been for ye now, anyways? Fifty years?"

"Close," Jim said. "Twenty-nine. Time flies, ain't it? Anyways, you're a fine one to talk, Moses."

Regan shook his head in mock pity and added, "God! Poor Hannah! If you ever do take your retirement I don't think there'll be much chance of you livin' long enough to die of natural causes in such a case."

They shared a good laugh over that bit of truth.

The trip proved much faster in the automobile for sure. Despite the protests of one of the more outspoken Common Council members, it was at long last voted that the Buffalo Police be provided a number of motorized vehicles. Even the suburban Lockport police had a motor patrol wagon by this point. Buffalo's recalcitrant city fathers had proven yet again an embarrassment to the supposedly progressive city.

"All them pouty little eunuchs down there at the city hall playin' politics at our expense so's to prove to their jealous playmates that they still wield some little measure of power," sniggered Regan. "Especially them who's on their way out. Fuckin' bastards."

On arrival in Hamburg they were quite surprised to see the courthouse corridor all abustle and the courtroom packed to capacity.

"Say, have we arrived at some sensational murder trial somebody forgot to tell us about?" Regan asked his old friend.

"Sure looks that way Mike," Jim replied.

Neither had expected such a public outpouring over what at first appeared to be only a routine case. Judge Stratmeir presided. It turned out that many of those in the courtroom observing the proceedings had suffered Emma Gunn's same unfairness.

Mrs. Robert Gunn of Hamburg N.Y. was suing Meyer Brown, a pawnbroker whose shop is located at N.º 136 Seneca Street in Buffalo. She was attempting to recover from Brown a watch that had been stolen from her.

Her home on Sandra Place had been robbed on January 16. A list of the articles that were stolen was sent to the Buffalo police. A few days later Detective Sullivan notified Mrs. Gunn that he had discovered a watch answering the description of the one taken from her home and that it had been pawned with Brown.

Mrs. Gunn was compelled to make the trip into town to retrieve her property at some inconvenience to her family, whereupon pawnbroker Brown demanded Mrs. Gunn pay the $10 he had advanced the thief on the watch.

Of course she refused.

"It's an outrage! Why, you're making a business out of supporting the dastardly activities of crooks and thieves!" she accused the pawnbroker.

Brown rolled his eyes condescendingly while sharing a smarmy smirk with his clerk.

"Sorry lady. That's our policy," Brown droned in a mocking sing-song tone, much to his clerk's amusement.

"Well now! Allow me to establish an example of my own policy, Mr. Brown!" Gunn fumed as she cracked her umbrella sharply on the glass case displaying dozens of gold watches, silver brooches, diamond hairpins and the like.

"How dare you!" Brown admonished her. "You must leave my business at once! I'd gladly place your watch under a wagon wheel and have it smashed to bits against the cobbles rather than allow you to have it now! Go! Get out!"

The following day Meyer Brown was served with a lawsuit to regain Mrs. Gunn's property.

Chief Regan, Detective Sullivan and Brown and his clerk—no longer smirking—

were all called as witnesses. The proceedings took less than an hour. Judge Stratmeir ruled that a citizen is entitled to his or her own personal property wherever it might be found. Brown was incensed and the notice of the ruling in that evening's newspapers would infuriate pawnbrokers citywide.

On the trip back downtown the two old friends mulled the audacity of pawnbrokers in general. They concluded they needed to be reined in. "You and me, let's lobby yer brother to end his nonsense," Regan proposed, "and begin the process of enacting a city law that places the entire responsibility for receiving merchandise, legal or otherwise, squarely on the shoulders of the pawnbrokers."

"Yeah," agreed Jim. "If nothin' else, it'll free up the courts. But beyond that, this whole thing's gotten way out o' control. As long as things remain as they are presently, these pawnbroker bastards might as well hang a sign out front of their store sayin', "Attention All Crooks & Shoplifters: Pawn Your Stolen Merchandise Here With Impunity."

Later that day the two paid a visit to Alderman Sullivan's office at the city hall to make their appeal. They found the Alderman mid-pow-wow with news reporters concerning his imbroglio with the Buffalo Union Furnace located directly across Hamburg Street from the Sullivan brothers' homes. The brothers had spent their entire life in the First Ward living on Hamburg Street tooth and jowl with the mammoth polluting enterprise, its filth and round the clock racket a thorn in their sides. At one time both had been employed there and both still resided with their families amidst its air and water polluting filth.

The reporters were jesting with the Alderman in between his serious chatter about the Union Furnace's accusation against him that the company was being unfairly targeted for persecution.

Fredrick C. Slee, attorney for the Buffalo Union Furnace Co. had charged in a communication to the City Councilmen that Alderman Sullivan was carrying out an ongoing vendetta by the persecution of his client by introducing various resolutions against the company in the Board of Aldermen.

The principal battle at this point was that Alderman Sullivan was demanding the Furnace, for the public benefit, tear up the rail tracks it had laid illegally in the First Ward's Katherine Street. Attorney Slee charged the Alderman's demand was not at all "for the public benefit" but rather it was part and parcel of an ongoing personal blood feud.

It was in fact partly personal, JP admitted, since two children and one adult—his constituents, neighbors and members of his own church—had thus far been killed by trains running the tracks down the very narrow and densely populated residential street since the rails had first been laid in 1906. It was the Mayor's policy, absconded from one of Charles Feldman's pledges back when he ran against Adam for office of Mayor, that all tracks illegally laid within the city be removed and the repaving paid for by whatever enterprise laid down the tracks to begin with. Officials placed the number of miles of unpermitted lines to be disinterred from Buffalo's streets at a staggering 150 miles of track.

JP addressed the newsmen, pads open and pencils racing.

"You notice that the company doesn't deny that it laid its tracks without a permit. It says it didn't know it was a street—despite being lined end to end with people's homes fronted by concrete sidewalks! And doesn't he know that the city has had lights and water in the street for 30 years? Does Mr. Slee mean to say the company didn't know that the Erie Railroad had to apply to the city when it got its permit to lay one track the full length of the same street away back in 1871? The tally of our citizens who have been maimed and killed by trains running on all these illegally installed tracks is horrifying. For mothers and fathers especially, to realize that their dead little ones would still be with them today had the railroads not scoffed at our laws and placed their own selfishness ahead of the welfare of our precious children, is heartbreaking."

The Alderman wrapped up.

"Now thank you gentlemen. We don't know what we would do without you here at the city hall. You keep us honest, and the defenseless public informed and safe."

The Chief and the Detective both smiled at the charming effect the Alderman's smooth diplomacy had on the reporters.

"Yep. Yer brother's still got it, Sully."

His Lips Forgot The Taste Of Truth

THE FIRST WARD IV

Wishing And Hoping, Planning And Dreaming

As the months passed, Nezla Joseph became a mere ghost of her former self. Every day she peered out the windows of her home intently, wishing, worrying, hoping, dreading. She refused to believe that her little boy, who everyone agreed was beautiful and kind, who enjoyed singing songs to his admiring little friends and sharing his pennies with them, would not be coming home. With each sound at the door she ran to open it convinced she would see him standing there.

Many a day she could not get out of her bed. Her daughter Nora, newly turned fifteen, supplanted her mother's role as cook, housekeeper, diaper-changer and disciplinarian. Nezla no longer had the heart to so much as raise her voice to her remaining children. It was Nora who now cared for the baby, who kept track of her brother Edward, who demanded he refrain from ever speaking to strangers, who insisted without exception he come straight home from school forbidding any and all diversions.

During periodic bouts of hysteria Nezla was wont to march up the street and enter the police station and inquire insanely about the progress in the search for her boy. The police assured the distraught mother that the hunt for Joey was ongoing, but in the eyes of the police all leads had run out—the disparaged postcards from Boston notwithstanding. The Lackawanna Police Dept. had initially put up a $500 reward for the return of the Josephs' son. The parents were entirely convinced that he had been kidnapped.

Back in November George Joseph had asked Lackawanna police to give up their efforts to catch the alleged kidnappers. He requested they rescind their $500 reward. He then publicized that he himself was offering a $500 reward for information leading to the return of his son. Certain that the police activity would frighten away the kidnappers, Mr. Joseph wanted it known that the police were out of the matter as an impetus for the kidnappers to contact him directly.

"I will ask no questions of the parties returning my boy," he promised.

It was a familiar move to Chiefs Gilson and Regan. They were thoroughly convinced now that George Joseph had received a letter from the kidnappers ordering him to act as he had. Mr. Joseph strenuously denied that this was true. Gilson said that kidnappers frequently threatened wronged foreigners to keep the police out of such cases. The fact was, George Joseph was advertising in the New York City newspapers that he had withdrawn the case from the police. Gilson regarded this development as significant. He theorized that it was probable that members of some New York gang, perhaps the Black Hand, were preying on the father's fears, threatening harm to the boy unless the hunt was called off.

Throughout the year following Joey's disappearance, George Joseph untiringly searched for his son. He was perpetually on high alert for any particle of a clue, any tip or notion or trace or prospect. No detail was too insignificant. He had purchased an automobile in the weeks following Joey's disappearance for the sole purpose of conducting his ceaseless quest. Sundays were spent with the entire family loaded into the car driving for many hours all over Western New York, looking and searching. The children were told they were on a sightseeing tour. Only the baby failed to fathom the true purpose behind these weekend excursions.

"Being Syrian, we have an advantage that the parents of missing white children do not," George Joseph told the *Buffalo Express*. "Children matching Joey's description are rare here, so he will stand out. Unless he was taken by other Syrians, he will certainly eventually be noticed."

The Syrian community was tight knit. They socialized almost exclusively among their own group. It would be almost impossible for a Syrian to be keeping Joey without his comrades knowing about it.

On May 8, 1912, eight months after Joey disappeared, Chief Gilson had received a phone call from a shopkeeper in Nunda N.Y. named E.W. Sheppard. The merchant swore he had seen a boy exactly matching Joey's description traveling with a band of gypsies in their covered wagon caravan as it passed through Nunda. The gypsies had stopped at his store for supplies. With them was the boy. Shepard was the friendly sort, and he got the leader to reveal where they were headed under the guise of having knowledge about merchants along the way he could recommend where they would not be taken advantage of. The leader revealed they were traveling west along the southern shores of the Finger Lakes, to Ithaca.

Lackawanna Police Chief Gilson was at first skeptical, but the storekeeper was as insistent as he was excited. Gilson called George Joseph with the news.

※※※

As George locked up the store, Nezla called down from an open window.

"Where are you going? It's the middle of the day."

"Oh, I just have to run some errands. And I'm expecting a shipment from Boston downtown, so don't worry if I'm late," he said in an uncharacteristically vague manner. She watched him get in the car parked at the curb and drive off. She was suspicious. Did he receive a message about Joey? Was he trying to protect her from hope by investigating in secret? This possibility renewed her massive headache. She shuffled to the bedroom and dropped onto the mattress like a rock and put a pillow over her eyes to try and block the light. She was convinced George had gone off on another mission to find Joey, and she prayed for God to protect him.

An excited George Joseph collected Detective Daley in front of the Lackawanna police station for the drive to Nunda. Once there they questioned store keeper Sheppard. He was convinced the boy he had seen was Joey. With this news George Joseph's heart pounded in his chest out of anxiety and unceasing hope. The storekeeper was so insistent that the boy was Joey that he offered to accompany them on their quest. He left the store in the care of his grown son and together the three set out in hot pursuit.

Nearly forty miles away, near Ithaca, they caught up to the caravan. The leader admitted that he had a boy in his company answering the description of the missing child. He walked down the line to one of the covered wagons and assisted the youngster out of the conveyance as the searchers looked on.

George Joseph's heart nearly leapt out of his chest.

"Oh my God! It's Joey!" he screamed.

Eight months of grief and worry exploded from his throat. "That's my boy!" George ran down the line, tripping over himself, tears pouring from his eyes. He grabbed the boy and hugged him tight, sobbing and wailing, "Joey! Joey! My little Joey! Thank you God! Thank you, thank you, thank you!"

Detective Daley and storekeeper Sheppard hugged each other and jumped up and down like children out of sheer joy.

"What a wonderful, wonderful thing you've done here, Sheppard!" exploded Detective Daley, eyes tearing with emotion. He planted a big smooch on the shopkeeper's cheek. "You're my hero!"

George pressed his face, now lined and aged by eight months of excruciating anguish and heartbreak, so forcefully into the boy's that the child yelped in pain.

He held the boy at arm's length to gaze lovingly into his dark eyes and absorb this moment of triumph. As he did, something looked wrong. The boy's expression was blank. He did not react or seem to understand what was going on.

"Don't you remember me, my son?" questioned George. The boy did not answer. "It's me, your Papa!"

❦❦❦

Nezla startled awake, alerted by a noise outside. She gathered herself and moved to the window to see George's auto approach. He stopped and parked, then got out of the car. He walked around the front and opened the passenger door, reached in, and scooped up the handsome dark haired little boy, kissing him all over. Both were laughing. Nezla could not believe it! Her heart rose into her throat, choking her. George put the boy down, brushed him off, took his hand and led him up the sidewalk toward the house. Nezla shrieked and flew down the stairs and out the door. She bounded along the walk aware that as fast as she was running her feet were failing to touch the ground. As she reached her boy she fell to her knees on the rough cement without experiencing any pain and wrapped her arms tightly around his ample little body. She shrieked and laughed and cried as too did George and the boy. All were ecstatic. A river of tears flowed down her cheeks. She was incoherent with joy, screaming and shouting. Months of dammed up anger, grief and rage escaped like live steam from her weakened frail form.

"Mama, what's wrong? You're scaring me!" cried Joey.

"Oh, I'm so sorry my beautiful little Joey! It's just that your mama is so happy to see you again!"

"Mama, you're scaring me! Wake up!" Nora pleaded after rushing into her mother's room. She shook her mother awake. Nezla looked up at her from her pillow, dazed. Realizing she had only been dreaming, she fainted dead away.

❦❦❦

"Here, Joey, let me see your arm," George Joseph proposed, kneeling by the caravan as he rolled up the boy's sleeve. The three inch scar from a gash Joey had received as a five year old from a broken window was not there. In a fright he wheeled the boy around and inspected the nape of his neck for the funny little birthmark shaped like a small insect. It wasn't there. He rolled back the boy's top lip with his thumb. The boy's baby teeth were intact. None were missing. The closer he scrutinized the more George Joseph was dumbfounded by the absolutely uncanny resemblance. Upon the ultimate horrifying realization that this doppelgänger was not his little Joey after all, the distraught father became lightheaded and dizzy.

Oh! No, this cannot be, he thought to himself. *Please, God, no.*

After talking with the child and reexamining him more closely George Joseph was forced to conclude that although the boy's appearance was so near like that of his son as to deceive anyone, even his own loving father initially, this was not his child. Detective Daley, his incipient joy now demolished, wiped away grief-infused tears.

The storekeeper felt mortified and kept muttering, "I'm so sorry. I'm so sorry."

On the way back to Lackawanna George was so upset that he could not drive, so Detective Daley took over the wheel. George's heart pounded so tortuously that he was afraid he was having a heart attack. Daley had to stop the auto twice so that George could get out to vomit. On his hands and knees he retched laboriously until there was nothing left to expel.

Whatever would he tell his Nezla?

Once home, George feigned nonchalance. He told his wife nothing of his journey, of the boy, or of the boy's dismaying uncanny resemblance to their Joey.

She told him nothing of her dream.

Keeping this grievous misadventure from his wife as he did oppressed him, resulting in a most terrible burden. George Joseph had no one at all in whom to confide, no one with whom he could seek relief or comfort. Nezla was teetering on the edge of derangement he believed, and every effort was made by him at every opportunity to protect her fragile and precarious condition.

One week after the trip to Ithaca, George suddenly disintegrated. So exhausted was he, so depleted of spirit and bereft of hope, that in bed one night he began to sob so uncontrollably that friable, delicate Nezla was put to a severe fright. He had as yet still not told her any of the details of the encounter with their son's doppelgänger.

But now it all poured out.

For the first time Nezla was able to look beyond herself in her solitary anguish to realize that her husband was suffering as least as much as she, and with that awareness she gathered what infinitesimal strength she had yet remaining. She enfolded her broken husband in her dissipated arms and caressed him against her bosom, stroking his forehead, comforting him with red hands wrung raw, allowing his despairing tears to mingle with her own.

"I had a dream..." she confessed.

They spent the rest of the night revealing their secrets to each other and sharing their pain, just as they once used to.

THE FIRST WARD IV

Lost And Found

On the first anniversary of Joey's disappearance an overwhelming silence filled the Joseph family home. Neither they nor the police were any closer to understanding the little boy's disappearance. Nezla on that day paid another visit to Police Chief Gilson. He offered what comfort he could.

"Today my son, my Joey he is gone one year. Sir, please! Can't you find Joey? Can't you find my boy?"

Dejected, she left. As she exited she brushed by the mailman on the sidewalk out front. He tipped his cap and said "good day," but she was deafened by her own chaotic thoughts. The mail carrier entered the station and there, mixed among the usual, delivered yet another postcard. Gilson bristled: *Another one?*

It had been preceded by half a dozen others during only the past six weeks. All had been dispatched to Gilson's junk drawer. This newest one too was postmarked Boston. He sat to read it, a bit intrigued by its arrival on the first anniversary of Joey's gone missing:

> I lied to you about not having money. Unfortunately I have too much money. Wish I were poor like Joseph or Job or poor like our savior Jesus. I am a Freemason of the 32nd degree honored and respected by all who know me. I have a son who married well. Can I, under the circumstances, give myself up? Yes I can of course. But there are still more murders I have not told you about, and they haunt me at night by my bedside. Oh God: I cannot live!"

The police up until then, with the exception of Chief Gilson's undisclosed postcards, had not received a clue. George Joseph had received a number of postcards and letters from Boston as well. He took these to Chief Gilson who continued to insist they were the work of a cruel trickster. He kept their existence entirely to himself. But now even the thick-headed Gilson wondered, what trickster would not tire quickly of such a stunt? A full year had passed and yet the postcards were still forthcoming, now at an even accelerated pace. He re-read a more recent one:

On Thursday November 2, 1911, at 3:30 p.m., Joey Joseph was enticed by me to the rear of a saloon to an outhouse and there abused by me and afterward strangled to prevent him from telling. The next morning I tried to kill a little newsboy who always stands in the morning at Seneca Street or near the hotel at N° 121 Seneca Street. The boy knows me. Ask him.

Chief Gilson noted that Joey was killed October 12, not November 2nd. He sneered knowingly, interpreting the mistaken date as more proof that the author was a crank. He ruefully tossed the card into his drawer to join its little mountain of predecessors. Almost a full year after receiving the first of many, he had neither shared these with anyone nor revealed their existence. Despite his being convinced the postcards were fakery, nonetheless as each arrived he saved it into his top drawer with the others before dismissing the collection from his thoughts.

❧❧❧

On October 14th Buffalo Police Chief Mike Regan was taken aback by a cryptic postcard that arrived in his mail from Boston:

> Dear Mr. Regan. I am sick of trying to fool myself. I am a homicidal maniac. I killed Joey Joseph, of Lackawanna N.Y. I strangled him as I did the others. Please advertise the fact. Post it or write for the information. Come to...

The last word was smudged illegibly. Regan read it over and over wondering about its authenticity. He immediately placed a telephone call to Chief Gilson. Regan told Gilson about the troubling postcard he'd just received in the mail concerning Joey Joseph's murder.

Without so much as a whiff of irony or accountability Gilson replied glibly, "Oh, yeah—*that*. Yes, I've received about a dozen of them myself. Obviously the work of a deranged crank."

Regan shot to his feet at Gilson's revelation. He did his utmost to stifle his shock and modulate his voice. It required everything he had at that moment not to explode.

"Oh, about a dozen you say?" Regan chirped calmly. "Well yes, that is interesting. How about I come there with the postcard I just received so that I might compare it to yours?"

"Sure, Mike," said Gilson. "How about sometime after lunch?"
"Actually, Gilson, I was just on my way out there anyway on other business," he lied. "I'll see you in about forty-five minutes."
Regan hung up the phone before Gilson could object.
"Sully!" he shouted. Detective Jim Sullivan had just walked in the door. "Let's go!" As the two raced for his automobile, Sullivan blurted, "Jesus, slow down Mike! Where's the fire?" Regan was wordless, broiling. Despite the morning chill he began to sweat.
"That God damned fuckin' son of a bitch moron! I feel like stranglin' the empty-headed bastard!"
"Who?" exclaimed Sullivan, alarmed.
"That asshole Gilson! What a fuckin' useless hack!"
Too much time had already passed since Joey's disappearance. Regan was made sick by Gilson's bizarre dereliction. The Chief blurted his frustration to Sullivan as he drove wildly out South Park Avenue to Ridge Road, tires squealing around the corner, to Gilson's office. Jim was incensed. "What a fuckin' idiot! How did such a stupid incompetent ever make Chief?" he exploded.
"We gotta stay calm, Sully! We gotta play nice and string Gilson along and not make waves so he don't shut us out."
Upon arrival the two professionals acted friendly and nonchalant. They inspected all the postcards calmly. Regan compared the writing on those addressed to Gilson with his own postcard. The script appeared to him without a doubt to be identical. Sullivan readily agreed. All were postmarked Boston. Regan thought the evidence was breakthrough, but cautious of insulting Gilson for his obtuseness, diplomatically agreed that the postcards' meaning was at best a bit tantalizing.
"I gotta admit it, Ray. I'm stumped. You're stumped. We're all stumped."
Sullivan nodded in agreement.
"It's been a year now and we're no closer to finding little Joey today than we was the day the poor kid went missin'. What say we show these here postcards to the public and see if any amateur sleuths might recognize something contained in these that we do not? Some telling detail, or perhaps someone'll recognize the handwriting. Anything at all might help at this sorry point."
Gilson somewhat grudgingly agreed, adding with a sniff of arrogance that he believed it best that police work be left up to the police, not the press, and certainly not the plebeian public. His prejudice confirmed all that Regan had deduced about Gilson up until then, and he reeled at what other useful clues may have been missed along the way during the previous year due to Gilson's brainlessness.

Regan strained at the seams to contain his exasperation.

Both officials issued a call to all the Buffalo newspapermen to come to Lackawanna to review the postcards and make reproductions. Gilson wanted to limit the number of reporters to two or three, but Regan's diplomatic maneuvering prevailed. Seven newspapers ran facsimiles of the postcards in their next editions.

Although Regan was now aware of the precise directions to Joey's body provided in the postcards written to Gilson, he did not immediately urge the Chief to search the location a second time, assuming Gilson himself would immediately come to that obvious conclusion.

Maddeningly, he did not.

Regan now realized the full parameters to which Gilson had botched the entire matter, but was not at this point going to allow for anything that might get him banished from the Lackawanna jurisdiction. He continued to acquiesce to Gilson's leading the investigation, keeping his counsel diplomatic and to a minimum.

Mike Regan's primary goal at this late stage was to just find Joey. They'd waited this long, he thought. A few more days wouldn't hurt if it meant being able to finally solve this crime.

※※※

One of the superintendents of the Lackawanna Steel Company, Talmage Blass, saw the postcard reproductions in the newspaper. He thought the distinctive handwriting looked familiar. He rustled through his own desk drawer and found a letter J. Frank Hickey had written to him. He studied the two side by side. The similarities were striking. His stomach sank, his heart raced. What should he do? Who should he tell, if anyone? He liked Hickey, mostly. What if he were mistaken?

He left the house that morning for work, his mind roiling.

He decided at first not alert anyone, but found himself entirely upset and distracted for the rest of the day. After work he had himself a drink or two to help calm his jitters. He had difficulty falling asleep and awoke in the night numerous times, stomach tied in knots. He was faced with the very real possibility that the man with whom he had a cordial relationship was a child murderer who had authored the diabolical postcards and letters to Joey's father and Police Chief Gilson. Blass was up at first light. He again compared the letter in his possession with the postcards in the newspaper. There was now no ignoring the similarities. He went to work as usual. His men, noticing him distracted and quite discombobulated, inquired whether he might be ill.

"Maybe yous should go home 'n' have a rest, Boss," suggested one.

Blass took the suggestion, but once home his thoughts fragmented wildly and his heart pained in his chest. Sitting in his new Barcolo chair he tried reading a book but found that upon finishing a paragraph he had no idea what he had just read. Resigned, he suddenly jumped up from his resting place, put on his coat, and walked briskly to the Lackawanna Police Station. There he showed the evidence he had and made a statement as to his suspicions.

Gilson took out a couple of the postcards, compared them to Blass' letter, shook his head, and said, "Nope. These weren't written by the same hand."

Blass was stupefied. He stood at the Chief's shoulder, positive now that it was Hickey's scribing on all the examples. He thought the Chief an idiot.

"But Chief! Look. They are not just similar, they are indeed identical!"

"Sorry," Gilson patronized with a slight smirk. "Thank you sir. Please, be on your way now. I have important work to do."

❦

On Saturday morning November 16, 1912, one year and one month after Joey's disappearance, the mailman delivered a letter postmarked Boston to George Joseph.

He waited until the store had been vacated by an exacting customer before opening it.

He was horrified by the nightmarish contents.

In the most foul of language the writer described the murder of his missing son in outrageous detail, sparing the parent nothing in describing how the rape and cruel murder was committed, even describing with glee how the meek terrified child failed to struggle or even try to scream for rescue.

It read in part:

> I watched the boy enter the candy store between 3 and 4 p.m. on October 11, 1912. When he came out I enticed him into the alley leading to the outhouse behind Doyle's. I killed your boy Joey because I abused him first and then I strangled him. He died very quiet, just stuck his tongue out and never moved. He is the first kid I killed that never fought. He just laid down and died; his tongue stuck out and when he was quiet I took him up and cast him down in that outhouse. I also am the murderer of 12 more kids. Just wait till Wednesday November 13th when I shall come to your store. Catch me if you can.

George instantly vomited into the metal wastebasket he kept under the counter.

When he'd recovered somewhat he read the entire missive again. Then once more. He could not accept its horrific claims. He did not want to believe that any human was capable of carrying out such cold blooded acts, most especially against his own sweet helpless baby.

The letter revealed the exact whereabouts of Joey's body.

The killer described how, after committing the hellish atrocities, he had forcibly crammed Joey's little body through a poop hole in an outhouse. He stated it was necessary for him to climb up onto the seat and stomp the little child past the opening with his boots, breaking Joey's little bones in order to force him through. He claimed he listened intently as the child's bones cracked and snapped. He provided the address: N♀ 121 Ridge Rd., behind Doyle's saloon.

With horror and disbelief George Joseph shot his gaze out the window and diagonally across Ridge Rd. to the purported location. Could little Joey really have been murdered within steps of their family home? Could his cherished Joey really have been so close by to his distraught loved ones all this time?

George Joseph began to tremble in dread and trepidation. A full year of the most extreme sort of stress had turned him into a jittery skittish nervous wreck. He had aged ten years in one. He feared constantly for his remaining children whenever they stepped foot out the door.

He knew he had to go across the street to investigate, as terrified as he was to do so. It took superhuman effort to get his protesting limbs into forward movement. He threw on his coat. He exited the store, forgetting to lock the door behind him. Dead leaves crunched beneath his feet as he went, the sound sending his stomach contents seeking escape in both directions. The letter's description of fragile little Joey's body being stomped through a shit hole by the barbarous monster haunted his every dizzy step. He crossed the busy thoroughfare, barely dodging the rumbling Ridge Rd. streetcar. He walked faster. He had to know.

Next to the saloon was a narrow vacant lot behind a rickety wood fence through which he stepped in a controlled panic. There, rubbish and papers and other discards were strewn among the brown overgrown weeds. Then he saw it. It was rarely in use anymore since the saloon's having installed indoor plumbing. He pushed open the creaky outhouse door. It was very dark inside. Along the top of opposing walls ran a transom accommodation covered with screening, torn and littered with the impaled corpses of a thousand mummified flies glittering like emeralds.

There were not three seats, as the letter in his hand claimed, but two. He took a smidgen of temporary comfort from this mistake.

Perhaps it was entirely a cruel bluff after all.

The two openings were simple holes crudely cut into a wood bench for the accommodation of defecators who no doubt afterward were left with slivers embedded in their rumps. He peered down into these black holes with trepidation, but all he could discern was obscurity. The smell on the other hand made itself abundantly vivid. George Joseph's trembling left hand grasped the perverse letter. He dared not share it with his wife, for it would kill her. He knew he had to deliver it straightaway to the police.

He flew from the outhouse forcing back his rising vomit. Leaning on the fence for support he bent and retched, heaving, until nothing was left inside. He looked over at the upper windows in his house across the street to make sure Nezla wasn't watching. The kids were at school. A few minutes later he arrived at the police station having no memory at all of how he got there, so entirely undone was he by the contents of the monstrous dispatch.

Gilson pulled the postcards from his desk drawer. He and George Joseph studied and compared them. George insisted that the handwriting was unmistakably the same. The Chief, just as in times previous, doubted it.

"He says Joey's buried in the cesspool! We must go there and search!"

"But Mr. Joseph," Gilson softly and unthinkingly responded, "we already searched there and found nothing."

"What? When? When did you search?"

Gilson was trapped. He had never told Mr. Joseph about the first postcard, received over a year previous, detailing exactly where Joey's body could be found. Rather than admit to that truth and have to offer some explanation, he instead thought it more expedient to quickly agree with George Joseph.

"Yes, I'll gather some officers and we will go there immediately."

The Chief and two officers, Wiley and Jasper, the two who had originally been sent to investigate the outhouse, immediately accompanied George Joseph back to the cesspool. Together they perused the unpromising scene. Gilson had pulled Wiley and Jasper aside to strongly caution the two officers to not under any circumstance reveal to George Joseph that they had previously searched the scene.

Gilson ascertained what tools might be needed to commence a proper search. Nearby a pile of wood and shingles gathered for the repair of Doyle's roof contained a long pole with a hook arrangement at the end. Gilson entered the outhouse. George stood behind him almost touching. Gilson poked the pole through the shithole. He first gauged the depth of the pool. Then he swirled around in the slime whereby he almost immediately hit something solid. An object was detected and a few jabs attached it to the end of the pole.

As Wiley and Jasper stood nervously outside, Gilson carefully raised the pole hand over hand. As it broke the surface, it could be seen through the shit hole that it was a small human leg, intact from thigh to foot, the latter being still clad in a stocking and a little shoe.

George Joseph gasped in horror as he recognized Joey's little stocking and shoe and shouted, "That's Joey! That's my Joey!" He felt the blood drain from his head. He collapsed into a heap, tumbling out the outhouse doorway flat to the ground. In hysterics he howled, having now seen with his own eyes the tragic truth.

"See?" Jasper whispered to Wiley. "I toldja then we shoulda found ourselves a pole. Now we'll be in deep shit ourselves."

Chief Gilson called in laborers to the scene. It was decided the structure be removed to gain full access to the soup of putrid defecant. The task of dismantling it required almost an hour. George kept his eye on his house across the street, hoping the activity would not attract Nezla's attention. The construction debris was removed off to one side. Then grappling hooks were utilized. These were sunk into the quagmire. The handler walked to and fro along the edge of the pool attempting to snag any solid object.

George Joseph watched furtively, shivering from equal parts terror and cold, sick to his stomach. He kept glancing toward the street, apprehensive about Nezla or the children being alerted to investigate. He had not yet thought of how he was going to break the news to his wife without her disintegrating entirely. The heavy traffic and noise on Ridge Rd. sufficiently obfuscated their activity.

"The only advantage to this damn cold," crasslessly stated the obtuse Gilson to George Joseph, stomping his feet, "is that it keeps the stink down."

Soon enough another bone was raised, followed a few minutes later by yet another. George Joseph went numb as he witnessed his child's remains retrieved piecemeal from the stinking muck. Each piece was placed on the brown grass so as to drain it of its disgusting coating before being placed in a bucket. Added to his anguish was the looming finality of having to inform his still-hopeful family that all optimism had now been extinguished. At long last, their little Joey had been found, dead.

The search continued for hours. Arm bones and ribs were pulled out. At 3:30 o'clock with November darkness already threatening, a pump was brought in. Drained of its feculent contents the pool surrendered Joey's other leg, then more ribs.

The Joseph children, returning from school, found the door to their father's store unlocked, but he was nowhere to be seen. They also noticed quite a bit of activity across the street, but did not think it entirely unusual. As was often the case their mother was asleep in bed in the parents' bedroom.

Nora shook her mother awake.

"Where's Papa, Mama?" Nora asked. "The door to the shop is unlocked."

Panic filled Nezla's face, as any hint of threat connected to her husband or children sent her into a tailspin. She jumped up from her bed and put on her dress, panicking.

"Mama, please, calm yourself. He probably just went to the grocers and forgot to lock up. I'll go look for him, alright? You just stay here and let me go get him. Please?"

Nezla stopped herself and sat on the edge of the bed. She was aware of how reactionary she had become.

"All right, Nora. You go. I stay with baby."

As Nora departed, her brother Edward came up the walk. "Eddie, stay with Mama. I'll be right back," she ordered.

Nora's attention was again drawn to the commotion across the street at Doyle's. The police were there. She wondered if there might have been another shooting. She continued up Ridge Rd. to the grocer's.

Nezla cradled the baby in her arms and paced. The infant was disturbingly quiet, unlike her other children when they were babies. She wondered if this child, born into a family situation saturated in chaos and fear, had been so damaged by the circumstances as to render him mute. She walked to the front window and looked out. She noticed all the men standing at the fence next to Doyle's. She took note that they were mostly policemen. Then she saw a flash of red plaid, identical to that of the plaid of the coat she had given her husband two Christmases previous. She caught a glimpse of face. It was George. She yelped aloud. She called to her son.

"Edward! Come here!"

Edward appeared almost instantly.

"Watch baby while I go cross the street a minute."

Edward took the baby from her gently, cradling his head. Nezla threw on her shawl and clumsily zig-zagged Ridge Road's heavy rush hour traffic. At the fence a policeman stopped her.

"Ma'am, you can't..."

"George!" she screamed. "George!"

George was standing at the edge of the cesspool engrossed in the nightmarish activity, the pail just feet away from which a young boy's bare bones jutted out the top askew in all directions.

Nezla's eyes then riveted to the pail. At first she did not recognize the odd collection as being bones. Then she burst. "No! It cannot be!" she shrieked.

George was frozen for a few seconds until the expression on her face, like a spear through his heart, jolted him from his paralysis.

She continued to shriek like a banshee, and with both hands rammed the policeman's chest, sending him toppling. She jumped over him and bolted to her husband's side.

"Joey!" she screeched in an octave no human voice had ever previously achieved. "Joey! Joey! Oh, can't be my little Joey! Say me this not my baby!"

George, sobbing, enfolded her as she collapsed in hysterics. He refused a policeman's help, lifting her himself and carrying her back across the street just as daughter Nora returned.

"Papa!" Nora screamed. "What on earth is happening?"

George, face contorted in horror and grief, did not answer. He just wanted to get his family safely into the house.

"Come Nora!" he cried, tears falling onto his jacket. Nora obeyed, even as her eyes were transfixed on the scene unfolding across the street.

Nezla's shrieks quickly resumed and with them Nora had her answer.

"Is Joey over there, Papa?" she asked incredulously, her voice breaking into a wail. "Tell me he's not...please!"

He could only but nod yes, his voice dumbed by the choking spasming of his throat, whereupon Nora halted in place, then stiffened and keened primitively like a mortally wounded shewolf, liberating a full year's bounty of bereavement and lonely despair. Edward appeared with the infant, stunned by the emotional scene. The baby, sensing it was no longer required of him to remain still and quiet, erupted in bawling. Across the street officers observing the family's agony, unable to contain their own emotions, broke down in empathy.

Inside the house George picked up the telephone and recited the number he had well committed to memory to the operator.

"Hello, Dr. Wellington Ross speaking."

George could barely get the words out.

"Doc...Doctor Ross, they...they found our little Joey!" he blubbered almost incoherently.

Ross didn't need to ask who it was on the line. He bolted to standing and grabbed his medical satchel.

"I'm on my way, Mr. Joseph. I'll be there as quickly as I can."

From across the street, piercing right through the busy traffic on Ridge Rd., overcoming even the heavy rumbling of streetcar wheels on the rails and the clanging of bells, the shrieks of Nezla Joseph shivered up the spines of the police officers. They all stopped to gaze toward the house as the primeval screams and collective wailings of the Joseph family poured forth from between its clapboards. Solemn policemen, fathers and husbands themselves, peered furtively, unsettled by the family's excruciating howls of agony. All stood there transfixed, motionless, silent, holding their breath, lips quivering, tears wiped on sleeves in response to the unfolding tragedy.

"All right, fellas," sniffled Chief Gilson, "Let's try and finish this damnable task before it gets too dark."

Less than fifteen minutes later Dr. Ross was in the door trying to prevent Nezla's complete disintegration. He prepared bromides as she flailed and howled. Although Dr. Ross had stuck her without any forewarning, the needle elicited no reaction from Nezla. It took but a few minutes for her to settle.

The Joseph children lingered in their solitude, overlooked by the adults as if they were little more than apparitions, as if their searing despair and torment were not equal to that of their parents. They had been required for more than a year to stifle, as best children were capable, their fear and pain and grief for the sake of their fragile mother, and now here they yet stood, still stifling. It was as if their parents had only one child, or more accurately, only one child who really mattered.

As Nezla faded into stupor, George got up to return to the dismal undertaking across the street. He forbade Nora and Eddie from leaving the house.

Darkness descended quickly and the temperature with it. Finally, around six o'clock, in the bitter cold, under the glare of a dozen kerosene lamps, the final portion of little Joey Joseph, the child's head, was recovered, its two front teeth missing.

Nora had sneaked out of the house.

Standing there shivering in the shadows, she witnessed a sight she would come to regret for the rest of her life.

THE FIRST WARD IV

Partners In Crime

Outrage spilled out in heavy black ink splattered across the front pages of the region's newspapers, and from there to the important dailies coast to coast. J. Frank Hickey's heart skipped a beat as he read the headline: MISSING JOSEPHS BOY'S BODY FOUND IN CESSPOOL.

It was 9 a.m. in Lowell. He immediately left work for the nearest saloon. There he spent the entire day and well into the evening downing prodigious amounts of alcohol.

The saloonkeep had never witnessed anything such as this.

"Another man would have been unconscious by noon, and dead from alcohol poisoning by dinnertime at the rate he was drinking," stated the bartender later. "But that man drank until we closed, and even then was able to leave the establishment under his own leg power. Then around noon the following day he arrived again in a drunken state and sat on the same stool for almost eight hours downing one drink after another arising only to visit the W.C.

"He spoke to no one. He was polite. Somber. That day too, despite his condition, he was able to get up and walk out of the saloon with nary a wobble."

On Tuesday at noon Hickey arrived on the train at Whitings, New Jersey. Immediately he made his way to the Keswick Colony, ten miles outside of town. He knocked upon the familiar door. It was opened by Mother Rawes, matron of the institution. Mother Rawes welcomed him into her waiting arms and led him gently into the parlor. He was in a pitiful state, extremely upset, submerged in another of his historic debauches.

❦❦❦

Telegrams, phone calls and letters poured into the Lackawanna precinct requesting details as police in far-flung cities throughout the United States and Canada sought to link Buffalo's unknown killer with similar atrocities in their own communities. The Police Chief of Hamilton Ontario drove across the International Bridge at Niagara to personally meet with Lackawanna Chief Gilson in hopes of solving the disappearance of a little boy from his own neighborhood. Newspapers across

North America printed photographic reproductions of the postcards beneath inflamed headlines.

Out of the woodwork at lightning speed emerged valuable findings.

Talmage Blass, the foreman at the Lackawanna steel plant, was revisited by Chief Gilson, now a bit more willing to hear what Blass might have to say. Blass reiterated his belief that Hickey had written the postcards. Additionally he imparted the amazing news that he had confided his suspicions in Jack Jepson, superintendent of the coke ovens, who also had in his possession a letter from Hickey that appeared to be in the same handwriting as the postcards. The letter, outlining Hickey's idea for an invention, was signed. Blass told the Chief that John Jepson lived at N⁰ 144 Macamley Street, that Jepson knew Hickey very well, and that the police should pay him visit.

Hickey it turned out was a habitual communicator. He wrote to friends and colleagues religiously, and many of those retained his letters, much to Hickey's liability.

❧❧❧

As the little pile of what remained of Joey Joseph lay on the copper table in his funeral establishment near the Lackawanna Police Station, undertaker William F. White suffered an unsettling flash of wooziness.

This was not due to what the experienced mortician was observing in front of him, but rather about what he was suddenly recalling. He remembered something his old friend and drinking partner had said to him one day as they sat at a table at Doyle's saloon, gazing out the window at small children playing. At the time White thought it a bit disconcerting, out of character from the man he'd known so well all those many years. Since they had both been drinking heavily White had dismissed his remark as the result of wanton intoxication.

But now his habitual drinking partner's sinister utterance came back to him, and in light of the circumstances, it seemed terribly foreboding.

❧❧❧

Alerted as to their imminent arrival by his friend Talmage Blass, John Jepson welcomed the police. He well remembered Hickey and produced for the police a letter Hickey had written to him two years previous.

"Hickey worked for me in 1910 but I discharged him because he was a heavy drinker," Jepson stated. "But there's someone else you might want to talk to—John Hoskyn. He lives at N⁰ 89 Montgomery Street."

Hoskyn too had in his possession a recent letter written by Hickey in which he revealed where he was and who he was working for. Hoskyn had ascertained that the writing on the postcards and in the letter he'd saved from Hickey were the same, with a very distinctive capital D. The letters a, d, and t were all connected in the same unique way, as was the phrase "Buffalo ~ N.Y.", having a tilde inserted between the "Buffalo" and the "N.Y." He carefully pointed out these examples to the police.

Jepson stated that while employed by him Hickey had boarded with Mrs. E.A. Jones at N̄o̱ 77 Aldrich Pl.

Mrs. Jones told police, "Hickey was a heavy drinker. He often came home drunk but he was never arrested for being intoxicated. One day I told Hickey he could not stay here any longer and that he must get out. When he left he took the front door key with him and then borrowed $3 from me and purloined $5 from the trunk of my sister, Mrs. Mae J. Kidd, who lived with me at the time."

After Jones kicked him out, Hickey went down the street to board with Edward Maddigan at N̄o̱ 59 Aldrich Pl. Mrs. Maddigan told police that Hickey was a heavy drinker and that he often came home intoxicated. She too kicked him out.

Next the police visited Mr. Shoemaker at his boardinghouse at 31 Seneca Street who also produced a letter from Hickey written right after he fled Buffalo. In it Hickey asked for a loan of one dollar with which he could repay one of his former landladies from whom he said he had borrowed money.

On the previous Sunday, the day after the discovery of Joey's remains, great crowds of the curious gathered outside the Joseph family home. Hundreds of others ghoulishly tried in vain to view what remained of the little body lying in William White's undertaking establishment. The newspapers reported that only a few intimate friends of the family were allowed to see the bones. At three o'clock Father Nelson Baker called at the house to make arrangements for the funeral. Nezla Joseph lay there in critical condition. Family physician Dr. Wellington M. Ross in a statement said that Mrs. Josephs was in a semi-conscious condition and was being kept quiet with administered bromides.

On Tuesday, prominent Buffalo alienist Dr. Nelson W. Wilson felt compelled to speak out.

He had read, and was disturbed by, what he declared a "reckless" article in that morning's *Courier* newspaper. The *Courier* furnished a reporter to record his argument and subsequently published his rebuttal.

"The Courier this morning paralleled the little Marian Murphy murder case of a few years ago with the Josephs boy murder. There is a wide difference in the two cases. Their only similarity lies in the fact that both were sexual crimes against defenseless children. The Josephs case entailed a high degree of sadistic murder—a case where death or the mutilating of the victim was a necessity for the fulfillment of the sexual appetite of the murderer. It was not a killing as an accompaniment of rage or fear. The murder was as necessary a part of the sexual assault as was the attack itself.

"In the case of Marian Murphy there was an assault of particularly sexual type. It was not necessarily the act of an invert. It was more the crime of a mental pervert, and the killing which followed was the result of the suddenly awakened panic of an already diseased mind. Marian Murphy was strangled with a rope which bound her neck. I investigated that case from the sexuo-criminologic standpoint at the time. I am fairly certain in my own mind of the identity of the murderer, and he bore few if any of the stigmata of the true sexual invert.

"There were some of the individual marks of an invert in the Murphy crime. It was merely a sexual assault on a young child whose subsequent murder became a necessity through fear of exposure. The Josephs case, on the contrary, presents to the student of sexual criminology easily read signs of a true inversion and the act of an hereditary sanguinary sadist whose capture appears to be imminent as a result of his intense egotism and his misguided cunning."

The reporter responded, "Dr. Wilson, did I just hear you say you know the identity of the killer of little Marian Murphy?"

"Yes, I believe I do," he responded.

"Who is it, and why after all this time has he not been arrested?"

"I cannot say why the police have allowed him to remain free."

"Doctor," continued the reporter, "I was in the employ of the Buffalo Express at the time of the little Murphy girl's murder. I caught her father outside the morgue after her body was found and interviewed him there. I became convinced then that it was he who killed his own child. Are we in agreement? Do you believe it was her father who murdered her?"

Dr. Wilson responded with a wry smile. "I am not at liberty to accuse any individual publicly, sir, not legally at any rate. Now if you'll excuse me, I have another commitment for which I am already tardy."

In the next morning's newspaper Dr. Wilson in a critical study of the case from the viewpoint of a criminologist, provided the first known example of modern criminal profiling.

He was quoted as stating that the criminal would probably prove to be:

— A man less than middle age.

— A careful dresser, probably inclined to foppishness.
— A very apparent egotist.
— Living in or near Buffalo and making frequent trips out of Buffalo.
— A man of education and a victim of an inherited inversion.

Wilson had initially offered this profile of the killer to the police. They dismissed it out of hand without first asking any of their suspect's friends if the description fit.

※※※

Lackawanna Detective Daley discovered that Hickey had previously resided at the Grand Union Hotel in Lackawanna. He was taken aback, to say the very least, upon questioning the manager there to discover that Hickey had enjoyed a close and lengthy friendship with well-known Lackawanna undertaker William White, the same mortician who was at that very moment preparing Hickey's latest known victim for burial.

Daley paid White a visit.

At his funeral establishment White feigned shock upon learning Detective Daley's revelation. He pretended that only at that very moment was he learning that his friend Hickey was believed to have murdered the little boy.

"I know how this must look! Certainly you can't think...! No, I had no idea that Hickey was in any way a degenerate! We were drinking laddies, that's all!"

"Yous two ever drink at Doyle's Saloon?" asked the detective.

"Doyle's? Oh, I'm not sure where that is. There was a saloon next to the Grand Union Hotel where we frequented quite often."

"Were you acquainted with the Joseph family before you provided your funeral services?"

"Oh no. They are Syrians. What reason would I have to be acquainted with Syrians?"

"Had you ever seen little Joey before, when he was alive?"

"I don't believe I did."

Detective Daley next paid a visit to Doyle's Saloon. He was told that over the years undertaker White had certainly been a frequent customer there, both alone and in the regular company of a certain friend. Daley was angered by this revelation. He wondered now if undertaker White might be involved in Joey's murder.

The detective returned to White to confront him with this latest information. White deflected ridiculously. "Oh, you meant *Dovles* Saloon. Yes we drank there at Dovles together a few times.

"It's not called 'Dovles'—it's 'Doyle's,' Mr. White."

"Allow me to correct you detective, but no, it is Dovles. Rhymes with 'lovelies.' 'Lovely Dovles' we used to call it. Just read the sign out front."

The detective returned to the saloon to see that the letters attached to the sign were carved from painted wood and that the Y in the word Doyle's had split and lost its tail, reading as a V at first glance. Undertaker White's foolhardy attempt at distraction in no way diverted the detective from the established fact that for years White and Hickey had drunk together in the saloon located directly across from Joey Joseph's family home. With regards to this surprising revelation, Daley's suspicions were accelerating.

"Where were you on October 12, 1911 Mr. White?" he asked after returning to the funeral parlor.

"Why, I was right here, preparing Mrs. Arthur Beck for embalming."

"Just like that? You have a ready answer for a date more than a year ago? What about April 10 of this year?"

White hesitated only a bit before proclaiming "I was attending to the Smith child from Electric Ave. I have an excellent memory, Detective Daley. But regardless, everybody around here knows exactly where they were and what they were doing the day the Josephs child went missing on October 12."

"Let me see your appointment book so I can verify that," Daley asked.

"Oh, sorry Detective. The representative from my insurance company currently has it. He's investigating a claim."

Daley was more wary than impressed with White's ready answers. He got up and headed for the door calling back, "I'll be paying you a visit again in a few days, Mr. White. Best you have that appointment book of yours here for me to inspect."

❦

As the avalanche of incriminating evidence against Hickey quickly mounted, Detectives Jim Sullivan and Jerry Lynch came under heated scrutiny when it was recalled that the two partners had arrested Hickey ten years previous, soon after the murder of newsboy Michael Kruck in New York's Central Park. In 1907 a disastrous fire had completely destroyed Buffalo Police Headquarters along with tons of evidence and records. Among the ashes was the signed confession of President William McKinley's assassin Leon Czolgosz, as well as Sullivan and Lynch's 1902 report on the arrest of J. Frank Hickey.

One fact to which Jim Sullivan was privy was that his partner Jerry Lynch kept a personal journal at home containing, in addition to personal musings, various details in connection with the two detectives' exploits and arrests. Sullivan had never read his partner's private journals, but as a writer who had been encouraged in that esteemed art by none other than Mark Twain himself, Sullivan periodically chastised himself for not following Lynch's example. Now he feared what might be contained in those notes, if indeed Jerry had written about the incident at all.

Sullivan decided not to bring up the subject, rather to allow Jerry to decide for himself what he may or may not wish to do. Only a colleague or two other than Sullivan also knew Lynch kept a journal. When asked about this by Chief Regan, Lynch claimed that he kept no such journal. The matter was dropped, that is, until the newspapers got wind of the rumor somehow.

After questioning those men who had retained letters from Hickey which compared favorably in writing style to the killer's postcards, Chief Gilson wasted no time informing Buffalo Police Chief Michael Regan of his findings. Never before had the police accumulated crucial evidence so quickly or moved so decisively. By Monday morning the newspapers were headlining the police's identification of the killer. Although newspapers' headlines screamed that the police had named their suspect, the press was not told his name.

After more than a year of lethargy in the case there was an explosion of activity.

The search was on for J. Frank Hickey.

THE FIRST WARD IV

Unnamed

Shaking her head in disgust, Hannah Sullivan sat reading Dr. Wilson's profile of the killer as printed in the newspaper. With no more babies at home to care for, her morning habit was coffee and toast with Zeke, who obligingly waited under the table at her feet for his share.

"Now don't go tellin' your father," she said, handing Zeke a chunk of toast spread with strawberry preserves. She had both the *Express* and the *Courier* opened to the heart-wrenching Joseph family story. She sat there sipping her coffee, comparing the two newspapers' reports. As usual she was troubled that details of the very same story or incident varied significantly in competing newspapers. This was more often the case than not. Even the quotations attributed to officials and transcribed by the assembled newsmen varied once put to print. This begged the question, which was the real story? What was actually said? What are the true facts? Just how competent are some of these so-called reporters anyway?

Ruth McGowan had suggested to Hannah that none of the papers ran the "true" story, but were carrying varying degrees of it, as provided by the authorities, interpreted by reporters possessing varying levels of expertise, and as censored by their editors.

Hannah had nagged some intriguing details of the case out of Jim, but mostly he held back protectively.

"You don't want to know, Hannah. It's all too disgusting for words."

She was obsessed by the killer's postcards and the letters he sent to the little boy's father. The newspapers stated that these missives contained sickening, cruel, graphic details of what the monster had done to the innocent child. The killer's revelations enraged the police and made violently ill the victim's father. George Joseph had kept these mailings entirely secret from his wife. Her emotional frailty and extreme suffering made it all too clear that something like that might in all likelihood propel her directly over the edge of sanity. As a mother who had lost four of her own children, Hannah could relate.

Jim had revealed some heartbreaking details. The monster had delighted in torturing the father with the detail that poor little gentle Joey, once Hickey began choking him, had not struggled or fought for his life. The sadistic murderer may well have been lying as to this claim, as he had admitted deriving great pleasure in the damage he inflicted on the parents of his victims. Joey died with his eyes open, Hickey stated, probably correctly, staring into his killer's. Hickey had been unnerved by this, and thus proceeded to stuff the child through the shithole head first to quickly exorcise himself of his victim's indelible gaze.

Hannah's eye caught in the *Express* article a familiar disturbing theme. It was a boast on the part of Dr. Wilson echoing the predictable blustering of the police—a firm scolding directed at the killer, and those like him, that their kind are "always caught eventually." This laughable claim was made in relation to what Wilson termed "serial killers." According to the all-knowing Dr. Wilson, all of these serial killers had been successfully apprehended and brought to justice, except for London's infamous Jack The Ripper.

This absurdity revealed itself in Wilson's next breath when he acknowledged that the killer of little Marion Murphy ten years previous had never been apprehended, even as Wilson professed that he was positive of the murderer's identity.

"Are these so-called learned men absurdly, intentionally oblivious?" Hannah asked Zeke. The wizened dog raised his head to hear her out.

"Do they not have the common sense to even suspect that hundreds—if not thousands—of past murders, of children missing outright, that have gone unsolved in this country might not in some large part be the work of such 'serial killers' too clever to tip their hand to police who are too stupid to even recognize that such a phenomenon exists? That the police refuse to acknowledge that what they claim to be a rare occurrence is in fact quite commonplace in order to obscure their gross failure at solving these disappearances?"

This pompous claim truly got Hannah's goat. She knew nothing could be further from the truth; after all, she was married to a detective. It echoed all she knew as wrong concerning the conventions of law enforcement. The department's own statistics proved that less than one serious crime in ten resulted in an arrest, much less a conviction. She denounced Wilson's preposterous claim as being made in conspiracy with the police to keep the public from panicking and from making judgments against the police, especially in light of the many murders committed in Buffalo in recent years that had completely eluded their solving.

Hannah marveled at the supposed educator's audacity, that despite all proof to the contrary available to any reporter who might wish to find out, the police and other officials continued to make this vacant statistical boast. Hannah knew from being married to a police detective for thirty years that the great majority of all crimes would remain forever unsolved. Officials who claim otherwise she believed deserved to be in prison themselves for their deception of a trusting, tax-paying public .

THE FIRST WARD IV

Joey's Funeral

Tuesday morning dawned cold and dismal.

The spotless little coffin containing the desecrated bits and pieces of the cherished boy was covered by a blanket woven of perfect white roses. By eight o'clock the crowd outside of White's undertaking rooms had grown beyond one hundred people. A police detail was sent there to keep order and maintain privacy.

The service at the church had been scheduled for nine o'clock, but it was a quarter hour after that before the procession even left the undertaking rooms. Flags on all public buildings flew at half-mast. Every house of business in Lackawanna was shuttered between the hours of nine and ten-thirty o'clock. The steel-plant city with its population of 15,000 had 120 saloons, but even these places locked their doors to pay respect to the little victim.

At nine fifteen o'clock the white coffin covered in white roses was carried out of White's undertaking establishment and placed in a white hearse drawn by two stately white horses driven by undertaker William F. White. Detective Daley watched intently every change of expression on the undertaker's face. He was highly suspicious that White may have participated in some manner in Joey Joseph's abduction and murder. Daley had taken it upon himself to research old police files related to unsolved crimes against children during the period now known to be when Hickey and White were habitual drinking buddies. Upon questioning White's neighbors and associates, word spread quickly of the detective's suspicions, and people began to wonder.

Undertaker White tried to focus on the miserable task at hand but could not avoid noticing Daley's unrelenting gaze.

Several black carriages filled with city officials followed behind the hearse. Municipal Court had been adjourned for the morning. The judge, along with every member of the Lackawanna police force, acted as escort. Headed by Chief Gilson, the funeral cortege proceeded to the Joseph family home on the lower Ridge Road. In addition to the Chief, patrolmen Davis, Clancy, Bowen, Daley, Wiley, Jasper and Schultz acted as honorary escort, marching alongside the hearse bearing the child. The funeral party wended its way down Ridge Road in the direction of Lake

Erie toward the Josephs home at the farthest end of town.

Public School N° 4, which the Joseph child had attended, was closed. The teachers and 300 students assembled at eight-thirty in front of the school as usual, only on this sad day to march in a procession of grief down Ridge Rd. to the dead boy's family home.

Approximately one thousand persons lined the sidewalks along the route. Men removed their hats as the hearse passed mournfully and all those assembled bowed their heads. Upon arrival at the Joseph home it was met by eight of Joey's schoolmates. They were John McCann, Joseph Miscall, Henry Rather, John Monahan, Brandon Eagen, Wilson Cullen, Walter Gurstine, and Leonard Reed, son of Lackawanna Mayor Reed.

The young boys carried the coffin into the house.

Joey's mother broke down and wept bitterly at the sight of the casket holding what little was left of her once-beautiful son. His black piercing eyes encircled by impossibly thick lashes haunted her thoughts; the realization that hers would never again look into his wounded her as searingly as a red-hot knife to the gut. As it was borne through the door Nezla ran forward and threw herself on the casket, shrieking and crying.

"Give me back my boy! Give me back my boy!" she wailed.

The surviving Joseph children, witnessing their mother's breakdown, stood wide-eyed and trembling. Their father sobbed unceasingly. The couple might have consoled each other, and their children, had they been at all capable of extricating themselves from the solitary depths of their individual grief. Each member of the family was as paralyzed as the next.

Dr. Wellington Ross and Dr. John Smoja, who were present, had to attend to Nezla before she was able to leave the house. She tore her hair out of her scalp in clumps as she shrieked. Joey's body remained in the home less than five minutes. By the time the procession was formed for the church, Nezla Joseph was so weak that she was unable to stand. She had to be carried to the street. Several hundred people had gathered outside the house. There were few dry eyes as the crowd witnessed the difficulty the sobbing mother, who necessitated being held up on both sides, had entering the funeral carriage. Dr. Ross followed behind the carriage on foot all the way to the church in anticipation she might suffer a total collapse.

From the family home the body was taken to the little wooden St. Charles Church on Ridge Rd. Nezla Joseph did not like the church. It was not Syrian. More so, she did not care for the pastor, Father Blakeney. He was neither Syrian nor did he care much for Syrian people, something he had made abundantly clear on a number of occasions.

Long before the service began the church was crowded to the doors and the police were obliged to turn several hundred mourners away. The members of Stony Point Fire District N⁰ 1 under command of Capt. Norman Smith acted as an escort to the casket as it entered. Each member of the Lackawanna firefighters wore a spray of memorial evergreen in his coat.

The service in the little church, as reported in the *Buffalo Express*, was "pathetic to an unprecedented extreme." The solemn requiem Mass was celebrated by Blakeney, assisted by the Rev. P.C. Santa of Our Lady Of Victory Church, Rev. C.F. Killeen of St. James Church, Depew, and Monsignor Francis Shemalie, pastor of the Syrian community's St. John Maron church on Seneca Street.

Amid celebrating the Mass the Reverend Father Blakeney delivered the funeral oration. In his sermon he paid high tribute to the sterling qualities of the Joseph boy with whom he had not been acquainted in the least. He took as his text "Render to Caesar the things that are Caesar's and to God the things that are God's."

Joey's mother wept bitterly all during the funeral. Many times the father had sobbed aloud. Their children, seeing their parents distraught to the point of near-collapse, and not fully understanding the events that led to their brother's death, found some solace at the breasts of their aunts.

Blakeney's sermon was scolding and heartless. Monsignor Shemalie especially seemed horrified, sitting at the side of the altar with the other priests. Blakeney lorded over the congregation smugly. It was clear he believed his talents were too precious to be wasted on such a poor little church and all these predominantly dark-skinned congregants.

"There is something more important at this time than to eulogize the little Joseph boy," he continued crassly.

Blakeney coldly addressed the suffering parents and their traumatized children as he applied the impersonal phrase "the little Josephs boy" rather than offering something more respectful, more consoling and appropriate, an endearment perhaps akin to "your beloved son and brother."

"We must bear up under the circumstances," he admonished as he fixed Joey's mother directly in his steely gaze, "And you, my dear woman, must bear up for your good children who survive. This little boy was ready to receive God! You should not regret that he is gone! God's will has been done! Dear mother and father of this boy, God called him! Why should you begrudge what God wants? If the boy should have lived and gone down through manhood, would you have the same satisfaction that he would have been saved that you now have?"

The deeply grieving congregation seemed stunned into silence by the priest's bizarre rationalizing.

Inside her own head in her native language, Nezla Joseph screamed at him. *What would you know? You have never received the precious love of your own child! You have never fathered a son, nor will you ever! You have never had to suffer your child's illnesses, much less his diabolical murder. How dare you lord over us with your sanctimonious stupidity at our most vulnerable moment, as we drown in the depths of our grieving, as if we are nothing at all, as if according to your high and mighty summation we are no more than spoiled children! It is you who are nothing! It is you who are clearly damaged beyond salvation! Go to hell, priest!"*

Embedded in the passionate culture of Syria, recrimination and vengeance are dispositions more ingrained than in America's. That being the case however, even the peaceful Monsignor Shemalie entertained certain dark thoughts against Blakeney as he listened to him chastise the murdered child's parents from the pulpit.

Nezla Joseph cursed at that moment the family's no longer being parishioners at St. John Maron, that the lovely Monsignor Shemalie was not leading the service honoring her dead child, a boy he had baptized and knew personally and mourned authentically. She knew that Monsignor Shemalie would have provided her the comfort and solace she so desperately needed rather than the interloper Blakeney's cold recriminations.

"May God give you the consolation that no human being can give," was Blakeney's chilly conclusion. Then he turned his attentions back to the altar.

It was nearly noon before the procession reached the outskirts of the cemetery.

As it passed Father Baker's Home for Boys, nearly a hundred of the young inhabitants marched down the steps and joined in with the Joseph family, the schoolchildren, the police and firemen, the city officials, the priests, friends and neighbors and a large contingent of the Syrian community to pass through the gates of Holy Cross Cemetery. Over one thousand additional persons awaited them in the graveyard, mostly Syrians, gathered at the gravesite. It took more than twenty police officers to open a passageway to allow the funeral procession to enter and proceed unhindered to its destination.

Owing to the serious condition of the boy's mother, Dr. Ross advised against allowing her to leave the carriage, but she begged for one last look at her son.

The Rt. Rev. Monsignor Nelson H. Baker helped her to the side of the casket and comforted her there as he conducted the graveside ceremony. The parents' sobs punctuated Father Baker's tender eulogy, its loving sensitivity in deep contrast to that of Father Blakeney's bizarre scolding lecture. Only sometime later would

Father Baker hear the details of Blakeney's sorry episode and respond to him personally and decisively.

As soon as Father Baker had finished speaking, a tall wild-eyed black-haired Syrian man in the crowd began causing a ruckus. He made his way determinedly toward the prelate and the Joseph family, waving his hand in the air excitedly above his head, demanding to be heard.

The crowd protested loudly, insisting the man was conducting himself inappropriately. Baker tried quieting the intensely emotional throng. The police stiffened, poised for a riot.

"Please! Please, let's hear what this man has to say!" implored the beloved priest.

The man stepped up to the open grave and cast his eyes downward onto Joey's waiting casket. He reached inside his coat pocket. Some in the crowd, including Father Baker, momentarily feared a pistol. Instead he pulled a long manuscript from his coat. It was written in the Syrian language and he spoke in that tongue so that only his fellow countrymen could understand. His voice was loud and emotional. The crowd was quickly agitated into near frenzy. He made an impassioned appeal that the wrath of God might descend mightily upon the murderer of Joey Joseph. He reviewed the career of the boy and told of the terrible agony of the parents during Joey's year-long disappearance. At the top of his voice he begged that God would wreak a terrible vengeance on the animal responsible for the little one's desecration.

"We pray that he may not escape the punishment he so richly deserves," cried the Syrian. "May God prevent him from committing further atrocities upon helpless children, and may God in his mercy deal with this monster in the way he deserves so that his fate may be a warning to other evildoers. Let his punishment befit the crimes of this terrible monster."

A few women standing closest to the open grave almost went into hysterics, but overall the crowd was mostly stoic.

Determining the man had finished, Father Baker signaled the young pallbearers. They struggled to lower the ropes supporting the coffin into the grave as gently as could be managed by boys wholly unpracticed in the custom. As it disappeared out of sight, Joey's mother resumed screaming and crying piteously.

"Oh, my little Joseph, my little Joseph, my little Joseph!" she wailed, then unexpectedly catapulted herself into the grave with her son. Thereupon a pathetic tug of war ensued between Nezla's husband and the child's coffin accompanied by a chorus of wounded cries and wails and eerie keening from the women present. With the assistance of her children and Father Baker himself, Nezla Joseph was brought out of the grave bruised and limp with delirium and carried into a waiting carriage. The Joseph children remained graveside appearing completely bereft. Dr. Ross followed their mother. As he administered stimulants he was heard to express concern for the woman's racing heart.

The police presence at the cemetery was extraordinary. It included fifty Buffalo police officers. A rumor had spread wildly that the killer in a letter to Chief Gilson had boasted of an outlandish plot to personally appear at the burial ceremony in order to further torture the Joseph family. The police knew that a full-scale riot could be the only result, with the killer torn apart into at least as many pieces as little Joey had been found.

The Syrian's impassioned speech coupled with the resultant clamor following Nezla Joseph's public prostration had the predictable effect of enlivening the police. Chief Gilson gave orders to clear the cemetery. The officers invaded the crowd, nudging mourners none too gently toward the cemetery gates. Fearful of a full scale riot, Gilson was relieved upon seeing people begrudgingly disband as ordered. However some of these began gathering on Ridge Rd. outside the cemetery where they halted traffic and commiserated angrily. Two men were stopped in the act of prying up cobbles. The police drew their clubs and again demanded that the crowd dissipate. After some strong urging they finally did as told without further incident.

The tall wild-eyed black-haired man was named Salem Morad. He was a member of St. John Maron, the Syrian Catholic church on Seneca Street. In that evening's newspaper his entire speech had been translated for all to read. He said that when the child was born he was bathed in holy oil, but when his slaughtered body was dumped in pieces into a cesspool of human shit by the murderer, it had been disposed of like just so much effluent in filthy ground unfit for the beautiful little boy. He expressed the hope that the murderer would be caught personally by himself or his fellow countrymen rather than the police, with justice meted out by them in appropriate proportion, an eye for an eye.

His Lips Forgot The Taste Of Truth

THE FIRST WARD IV

WHITEWASH

Lackawanna Detective Daley was not exactly an admirer of Buffalo Detective Jim Sullivan. He thought Sullivan projected superior airs—even though he never directly said anything outrightly disparaging about him or the town of Lackawanna's small police force. It was just a feeling he had. Despite this, Sullivan did give the impression he could be relied upon and trusted.

Daley was bewildered by the ongoing revelations as to his own police chief's stumbles and fumbles, and thus did not share with Chief Gilson his suspicions about White the undertaker. If Gilson could scoff at and dismiss evidence as obvious as the dozen postcards he'd received, Daley assumed his suspicions about the undertaker might be brushed aside as well, or even mocked.

"Thanks for meetin' me here, Sully," Daley said. They sat at a little table in Doyle's saloon at the front window.

Jim Sullivan said, "Sure. Anytime, Daley."

"I discovered somethin'...disturbing...,Sully," Daley said. "And I thought you might have had experience whereby you might agree with me that what I learnt might be, could be...well, maybe the tip of an iceberg of sorts," Daley began.

"What's that?" Sullivan asked, sipping his beer.

"I found out that the undertaker—the one who's handled the remains of little Joey—that he's a longtime friend of Joey's murderer, Hickey."

Jim was stunned to silence. Gobsmacked, it took a few moments of processing that revelation for him to respond.

"*What?*" Jim erupted loudly. "Wait! You mean Hickey? Them two're friends? The killer and the undertaker? Yer fuckin' kiddin' me!" Jim nearly knocked the table over.

"Nope. Wish I was," Daley groaned.

"What *kind* of friends, Daley?" Jim exclaimed.

"Drinkin' buddies, Sully! *Drinkin' buddies!*—for ten years almost! Can you believe it?"

"Jesus Christ—*ten fuckin' years?* Holy shit!" Jim was bowled over.

"And right here, where you and me are sittin' now, right here at this very window is where them two sat together time and again. Tell me, Sully. Whaddya see—lookin' out from here now, from our point of vantage?"

"Holy Mother! Joey's house is right there."

"Yep. I went over there to White's morgue a while ago to question him about Hickey, and he was evasive to say the least, claimin' he didn't know nothin' about this here Doyle's saloon, when in fact the barkeep over there went 'n' told me the exact opposite."

Daley called, "Hank! C'mere a second, will ye?"

Barkeep Henry Goldsmith approached.

"Good day, Detective," Goldsmith greeted.

"Hank, this here's Buffalo Detective Jim Sullivan."

"Pleased to meet ye, Hank," said Sullivan.

Hank smiled and nodded.

"Hank, tell Detective Sullivan here what ye told me. About Hickey an' that undertaker."

"Okay. Well, that Hickey feller used to come in here on a regular schedule with that undertaker. One time some little girls was playin' jump rope outside an' the undertaker was sniggerin' in a dirty kind o' way not knowin' I was standin' right there and when he looked up an' saw me, he an' the other one got all sheepish 'n' red-faced like I caught 'em doin' somethin' they ain't oughta."

"Did they snigger like that oftentimes, Hank?" asked Jim.

"Well, times after that I'd see them move close to one another like they was sharin' a secret and they'd always look up beforehand like they was lookin' out t' see if I was in earshot. But I never overheard 'em again direct sayin' nothin' dirty 'bout little girls after that one time."

"Thanks, Hank," Daley said, dismissing him with an appreciative smile.

Hank went back to work.

"I been pullin' records alludin' to any crimes against children around here for that interval them two was friends, Sully, an' I was hopin' you might do the same. 'Specially fer anythin' suspicious that happened close to the border of our two cities, 'specially in South Park proper, you know, in the woods around South Park Lake, an' the Botanical Conservatory."

Just at that moment who should stroll by Doyle's Saloon but Undertaker White. The cops exchanged flabbergasted looks. White entered Frank's Candy Store next door to Doyle's. The cops waited. They saw White emerge shortly thereafter. He held no package nor did he appear to be eating anything.

"What the hell? Why'd he go in the candy store if not to buy something?" Sullivan said.

"Let's go," ordered Daley jumping to his feet. They exited and waited on the sidewalk a few moments following White with their eyes until he rounded the corner, then they entered the candy store.

Tony Frank looked unsettled to see them.

Sullivan glanced to the place that once held the little gambling machine Daley had ordered the proprietor to get rid of. It was still gone.

"Why was Undertaker White just in here, Mr. Frank?" asked Daley.

"Who?"

"Don't be coy. The undertaker, White."

"Oh. He was buying candy." Frank stammered.

"What kind of candy?" asked Sullivan.

"Um—licorice blocks."

"How much did he buy?" Jim asked.

"Not much. Five blocks I guess."

"You *guess?* It was less than two minutes ago, Frank," shot back Daley.

"No, it was five blocks. I'm certain," replied the candyman.

"Are these the same licorice he bought?" Sullivan said, pointing to a tray of large licorice blocks on a tray in the glass case.

"Yes, that's it."

"And did you put the licorice in a bag? A box? Which?"

"Why...yes. A little bag, like this." Tony Frank held up an example.

"OK, gimme five blocks in that same bag." ordered Daley.

Frank complied and handed Daley the bag. He held it up as if thoroughly examining it. Sullivan nodded his approval. Then Daley put it into the inside pocket of his jacket. It created a very visible bulge. He then put the bag into his trousers' front pocket, then the back. Both created a very ostentatious bulge easily seen to be out of place. Frank watched, perplexed.

"You notice, Frank, ain't no place you can stash this bag on a body where it ain't obvious yer carryin' somethin'. We watched that undertaker come out yer store and there was no bulge anywheres. He had nothin' in his hand, and nothin' in his pockets."

"Uh, well, he stood here eatin' it while we talked."

"Talked? 'Bout what?"

"Hmm. The weather. The steel plant..."

Daley crammed a whole block into his mouth and offered another to Jim Sullivan. The two stood there chewing with difficulty, seeing how much time it took to thoroughly chew it, sufficiently so as to swallow it without choking.

"Notith we can't thalk wit' our moufs full," Daley demonstrated.

Tony Frank looked as if he didn't care a whit.

"He ate that whole bag of licorice in less than three minutes, yer sayin', talkin' all the while? Come on!"

"No, he ate a couple or three, then he put the rest in his pocket. He's a fast eater."

"Impossible! We were watchin' him like a hawk, Frank. We watched him go in and we watched him come out two minutes later. He weren't eatin' nothin' when he came out yer store, nor was he pickin' his teeth."

Frank just shrugged as if to say *so what?*

"What were you two really talkin' about, Frank? Huh? *Kids?* Were you talkin' about the little children who come in here? Children maybe you both got yer eyes on?"

"What?" he countered in an offended manner. "No! I don't know what you're talking about, detective. We were just talking to pass the time."

The two detectives were stumped at that point. Obviously they were beginning to piece together a twisted puzzle that they suspected equally, but Tony Frank had answered all their suspicions adroitly with no hemming or hawing. They stood in silence for a minute, picking their teeth, looking around for anything amiss, but drew a blank.

"All right," Daley said. "Better for you we not never see that shady gamblin' machine in here again."

Frank stood his ground poker-faced, not responding. The two cops left.

"Either that Syrian is the smoothest liar in this here ward or he's tellin' the truth," stated Sullivan.

"I believe neither of them two things is true," answered Daley.

Tony Frank stood at his shop window watching the cops as they put distance between him and them, and scoffed.

❧❧❧

"Hey! Yous in some kinda trouble or somethin'?" asked Hank Goldsmith. He had run into Undertaker White at the hardware store on South Park Ave. the next morning.

"Excuse me?" White responded. He didn't recognize the bartender at first.

"I says, you in trouble? Wit' the coppers I mean."

"Oh, Mr. Goldsmith. Hello there. Sorry. I didn't recognize you in broad daylight. Uh, no. What do you mean?"

"Detective Daley and some nosy little Buffalo higher-up was in Doyle's yesterday askin' all kinds o' questions about ye and about that murderin' fool friend o' yers, Hickey. So I was supposin' you was in hot water with 'im."

"I don't believe so. What did they ask you about?"

"They wanted know if you been buggerin' little kids—more or less."

THE FIRST WARD IV

Wild Women

The Buffalo Police Department was quite adept at the public relations game. Feeding interesting stories and accounts of arrests and police heroics to the newspapers allowed the public to conclude the police were doing their job admirably, and if the circumstances of an arrest were unusual or dramatic or humorous, all the better.

Both Sullivan brothers knew the value of publicity. Before becoming a cop, Jim Sullivan had been masterful in publicizing the Mutual Rowing Club from its very inception, scheduling community picnics, fundraisers and other events, and getting the Buffalo newspapers excited about printing accounts of these.

JP as alderman had surpassed his brother in the art of PR, even. He filled willing newspapers' columns with entertaining stories about his large family and his travels as a way to offset the bad publicity surrounding his devious political doings.

In short order two stories appeared in the local papers involving Detective Jim Sullivan.

The Amazonian Negress

Margaret Schaning, an Amazonian negress, living at N⁰ 48 Union Street, made a murderous assault upon her white husband, Fred Schaning, last night.

She slashed him with a razor across the back and side from the end of the shoulder-blade to a point directly over the heart, cutting a gash fully eleven inches long, and quite deep.

Schaning is at the Fitch Hospital, and his condition at this writing is critical. In fact, his chances for recovery are not considered favorable.

Inspired by Jealousy.

Jealousy was the cause of the trouble in the Schaning household, the neighbors say. Fred is a white man of French extraction, about 30 years of age. He is a fairly good-looking chap, of gay manners, and his ebony-skinned wife formerly thought that he was perfection.

There were others (female) who entertained like views and Mrs. Schaning it seems found it out. She proceeded yesterday morning to call Fred to ask about his alleged trifling. He resented and Margaret is said to have called her hubby a liar whereupon Mr. Schaning smote her with a right hander on the forehead, sending her to the floor. Schaning then left the house and when his wife came to her senses she went to Fred's dressing case and there, taking out his Sunday razor and whetstone, she proceeded to put the keenest kind of an edge on it. Stowing the deadly cutlass away in her skirt pocket the Amazon then started out to find Fred.

She said that she would not spoil his good looks by cutting his face, but she vowed that she would carve her name upon his back the moment he would come within her sight.

Schaning was not discovered by his irate wife until 9:45 o'clock last night, and then he was seated in the back part of Edward Manuel's barroom, talking to a few friends.

Suddenly a dark figure rushed up to the rear door, and with a spring like that of a tigress, the woman was at Schaning's back. Without an instant's notice that glittering blade flashed around her head and instantly it was brought down with a semi circular motion on Schaning's back, cutting deep through his clothing. By a dexterous twist the infuriated negress ripped the blade around the clothing, bringing it towards the breast and in the region of the heart.

Blood spurted out in all directions and Schaning with a startled cry leaped to his feet and escaped from the room. He staggered around to Dr. Watkins' office where he was met by Special Talmadge who assisted him upstairs and aided the doctor to remove the torn clothing. Dr. Watkins dressed the wound and put several stitches in it, after which he ordered Schaning to the hospital.

The would-be murderess was caught in McElwaine's saloon by Detectives Sullivan and Lynch a few minutes later. She fought desperately kicking punching and biting. She sank her fangs into the arm of Detective Sullivan, making a painful wound which was attended by police physician Armstrong at Police Headquarters. There Schaning was charged with assault of the first degree.

Important Capture By Detective-Sergeant Sullivan

Detective Sergeant Sullivan made a "catch" yesterday afternoon which is regarded by police officials as one of the most important made in Buffalo in a long time.

He arrested Mrs. Anna Kurzman and her daughter Clara Bork, two of the most cunning pickpockets and shoplifters in the country, and received stolen property from them valued at $500; besides a number of pawn tickets representing property to the value of $300-$400.

About 3:30 o'clock in the afternoon Det. Jim Sullivan while strolling through a Main street store noticed the Kurzman woman and her daughter, both of whom were known to him, elbowing their way through the aisles in a way that excited his suspicion. They saw the detective looking at them and at once started towards the door. Sullivan followed, and overtaking the women on the sidewalk promptly arrested them on suspicion. The prisoners were conducted to police headquarters and upon being searched a new pair of shoes and several handkerchiefs were found in their possession. It was learned later that the goods were stolen.

The prisoners acted in a sullen manner at Headquarters and for a long time refused to tell where they lived. The daughter finally broke down and fell in a dead faint from which she did not recover for some minutes. The officers bathed her temples with ice water and other restoratives were applied. The girl bore the appearance of a corpse for a time but finally recovered consciousness.

The heartless mother afterwards rebuked her daughter for her "babyishness."

The officers worked at the women for a long time before they would give the location of their home. Finally it was learned they lived at N⁰ 469 Sherman street.

Detective Sullivan accompanied by Detective Holmlund then repaired to the Sherman Street house and made a search of the premises. The officers were amazed at their findings. Drawers, trunks and boxes in all parts of the house were found to contain stolen merchandise from half a dozen of the more prominent emporiums of the city.

The booty consisted of silverware, velvets, ivory-handled knives and forks, corsets, pieces of dress goods, silks, cut glass, tapestry and imported dishes.

The pawn tickets recovered numbered 25 and represented diamond rings, clocks, overcoats, lamps, suits of clothes, a sealskin cape and various other articles which had been pawned at different shops throughout the city. Mrs. Kurzman is 36 years old and her daughter 18. Both have served time in the penitentiary and their photographs appear in the Rogues' gallery. Detective Sullivan will be kept busy visiting the pawn shops to recover the stolen items.

— *Buffalo Express*

His Lips Forgot The Taste Of Truth

Dear Mother Ross

"J. FRANK HICKEY."

The suspect's name was now universally known. Newspapers across the nation screamed it from atop their front pages in large uppercase alphabeticals in damning ebony ink.

Hickey was at that very moment being transported to Buffalo on the train.

Mrs. Isabelle "Mother" Ross read these disturbing words in the *Buffalo Express* as she sat at her breakfast table at the White Light Mission located at Elm Street and Broadway. She just shook her head pitifully.

"That poor, poor man!" she exclaimed.

What Hickey had confessed to Mother Ross one year previous concerning his purported transgressions—transgressions that she had failed to report to police—was, it seemed now, true. She had felt no urgency to go to the authorities with this terrifying information, for it had been confessed to her in confidence with the expectation of something akin to the Catholic Seal of the Confessional. She had always scoffed at the miserable Catholics' claim that only their own shameless cult held entitlement to the confidentiality inherent in that sacrament.

Hickey had interpreted it as a sign from God that he had been led to the bosoms of the similarly named Mother Rawes at the Keswick Colony for Inebriates in New Jersey and Mother Ross of the White Light Mission in Buffalo as worthy and trusted confidantes.

Mother Rawes and J. Frank Hickey had become intimate friends over the years during his many intervals drying out at New Jersey's Keswick Colony. He was extremely popular with the staff of that institution. A few days after arriving on his most recent and what was to prove final visit, while only just beginning to sober up, he took charge of the pouring of a concrete foundation for the installation of a bridge on the colony property. It was there as he supervised workers on the construction that Sheriff Tilton arrived with a warrant signed by Buffalo Police Chief Michael Regan.

Nonplussed, Hickey read it and mused, "Hmm. That's a mighty serious charge."

The police took Hickey into custody right then and there. Mother Rawes was beside herself, screaming that they surely must be making a mistake.

Before taking possession of their prisoner they respected his wish to change out of his dirty work clothes into a suit and tie. Mother Rawes pinned a rosebud onto his lapel and straightened the kerchief in his breast pocket, tears rolling down her face. "There. You look real nice now, Frank. I'll be prayin' for ye, I will" she rasped.

Hickey admired himself in the mirror by the door as he was escorted out. He was pleased. He understood full well the importance of public image. This awareness stemmed from childhood and had been reaffirmed to him time and again ever since.

Hickey's interest in American history had as a twelve-year-old led him to a book reproducing a document signed by General George Washington in 1775. In this document Washington laid out those attributes most desired in candidates being considered to act as his personal life guards. Hickey found it remarkable that Washington stated these candidates should be "handsome, between the height of five-foot-eight and five-foot-ten, of a fine physique and possessing the attributes of cleanliness and sobriety." He was impressed to learn that the character of an individual at that time in American history was judged almost entirely on such superficial traits; that those possessing these were considered good and capable people only for their boasting such cosmetic qualities. He did think it odd that Washington did not prefer that those who would be expected to fully protect him from assault and assassination be well over six foot tall or of exceptional strength and musculature. Had he read further he would have found that Washington himself was five foot ten, and surmise that his hero did not wish to appear to others as weak or diminished by having his guards towering over him. Washington too well knew the importance of public image.

Hickey had thus modeled himself as best he might on Washington's ideal, including pursuing sobriety by his continued revisiting of Keswick. He learned that by following Washington's archetype that he was able to extricate himself from predicaments thick and fast, circumstances that some lesser-well-kept man might not.

Indeed, it was the folly of human beings in general from all past and present ages to judge a person overwhelmingly on his physical appearance. It was this same foible in humanity which allowed Hickey to so successfully pursue his evil ways and evade detection for all these many decades, for he did not look like a killer of defenseless children.

During the autumn of 1911 Hickey was employed as a concrete inspector by the Stewart Construction Company of New York which had the contract for laying the foundation of the new Rogers, Brown & Co. furnaces in South Buffalo. Hickey worked there steadily until October 12, 1911, the day Joey Joseph disappeared, at which time he too coincidentally went absent. Timekeeper's books revealed Hickey did not work on the 12th. He had arrived on the job drunk that morning, late, and was sent away by his supervisor recommending he go home and sleep it off.

He did work on the following day, the 13th. Not previously known for his absenteeism, he was also a no-show on the 15th and the 22nd. At the time he was boarding at a house at 31 Seneca St. owned by Roscoe Shoemaker. There the proprietor also ran a restaurant on the ground floor at which Hickey took meals several times. On October 24th Hickey arrived to work drunk and was sent home once again. On the 25th he arrived again drunk and was immediately fired.

For two entire days after that, he drank without cessation, conveniently claiming later it was to block the memory of his murderous assault on Joey Joseph. He sought familiar refuge in Buffalo at Mother Ross' White Light Mission for a few nights, the lost lamb begging for her help in finding Jesus once again. There he and she shared their confidential heart-to-hearts. Afterward he boarded a train that would ultimately take him to his recurrent drying-out refuge, the Keswick Colony.

Hickey's name now widely vilified, the Reverend N.S. Methfessel stepped forward. He had been pastor at Bethel Presbyterian Church in Lackawanna, where Hickey had been a member.

He described the two of them as "intimate friends."

"I know Hickey well," Methfessel stated. "He joined the church in the Spring of 1910 and for almost a year attended services regularly. He was a real gentleman, always courteous and polite, neat, clean, well-dressed. He was very sincere but I am sorry to say he was a drinker.

"He came to me personally before he joined the church and declared he was addicted to the drink habit and that he thought if he joined the church it would cure him. He declared he wanted help from God and asked me to pray for him. For several weeks he took great interest in church work and then one Sunday he signified his intention of joining. Hickey often came to me and told me how hard it was to keep away from liquor and how he fought against the habit. All of a sudden he stopped coming to church. I learned he had been on a drunk. After that he dropped away from church work and then he stopped attending altogether.

"I never noticed that he paid much attention to children and always thought he was a bachelor. He always spoke highly of women members of our congregation and was a man who could pass in the best society. He appeared to be well educated and acquainted with the Bible.

"It was a horrible crime, and I was surprised to learn yesterday that the police were looking for him. I hope the police will soon catch the murderer and give him his just desserts."

Methfessel ended his statement with the frivolous self-serving chestnut on which those whose reasoning is addled by religion depend: "I am certain that God will punish him if the police do not."

On his way from Keswick Colony to the New Jersey town of Toms River in the police wagon, the arrestee calmly defended himself in a personable manner, answering his captors' questions, attempting to charm them.

"I never wrote any postcard or letter to any Police Chief nor police department in my life," lied Hickey almost convincingly. "I am a dipsomaniac, and have been at the Keswick Colony three times. I was there from December 4, 1910 until April 2, 1911. According to your information this Josephs boy was killed in November 1911. At that time I was working in Lackawanna for a cement and concrete construction company but I never knew anybody by the name of Josephs nor did I ever write a letter to anyone in Buffalo. I live in Lynn, Massachusetts. I am divorced from my wife. Alcohol was my undoing. I have one son, twenty-one years old. I never wrote from Whitings. I believe someone is using my name. I never heard of Michael Kruck and can prove I was not in New York in any part of 1902."

The next day's newspapers laid it all out. Mother Rawes sat at her breakfast table at Keswick Colony staring unseeing past her soft-boiled egg going cold in its shell, absorbing what she had read and could no longer deny. She acknowledged to herself that she did have questions in the past about Hickey, things that troubled her about him. He was an odd sort, she could agree. And he sometimes said queer things that compelled her in her discomfort to change the subject.

"I know he has fought his weakness for liquor," she stated, "but I guess it is constitutional. We have never had any occasion to even suspect he is a degenerate," she lied. "I just cannot believe this is the same man they've been looking for."

Several of the Keswick inmates were obligated to corroborate Mother Rawes' statement. One of them, who was Hickeys roommate and was paired with the accused man in the early part of the year at meals and at work, said Hickey had been of great service to all the men in the colony library and in other ways.

In preparation for Hickey's extradition to Buffalo, it was decided he would reside at the Erie County jail in Buffalo rather than be jailed in Lackawanna. Threats of avenging mobs overtaking the small Lackawanna facility was the reason.

Nezla Joseph continued to suffer mightily. Upon being told an arrest had been made of her boy's killer, she received the news apathetically at first, in striking opposition to the hysteria that had branded her behavior previously.

Erie County District Attorney Wesley C. Dudley and Lackawanna Police Chief Ray R. Gilson traveled to New Jersey to take Hickey into custody. On the train journey from New York to Buffalo, Hickey was in a confessional state of mind. A full series of admissions were forthcoming. He detailed the murder, by his account accidental, in Lowell Massachusetts of the alleged drunk, Edward Morey. He admitted to strangling newsboy Michael Kruck in Central Park. He admitted torturing and raping little Joey Joseph in Lackawanna. He confessed to a total of twelve attacks on boys, but on this occasion admitted to killing just three, despite having claimed twelve murders in one of his postcard messages.

"Hickey apparently is a man with a dual personality," stated District Attorney Dudley to waiting reporters during a stop in Syracuse. "He is intelligent. He is overcome with remorse and says again and again that he cannot comprehend what possessed him to commit the crimes. He asserts he became a maniac only when filled with whiskey."

More than one reporter present interpreted District Attorney Dudley's statements to be oddly more apologist than damning.

Upon arrival in Buffalo, Hickey was shackled to Sheriff Frederick C. Becker and taken to the D.A.'s office from the Erie County jail through a tunnel connecting that facility and the city hall. The underground passageway had not been used since Leon Czolgosz had been taken through after being sentenced to death for the assassination of President William McKinley. This was done in order to protect the assassin from huge and furious gatherings of Buffalo citizens brandishing nooses awaiting his exit from the court so that they might lynch him.

There in the D.A.'s office Hickey signed a confession. In addition to the murders, he confessed to numerous other violent attacks on boys, the most recent being committed the previous August 5th in Lawrence, Massachusetts. He said all his crimes were carried out wholly under the influence of alcohol. He claimed that such thoughts never entered his mind when sober, but once intoxicated he felt overwhelmed with the desire to kill small boys. He admitted torturing his helpless victims.

D.A. Dudley in his notes stated the following about the confessed murderer:

> "He is about five feet seven inches tall and weighs about 150 pounds. He is partly bald. His mustache is short and sandy. He is nervous and continually chews his upper lip. He is forty three years old. His shoulders and arms are powerful. Two thirds of the man's weight lies above his waist. His hands are long and narrow and move quickly and nervously from two muscular

wrists. He has features that once were ingenuous but now are marred by hard lines of dissipation. His chin is not weak, but hardly what might be called firm. His jaws distend below his ears. His blue eyes beam in the most amiable manner. He is soft of manner and speech. He has an ingratiating personality that engages anyone talking to him. He is extremely popular with the inmates at the Keswick Colony For Inebriates."

Once Hickey was securely installed in the county jail in Buffalo, Mother Ross of the White Light Mission contacted Police Chief Regan and asked permission to visit the prisoner.

"My husband the Reverend Ross and I have previously ministered to Mr. Hickey," she stated. "We wish to provide him some comfort at this time when the whole world seems to be against him."

Her request was approved without anyone's curiosity over the nature of their previous relationship being piqued, or any detective being dispatched to gather information from her. Hickey was relieved to lay eyes on a friendly face, one in whose confidence he could trust completely. He had previously confessed to her his killing of the Joseph child, the newsboy Michael Kruck, and the drunk in the drug store. She continued to keep his secrets from everyone, from her husband the Reverend, and most crucially from her son the doctor.

Hickey asked about her son. Would he come visit him in jail and have a look at an open sore on his foot?

Mother Ross claimed he was traveling, knowing her son would have nothing to do with providing any comfort whatsoever to the accused monster. After all, in an unfathomably curious coincidence in the case, Mother Ross' son Wellington Ross was the physician who had been faithful attendant to Joey Joseph's mother Nezla in her hysterical sufferings since the little boy's disappearance.

The mother provided comfort to the murderer while her son provided comfort to the mother of the boy he murdered.

Hickey then asked about her husband. Mother Ross told him that he was over in Welland but was expected to return from Canada that evening. Hickey asked Mother Ross if she might ask Father Ross to come visit him.

"I'm afraid I must leave you now, Frank," she said, "but I surely will ask Father Ross tonight if he will come see you."

"Oh, thank you, dear Mother Ross. God bless!" Hickey exclaimed.

Upon her return to the White Light Mission forty minutes later, awaiting Mother Ross on the stoop was her son, Dr. Wellington Ross.

"Mother, have you heard the good news? They finally have that hideous monster Hickey in a cage where he belongs, even as we speak! I pray he burns in hell for a billion years for what he's done. That little boy's family has been destroyed. I can't begin to tell you the terrible suffering Mrs. Joseph has been through in the past year and how trying it's been for me to keep her from tipping over the edge of sanity."

"Well son, she is a very lucky woman to have such a caring doctor on whom she can depend," soothed Mother Ross with a knowing smile, patting her son on his shoulder. "I'm very proud of you."

"Where have you been Mother? I've yet to visit my patients in the hospital. You asked me to come and I've been waiting here for you almost an hour now."

"Oh, Wellington, I do so apologize, dear. I was off doing the Lord's work and the time just ran away from me. Can't you stay and visit with your poor mother just for a few minutes?"

At that moment the door swung open. A bedraggled man exhibiting a distressed look on his face exited.

"Mother Ross, come quick. Mr. Lewendowski is drinking again!"

"Oh Lord! I'm sorry, son. I have to attend to this poor soul. I will telephone you tomorrow. Your father will be coming back from Welland this evening. Can we see you for supper on Sunday?"

The good doctor hadn't even the opportunity to respond before Mother Ross turned and disappeared inside to continue her all-important godly works on behalf of more deserving men than her own son. She gave no thought at all to her ongoing deception—not the ramifications of that to Hickey's many victims both historic and recent, not the stresses her only son was suffering, not what her son might feel upon learning the truth about where his own mother's true loyalties reside.

Mother Ross informed Father Ross immediately upon his return that she had visited Hickey and that the prisoner had requested a visit from him.

"Wellington was here earlier, Father. He doesn't yet know. He doesn't recall that Frank has stayed here with us, and I think it will be prudent for us not to remind him, all considering."

Father Ross agreed despite his mind being elsewhere, then immediately departed the White Light Mission to visit the jail.

He was allowed in to see the prisoner.

As the Reverend John W. Ross entered Hickey's cell, police and reporters retreated from earshot at the preacher's request to ensure privacy. The two commiserated for over an hour. Hickey said that a story told by Reverend Ross some years previous on one of his visits to the mission about a degenerate drunk not unlike himself had inspired him to try and become a reformed man.

Neither the police nor the reporters seemed to attach any significance to the suspicious fact that Hickey was acquainted with Father and Mother Ross. Father Ross told the reporters at the jail that he and Mother Ross had known Hickey for ten years or more and that he had in fact resided with them at the mission on at least three occasions. When reporters asked about what was discussed between him and Hickey, Ross claimed the information was privileged "as between a shepherd and his lamb" with respect to customs relative to spiritual advisors.

Immediately after Father Ross departed, Hickey consented to receive a number of the newsmen. Hickey praised Mother and Father Ross highly to the reporters. He interrupted the newsmen's questions numerous times to read to them from his Bible, namely St. Paul's Epistle to the Corinthians and other holy passages related to forgiveness.

One newsman whispered to the others that seeing Hickey sitting at the little table in his cell puffing on a cigar he looked like the sort of character that most any child would flee from in terror. They all snickered in agreement. For a while Hickey replied to the reporters' questions, admitting he murdered Joey Joseph in the outhouse under which the boy was found. He was asked if his own father had attempted a sexual assault upon him as a child, which was both an event widely rumored to have occurred as well as a logical conclusion considering his obsession.

"I am not going into that," he emphatically stated.

The newsman told him that it was said he had recently made just such a claim to alienist Dr. James W. Putnam.

"I cannot go into that," again dismissed Hickey. "If I can tell you anything about my life I will gladly do it. I want to help you boys out, but these continued questions about that particular subject are making me tired. They get monotonous."

"What was the murderous assault your father committed on you when you were twelve years old?" one newsman persisted.

"I will not tell you. I won't tell you any more," replied Hickey.

"Do you study the Bible?" another asked.

"I wish I had paid more attention to it when I was a boy," replied Hickey.

"Why do you want to kill little boys?" was asked next.

"I do not know. I have no desire for women or men—only to kill little boys."

"Why did you kill Morey in Lowell? Did you have a craving to kill even back then?"

"No, that was accidental—I was rather like the boy who did not know the gun was loaded."

"Did you want to stop Morey from drinking?"
"No; I wanted to make him drunk—quick."
The *Express* newsman did not hold back.
"Whatever one's personal sexual obsession might be, Mr. Hickey, the urgency to satisfy it surely doesn't arise only once very few years," stated the reporter. "It must be necessary then for any logical person to acknowledge that no matter what one's sexual urges are, they are in need of satisfying on a regular basis regardless of what might be claimed to the contrary. Someone who kills repeatedly as in your stated case for sexual pleasure, certainly does not allow years to go by between satisfying uncontrollable sexual urges."
At this Hickey stood, signaling the end to their conversation.
"Gentleman, I need to get some rest for the trial ahead. If you'll excuse me, it is time for you all to go."

❧❀☙

Father Ross arrived home from the jail to the White Light Mission after lights out. He tip-toed his way quietly past the indigents snoring in the dormitory and up squeaky stairs to the family quarters where his wife slept in her own room.
He knocked.
"You awake, Mother? Might I come in?"
"Yes, I'm awake."
She switched on a light. "What is it, husband?"
"I sat for quite a while this evening with our dear Mr. Hickey. We read passages from the Bible together. One of the newsmen—the place was swarming with them—recognized me. I wouldn't tell them anything, but they will surely mention me by name in the morning edition. We have to call Wellington and tell him. Tell him the truth. Before he reads it in the newspaper. Or worse, before someone surprises him about it blind."
"All right. I'll call him first thing in the morning," she said, reaching for the light switch.
"No! We have to talk to him now. Right now. Tonight. But first we have to explain to him this awkward circumstance, about why we're only telling him about all this now. And for God's sake, we can't ever let him know about Frank Hickey's confessions to us. He might never speak to us again."
"Oh come now, Father! Our own flesh and blood would never scorn us."
"What if Wellington finds out," Father Ross continued, "that the hell he's been put through during the last year caring for that poor hysterical woman was

unnecessary because we knew all along that Hickey had murdered her boy? That we might have prevented our own son's torment, as well as that of the mother also, over that little boy? What then? I'd say he might well see that as a betrayal on the part of his own flesh and blood!"

"Betrayal? Hogwash!" she scolded. "Wellington knows better than anyone the importance of the work that we perform in God's name. He'd surely understand if he found out. But there's no reason at all for him to know everything! All we need to tell him is that we were acquainted with Frank Hickey from his staying with us here some years back, and that upon arriving in Buffalo after his arrest he remembered us and asked for our counsel. That's all! He doesn't need to know any of the rest. There's no reason."

The Reverend neglected to tell her that he had spilled incriminating details to the newsmen.

"Wellington has been put through enough already," she continued, "treating that hysterical dark foreign woman. And think of our poor Frank! Remember, right now he's suffering just as severely as that dead Syrian's mother, if not more so!"

❧❧❧

Dr. Wellington Ross could not sleep. He sat upright in bed reading a book, unable to concentrate fully. Hickey's arrest had that day resalted Nezla Joseph's gaping wounds and he had spent an arduous hour and a half with her at the family home earlier that evening. He felt terrible for her remaining children, for they were motherless essentially, with no one but each other to comfort or administer to them.

The telephone rang.

"Hello?"

"Hello Wellington. It's your mother."

"Mother, what's wrong? Are you ill?"

"Oh, no, son. I'm fine. We're both well. Listen, we wanted to tell you of a...well, a very strange coincidence. It's a trifle bit unsettling perhaps, or you might even find it amusing. Do you recall that man they arrested for killing that little Syrian boy?"

"That little Syrian boy has a name, Mother. It's Joey. What about it?"

"Well dear, it turns out this same man stayed with us here at the Mission some years ago," she said in a sing-songy voice, as if such a horrifying revelation were negligible.

Dr. Ross paused in utter disbelief, trying to make sense of the shocking admission.

"What? Jesus Christ! Tell me that's not really true, Mother!"

"Please Wellington. Don't take the Lord's name in vain."

"That is...shocking, Mother. Shocking! When did you realize this fact?"

"Well, we didn't remember him at all at first, dear, but when they brought him to Buffalo he somehow recollected us, and asked the jailer if he could request your father and me come read the Bible with him."

"The Bible? *The Bible?* That vile monster wants to read the *Bible?* What on earth could be more of an outrageous manipulation of you and Father than that? Dear God in Heaven, Mother! Well, I'm certain you recognize he just wants to use you for his own evil purposes. Surely you told the authorities you would cooperate in doing no such thing! Oh my goodness! The sheer audacity of that malicious pig!"

"Wellington! I am truly shocked at your lack of charity! This is our Mission. This is what we, your father and I, have devoted our entire lives to building! To helping the helpless. To saving souls for Jesus!"

"Saving souls?" he responded incredulously. "You want to save the soul of this sick degenerate? Chief Gilson told me details Hickey confessed to him on the train as to the rape of that poor sweet child! To choking the life out of him and stomping him through a toilet hole into a filthy wretched cesspool, breaking his little bones! His crime is no less than completely unfathomable! You and Father can save all the souls of drunks and vagrants that you wish, Mother! But not degraded forms of low life unworthy of the skin they are wrapped in, such as that Hickey animal!"

"Wellington! I will not have you speak to me like that or try and direct my mission! God's Fourth Commandment demands 'Honor thy father and thy mother!' We minister to those who need us most, Wellington, and this man is in greater need that anyone we have ever previously encountered."

Something dawned on him suddenly.

"When did you first meet this man, Mother?" Wellington asked, his alarm now raised. "When did you allow him to stay there with us—in *our house?*"

"Well, it was about...ten years ago or so, I believe," she lied, partially. She evaded the fact Hickey had in truth stayed on three separate occasions, the last being the year previous, right after Joey's murder, during which time he confessed to them his heinous act.

"Ten...*ten* years ago? That means...that means I was sixteen! I was sixteen when a murdering monster, a murderer of boys by his own admission, was welcomed into the very house in which I slept! Oh dear God!"

"Wellington!"

"No! Wellington nothing! You cannot do this, Mother. You cannot disrespect our family in this way. Our family comes first! Your own son comes first—not some subhuman evil garbage! Neither will I allow you to disrespect the Joseph family!

This is so absolutely scandalous that I cannot even begin to name all the reasons why. And my medical office! What ever will I tell people? What would I tell my patients? My esteemed colleagues at the hospital—and everything I've worked to achieve? That my own parents are praying with a vile murderer and rapist of innocent little children in his filthy jail cell! If Mrs. Joseph finds out it will send her past the point of reason. As it is her mind is almost lost already!"

"Get a hold of yourself, Wellington Ross!" Mother Ross denounced. "We did not raise you this way! Now you listen to me, young man, and listen well! We are ministering to that man because that is God's purpose for us. God Himself called us to His ministry! He…"

Wellington Ross was now uncontrollably outraged.

"I can't listen to your shit any longer! Who the hell *are* you anyway, Mother? This is absolutely despicable! Put Father on the telephone right this second!"

Mother Ross angrily handed over the receiver to her husband.

"Father, take your recalcitrant son in hand!" she ordered furiously.

"Wellington, listen…" his father began calmly.

"No! You listen to *me*, old man!" Wellington cut him off. "Neither you nor Mother will have anything whatsoever to do with that cretin. Understand? You will not shame our family before this entire city! The entire nation! You will not defame my medical practice and all I have worked for all these many years! You will not debase yourself for Mother's sake *yet again*, like some simpering spineless coward.

"Stand up like a man for a change and grow some balls and take charge of that woman, because if you do not, I will! I will have her sent right back into that Asylum where she clearly belongs, and this time I'll make sure she's locked up for good and all! I will swallow the key myself if I have to!

"Time and again you two have failed to protect me throughout my life. You welcomed criminals and perverts and ingrates into the very house in which I slept as a child with no regard whatsoever for my well being or for my safety! I didn't know the meaning of a fearless uninterrupted night's sleep until I went away to university! How many times did I have to awaken in the night to fight them off, screaming to you for your help? "All in the name of God, for His sake," you both claimed to me back then! You told me that God expected *me*, just a *little boy*, to sacrifice! I was but a defenseless child, terrified and alone, my parents' tender attentions withheld from me yet freely given over to dirty degenerate strangers—and in God's name, no less!

"Well all that ends right here and now this very second, Father! So help *me* God!

You two are finished putting me last!"

THE FIRST WARD IV

GORDIE PITTON

Thanks to a telephone call, Detectives Jim Sullivan and Jerry Lynch quickly tracked down Gordon Pitton, the boy who was with Joey Joseph when Hickey abducted him. While Gordon's mother had recently told her sister the truth, she had refused to agree to tell the police. Her sister, a loving mother of two little boys, felt rather differently on the subject. She had the police standing at her sister's door in a flash.

The Pitton family had moved three times in the previous year, from Lackawanna to Buffalo to Detroit and back to Buffalo again. It did not escape Sullivan the bizarre irony that Gordon was found living with his family on West Avenue, a few doors away from where little Marion Murphy, the victim of Buffalo's last notorious child murder, had also lived.

"What are the goddamn chances of *that*," Sullivan asked his partner incredulously, "in a city having well over 2000 other streets to choose from?"

"I sure hope that ain't no fuckin' omen," worried Jerry Lynch, "'cause I ain't no believer in coincidences."

They climbed the front steps and rapped on the Pittons' door. The detectives requested that Gordon accompany them to Police Headquarters. Sullivan made note of Mrs. Pitton's odd, although not strictly uncooperative, manner.

"I wanna talk to him fer a minute first," she said, trying to lead Gordon away, "in private."

Her sister had warned the police of her ways and methods.

"Sorry ma'am. He's comin' with us," Sullivan said.

"Then I'm goin' witchas. I ain't lettin' my little boy go off alone with no strangers," she protested.

"Interferin' with police business is a cause for arrest, ma'am. Is that what you want?" Jerry said, dangling his handcuffs in front of her eyes.

"I wanna go with them, Ma," Gordon insisted. "Please?"

Mrs. Pitton didn't answer, but withdrew her hands from Gordie's shoulders, allowing him to join the detectives.

"That bird's more'n just a little strange," Sullivan mumbled to Lynch once out of her earshot.

When they arrived at their destination, to gain Gordon's confidence Sullivan allowed the boy to handcuff him and put him in a cell. Gordon glowed in the cops' attentions.

The detectives asked the boy if he might want to see if he could recognize someone.

"Who?" asked the boy.

"Well, we don't know, Gordie. It's up to you," Jim Sullivan said. "We'll have you observe some men and you'll tell us, um...oh, I don't know...if you know any of them from somewheres. You might not—it's just a silly game after all. It's just for fun."

"If I recognize some, will I get a prize?"

"We can't promise nothin' like that Gordon," answered Detective Lynch. "We just want your opinion, because you're such an intelligent boy. And a good boy too I hear."

Joey's name was never mentioned by the detectives nor the reason for Gordon's being brought to jail to play the game.

"All right," the boy agreed.

As a group of men were paraded out for inspection, Gordon visibly stiffened upon the sighting of Hickey.

"Oh no! It's him!" he gasped.

"Him? Who are you talking about?" asked Sullivan.

"That bald man—there. Right there!"

"They're all bald, Gordon, more or less."

"No, that man there. The third one. With the spectacles. That's the man who bought us candy, me and Joe!"

❧❧❧

"Hickey's mind is a seething mass of fiends and devils," stated Ernest W. McIntyre, lawyer, whom Hickey called to his cell yesterday to consult regarding his defense at the trial for the killing of Joseph Josephs, the seven-year-old Syrian boy, in Lackawanna.

"The only defense for this man is an insanity plea," said the lawyer, after having talked with Hickey for about two hours. "His story is the most repulsive I ever listened to, and I was glad to get out into the fresh air again after talking to him."

—*Buffalo Courier* December 1, 1912

McIntyre was just the first in a parade of attorneys who were in and out of Hickey's cell all day. Hickey requested a visit from a number of lawyers who spent as little time as possible with him and departed with a look of deep disgust on their faces, all except for one.

Attorney and former first assistant District Attorney Daniel V. Murphy arrived in the late afternoon and within less than fifteen minutes emerged wearing a resolute expression revealing his full intention of representing Hickey.

Hickey, who claimed pennilessness, had to rely on the goodness of Justice Charles H. Brown to select a capable lawyer to represent him. Erie County allowed $500 for this purpose. The following morning at 10 o'clock at Hickey's arraignment Daniel V. Murphy won the assignment as Hickey's defense attorney. Ironically, Attorney Murphy had also represented the Chinaman initially accused of the infamous killing of little Marion Murphy ten years previous.

Hannah Sullivan realized this as she sat reading the news with her sister-in-law Annie. A devoted attendee of high profile murder trials for entertainment, Hannah recalled that Attorney Murphy had exhibited a record of queer attraction to such cases. She took notice of Attorney Murphy's home address: 96 St. James Place.

"My goodness gracious, Annie!" she harrumphed. "I wonder how many missing children they might find over there on St. James Place buried in Attorney Murphy's own backyard?" Her hackles had been raised by Murphy's historic and strangely enthusiastic defending of the most repugnant of the accused.

Annie was stewing about something, but Hannah didn't realize the boiling was partially about her. Annie was having a day. She was short with everyone; her children, her husband, Hannah, the dog, the milkman, Hannah's going on and on about her strange friend Ruth, JP's constituents showing up on her porch throughout her busy day wanting some favor knowing full well the alderman didn't get home from the city hall until supper time. She'd had her fill.

"What do you think makes someone like Murphy tick, Annie? He wants to put that Hickey degenerate child murderer back out on the street? What makes him take precedence in that over the safety of his own children and everyone else's for that matter? My word!"

"You *are* joking, right Hannah?"

"Joking? Why no, of course not. What makes you say such a thing Annie?"

"You! You and your murdering brother! I recall what a state you were in during *his* trial, since we're now speaking of sensational trials, you being so afraid he would have to go to prison! He shot three men with the intention of shooting twenty more, Hannah! Your own flesh and blood brother! You are a hypocrite of the highest order, Hannah dear! When it's anyone else, they should be hanged in the town square by the piano wire method according to you, but when it's your own brother David Nugent—who rightly deserves to be hanged with piano wire—it's quite another story, isn't it? You were perfectly content with having *him* walking the streets freely after shooting innocent men, now weren't you, Hannah? Balderdash!"

"How dare you say such terrible things to me, Annie! What's gotten into you?"

"How dare I? Even while free on appeal after his rampage, your brother continued going to the rail stations with Pete Dalton to collect and to supervise the dreadful murdering shites that Fingy Conners still to this day imports from New York's Bowery to maim and kill our own good neighbors who are only trying to unionize! Stop all your nonsense Hannah! Stop it right now! Your brother is, is...he's a pile of shite needin' a good shovelin' right down into the sewer that is his rightful place! How dare you year after year not disapprove of what David Nugent does while pretending to be a good Catholic all the while, all the while you're castigating priests for their wrongdoings and pontificating while out the opposite corner of your mouth you defend your terrible, terrible brother! David Nugent is a murderer, and so is your cousin Dick Nugent and your stepbrother Maurice Halleran! All pieces of Fingy Conners' loathsome murderin' gang! All killers of men! You certainly do come from a depraved family, now don't you?"

"Annie! I never!' cried the incensed in-law.

Hannah jumped to her feet and stormed out of the house, nearly colliding with the Alderman as he limped up the walk. She neither stopped nor apologized.

"What was *that* all about?" JP asked Annie as he hung up his hat and coat.

She told him what had been said.

"What's taken you so long, dear heart?" he replied, kissing her on the cheek. "I've been waiting patiently for you to finally wake up to the ways of that foolish woman for some twenty years now."

At his arraignment Hickey pleaded "not guilty" to the charges against him in a strong and confident voice. He showed neither fear nor emotionality of any sort. He yawned widely and repeatedly during the proceedings and wore a look of detachment and boredom throughout.

Although Hickey admitted three murders, he adamantly denied committing any other death crimes. The Erie County authorities were extremely doubtful of this. All seemed to agree with the widely-held notion that any man having such a perverted sexual mania for raping and killing small boys would never allow ten years to lapse between such crimes. Hickey now claimed that although he tried killing twelve additional boys, he failed. The authorities believe a man with the strength in his hands to crush out life so easily who attempted twelve murders against defenseless boys would not have failed so many times after the so-called "first" murder of newsboy Michael Kruck ten years previous. They believed poor Michael Kruck was not his first child kill, nor was Joey Joseph his last.

THE FIRST WARD IV

The Interview

Detective Jim Sullivan felt an unrelenting nagging need to relieve the gnawing in his craw. He had a desire, borne of frustration and self-recrimination, to question Hickey, as it was he who had initially arrested Hickey ten years previous.

He paid a visit to the prisoner in jail. He brought Hickey a cigar and a Hershey bar. Jailer Fink unlocked the cell and Sullivan entered.

"I want to speak to the prisoner in private, Fink. Have a seat down there by the stairway," he motioned. "I'll call you when I'm done."

Fink did as told. He dragged his chair noisily to the foot of the stairwell at the far end of the row of cells, then sat to read his newspaper. When assured Sullivan's attentions were solidly focused on Hickey, Fink sneaked down the stairs to inform D.A. Dudley. Fink had grown quite fond, and protective of, his charge.

Hickey tore open the chocolate immediately and feasted on the sweet.

"You remember me, Frank?" Sullivan asked.

"Have we met previously?" Hickey responded coyly.

"I arrested you some ten years ago after you involved yourself in a brawl outside a saloon on Seneca Street," replied the detective.

Silence. Hickey wordlessly enjoyed his treat.

Silence was a technique Sullivan employed in his own dealings with people of all sorts: criminals, busybodies, errant children, his wife. People generally are made very uncomfortable with silence, and Sullivan knew if he waited long enough, the person he was dealing with would soon have the uncontrollable desire to fill the void with their own words.

Such was not the case with J. Frank Hickey, however. At long last it was Sullivan who was compelled to speak up.

"At the time I arrested you back then, Frank, you confessed to me the murder of the newsboy in New York's Central Park. Michael Kruck."

Hickey simply shrugged.

"I know you killed other boys besides him, Frank. Besides the Kruck boy, and little Joey. Why don't you tell me somethin' 'bout them other boys?"

"Nothing to tell, Detective. I admit that I had tried on occasion to kill other boys, but I was not successful."

Sullivan had no doubt whatsoever there were additional victims.

"Who were some of them other boys that got away from you, Frank? You recall any details? Names?"

Due to there being an official record of the incident, Hickey confessed to Sullivan that he had just recently attacked a boy in Lawrence, Massachusetts the previous month. He claimed the boy stopped him on the railroad tracks there to ask him for a light. He recalled he immediately set to wrapping his hands around the boy's neck and strangling him. A local newspaper report stated that two railroad workers nearby were shocked to see this occur in broad daylight right before their eyes. They ran to the aid of the boy, rescued him, and held Hickey prisoner for the police. Hickey appeared before Judge Maloney in Lawrence who, quizzically, despite the obvious murderous intent of such a escapade, fined Hickey just $5 and then set him free.

"No one would believe I was the devil incarnate because I always dress well and always associated with the finest sort of people," Hickey boasted. He told Sullivan he first took to drink when he was 17, after he had mistakenly killed the drunk named Morey with laudanum. Then at age 22, Hickey said, he tried murdering two boys.

"Why don't you tell me about that?" urged Sullivan.

"I believe I was obsessed at the time," Hickey shrugged.

Hickey had met the two boys, Harry Bennett and John Lee, both fifteen years of age, in Pi Alley in Boston on November 11, 1905. Pi Alley, like the earlier Central Park location where Hickey met newsboy Michael Kruck, was in the very shadow of a busy local Police station, this one being at Boston's Court Square. The two boys asked him for money. He invited them to his room in a boarding house on Hanson Street. Then he went out for whiskey.

"It came over me all of a sudden that I was going to settle them. When I came back with the whiskey we drank it all, and they fell asleep. I stuffed up all the cracks and corners in the room tight, then tore the gas fixtures from the wall and lay down on the bed to die with them."

By his account he woke up three days later in the hospital with the boys. He was arrested and removed to a police station where he attempted to kill himself, or so he claimed, with cyanide of potassium which the police had overlooked in searching him. He was discovered and again rushed to the hospital and revived. Two days later his case was presented to the grand jury, which failed to indict him.

"I can't understand it," Hickey told Sullivan. "I have had chance after chance and yet I have always gotten away." He smiled beatifically. "It seems as if God was always giving me new opportunities to make good."

"You ain't got no cyanide hidden someplace on you at this time, now do you Frank?"

"No, I am going to see this through, Detective," Hickey declared.

He continued his remembrances, telling of meeting a boy tramp two years previous in Quincey Massachusetts who asked him for a place to sleep. Quincey was a no-license town.

"I procured a bottle of whiskey and took it to my room. We both drank. The desire to kill the boy came over me. While waiting for the boy to fall sounder asleep I myself fell asleep. When I awoke in the morning the opportunity had already passed. I was disappointed that I didn't have the chance to kill him."

Sullivan smiled wryly. He thought perhaps something otherwise.

"Let me tell ye exactly what I think about your little stories, Frank," Sullivan said, buffing his fingernails on his pant leg. "Them're just stories.

"The boy who asked for a light on the railroad tracks?" Sullivan surmised, "You knew that boy. You knew him. You'd had your eye on him for some time. You'd been watchin' him for a while at that point. You watched him and learnt his habits. Then when you thought the time was right, you took yourself a couple o' drinks as you waited for him to pass by. This was your customary scheme so as to defer the blame to an alcohol habit rather than to your true nature.

"Then you approached him and proposed he come back to your room. You offered him drugs of which you know all about from your previous work in the drugstore. But he was repulsed by you and your very odd manner. He laughed at you. He called you a pervert, but I'm bettin' he used a more earthy term, a derogatory name which injured your delicate sensibilities. He called you exactly what you are, Frank. And then he punched you, isn't that right? He didn't even know you, but he didn't have to know you to see so plainly what the rest of us also see—a cowardly little man who was laid down by his own father and fucked up the ass night after night for years on end, who didn't have the nerve to just take a baseball bat to make mincemeat outa yer father's cock and balls as he slept. And you also didn't run away although you had every chance and every reason to.

"Why is that Frank? Perhaps you thought you deserved it? Your own mother refused to believe you when you finally told her about it. But she knew, Frank. Believe me, she knew all along—and she was happy and relieved that the old wreck wasn't botherin' her no more. She slept like a baby with a smile on her face from then on, while your father was stickin' it to you like a pig, hellish night after hellish night. When that boy on the tracks punched you, you grabbed him around his neck, and that's when the good Samaritans arrived to break up the fight. That's why the judge let you go with little more than a $5 fine, Frank. Because it was a fight, a fight you were losing. Your story about just grabbing some innocent kid for no reason at all in broad daylight and choking him like a crazy man? It's rubbish. It's a story like all them others, to support your future claims if you were ever caught. All these stories you conjured up to support just one thing, your claim of insanity, a contention that you are now putting forth to avoid being sent to the electric chair at Auburn Prison."

Hickey sat expressionless, seemingly unaffected by the scenarios Detective Sullivan had assembled in an attempt to elicit an impassioned reaction from him. But Hickey did not break, nor did he even bend, not even a little.

Hickey acted as if he hadn't heard a word Sullivan said. He picked up where he had left off before Sullivan began outlining his theories. Hickey claimed he had written the postcards relating the Joseph boy's killing as an act of compassion "to quiet the boy's family." He claimed he sent the first postcard three weeks after the murder to tell the family exactly where Joey was so as to end their suffering. He again expressed surprise that the body was not looked for then.

"So you're claimin' the impulse to murder comes over you only after you've gotten drunk? Never *before* taking a drink, Frank?" Sullivan probed, trying once more to get a response revealing something useful. Anything at all would do. He knew he was on the right track. Hickey wasn't insane. He was just evil. Pure filth. Diabolical, cunning, subhuman.

"Before I drink," Hickey said. "I drink to forget it, to forget Morey's face there in the drugstore. I see Morey's eyes before me, staring up at me from the floor wide open, dead. That comes over me at any time, night or day, drunk or sober. It terrifies me. Fills me with shame and guilt. The only respite I can find is alcohol. But once I am drunk, my thoughts become uncontrollable. I can't help myself."

Sullivan chuckled, shook his head at Hickey's obviously well-rehearsed self-serving anecdote, and rolled his eyes.

"Yes, Hickey, now you've convinced me. It's the dead eyes of a hopeless pestersome drunk man from thirty years ago that torture you, rather than the much more recent dead eyes of innocent and kind, helpless, sweet little children who did nothing whatsoever to annoy or provoke you!"

For the first time, emotion clouded Hickey's expression. Jim sensed at last that a breakthrough was imminent.

Just at that moment D.A. Dudley arrived with jailer Fink and entered the cell. He nodded to Sullivan in an unfriendly manner. Dudley remarked to Hickey that if he was going to be giving details about the killing of the Kruck and Joseph boys to Detective Sullivan, that such information might be used against him.

Sullivan was incensed that the D.A. in charge of procuring justice for the murdered boys would in any way advise the confessed killer that might be of benefit to him. He glowered at tattle-tale jailer Fink.

"I'm City. You're County," Detective Sullivan summed up, hissing. "You 'n' me Fink...I'm seein' a little discussion in the future, just between us two, you 'n' me."

Sullivan stormed out heatedly without another word to either Dudley or Hickey, trembling with frustration as to how close he had come to getting something useful out of the murderer before Dudley interrupted.

※※※

The police of Bridgeport, Connecticut wrote to Lackawanna Chief Gilson asking him to investigate the killing of Philip Mastroni, seven years old, who was strangled to death there October 4, 1907. A letter was received by District Attorney Dudley from the Chief of Police at Providence, Rhode Island in which it was stated that William Mather, twelve years old, was found dead in a woods at North Providence under circumstances similar to those described by Hickey in his confessions.

In all, scores of such letters and telegrams were received by Chiefs Gilson and Regan and D.A. Dudley. They revealed a previously unrealized phenomenon, an epidemic of deadly attacks against boy children. The sheer numbers were horrifying. The scope of these killings had up until then been unknown due to police departments' deplorable failings to communicate amongst each other.

And despite the horrifying number of these child murders, these were only those killings that had been discovered before the victims' little bodies decomposed and disappeared forever. What about the thousands of missing children nationwide over the past decades, many of whom were dismissed as "runaways" never to be seen again? For every murdered child found in the woods, how many more would never be encountered by anything other than a scavenging animal hopelessly scattering their little bones among camouflaging fallen branches, leaves and undergrowth, never to be discovered by anyone, ever?

To underachieving police departments with dismal records of crime solving these revelations added to their already heavy burden. They did not relish their citizens, already highly critical of the failure of police either to stop or solve local crimes, being provided entirely new information of additional egregious examples of previously unknown criminality and police ineptitude.

That evening Jim Sullivan, angered and in a mood, confessed as much to Hannah. "Nobody believes children just run away to begin lovely new lives somewhere else in anonymity, never contacting anyone at all from their past ever again, somethin' which many wishing to make themselves feel better claim is the case. Children are of course defenseless. None are equipped to survive alone. We think most of these children have been murdered by a parent or an abductor and buried in some out-of-the-way place where no one will ever find them. There's no tellin' how many boys Hickey's murdered, Hannah, but it sure as hell ain't only just been them two."

At Headquarters Jim paged through Chief Regan's Telegraph books in which every call to the police was logged with a full explanation of the complaint. The number of missing children entered in these journals was appalling. A few would on a following page's entry be logged in as having been found or returned home, but three times as many were not. Scores of similar volumes cataloging similar losses rested in shelves behind the telegraph desk filled with woeful entries stretching back years. Jim wondered how many of these children may have disappeared at the hands of J. Frank Hickey or some as yet undiscovered murderous scum just like him. No one wants to be made aware of these monsters, to acknowledge they exist, to initiate the near-impossible task of hunting them down and proving them guilty, which is why so many of these killers are successful.

※※※

On November 30, with Hickey already in custody, Lackawanna Police Chief Gilson received yet another postcard from Hickey. It was postmarked November 9th and had been delayed in its delivery for a number of weeks. "Goddamned post office!" he sputtered.

The card read:

> "Will you arrange for my carfare to Buffalo to meet justice if I tell you how? Will you telegraph the Boston Sunday Post in the want column that Mr. Gilson will arrange for transportation to Buffalo for me? I will come. No Boston Police for me."

The city was in an absolute uproar over the developments in the Joey Joseph tragedy once the initial shock of recovering the child's body had sunk in.

But things really exploded when the postcards were widely scrutinized and in the process revealing the unfathomable incompetency of Lackawanna Police Chief Ray Gilson.

Three weeks after Joey first went missing, Gilson had received a postcard from Hickey telling him exactly where Joey was buried. Two department underlings were sent to the outhouse location to investigate. Despite the unique details that the postcard provided, the officers carried out only the most superficial of inspections. For whatever reason—laziness, revulsion or ineptitude—the cops made no attempt at examination of the very pool in which Hickey stated he had sunk Joey's body. They returned from their careless search to report their findings to the Chief, who expressed no criticism regarding their stated "efforts." Gilson, upon hearing their report, demanded nothing more detailed from them.

The morning of December 1, 1912 Hickey made a statement to reporters gathered outside his cell. The meeting was overseen by prosecutor District Attorney Dudley: "What I don't understand, fellas," Hickey said, "is that I wrote a postcard to Gilson three weeks after I killed the boy. I told him just where to find the boy. There were no different directions in that postcard than there were on the later postcards."

An inveterate apologist by habit, District Attorney Dudley interrupted Hickey's statement to defensively remind him that the Lackawanna police indeed did look in that place. Hickey laughed out loud and mockingly shot down the sophist D.A.'s defense of the Lackawanna department's incompetence with a powerful retort, eagerly reported in the city's dailies:

> "They didn't think to stick a rake down into it? And with a straight face they have the nerve to call themselves 'investigators'? I cannot understand why this was not done. At that time the body would have been still intact. The family's suffering could have been ended! I wrote these postcards to ease the minds of the mother and father! I wrote them publicly on the desk of the money order division of the post office. People were right there and it was right out in the open. I didn't care. I was totally indifferent to everything. It was in the Boston post office and when someone jostled against me I thought right then and there they had me. I was utterly indifferent to what transpired. The thing would get me and I would get the drink and get rid of it."

With the information of Lackawanna Police Chief Gilson having received such specific directions to Joey's burial spot so early on and the revelation that the subsequent police investigation had been carried out so shoddily, Gilson was universally vilified in the newspapers. Headlines blared. Fiery editorials condemned him. Answers were demanded.

The *Buffalo Enquirer* in an editorial accused the police of being delinquent. The paper questioned how it was possible, while in police custody confessing loudly to the murder of newsboy Michael Kruck, Hickey was then allowed to walk free. The *Enquirer* was additionally infuriated that the public had not been informed of Hickey's confession to the Joseph and Kruck murders until a full two days after he provided it:

> Hickey was known to be in the vicinity when the Joseph murder was committed. He was known to have been arrested as a suspect and to have in a maudlin manner implicated himself in the Kruck murder. He has been obliged to write letters to the authorities in order to convince them that he was the man they were after. Despite the incontestable number of postcards and letters received by the authorities, these were nonetheless dismissed as crank. This was not done based on any evidence but rather on a mere whim of opinion by Lackawanna Police Chief Gilson. The law, which has the habit of demanding full penalty from criminals, nearly allowed this arch fiend to escape."
> —*Buffalo Enquirer*

Chief Gilson attempted to justify his actions, or lack thereof, in a most preposterous manner. In doing so he revealed that he was the sort as equally incapable of taking responsibility as was Hickey.

Gilson argued in the *Buffalo Times* that his dereliction of duty was in fact quite beneficial to the case. The *Times* news story containing this quote mocked the absurdity of Gilson's justification by headlining the story under which it appeared thusly:

> ### Amusing Theory Advanced by Lackawanna Chief Of Police to Cover Incompetency of His Department.

> "Well, I just don't know," he justified. "They did not do so (search the cesspool) and it seems to me now that it was the work of Providence. For I have not the slightest doubt that we never would have found Hickey if we had recovered the body at that time. Hickey has stated since, that his purpose in writing the postcards was to ease the mind of the parents insofar as the finding of the body would do so. You see, had the body

been found then, Hickey would in all probability have stopped writing the cards and we never would have located him."

As outwardly disturbed as Gilson might have portrayed himself by the universal condemnation of him, internally he let out a sigh of relief.

He had in his possession the tardy postcard written November 9th but not delivered to him until after Hickey's arrest. In it Hickey asked for carfare to Buffalo so as to turn himself in. As was Gilson's proven habit, had the card arrived 3 or 4 days after mailing, as would be the usual delivery window, Gilson would have dismissed it like all the rest and tossed it into the drawer with the others.

Had he done that, considering the furor over his earlier transgressions, news of his failure to follow through with Hickey's offer to travel to Buffalo for surrender would have most assuredly ended his career.

※※※

Hannah Sullivan continued to find comfort and solace in her afternoon tea dates with her friend Ruth McGowan, with whom she discussed such travesties, especially since her recent blow up with sister-in-law Annie. Hannah habitually registered opposition and surprise at the continual absurdities of men holding public office, while Ruth seemed calmly accepting and resigned. Their different outlooks allowed each to learn something from the other.

"What does your husband have to say about all this, Hannah, him having arrested that degenerate all those many years ago?"

"Obviously he is upset, Ruth. Upset because Hickey was released, but more upset in this moment, now that Jim's good name has been dragged into it."

"Did you know, Hannah, some people are saying that if your Jim had only done his job right, that little Joseph boy would still be alive."

"Who is saying such a terrible thing?" she exploded.

"Just people, here and there. It's a normal conclusion for people to reach, Hannah. People need someone to blame. Come on—we both discussed many examples of that, together you and I. Did Jim tell you why Hickey was allowed to go free back then?"

"Honestly, Ruth, it's driving him crazy because he can't remember. He recalls that while in jail after he arrested him that Hickey in a drunken state was yelling to the heavens that he had murdered that poor little newsie in New York."

"And yet they allowed him to go free? Doesn't a man's confession mean anything anymore?" Ruth sighed.

"Jim told me his partner Jerry Lynch had the habit of keeping a journal and that he asked Jerry to search at home to see if he had written something about it, that perhaps there he might find details allowing them to better defend themselves. At any rate, it wasn't up to them to release Hickey or not. That was the Chief's decision. They just carried out the orders of the higher-ups. Jim and Jerry had no recourse but to follow though on orders."

"Then why is Jim under such criticism? He should be credited with bringing Hickey in in the first place. It was his superiors and not him who allowed Hickey to go free, correct?"

"Yes, you would think so, but I don't know, Ruth. It was a real kick in the head to Jim when it was brought out that he had previously arrested Hickey. He didn't say as much, but I'm sure he thought the same as everybody else. If he had been able to keep Hickey in jail back then, little Joey Joseph might still be alive and his poor mother not within a hair's breadth of being locked up in the lunatic asylum."

Ruth thought in silence for a few moments. Hannah inspected her face, unsure if Ruth was still taking morphine. She was on the brink of asking her outright when Ruth advanced the conversation.

"You know Hannah, it's all about these men in charge failing to do their duty, and having failed, they refuse to take any responsibility for their failure. They are all scrambling to cover, to shift the blame to someone or something else. That absurd statement the Lackawanna Chief made? Oh my goodness gracious! An intelligent man would be mortified to claim such a preposterous thing. Moreover, the city should be questioning why they are employing someone so ineffectual in that position. No wonder we have the amount of crime that we do! Criminals can read, we must assume. When they hear or read such stupid words come out of a police official's mouth, it's almost an invitation to them to remain in the business of stealing and killing. The chances of their getting arrested seem to be microscopic these days."

Hannah shivered. "That one postcard, where he referred to Banquo and Shakespeare...that really boggled some people. To think an intelligent and educated and well dressed man—someone they might well invite into their very own homes among their children—would be capable of such horrible crimes!'

"You're right. People have been disturbed to learn that such depraved acts were carried out by an educated man. Throughout history, the great failing of humanity is the refusal of people to accept that evil has no relation to social status. The bizarre need of people to believe that terrible things are only carried out by those they themselves would by choice never come in contact with is absurd. Education, status, wealth, prominence, social standing—none are a barrier to man's ability to commit evil."

Hannah mused over that for a few moments.

"People like me and Annie," Hannah said mournfully, "we held our sick and dyin' babies in our arms, our minds absolutely addled by fear and filled with horror and helplessness and grief. So to accept that there are people out there who intentionally hunt down and murder *children*...it's all too sickenin' to fathom."

❦❦

District Attorney Dudley appeared at Headquarters to see Chief Regan. Regan had not arrived yet. Detective Sullivan was also there awaiting a few moments with the Chief. The two adversaries found themselves seated outside Regan's office together. It was an uncomfortable situation for both. Told that Dudley was one of those who was inexplicably criticizing him and Lynch for "letting Hickey go," Sullivan was angry about that, as well as Dudley's warnings to Hickey not to talk to Sullivan that day at the jail.

"Mr. Dudley, I hear you been bad-mouthin' me and Jerry Lynch for what happened back there in aught-two. We got no credit from you for arrestin' Hickey in the first place back then, but now yer givin' us grief for somethin' we had no authority over. You know full well only a Captain or higher up can order a prisoner released. So I'm not interested in all the reasons why you made up your mind to oppose me. I have no say over your likin' me or not. But I am interested in your mild manner concerning yer handlin' of Hickey."

"I beg your pardon!" sniffed the Prosecutor. "Just *who* do you think *you* are?"

"Murphy wants this monster in the State Hospital, which means Hickey could be out on the streets killin' more little boys in no time once he's done charmin' them fool alienists down there at the Forest Avenue Crazy Hotel into believin' they cured him.

"I heard you sayin' you're plannin' on protectin' the tender sensitivities of the men on the jury, as if they are children who might faint dead away at hearin' the awful details of Hickey' crime. You can bet Murphy's heard this same thing about you, and he will do all he can to play into that. Murphy is hell-bent on gettin' the jury to see Hickey as insane, so you gotta tell that jury every disgustin' detail to support the truth—that Hickey is just plain fuckin' pure evil."

"Again, just *who* do you think you are, Sullivan, instructing the District Attorney how to prosecute a case?"

"Well if you'll just go back to Murphy's defense of the Chinaman..."

"In that instance, Detective," Dudley interrupted, "the case against the Chinaman was very weak as opposed to Hickey, who has confessed all the sickening details, so there is no need to be heavy handed about it. That little boy's grieving parents will be in the courtroom after all!"

How do so many fuckin' lunk-heads manage to get themselves into these positions of power? wondered Sullivan silently in his head.

Trying diplomacy, Sullivan suggested a strategy.

"You need to remind the jurors that they are all good Christian men, that their Christian beliefs include a very heavy warning from God Himself about the power of Satan, about the influence of the devil and his devious ways. Yes, it might be hard to understand that an educated man like Hickey is so evil that he could commit such dastardly crimes—that is probably only natural. But it goes against these jurors' religious beliefs to reject evil as his sole reason for killing, in favor of insanity, simply because they are uncomfortable accepting the evil which permeates this world we all live in.

"Denying there is a Satan when God Himself tells us the devil exists, is that not itself blasphemy, Mr. Dudley? Rejecting God's own warnings is not a sin? The jurors cannot have it both ways, They cannot claim this man is simply insane due to the fact their very own religion demands they remain vigilant for the presence of the devil. Providin' Hickey an out like insanity goes against their religion, yours, and mine. The jurors cannot believe two opposing things at the same time. The jurors must choose. They must be true to the basic foundation of their Christian beliefs and reject the ridiculous notion that this savage is somehow not responsible for his hideous crimes because Murphy wants to trick them into believing Hickey's insane.

"I personally find it suspicious what Murphy is doing. Perhaps you might while you're at it consider what motivates Murphy so strongly in this regard. The only answer to such vile crimes as Hickey's is pure evil. It is absolutely the work of the devil himself. The Bible warns us repeatedly. Tell the jurors they need to honor their Christian beliefs and find this vile excuse for a human guilty of the intentional premeditated murder of a terrified, tortured, completely innocent and beautiful little boy."

At that instant Chief Regan walked in. Dudley scoffed at Sullivan and stood to greet Regan. Sullivan persisted as Dudley walked away with the Chief, shouting after him.

"Mark my word, Mr. Dudley! It's a terrible mistake coddling the jury when the exact opposite is called for! There can be no doubt left in the jury's mind as to the depravity of Hickey. He done abhorrent things—and the jury must not be spared the graphic details!"

With a loud *bam* Dudley wordlessly slammed Regan's office door closed behind him.

THE FIRST WARD IV

Secrets & Lies

Hannah had tried to entice a reluctant Ruth to follow the jury proceedings in the newspapers along with her. She had also tried to enlist Ruth's attendance at the trial itself, just as Annie had previously attended so many others with her. Hannah and Annie had only just the previous Thursday enjoyed a lukewarm *rapprochement*, but between them things were not now friendly in the way they were once. Annie no longer considered attending sensational trials as an exciting diversion in the way she formerly had, but to Hannah they were as fascinating as ever. As Hannah had grown older she assumed answers to life's mysteries would eventually reveal themselves, but had recently concluded she knew less than she ever did when it came to the conundrum that was human behavior.

Ruth held the opinion that trials, especially high profile murder trials such as Hickey's, served more as sensationalist advertisements for attorneys chasing their political ambitions, as well as an avenue for politicians and their appointees to keep their names in the news. She claimed her attending one would not just be tantamount to approving of the ensuing circus and its passel of stupid clowns, but her contributing to the charade.

Despite Ruth's misgivings, since the newspapers were full of minute details of the case, and people she met on the streets were speaking of little else, she and Hannah did discuss some particulars.

Most people with children despised attorney Daniel Murphy's obsession with having Hickey declared insane.

Hannah recalled the horrifying cautionary tale of Sadie McMullen. The story had recently resurfaced among those who feared that if Hickey were indeed declared insane he might be put back out on the streets again in very short order, much to the detriment of vulnerable children, just as had Sadie McMullen.

McMullen, a native of the nearby town of Akron N.Y., had been in the employ of well-to-do George Dunbar as a housekeeper at his mansion on Delaware Avenue in Buffalo. Dunbar was the owner of Buffalo's Eagle Ironworks. Sadie had taken her two week vacation from her position at the Dunbar household to visit her family in Akron—but that was not all she took. Dunbar accused her of stealing articles from the house and sent her replacement, Jessie Jessamyn, to Akron to confront her. Sadie denied the crime, but the accusations rattled her to the extent that she wrote a suicide note to her aunt, Nancy Morgan of Michigan Street in Buffalo, who was a member with Hannah in their local close-knit weekly pedro club.

Sadie then took two small children out along the railroad trestle spanning Akron's aptly-named Murderer's Creek and threw them over the edge where they crashed into the deadly rocks 72 feet below.

Sixteen year old McMullen had enticed the innocents shortly before dark under the guise of going to the store to purchase butter with which to bake them cookies that evening. On the way, passing the bridge, she fabricated a story that a man with a gun was pursuing them with the intention of murdering them. Their only chance of escape, she said, was across the bridge.

Warned never to set foot on the bridge, Sadie had to virtually drag the protesting children across the span. The bridge, being intended solely for the passage of trains, had no guardrails or footpath, only a foot-wide plank walkway, and light was fading fast, making transversing it precarious. The children were terrified. Reaching the highest point, Sadie attacked and tried to throw off 11 year old Lily May Connors, who struggled fiercely against her assailant before ultimately being overpowered. Six year old Delia Brown tried to run away but was caught. She too was hurled over the edge.

Lily May was found, skull split open, brains spilled on the rocks, with virtually every bone in her body broken. Next to her was the presumed lifeless Delia, who somehow had miraculously survived, her fall cushioned by the body of the dead friend who preceded her. Six-year-old Delia, once recovered, was able to testify lucidly in court against the killer.

Sadie's attorney's defense was insanity. He prevailed, and she was placed in the insane asylum on Forest Avenue. Astonishingly, only two years later, with "Reason Restored" proclaimed on her record in vivid red ink as her most recent diagnosis, she was freed, at liberty once again to live among susceptible children. The people of the killer's beloved town of Akron ran her out when she attempted to return. No one knows for certain where she eventually wound up, or what dark events involving her may have eventually transpired.

"His argument is that no sane person would ever do what Hickey did," Hannah exclaimed of Daniel V. Murphy. "That attorney has three children of his own!" she raged. "How *could* he? That animal Hickey needs to be strapped into the electric chair at Auburn Prison immediately. I'll volunteer to throw the switch myself! Seems clear to me Murphy would like to ultimately have Hickey set free in order to kill more children."

Well," Ruth agreed, "you know how I feel about attorneys by and large. They are sick parasites. Anyone who can defend an animal such as Hickey is more like Hickey than he is similar to the rest of us. I say if he wants Hickey out of prison so badly, Murphy should be required to take him into his own home and provide him a bed next to his son's in his son's room and close the door. Then we'll see how eager Murphy is to save that monster's life!"

Hannah thought that was a brilliant strategy. "I say in the meantime we demand the police visit Attorney Murphy's home over there on fancy St. James Place," suggested Hannah, "and dig up his backyard. It would be no surprise to me if they discovered the bodies of children buried there. Like I always say, 'You are who you defend!'"

Ruth continued, "It is very troubling Hannah, that Murphy would try to influence the jury's perception of wrong as being right and down as being up. To take advantage of the ignorance of simple men and intentionally create confusion in their minds.

"How do you mean, Ruth?"

"This is a very troubling aspect of human nature, the unwillingness of people to accept difficult truths—especially when revealed as being so abhorrent as Hickey's. And then we have the opposite ability—perplexing and confounding to be sure—of people to not just believe, but eagerly seek out, to pursue things absurdly fantastical and unreal like astrology and fortune tellers. These opposites are the two most important things that prevent crimes from being investigated, prosecuted, and successfully tried.

"How many killers have been found not guilty by juries unable to accept the obvious example of true evil sitting right there in front of them? These same people swear by their ridiculous Bible which is overflowing with countless examples of pure evil. Where in their Bible does any example of innocence in God's eyes due to insanity ever crop up? Well, it certainly does not, now does it? Yet these same men on the jury are raptly listening as that attorney tries to convince them that their faith in God alone should guide them to conclude that putting this man to death is wrong. These two things are in total opposition.

"The fact is, evil lives on our street, and for some people, right in their own home. It's a fact of human failing Hannah, that if these same people can accept and even celebrate a demon shite the likes of Fingy Conners, let's say, and even elevate that same evil man to admirable social acceptability, then they certainly will not acknowledge other evils in their midst either.

"The need for people to believe that we all share the same morals is a terrible human failing, even as the exact opposite is proven to us time and time again. We push it out of our minds, which is one thing, an understandable thing really, but to push it so far outside of ourselves that the next time we are confronted with the same situation we fail to recognize it for what it is, to recall the repercussions and consequences of what transpired previously, and the tragedy that came from that... it's all very troubling. I think I've lost just about all faith in the goodness of people anymore.

"It isn't that humans aren't capable of learning from the past, rather they are intentionally and willfully unwilling. The terrible truth that Hickey and those like him are not insane lunatics but rather evil yet normal-acting people who live and work and go to church among us, so rattles people to such a degree that denying this fact is their only way of coping. We expect a monster to look like a monster, but the reason monsters are so successful is because the worst of them look like everybody else."

"You're scarin' me Ruth."

"I'm sorry Hannah, but it is what it is. I won't apologize."

"No, I don't mean that. I mean you're scarin' me because everything you just said is also what Jim has said to me at one time or another. He's always sayin' 'people want it both ways' too. You two see things the same way. It makes me feel like I been asleep all these years."

Ruth remained silent as the wheels turned inside Hannah's head. She wanted Hannah to draw her own conclusions, to analyze her own behavior and beliefs. "What you're saying Ruth. It's...it's terrifying. I mean, I guess that I'm one of them who just doesn't want to face the evil, who don't want to believe evil is all around us. I wouldn't want to ever leave the house again if I fully accepted that."

"Accepting it won't imprison you Hannah—it will set you free. It will protect you. Being aware of danger helps us survive, because we know what to be on the lookout for. Refusing to face it makes us all the more vulnerable."

Hannah thought again, silently. Ruth got up from her chair.

"Can I get you more tea, dear?"

"Ruth, I got to confess somethin' to ye," she said with downcast eyes.

"What?" asked Ruth.

"She told me the whole story and made me promise never to tell no one. I intentionally stopped thinkin' about it shortly after Sadie McMullen was set free from the asylum. I had to, for my own sanity. I had to block it out so I could go on with my livin'. I was as shocked as anyone that they set that evil little girl free—and so soon after the murder too! I had to drive it out of my mind, Ruth, I *had* to. But ever since Nancy died last Christmas, I just can't get it out of my head. It's burnt into my brain. I feel so guilty!"

"Nancy who? What on earth are you talking about, Hannah?"

"Nancy Morgan from over on Michigan Street, Ruth. She's the aunt of the child murderess Sadie McMullen. She was a member of our pedro club. It was Nancy who Sadie mailed her suicide note to right before she threw them poor babies off the trestle. Ruth, I never even told Jim what Nancy told me. I'm so ashamed."

"What on earth did she tell you that was so alarming? Tell me, Hannah!"

Hannah was trembling now. She took a few deep breaths. Her cheeks flushed red.

"Nancy Morgan withheld information during the trial which could well have resulted in Sadie going to prison for the rest of her life, or even given the electric chair, rather than being set free."

Ruth had to take a step backward just to maintain her balance.

"Oh my God," she gasped.

"I kept quiet so's to stay out of trouble, and not just because Nancy asked me to. It's like Fingy Conners said at little Davey's Confirmation, "You can't be held accountable for sayin' somethin' you never said," and so I said nothing. Nancy was a wreck. She believed Sadie would be locked up for the rest of her life in that Asylum, which would keep her from doin' somethin' like that ever again. But, when they set Sadie free after only two years, Nancy was horrified at what she done. She was only tryin' to keep her niece from fryin' in the chair, Ruth.

"Only me and Father O'Connor knew the full story. O'Connor advised her she should come forward and tell the truth, but she was terrified they would put her in jail for keepin' it to herself so long, so she kept it just between me and her and Father O'Connor."

Ruth thought a moment, then said, "The tyranny of being asked to keep someone else's a secret is this, Hannah: they are burdening you with that which they themselves do not have the strength to bear."

"Oh my," Hannah nodded her agreement with this insight. "Why do I continue to keep others' secrets? Why won't I see things clearly, as they are, instead of trying to wish them away? My brother David *has* killed people, Ruth, just like you and Annie both said. I'd just pushed it out of my mind. As if such a thing should have no impact on me, or my kids, or his kids, simply because he's my dear brother. I wasn't able to bear the thought. I am not an eye witness nor has David ever confessed to me what he done, but there is just too much evidence to ignore.

"He's one of them people, Ruth—he lives among us, goes to church among us.

He's killed people, beaten people, and he's delivered Fingy Conners' hired killers to the saloons and meetin' places with the full intention to maim and kill unionizers. Then he protected them same scum afterward. And I ignored all of it...because how do you accept that your own dear brother who you love is so cruel?

"At little David's Confirmation party I saw fear in them dear children of his. They were so stiff and rigid, and his wife meek and silent. Everyone remarked about how polite and quiet and well brought up David's kids were. How shy and gentle his wife was. But they weren't shy, or well behaved, Ruth. I think they were all..." she gulped. "I think they were all just terrified of my brother."

His Lips Forgot The Taste Of Truth

THE FIRST WARD IV

Grave Matters

Throughout Alderman John P. Sullivan's life, bewilderment with regard to his late father had haunted both him and his brother.

Jim, being eight years old the day their father left, was gifted with many memories of him, but JP was only a baby at the time and thus had none at all. JP was only eight months old when his father marched off from Buffalo with the 49th New York Volunteers in the Summer of '61, shortly after the Civil War began.

In his darker moments JP deeply envied his older brother for his having so many stories to tell about his adventures with their father. Not the least of these was their outing to attend the public reception to meet President-elect Abraham Lincoln face to face on his journey to Washington for his inauguration.

Their mother had added conflicting bits and pieces through the years, not out of obfuscation he reasoned, but rather out of her own confusion over things. Upon John P. Sullivan Sr.'s death, the Union Army appeared to have few personal records relating to him. The government had maddeningly concluded, despite his marriage to Mary McGrady and their surviving two sons, that the dead soldier was unmarried and childless.

Left penniless, the widow was forced to place her children in the Buffalo Orphan Asylum for the sake of their survival, the government having denied her rightful widow's and orphans' pension. She could not immediately produce official papers certifying the marriage or the children's births as required.

She had married John Sullivan in October 1850 in Amsterdam NY at St. Mary's Catholic church. In her desperation to provide proof of her legal marriage, she contacted that church but was told there was no record of the union there. In fact, there were no records at all for any of the many marriages, baptisms or burials that took place from St. Mary's between 1848 and 1852. All records had been lost.

For both Sullivan brothers their protracted Buffalo Orphanage ordeal was a source of great upset and shame, despite JP's having been too young at the time to have clear memories of it. But his brother Jim's tortured recollections were as vibrant as if they had only just been recently formed.

In 1863, out of having no better chance of survival, their mother married another soldier from the 49th, Peter Halloran, and thereby was able to rescue her sons from the institution. The marriage proved tumultuous and violent from the outset, so much so that no one would have faulted Mary for entertaining the thought that husband number two might better meet a similar fate as husband number one. Indeed her heart raced upon notification the year following their ill-conceived marriage that Peter had been seriously wounded at the Battle of the Wilderness. Alas, he was sent home to recuperate, during which time the patient exhausted the patience of his wife-nurse to the extent she redoubled her efforts at making him well again so he might be sent back to the front lines.

After the war was over, Halloran returned angrier and more bitter than before. Within a few months he had been arrested for grand larceny and sentenced to Auburn Prison for two and a half years. On the verge of a nervous breakdown and once more in dire financial straits, Mary was compelled to once again place her sons, now aged 13 and 6, with the Buffalo Orphanage. Then she disappeared.

Mary Sullivan-Halloran had previously signed papers in 1863 appointing her pension agent, Samuel Lake, legal guardian of sons Jim and JP in the event of either her death or her absence, as revealed in Lake's correspondence with the government regarding her ongoing pension case. Neither brother spoke to anyone except each other about these unsettling episodes in their young lives.

Growing up amid chaos and abuse, culminating with their vile stepfather attacking their mother with a butcher knife and plunging the blade into her neck as they watched horrified, JP had always longed for his real father. He often fantasized about the perfect life they might have lived together as a family if only his father had survived the war.

❦❦❦

"I've packed your valise, husband," said Annie. "Remember your train to Baltimore is at 4:40."

"Annie, stop your worrying," replied JP. "Me and the fellas are all taking the same train. All of us together. I promise you they won't let me get lost. Trust me."

The fellas included newspaper publisher Fingy Conners of the *Buffalo Courier* and *Enquirer*, and *Buffalo Times* publisher Norman Mack, who had been provided the honor of opening the Democratic National Convention.

"Well, being a delegate is mighty important stuff," Annie said. "I don't want you to miss it."

"I can assure you that all the arrangements have been made, dear. No need to fret."

"How come I can't go, Pa?" asked little Mildred. "We're learnin' all about the conventions in school. I can help you, maybe. Please?"

"Honey, nobody but the delegates are allowed. Anyway, you're a girl. Girls and politics don't mix."

"Can't I just go 'n' watch?"

"Mildred, no. This is adult business, you know that. Maybe next time. Looks like women might be gettin' the vote after all, so maybe I can bring you to the next one."

"Oh, alright, Pa," she mumbled. Unsatisfied, the young girl sulked away.

After double checking his pockets to make sure he had his change purse, his medicine and his rail tickets, JP picked up the heavy valise, leaning to one side to compensate for his bad leg.

"Okay Annie, looks like I got everything. I know you'll have the situation under control as always. I left the telephone number of the hotel by the telephone there on my desk, in case of an emergency."

Hearing the trolley bell coming down Hamburg Street he gave her a quick peck on the cheek and limped hurriedly from the house.

❧❧❧

The convention proved an exhausting ordeal, from Norman Mack's being compelled to pound the gavel for a solid four minutes before bringing the Baltimore gathering to order, to the blistering hot venue, to the public shaming of William Jennings Bryant and Fingy Conners. On the last day, depleted from the cruel summer heat and the wild goings-on regarding the unending Tammany shenanigans, JP placed a call to Washington DC to his old friend and cousin-in-law, undertaker, Mutual Rowing Club brother and Buffalo Congressional Representative Daniel Driscoll.

Over the years JP had confided in his wife's cousin his frustration over having no clear answers as to the mystery of the whereabouts of his father. Driscoll conveniently invited JP to meet in Washington after the convention was over with, the aim of using his power of office to track down JP's deceased parent.

The family had been told Private John Sullivan had died in Washington on September 18, 1862. Had there been any other pertinent details, they seemed long lost to the mists of time. JP's mother had been dead now for almost thirty years, his father for over fifty.

As he awaited the operator's call back once having established a good connection he said out loud to himself, "How I wish I had asked more questions of my mother when she was alive!"

The phone rang.

"I have your connection to the Congressman, sir. Go ahead."

"JP? Are you there? Hello?" asked Driscoll.

"Yep, Dan. It's me. We've got a bad connection it seems. Listen, I'm about ready to leave Baltimore and I was hoping that you were still interested in helping me track down my father. I know you're busy running the Nation and all..."

The Congressman laughed. "Never too busy for my old Mutuals mate. How's your brother, by the way?"

"He's well, and as anxious now as I am to see if we can put some family questions to rest."

"Yes. I've arranged for us to visit Arlington Cemetery tomorrow afternoon. I had my assistant do some research at the National Archives and it turns out there are quite a number of Civil War-era John Sullivans from New York buried there, so we'll go take a look together. I'm sure he's in there someplace."

"That's real exciting, Dan. Thank you again for all your help. I've been waiting half a century for answers. I arrive in Washington at 4 o'clock this afternoon. You free to have dinner?"

"Sorry JP, can't. I have a committee meeting. No idea what time that might end. Let's just stick with our original plan. I'll come by your hotel and we'll head out for Arlington, let's say, about 2 o'clock tomorrow afternoon?"

"All right, Dan. See you then."

❧❧❧

The following day, having arrived at Arlington, Driscoll called up the records for all Civil War burials for the name John Sullivan. Upon providing Private Sullivan's date of death they discovered that no soldiers who died prior to 1864 were buried at Arlington. Sullivan died in 1862. The official suggested they might try the cemetery at the Soldiers Home up on Harewood Road.

As the auto puttered up the grade, JP refreshed Driscoll's memory. JP didn't realize that he did not have all the facts straight until he was made to recount them for his cousin. What he recalled were essentially what few he had been told thirty or forty years previous. Even those details were hazy now. Again he expressed regret at not having questioned his late mother thoroughly enough. He recalled certain facts not adding up back then, but wary of upsetting her he elected not to probe further.

"I was only eight months old," JP began, "and my brother was eight years old. My father left with other volunteers from Buffalo to Elmira, and from there to the front. We did not hear from him directly after that."

"Do you recall the date he left?" asked Driscoll.

"It was in summer, 1861. August, I believe," he stated.

"And he died…when?"

"A year later, September 1862."

Driscoll was silent for a moment or two.

"You say he left and was gone an entire year and your mother never heard from him?"

"Well, uh, yes, I guess. That's what she said: 'We never heard from him directly after that.'"

"Why would he not write for an entire year? That's very odd. And wasn't his pay sent home to support his family? I mean, that was the requirement. It all makes no sense."

JP hadn't ever thought about that. Suddenly he was left to question things he had long believed and accepted. "Holy mackeral! If the government was sending home his pay to his wife, then how could they claim they didn't know he was married?"

"Well, that is a corker!" Dan said.

"But as far as his not writing to us, he was illiterate, I believe," he stammered, befuddled by Driscoll's queries.

"Lots of those soldiers were illiterate, JP, but in that case they asked a friend or paid someone to write letters for them. Don't you think it's rather odd your father didn't do that?"

JP suddenly conjured a hazy fleeting memory of his brother Jim telling him that they did receive one letter.

"I'm not even sure now, Dan. Damn it! I should've had a good long talk about all this with Jim before I left. Well, that's something I never probed with my mother, much to my regret at this moment. I didn't even think in those terms, actually. Maybe he didn't write because he knew she couldn't read."

"She could have had someone at her church read the letters for her, right? And Jim was in school—certainly he could read and write at that time. So I wouldn't entertain that particular justification for your father not writing for an entire year—if indeed that was the case."

Dan paused before expressing a theory he'd held for a long time.

"JP, did your mother ever discuss why your father would leave her and your brother—and you, when you were such a defenseless baby—to just go off and join the army when that war was so new at that point? That detail has always struck me as odd. Who leaves a woman with an infant and a little boy alone to fend for themselves while he goes off to fight an adopted country's war, especially one so new at that time? How old was he when he volunteered?"

"He was 37," said JP, growing more uncomfortable.

"That's pretty old," returned Driscoll.

JP was becoming increasingly flustered. "I know he was a true patriot!"

"Patriotism is all well and good, JP. But family comes first. And in 1861 there was nothing in place at all to support the families these men left behind, not even a government pension program existed when your father joined up. It seems without logic why an immigrant like your father would march off to fight an adopted country's war so quickly at the expense of his own wife and two small children. Goodness, my own uncle flat out refused to volunteer until protections had been put in place for the family he was being asked to leave behind."

"What are you inferring, Dan?"

"Well, we both know your mother had a rough life. And she wasn't the easiest person to get along with, you'll agree. I wonder if your father might have joined the army just to get away from her."

"Dan!"

"Well, you have to be pragmatic about this, JP. He left you helpless at only eight months old! What kind of father does *that?* And in the dangerous, disease-infested, criminal-overrun First Ward! I mean, Jesus Christ! He left your brother. He left your mother. Your mother was forced by desperate circumstances to place you two in the orphan asylum, after all."

"Yes, but that was after my father died. She had no other choice," he argued, voice raised.

"Perhaps you might ask to inspect the records at the orphan asylum. There may be valuable information in these records, JP. Perhaps she placed you there before he died. Once she had been left alone by him, what in heaven's name did she manage to live on with you two in tow? She had no family to support her. If you discover that you and Jim were placed in the asylum before your father died, that might indicate money wasn't being sent home and that he might have been running away from a bad marriage."

"But you said it was required, that the government sent the money back to the families, so the men didn't drink or gamble it all away."

"That's true JP, but if in fact he never revealed to the army that he was married in the first place, his pay would stay with him. Maybe he didn't reveal he was married."

"Jesus Christ Dan! Old Doc Green drove us all to the railroad depot to see my father off when he left with his regiment! I didn't ask you to ruin my father's and mother's reputations after all! I only asked you to help me locate his gravesite!"

"Okay, okay JP. Calm down. I'm just asking the questions that certainly you must have already asked yourself. You are not one to be blind to such details, that's for certain. You were only eight months old at the time. How do you know for sure you all saw him off at the depot?"

"Let's just drop the subject!" JP shouted, flustered.

"Okay! All right. Sorry, JP."

They continued on in uncomfortable silence for a couple of minutes until the Alderman broke it.

"All right, Dan. I did wonder, truth be told. I did ask my mother why he left us behind to go fight a war that hadn't even been quite established yet at that time. Kids have lots of questions. And adults who don't want to answer those questions shut kids down. And I was shut down. I recall her getting angry when I asked too many questions about him."

Dan tread more lightly now.

"Did your mother, um, did she seem proud of your father? Or did she seem, I don't know, resentful perhaps?"

JP considered the question for a few moments.

"I don't know...neither, really. She hardly spoke of him at all unless me or Jim brought it up first, and even then she was vague. Yes, she should have been angry, certainly. Scraping by in the Ward is no easy picnic even today, but fifty years ago? Well, as you said, it was basically a lawless place back in those days. I always thought my father was spoken of so little at home when we were young because her remarriage to Halloran was such a disaster. There was so much upheaval and drunkenness and violence that all of us were preoccupied with just getting through another day in one piece. It wasn't until I got older, say, fourteen or fifteen, that I began to really contemplate all this and try to connect the various elements that seemed to make little sense. It was then I started asking questions. She always gave the shortest answer possible."

The sign announcing the Soldiers Home appeared roadside.

Driscoll's auto made a right turn into the cemetery. They first drove among a sea of identical white headstones before doubling back to the records office. In short order there they discovered the name of John Sullivan, 49th NYV, number 1450, along with other data that assured the Alderman and the Congressman that they had indeed found JP's father at long last.

As they pored over the records in his file, JP became more and more upset.

He had always believed the family legend that his father's life might have been saved had he not refused to undergo an amputation of one of his arms after having been shot at the battle of Bull Run. This caused much regret and resentment in him as a child, since he most surely wished to have a one-armed father rather than none at all. Then throughout his teens, up until the ordeal of his mother's illness and death when he was 25, and many more times since then, he alternately cried and cursed his dead father for making such a foolish, selfish decision.

But it wasn't until the present day, almost exactly fifty years after his death, that JP discovered the official details.

His father, having been wounded in the forearm by a musket ball, did indeed undergo an operation at Harewood Hospital by a surgeon named Weir, in which his ulna, one of the two forearm bones, was partially excised, leaving his arm intact. The surgery was a success, but he died less than a week later of typhoid.

His injury had been relatively minor. But in the aftermath of the operation he in all likelihood would not have been able to lift, much less competently fire, a musket or pistol, or perform manual labor. In fact it is most likely he would have been discharged from the army, leaving him free to return home to rejoin his family.

JP was absolutely shocked by this.

Fifty-year-old beliefs that had haunted him with what-ifs were immediately replaced with a whole other set of revelations and possibilities that opened a Pandora's box of brand new if-onlys.

The file also revealed that the 49th NY Volunteers did not take part in the Battle of Bull Run. So how could his father have been wounded there?

Further digging turned up months of records verifying that John Sullivan had fallen chronically ill and was bedridden in the camp hospital tent at Bull Run for months prior to the battle in which he was shot, his unit having moved on without him.

The records also enumerated the sad paucity of John Sullivan's worldly possessions at the time of his death: little more than a handkerchief, a razor, a comb and a ten cent Richmond note.

Digging further, JP was stopped in his tracks. In his hand was the cruel official document that was at the center of all their suffering.

In it, the spaces meant to include John Sullivan's particulars concerning his marital status, parental status and even his hometown all contained the word "Unknown."

"Unknown?" he uttered in astonishment. "How could the army not know he..." Then he thought, did he not tell them? Did his father keep secret from the army that he had a wife and children? Then he thought, no. There was no reason to keep his hometown secret, and anyway, being a member of the 49th New York, in which the majority of volunteers originated from Buffalo, that detail would be obvious.

Was the Army's record-keeping to blame? Some lazy or errant civil servant who couldn't be bothered to record the facts accurately? If his mother had been properly recorded as John Sullivan's wife, and JP and Jim as John Sullivan's legitimate children, perhaps there never would have existed the circumstances that resulted in their orphanage nightmare, or his mother's hellish remarriage to Peter Halloran. It was all too much to digest in a single sitting. His head was spinning with new information, the details of which changed everything.

"Come on, Dan. Let's go," JP said.

The two friends headed out into the vast field of white headstones to search, directions in hand.

"Here it is!" rejoiced JP.

John Sullivan's grave was found at the foot of a tree just a stone's toss from the roadway.

"Too bad neither of us thought to bring a Kodak," muttered Dan as they stood staring down at it. "You really should have a photograph of this occasion."

"Oh, dear. Look, Dan. It's broken," said JP pointing to his father's marker, "and somebody did a half-assed job repairing it. It's shameful."

The damaged marker had been repaired haphazardly. He surveyed the others all around. No adjacent markers were cracked or broken.

"How did this one stone alone become injured?" JP said, wondering to himself if it might have been done intentionally. In his imagination flashed a picture of his mother dressed in mourning black taking a sledge hammer to it.

"Don't know," replied Dan. "How about I just leave you here alone with your Pa for a while, JP?" Driscoll offered. "You two've waited a half century for this reunion. It's about time you got reacquainted."

The Congressman wandered off, studying the names and dates on various stones as he went. He shook his head mournfully, dismayed at the number of stones displaying the epitaph *Unidentified* rather than the men's names. He wondered how many grown children were still distressed and searching just as JP was, their father never to be found by them because he was lying under a stone having the designation *Unidentified*?

Driscoll glanced up.

Across the way JP stood looking down, hat in hand. He was absorbing the reality of at last realizing a life-long quest: reuniting with his father. It was almost like a dream.

He cleared his throat.

"Hiya, Papa," JP said quietly, choking up. "Sure has been a long, long time, hasn't it? You lyin' here all alone for half a century now with no family bringing flowers or stopping by to visit. Oh, it's me—your baby son Johnny, all grown up. I've been looking for you for fifty years, Pa. Fifty goddamn long years. And now here we are together. I finally found you."

His eyes filled with tears. He pulled the handkerchief from his pocket.

"How's Ma?" he sniffled, wiping his eyes. "Is she there with you? Are you both together? Kiss her for me, won't you?"

He blew his nose.

"I got a million questions Pa, if only you could answer me back."

He took an anxious breath. "Well...first off...why the hell did you leave us in the first place? Me and Jim, we needed our Pa! Was it like Dan said? Did you have it out with Ma?"

Driscoll glanced across the field of sun-bleached markers a few times curiously observing JP speaking to his father at length, wondering what was being said, although he had some idea.

"I know she could be a real pill, Pa. Judgmental. Even unforgiving sometimes. But is that any reason for you to leave your two loving boys behind?"

Dan kept himself busy, allowing his old friend his long-awaited reunion. After about twenty minutes he saw JP wading though the maze of markers in his direction.

"Look at this," said JP. "I chipped a piece." He opened his hand. "For a souvenir. Now I can take a bit of my Pa wherever I go."

Driscoll smiled. "You yourself are the finest part of your Pa, JP. You and Jim. So you've already been taking him wherever you go. He's been with you all along."

JP smiled and nodded in agreement.

"You about ready to head back, JP? Or do you need more time?"

JP again nodded. "No—yeah we can go, but first let's return to the office to see what I might do about having his stone fixed better."

At the records office JP was told that the stone had been discovered too damaged to be properly restored.

"What happened to it? How could just one headstone be so damaged while none of the surrounding stones are?"

"We have no idea, sir."

"Was it a vandal?"

"We have no way of knowing. It may have been already cracked when it was installed, and later, perhaps during a storm, fell apart. Perhaps a branch from a nearby tree fell on it."

"Can a replacement be made? I'd be happy to pay for it," JP said.

Dan Driscoll was taken aback by the unhesitant offer, coming as it did from such an historic skinflint.

"I'm sorry, sir, but we have no program in place at this time to craft a matching replacement. If you wish, you could order a stone and arrange to have it installed. There's a monument maker just a short distance back down Harewood Road."

❧❀❧

Shortly after leaving the cemetery they spotted the monument maker's facility and stopped the car to inquire.

"Sorry, but no similar white stone to those at the burial grounds is available to us, sir. Not for some time now, in fact. But you might order a conventional granite stone, even though it will not be a match for those surrounding. Given the available material though, it will be significantly more substantial than the government issued markers."

JP thought for a moment, tempted to keep looking for a close-enough match so as to not appear to dishonor the other dead soldiers. However, he knew himself, and he was due back in Buffalo the following day. He was aware that if he didn't make a decision right then and there, the task might fall by the wayside. He agreed to replace the stone with a granite marker.

"Now Pop will really stand out from all the rest," he said cheerfully. "Next time I come back here I'll be able to find him straight away. I'd like to bring my brother here to reunite with the father he knew so well. And I want my kids to meet their grandfather."

After leaving the monument maker, riding back downhill into Washington, a fragment of memory popped into JP's head.

"You know something, Dan? That letter I mentioned, the one my brother once told me about that our mother had received from our father? I think he said it had been dictated to a fellow soldier who was able to read and write. If I'm recalling correctly now, Jim told me that he had read the letter to their mother, and wrote back to him shortly before reading the terrible notice in the newspaper that Pa had been shot. Until this moment in fact that memory had disappeared from my head as completely as it seems the letter has, if indeed it had ever really existed, which after all that I've learned today about misinformation, I now must question.

"So much of what I had previously accepted as true is now disproven while newly discovered details have left my head spinning. I don't recall my mother having ever mentioned such a letter, not even in passing, nor did Jim repeat that story to me any time since we were kids."

He sat motionless in thought for a minute.

"I'm going to have to ask Jim about all this when I return home. Me and him, we got plenty to discuss now. I expected to get my final answers today, you know, answers that would wrap up all my questions. But now I got more questions than ever. At any rate, this story sure is a dandy, ain't it? I'm sure the *Express* will be interested in it."

"I bet they will too. Always thinking there JP," Dan said, smiling.

"Publicity is the key, Dan. We always got to be keeping ourselves familiar, always keeping our names in the papers for when reelection time rolls around."

"Yep. Always thinking," repeated the Congressman.

Pvt. John Sullivan's damaged grave marker was replaced by his son JP Sullivan.

"FINGY" CONNERS MAY FACE TRIAL

Whitman Believes He Can Convict the Buffalo Boss of Graft.

NEW YORK, Nov. 13.—The evidence unearthed today by Whitman's investigators was the strongest that has yet come to light and in the opinion of those close to the situation will form the basis for numerous indictments. George A. McGuire, the Syracuse bonding agent, has assured the district attorney's office that he will make a clean breast of all he knows in connection with the extortion of money by politicians from contractors.

In the opinion of the district attorney, McGuire knows enough to warrant the conviction of half a dozen men or more. Already subpenas are being prepared for several political leaders. Among the number, Whitman announced, was Wm. ("Fingy") Conners of Buffalo. Whitman also announced that he would investigate the charges made in Buffalo by John A. Hennessy, William Sulzer's investigator of graft, against Norman E. Mack.

Hennessy said this afternoon that he had given the district attorney the names of 300 contractors who said they had yielded to the extortions of grafting politicians.

Bringing Up Father

Fingy, weary of her nagging, had brought wife Mary along to New York for a brief vacation. The only way he could think of to make the ordeal bearable was to include his winsome daughter Kate. Fortunately Kate had inherited the looks and easy temperament of her late mother, Kate Mahany, Fingy's first wife, rather than those of her father.

Although sensitive to her stepmother's domineering nature, the two got on well enough that they could spend time together without killing one another, especially if shopping were involved. Like many children of the widowed, Kate was none too happy when Mary Jordan managed to wheedle her way into the Conners family. Over time Kate was wise enough to realize that throwing tantrums would not get her nearly as much, or as far, as playing nice.

Fingy had bribed Kate with a visit to Tiffany's to keep Mary off his back while, despite his swearing not to, he engaged in some private business dealings with his political cronies. He might no longer be State Chairman, but he still was a key player in New York Democratic politics.

The Conners were staying at the Waldorf Astoria at 34th Street and Fifth Avenue. Fingy much preferred the magnificent cast iron Park Avenue Hotel with its massive moose head mounted overhead the check-in desk and big feathered brass beds, but on this trip he deferred to his wife's inclination. The Waldorf's rooms were decorated in a style more befitting a grand lady such as Mary fancied herself to be, with canopy beds painted with scenes of 18th Century France looking like something Marie Antoinette herself might sleep in if she were visiting Manhattan, and a Grand Ballroom fit for Versailles, if only Fingy cared a whit about dancing.

On day two of their visit Fingy had committed to attending the Metropolitan Museum of Art with his ladies and enjoying an elegant lunch afterward at the Hotel Astor's Rooftop Garden.

It was the bane of his existence getting Mary off and running at the start of an outing. It was like pulling teeth, as she was wont to spend hours in preparation for her appearances in public. If this were true in Buffalo then it was triply so on New York's Fifth Avenue. After a number of false starts, the highly impatient

Fingy announced he was going down to the lobby and would wait for them there, "unless some pretty little thing lures me away." This chestnut still worked on Mary, she, having found the goose that laid the golden egg, fearing she might easily be usurped, if not replaced altogether, by someone younger.

"I'll be down in five, Pop," assured Kate. "I promise."

"Don't make no promises yous can't keep, Katie," he said as he walked out the door.

Fingy descended on the lift. In the Waldorf's crowded lobby he parked his hind end on a huge divan flanked by palms. He accepted a New York Times from an attendant.

"Do you mind, Sir?" asked the polite young man wishing to seat himself. "My appointment is quite late, I'm afraid."

Fingy said, "Sure, go right ahead, lad," in his gruff dockworker's voice and patted the seat.

"The name's McManus. George McManus," said the young man, thrusting out his hand.

"Conners. Jim Conners," responded Fingy, obliging a firm handshake. Fingy took an instant liking to McManus if for no better reason than he thought McManus' mug resembled his own quite strongly back when Fingy was his age.

"Say, lad, what're yous doin' fer a livin'?"

"Well, I'm a writer sir, and an artist."

"Ain't no money in that!" bellowed Fingy critically.

McManus, rather than taking offense, laughed in friendly response, "Oh, I think you might be pleasantly surprised, Sir."

The two conversed so easily and laughed so often that Fingy didn't realize his girls had still not shown up. By the time they finally waltzed into the lobby, Fingy and McManus had become fast friends.

The women just stood there as Fingy and McManus continued to carry on together. Finally Mary chirped impatiently, "Darling? Ready?"

"Hold yer horses there Mary," Fingy said, waving her away. McManus, getting his first look at Kate, abruptly shot to his feet, entranced. He held his derby at his waist to obfuscate his immediate attraction to her and stammered out a "hello." Kate smiled shyly.

"Mary, Kate, this here's George McManus. He's a artist."

"Hello," Mary shot back condescendingly.

Kate's response was much friendlier. "Please to make your acquaintance, Mr. McManus," she said warmly.

Fingy sensed Mary's chill, and in a knee-jerk reaction that had at some point become automatic to him, gathered up his coat and hat to leave. Then he stopped himself.

"Say, George" Fingy offered, "why dontcha join us? We're goin' to the art museum. It'd be real nice t' have a artist come along t' explain us things.

Mary turned livid. "Oh, I'm sure Mr. McManus already has plans, dear..."

"Yes! I'd love to, Mr. Conners! How generous of you, sir. It appears my appointment has forgotten all about me at any rate, so I would be more than delighted to accompany you. Is that all right with you, Miss Conners?"

"Oh my yes, Mr. McManus," Kate enthused, relieved to have another warm body to temper the icy company that was her stepmother.

As they departed, the concierge nodded to Fingy to indicate their car was waiting out front. The doorman ceremoniously held the portal open, and the four climbed into the magnificent 1912 Rolls Royce Silver Ghost. What would otherwise have been an uneventful automobile ride became instead a party on wheels. McManus was highly entertaining and even dour old Mary could barely keep herself from laughing once or twice despite her most resolute efforts.

All the way up 5th Avenue George directed his wittiest *bon mots* Kate's way, to her delight. He complimented Fingy generously for his taste, gushing over the magnificent auto with its tufted mohair divan seating and beveled glass windows. McManus was clever enough to both reference his own working class background, which pleased Fingy no end, and congratulate himself modestly for his own financial success at his relatively young age. By the time the car reached the museum, Fingy, George and Kate were firm cohorts.

Mrs. Conners on the other hand wasn't so sure. An inveterate gold digger herself, Mary's hackles were raised concerning George McManus' true motives.

Across town, New York's aggressive District Attorney Charles Whitman was plotting.

He'd had Fingy in his sights ever since he'd won that powerful office, but couldn't quite nail him. However, he believed he *could* successfully nail Fingy's friends, and then perhaps Fingy by association.

Rowland B. Mahany had once been Fingy's fiercest enemy during Conners' most vulnerable time. One of the cleverest weapons in Mahany's arsenal was his unsubstantiated but vigorously argued claim that he was cousin to Fingy's first wife Kate Mahany, and therefore, family. A graduate of Harvard, a respected writer and poet and champion of the Irish and Ireland long before it was fashionable, Mahany had been a Congressman representing Western New York in the nation's capital. He had been a close ally of the late Father Patrick Cronin, who at the turn of the century was Fingy's most virulent critic and fearless opponent. Both had railed mightily against Fingy during the infamous 1899 Grain Scooper's Strike.

This championing of the common laborer earned Mahany Fingy's eternal wrath, or so it then seemed. Fingy used the power of his Buffalo newspapers to take Mahany down despite Mahany being highly approved of by the populus. And as the claimed close relative of his late wife, so therefore too he was esteemed by Fingy's daughter Kate. However no one, blood relation or not, crossed Fingy Conners without paying a steep price. For Rowland Mahany that price was his Congressional seat.

But more recently things were different. Rowland Mahany had slowly but surely migrated over to the dark side, the side where Fingy Conners not only resided but ruled. The previous year Conners had appointed Mahany editor of his *Buffalo Enquirer* newspaper. However, Mahany was at the present time under investigation for highway graft by the District Attorney of New York State in regard to his dealings with Fingy Conners.

D.A. Whitman, who had been searching for Mahany for weeks without success, learned on this day that the object of his investigation was in a Harrisburg hospital.

Mahany, terrified by the feared District Attorney's relentless pursuit of him and the D.A.'s stated objective to award him prison time, had consumed fifty grains of strychnine in an attempt to end his own life. He was discovered in time by friends and rushed to the hospital where he insisted his name was Charles Brown. While recovering there, he took a straight razor to his own throat. That attempt too failed, and he survived. In his obsessive quest of checkmating Fingy Conners, D.A. Whitman hopped on a train to Harrisburg to question the ex-Congressman.

❧❧❧

George McManus, as he escorted Kate and her stepmother through the Met's vast galleries, had convinced Mary that rather than the Astor, the dining room at the Park Avenue Hotel was nowadays the most fashionable place for those who matter in New York Society to see and be seen.

He had quickly picked up on what Mary's priorities were. For her, creating the illusion of culture and social standing was of paramount importance. George's suggestion excited Mary. She took the suggestion to Fingy, who frankly didn't care where they ate.

The dining room at the Park Avenue Hotel, George schemed, would be an ideal place to continue his wooing of Kate. The room, although cavernous, gave the impression of intimacy despite its grand scale due to the many massive square columns that supported the carved plaster ceiling. Tables were arranged abutting these columns providing diners an air of seclusion from one another, yet the massive space would make for an opportune venue within which to take a private stroll with Kate shielded from the overzealous surveillance of her step mother.

Mary, despite her seeming to enjoy George's company, had already decided by meal's end his social status was inappropriate for her beautiful stepdaughter. As the younger couple excused themselves from the table before dessert to explore, Mary stated her objections to Fingy while at the same time trying to keep an eye on them.

"That boy is nice enough dear, but what has he to offer our Kate, I mean socially? Financially? *Tush!* Nothing. She can do so much better."

"Nobody's proposed marriage yet Mary, so relax. Let them kids have some measure o' fun 'fore ye bite his head off."

The waiter approached to ask permission to bring the dessert trolley.

"Come back in five minutes," dismissed Fingy, "but bring me a bourbon 'n' soda in the meantime."

"Yes sir," the waiter responded.

Five minutes later Kate and George had not yet returned. Mary was getting agitated, craning her neck to try and peer down the length of the room.

"These ridiculous columns," she said as she rose from her chair, "don't allow one to take in the scope of the room properly."

"Sit down Mary. Where ye think yer goin'?" snapped Fingy.

"Balderdash! She's my daughter too. That boy is not to be trusted. I feel it down to my toes!"

Mary took off in a flash, nearly knocking down the waiter as he approached with Fingy's drink.

"Jesus!" scoffed Fingy as his drink was set before him. "Don't mind her. Say, yous married, fella?" he asked the waiter.

"Unfortunately, yes sir, I am," he responded. The two shared a chuckle.

Mary quickly paced the full length of the room, silk skirts rustling, but could not locate the couple. She grew increasingly agitated. She asked hotel staff if they had seen the couple. Kate was conspicuous due to her wearing a red dress. They had been seen heading toward the Courtyard. Mary followed directions and discovered the couple on the veranda leaning on the rail overlooking the central Courtyard, shoulders touching, engaged in an intimate conversation. As she approached from behind she was shocked to see them kiss.

Mary bolted forward and yanked George away from Kate by the elbow.

"Just who do you think you are, young man?" she hissed.

"Mrs. Conners..." he began in protest.

"Come with me, Kate!" demanded Mary as she hooked Kate's arm.

"Mary! I am not a child anymore! How dare you embarrass me in public."

"As long as you are a member of this family, Kate Conners, you will conduct yourself like a lady. Canoodling in public no less? And with a boy you only just met?"

Mary turned her attention to George.

"And you can go young man, right this minute. I will convey to Mr. Conners your regrets!'

As the women stormed off George called after, "Kate!"

As she was hustled away Kate looked back with an expression claiming her helplessness. As George had heard Kate say herself with his own ears, she was not a child anymore. Yet she was allowing herself to be treated as such in public by her overbearing stepmother.

"Fucking bitch," George steamed under his breath.

Once out of sight, neither woman looked back to see that George was hot on their heels. The women returned to their table.

"Let me handle this," Mary said to Kate in preparation for explaining George's absence.

They sat with their backs to the room. Immediately George joined them, pulled out his chair and sat as if nothing at all had happened.

"Sir, I can't tell you enough how much I've enjoined spending this time with you, your lovely wife, and daughter. It may sound a bit old fashioned of me, sir, but might I ask your permission to call on Kate next Wednesday when I arrive in Buffalo?"

Mary was livid with rage at having been outfoxed by this brazen young interloper. Before she could utter a syllable, Fingy said, "Why certainly, George! Ye know, I do appreciate them old fashioned ways. Ain't often I meet a young man like yerself wot's still got manners like we learnt 'em when I was yer age. Wot say yous come to the house fer supper on Wednesday. How's yer favorite?"

Mary was steaming. She kicked Fingy under the table.

"Ouch, Mary! Watch them heavy heels, will yous?"

"Well sir, if I had to choose my absolute favorite," George McManus sleuthed cunningly, "it'd have to be corned beef and cabbage."

"By golly! I knew there was some reason why I liked yous so much, McManus! Corned beef is a favorite o' mine too—so corned beef it's gonna be! Our cook Moira makes the best corned beef 'n' cabbage this side o' Killarney!"

George looked at Kate and gave her a crafty smile. He ignored Mary's red-hot glaring.

"Ahh!" exclaimed Fingy as the waiters rolled up a huge elegant silver dessert cart laden with cakes, tortes, mousses and parfaits. "Perfect timin'!"

※❦❦❦

Fingy, who normally took little interest in the romantic lives of his son and daughters, leaving the gory details up to Mary, made an exception in George McManus' case. George was even more adept at manipulating people and situations than was his newest rival, Fingy's wife. Indeed, had Mary not been so blinded by her umbrage, she might have admired and perhaps learned a thing or two from George's skillful maneuverings. But Mary's techniques were borne more from a primitive insecurity, the fear of being bested and usurped, whereas George's were intellectual, originating from a sound, and perhaps a bit inflated, sense of self.

Mary was aghast at how skillfully George had seduced her husband. Fingy was no easy mark by any means and prided himself for getting the better of others before they could get him. But George had craftily read Fingy and Mary both and controlled a situation that put him at the elegant dining table in the Conners mansion, sitting across from the object of his desire, the beautiful Catherine Conners. There too sat the scowling stepmother now fiercely determined to get rid of the obtruder. What Mary had in common with her husband was the unwaivering determination to defeat at any cost anyone who got in the way of their dreams and schemes.

"So, Mr. McManus" said Mary acidicly, "What is it that you do, again? I mean, to support yourself?"

"I am an artist, Mrs. Conners."

"Do you mean in the vein of Leonardo da Vinci or Rembrandt?" she retorted in a snarky tone.

"Oh yes, very much so indeed. I invented Baby Snookums."

"Baby Snookums?" exclaimed Kate. "Really George? I love that Sunday comic! Pa, did you know that? George, Baby Snookums runs in Pa's newspaper, the *Courier*!"

"What on earth is Baby Snookums?" pretended Mary, as if she didn't know.

George ignored Mary. Another trait he shared with Fingy Conners was the intelligence to shut up and satisfyingly allow people to indict themselves with their own words. He would not be taking Mary's bait.

"As a matter of fact," George continued, "recently I took a new position with the *New York American*. I have a new strip that's becoming quite popular, perhaps you heard of it too, Kate. It's called 'Rosie's Beau?'"

"Oh. I don't know that one, George. Pa, do any of your papers run "Rosie's Beau?"

"Can't say they do, Kate. Say, George, wot's Rosie's Beau about?"

"Well, sir, it's about a fella and his best girl who can't quite seem to get to the altar."

"Autobiographical, perhaps?' snarked Mary.

"I find myself in a fine position, sir. I am thinking of new ideas all the time. One I'm working on now, 'Spare Ribs And Gravy' is about two lads who are forever having misadventures. If you might indulge me, sir, I would greatly value your opinion, that is, if I'm not imposing on your kindness."

"Imposin'? Son, that's my job—thinkin' o' new things the subscribers will enjoy and look forward to readin' every Sunday. Why, my *Courier's* got a bigger readership than all them other Buffalo newspapers combined! So sure, send 'em to me and I'll let me editors take a look."

"How much salary do you make annually?" asked Mary boldly.

"Mother!" scolded Kate.

Without a hitch, George responded, "About $12,000 a year, Mrs. Conners. But with each new strip and each new newspaper that options my work I will continue to make more and more. That way I'll be able to provide handsomely for my wife and family when the time comes."

"Didn't you say you've married previously, Mr. McManus?" Mary harassed.

"Mother, stop! You're embarrassing everybody!" scolded Kate heatedly.

"No, Mrs. Conners," he said slickly, sending a wink and a smile Kate's way. "Up until only just this past weekend in New York, I hadn't met the right girl yet."

Kate beamed at the boldness of this new suitor, so much like her father in that regard. Fingy too took notice.

That night as he crawled into bed, Fingy said to his wife, "I do like that young McManus fella, Mary. Reminds me a bit o' meself when I was his age."

"Well I don't trust him, Jim. Not one bit. He's vulgar and he's rude."

"Funny, he treats me 'n' Kate just fine," he said, rolling over and turning his back to her. "Yous sleep tight now, Mary. Hear me?"

1913
THE WITNESS

George McManus had tried his damnedest. Flowers. A gold locket. A professed love of children and puppies. Sherlock Holmes novels. Shared dreams. A passion for overseas travel. But between Mary Conners' relentless domineering and poor Kate's rubbery backbone, Mary Jordan Conners succeeded in weaning stepdaughter Kate from her infatuations regarding George McManus.

Mary claimed victory haughtily.

George had traveled to Buffalo three more times that month just to see Kate. But at each meeting Mary managed to make an appearance. The couple sparred over Kate's so readily buckling under to her stepmother's intrusions. George ultimately saw the writing on the wall.

George McManus professed to be heartbroken, but in truth he had foreseen that Kate's lack of gumption, most especially in regard to her stepmother's ceaseless interference, would severely test their relationship. Mary was an insufferable bitch having neither desire nor reason to disguise her machinations.

Fingy Conners busied himself at his desk at the *Courier*. He took up his brass Pan American Exposition souvenir letter opener and slid it under the flap of the envelope bearing the *New York American's* engraved return address. Inside were some news clippings with a note:

> Dear Mr. Conners,
> Admiring you and your publishing empire as I do, I thought you might be interested in examples of my newest comic strip for the American. It's called "Bringing Up Father."
> I still recall the wonderful corned beef and cabbage dinner at your beautiful home. It was the best I ever ate!
> Respectfully yours,
> George McManus.

Fingy smiled.

"Always liked that young lad," he muttered out loud. "Very well mannered. Too bad."

He then unfolded the comic strips. He stared. It was almost like looking in a mirror.

What met his eye was a caricature of himself not in the least bit disguised. A burley well-fed man short of stature with an ever-present cigar stump stuck between his lips. His favored style of suit. The hooked cane. Wealth and servants. His habit of corned beef and cabbage. His love of a good fistfight. The speech pattern.

"Jiggs" *was* Fingy Conners in caricature. Jiggs' beautiful daughter, "Kate" was, unlike her cartoon parents, drawn realistically to look just like George's lost love. And the foil, "Maggie," Jiggs' shrewish nasty threatening wife, was represented in visage as dog-like, accentuating self-conscious Mary Jordan Conners' weak chin in cruel exaggeration.

Fingy read through the strips, chuckling in recognition, especially at the one in which Kate's earnest suitor is driven out of town by Maggie.

"Wilson!" he yelled.

Editor Wilson raced into Fingy's office.

"Yes, Boss?"

"Here, take these 'n' show 'em around. I think we might be addin' this here new strip to the Sunday color comics. It's called "Bringin' Up Father.""

"Yes Sir."

As Wilson circulated, Fingy sneaked glances to see if they saw what he saw. They did. Peals of laughter and lots of elbowing ensued as McManus' none-too-thinly disguised homage to The Boss were pored over and passed around.

Fingy immediately called his secretary in to pen a note on *Courier & Enquirer* stationary.

> Dear George,
> Got the comics. My editors all like "Jiggs" a lot. Me too. We'll take it on. One note, though: change Kate's name to something else.
> Sincerely,
> William J. Conners
> Editor in Chief

The message arrived in the *American's* mailroom two days later. George chortled as he read it, then went back to the board he was drawing, took up an eraser and changed Kate's name to "Nora."

At that very same moment Fingy was in Buffalo rejoicing over two welcome bits of news. First, his efforts to block a subpoena and thus remove Rowland Mahany from the sights of D.A. Charles Whitman had been successful, and second, in even more welcome news, Peter F. Collier, the founder of *Collier's* magazine, was dead.

Collier's son Robert had immediately assumed the magazine's leadership.

"That fool son o' Collier's don't know his little dick from his old man's walkin' stick," Fingy snorted as he crowed aloud. "Get the lawyers on it," he ordered his office manager.

With *Collier's* chief newly dead and all his incriminating secrets against Fingy buried along with him, Conners felt it was now safe to proceed full force with his vengeful lawsuit, despite it already being a full seven years after the fact.

The late Peter Fenelon Collier had been a formidable foe. He had the dirt on everybody—not the least of whom was Fingy Conners. *Collier's* scandalous article printed in the July 1908 issue accused Fingy of multiple crimes, the principal offense being murder. However, Peter F. Collier personally knew much worse than what was revealed in that sanitized 1908 piece. He was more than willing to pay people for information, and pay them very well.

Collier and the revered Buffalo priest and Irish activist Father Patrick Cronin had been fast friends. The savvy Cronin was editor of the *Buffalo Union and Times* Catholic newspaper and a powerful and highly respected advocate for the welfare of the downtrodden. Cronin had preceded Collier in his naming Fingy Conners an outright murderer in his editorials in the *Union and Times*. Indeed these accusations, made at the very end of the 19th Century, were what first attracted Peter F. Collier to the priest.

Both Cronin and Collier were champions of the Irish and of the promoting of Irish identity among American descendants of the Irish. As fantastically wealthy as Peter Collier became, he never forgot his very humble beginnings. As for Father Cronin, poor people in dire straits made up the majority of the population of Buffalo's St. Brigid's Parish, and Cronin established himself immovably as their staunchest advocate and defender.

Both Cronin and Collier hated Fingy Conners, and much that Collier came to know about Conners was derived through long conversations the two cohorts, Collier and Cronin, engaged in. Collier was a generous contributor to Cronin's church and causes. Being confessor to his flock, Father Cronin heard in the confessional harrowing accounts, many first hand, of Fingy Conners' crimes against First Ward unionizer family men whose principal transgression against him was their desire to sufficiently feed their families. Some of Cronin's confessors were the very men seeking absolution for carrying out violence on Fingy Conners' orders.

Perhaps Father Cronin may have exercised a more pragmatic assessment of the Catholic Seal of the Confessional than most, just as so many fellow priests likewise maintained a more "pragmatic" attitude regarding the sacred vow of celibacy, the vow they had pledged to God as they lay pronated on the sacristy floor at their Ordination.

Cronin's parishioners well knew that there was only one possible way Cronin could be privy to so great a number and to such gory details of Fingy's crimes for certain, and that had to be his rigorous questioning of confessors during the Saturday sacrament. His aggressive cross examinations were said to have been not unlike those of a thorough and somewhat threatening courtroom prosecutor.

There were precious few lines that Fingy Conners would not cross, but maiming or killing a priest seemed to be one. Except for some comparatively tame Conners harassment, such as the kidnapping of Cronin's beloved Great Dane, the priest went largely unscathed. A devoted Catholic, Fingy's terror of burning in hell overrode his obsession for revenge in this case. Fingy breathed much easier once Father Cronin had taken his last breath in 1905, and now with Collier gone too, he finally felt it safe to poke his head completely out of the foxhole.

Known infamously for having left many a dead body afloat in Buffalo's network of canals and slips only to be discovered there come first light, people dared only whisper the sorry details. The Buffalo police guarded Conners' secrets and enabled Conners' lieutenants, the Nugents, Daltons and Hurleys, to continue inflicting punishment on Fingy's offenders at will. The owners of Buffalo's competing newspapers tread lightly around Conners as a matter of course. Unlike a Dillinger or a Billy The Kid, there was no bragging or expositioning of the many notches on Fingy Conners' guns, bricks or leaden pipes. As author Will Irwin wrote in his *Collier's* article, "There are no rules in his fighting."

Irwin could have said more than he did in his printed *Collier's* piece—a lot more. But he was sworn to secrecy by those who were brave—or foolhardy—enough to come forward and grant him an interview as they elaborated on the twisted tale of Fingy Conners. Just the same, Peter F. Collier had taken a heavy red pencil to Irwin's submitted article, excising details deemed too inflammatory to print without absolute evidence, or too dangerous to the well-being of those who spilled the beans. Indeed two of those interviewees got cold feet soon after their interviews and in a panic contacted Collier to beg him not to reveal the entirety of their statements so that they might continue through life breathing and uncrippled.

Irwin was surprised at the revelations some were willing to make, such as those of the editors of the *Courier* newspaper who Fingy had so off-handedly fired after becoming irked about their being able to afford to eat in some of the same restaurants where The Boss himself preferred to eat. Still, the details provided by them were interpreted by the wiley Irwin as substantially watered down and less detailed than the actual occurrences themselves.

"But Mr. Conners!" exclaimed Attorney Osborn, "certainly you must have entertained that upon filing a lawsuit against a periodical as formidable as Collier's Magazine that they would fight back with all the legal artillery at their disposal, which is quite extensive."

What Osborn failed to add to that caution was that the world had by now after seven years forgotten all about the old profile in *Collier's*, and Fingy would only be shooting himself in the foot by going ahead with this lawsuit and resurrecting that which otherwise had long been consigned to oblivion. Predictably, newspapers across the country upon learning of the lawsuit newly resuscitated all the sordid details to refresh everyone's memory.

> Former Democratic State Chairman William J. Conners has brought a libel action against Collier's Weekly for $100,000 damages. Will Irwin, one of Collier's special writers, went to Buffalo and had a long interview with Mr. Conners some years ago. Mr. Irwin, however, published a great many things about Mr. Conners which Mr. Conners alleges are untrue.
>
> The complaint sets up that the article was intended to bring Conners into obloquy, disgrace, ridicule and disrepute, and by the statement made it was intended to be understood, and it was understood by the readers of the magazine, that Mr. Conners was unscrupulous and dishonest in honest business and had employed unlawful and disreputable methods and thereby charged him with the crime of secret murder, the crime of inciting murder, of secret assault, the crime of riot, the crime of conspiracy and with an offense against the election law.
>
> The general charge is made that Mr. Conners bribed the freight agents of the carrying lines on the lake in order to beat his competitors in the freight handling business.
>
> The complaint in reference to secret murder is based on a portion of the article to the effect that when things became dull in his water-front saloon he would start an argument and that if he was unable to settle it with a bungstarter he resorted to the methods of the "highbinders."

The charge of inciting murder is based on the gross invasion of the propeller ship Mather during the grain strike. It was alleged that Conners inspired a number of his men to fire into the hold of the boat at men who were unfriendly to Conners, maiming some.

In the answer that has been filed, and which covers only two typewritten pages, there is no attempt at justification or mitigation and the claim is made that no damage was done to Mr. Conners by the publication, though malice is denied.

This looks, says the *Auburn Citizen*, like a square up and up test between Conners and Colliers which, if neither side backs down, must result in establishing the exact truth about a man who has been much discussed during the last few years.

— *Oswego Daily Times*

Fingy Conners' unhinged raging reflected neither prudent boundaries nor common sense. There was no thought put into it nor logic wrapped around it. Once his fuse was set off he just exploded. It behooved all in close proximity to run for cover. Fingy Conners may have had a flotilla of enemies, but none were more potent a threat to Conners' well being than he himself.

"So, whadder we goin' t' do *now*, Osborn?" Fingy shouted.

"We settle, Mr. Conners. That's your only way out I'm afraid," the attorney adroitly countered.

"I ain't settlin'! Conners don't settle—'ceptin' wit' his fists!"

Fingy jumped up and took a street pugilist's stance. "See?"

Osborn kept a poker face despite Conners' comical posturing—dangerous yes, but comical all the same.

Fingy Conners commenced every new relationship, every new transaction, with the threat of physical violence whether subtly inferred or otherwise. It worked for him at age four and it was still working for him at age fifty-four. Sometimes it was shamelessly overt. At other times, such as recently with President Woodrow Wilson, it was occluded, he being preceded by his storied reputation and capped off with a veiled facial expression coupled with an inapropos superior attitude.

Attorney Osborn was a master at keeping his cool. But with two high-stakes cases underway concurrently, Osborn was being stretched thin and his patience for Fingy's foolishness along with it.

"Mr. Conners, you wished to make a statement by launching this lawsuit. All right, statement made and finished. Point taken. But if Mr. Weir takes the stand in this trial, at the very least it's William J. Conners who'll be paying out a pretty penny to Collier's Magazine, not the other way around. Weir is on his way here from Ohio as we speak, ready, willing and able to spill the beans. *Your* beans. I urge you again, sir—*drop this lawsuit.*"

The actual amount being demanded in the lawsuit was $50,000, but for ego's sake and publicity purposes Conners inflated the figure to $100,000 in his newspapers, knowing all other periodicals would follow his lead.

Fingy chuffed up a thick glob and launched it into the spittoon, pulled the handkerchief from his breast pocket, wiped the excess, shoved his soggy cigar stub back into his viperish mouth, and sat back down behind his desk. A dark foreboding scowl came over his face, a grimace all too familiar to those who crossed him.

"All right, Osborn. Get outa here. I got t' arrange some things."

Osborne took up his briefcase and derby and said "Good afternoon, then," and left.

Fingy picked up the telephone and clicked the hook a few times to summon the operator.

"Yeah, git me Chief Regan at the Police Headquarters."

He drummed his four fingers impatiently as he waited for the connection. A full minute passed. "What's takin' yous so long, dearie!" he shouted to dead air. The operator clicked in just one second later. "I have your party on the line, sir," she pleasantly intoned. "Go ahead please."

"Yeah, Mike, it's me. What's say I buy yous a cold beer at Kize's place? Four o'clock? Yeah? All right, good. See ye then."

Kize's place was the Hotel Vega at the corner of Pearl and Eagle. Proprietor John J. Kennedy, former city alderman from the 19th, greeted Chief Regan with a whoop.

Regan teased, "Kize, ain't you supposed to be passing' laws over at the city hall right about now?"

Kennedy reminded the increasingly forgetful Police Chief that he was now the duly-elected Treasurer of New York State.

"Yeah, course I knew that Kize! Only kidding."

The chatter quieted once Fingy Conners walked through the door of the elegant establishment five minutes late.

"Two beers, cold as a witch's tit," he barked at the bartender. He wasted no time getting down to business.

"I need yous t' do me somethin', Mike."

Like everyone in Conners' orbit, Police Chief Mike Regan and Fingy had endured their share of ins and outs—mostly outs in more recent times. But finding himself in a real pickle the previous year, or more precisely, his son-in-law Tom Hagen having landed himself in a heap of trouble, Regan's reaching out to Fingy became unavoidable. Having a sixth sense for such things, not unlike a lion able to sniff out the sickly calf among a stampeding herd, Fingy pounced. Hagen's—and by association, Regan's—problems immediately evaporated like steam on wet asphalt on a hot summer's day. The public humiliation that the Chief and his wife Ellen would have suffered over the Hagen incident never materialized. Now Regan owed him one.

"I just got word from Osborn—that cocksucker at Collier's made a temptin' offer to that Weir stooge to come up here t' Buffalo 'n' testify at the trial," railed Fingy. "That's what all their fuckin' delayin's been about. Linin' up dirtbags willin' t' say any lies about me they tell 'em to."

Regan nodded expressionless as he silently calculated all those he knew about, just from this past year alone, who Conners had gone after based on little or no provocation or evidence. *You are truly one sick bastard, my friend,* Regan sighed to himself silently as he pretended to listen attentively.

The unabashed instigator and champion at retribution routinely lashed out at any and all perceived threats and enemies blindly as if convinced that none of his injured parties would ever dare retaliate. He conducted himself that way predictably as a matter of habit. But on the rare occasion when someone did seek, then win, their vengeance, the thin-skinned bully Fingy Conners responded initially not unlike a victimized little boy, hurt and wounded and disbelieving and on the verge of tears. But that knee-jerk reaction quickly segued into an oath of deadly vengeance every time.

"So, what yous expect me to do about it?" Regan asked.

"Shoot the fucker," Fingy said.

"You know I can't do that."

"Sure ye can. Put a tail on 'im when he gets here t' town and follow him 'round until he's in a position so's ye can put him on the ground fer doin' somethin'. Then maybe a gun goes off accidentally or he trips 'n' cracks his stupid polack skull on the curb or falls in front of a streetcar." Fingy shrugged matter-of-factly. "Easy. Just another accident."

"That ain't gonna happen, Fingy."

"Hold the weeds down 'n' they'll only grow sideways, Mike! Pull em out by the fuckin' roots instead!" Conners shouted, pounding his meaty fist on the bar for emphasis. "Yous owe me, Regan!"

"And you owe *me,* Conners!" Regan responded, pointing to his toe.

Back in '94 Regan had been scapegoated after Fingy's election-fixing scheme blew up in his face. The sole head to roll among all the many collaborators was Regan's. He'd lost the toe to frostbite after being stripped of his captain's rank, demoted to patrolman, and turned out onto the mean streets to pound the beat for three freezing Buffalo winters.

"I know of that Weir fella," offered Regan. "He ain't well, an' he'll be easy to scare. I'll have a coupla me lads put a good fright into 'im. But you of all people should well know the power of a good writer along with the publication that prints his words. This could end up bitin' you in that big fat lily-white arse o' yers."

Fingy unhappily considered the offer.

"Well yous better spook him good 'n' plenty. Put Jordan on it. That son of a bitch ain't got no conscience at all."

Regan gulped the last of his beer and with a wordless goodbye turned and left. On the way out Kennedy tried to stop and chat him up for some advice, but Regan kept moving. "Gotta get back to work, Kize. Maybe later."

Kize Kennedy watched as Regan walked out the door, dark worry etching lines into his face.

HUGH C. WEIR.

Hugh Cosgro Weir

The train rocked hard just as it crossed the Ohio-Pennsylvania line.

Hugh C. Weir jolted out of a half-sleep at the rail car's jounce. He'd been napping in the first class sleeper, paid for compliments of *Collier's* magazine. In the other bunk lay Lyndon Sanchez, a Pinkerton's detective in Robert J. Collier's employ. His job was to keep an eye on Weir, comfort his worries, soothe his nerves, keep him from getting too drunk and deliver him safe and sound to Buffalo. It was feared that an agent of Fingy Conners might be aboard vigilant for any opportunity to toss a wrench in the works or an inconvenient witness off the speeding train. Sanchez snoozed with his Colt 45 under his pillow and a derringer strapped to his ankle.

Weir dreamt on and off, reliving the events that had brought him to this point until the train finally pulled into Buffalo's Exchange Street depot.

Bodyguard Sanchez' job was finished once he'd settled Weir into his room at Buffalo's Hotel Statler. Weir was signed into the Statler under an alias. Reservations had also been made at the Iroquois Hotel under Weir's name to throw off any dastardly scheme Conners might have planned. A decoy checked into that room and was paid to remain ensconced there until the morning of the trial.

As Sanchez departed, the bodyguard literally bumped into Charles B. Sears, one of Collier's attorneys on the case, in the hotel lobby.

"Say, how'd everything go?" Attorney Sears asked.

"Well," Sanchez answered, "Conners had two agents aboard that train, Mr. Sears, and it was all I could do to keep Weir from gettin' tossed head first from the car. I even had to supervise the preparation of his food in the diner car, so certain was I that he might get poisoned."

It was a lie. The trip was uneventful, but Sanchez wished to paint his provided services as indispensable.

"Good work, Sanchez. You'll be hearing much more from us in the near future," congratulated Sears.

Sanchez smiled broadly and said "Just part o' my job, sir."

The two shook hands amiably. Sears bid him goodbye, then took the elevator up to the fourth floor and knocked on Weir's door.

"Who is it?" called the cautious witness.

"It's Attorney Sears, sir. I'm here alone."

The door opened and the very nervous Hugh C. Weir looked past Sears down the hallway to make sure he hadn't been followed.

"You look good, Mr. Weir. None the worse for wear. Was the trip tiring?"

"No, not at all. It was completely uneventful."

"Mr. Sanchez tells me there was some excitement."

"Oh? How's that?" asked Weir.

Sears caught himself. He surmised that the very professional Mr. Sanchez had admirably kept Weir in the dark as to the dangers that had been plotted against him.

"Oh, nothing. You know that the trial is taking place day after tomorrow at nine o'clock. Perhaps it's best you remain in your room and rest up until then?"

"What the hell for?"

"Uh, well," Sears chose his words so as not to frighten the witness, "because that way you'll be good and ready. I hear you're writing a new book? This idle time might well prove productive for you in that regard."

"Don't think so. I got plenty o' rest on that damned train. I got lots of friends here in town Mr. Sears, and some family too. Don't worry. I'll be at the courthouse on time. But I ain't holin' up' in this stuffy room 'til then, that's fer sure," he chuckled scornfully.

※※※

Hugh C. Weir was an extremely prolific writer. He became a newspaper reporter at age 16. He wrote for all the popular magazines. He wrote books. He wrote plays. He wrote screenplays for the new moving picture industry. He considered this trip to Buffalo a respite of sorts from all that writing, just for a few days, unless of course he might gain inspiration via some unexpected event.

Just such an event lingered on the horizon.

Hugh Cosgro Weir was so sickly, frail and slight of build as to belie his astonishing accomplishments and the many dangerous situations from which he extricated himself in pursuit of a good story. Placing himself in a Springfield Ohio prison to research a story in 1903, a riot erupted around him during which a door was forced and the Negro prisoner in whose cell he was incarcerated was dragged out and lynched. In Panama to write an article on the Canal, he had been attacked by an alligator, bit by a black scorpion and hit by a runaway speed boat. He was a Christmas fanatic, buying and individually wrapping the hundreds of Christmas gifts that he gave out each year. He became a personal friend of former President Teddy Roosevelt and was an avid collector of Charles Dickens memorabilia.

Weir was not a writer who had to rack his brain for story ideas. Many of these were provoked by events directly witnessed and people personally encountered. Lately he was finishing up a collection of stories having a female heroine: "Miss Madelyn Mack, Detective." The protagonist was inspired by Weir's good friend Mary Holland, "the mother of modern fingerprinting."

Miss Holland had been an editor on the magazine *The Detective*, a serious professional police journal. On assignment she was sent to the 1904 World's Fair in St. Louis. There Holland witnessed Scotland Yard's demonstrations of the new fingerprinting methods and technology.

The murderer Alfred Stratton had been the first person in the world to be convicted of murder based on a fingerprint. He and his brother Albert had robbed a shop in England at Deptford, and murdered the proprietor couple, leaving behind Alfred's greasy thumb print in the act.

Miss Holland became obsessed by this amazing discovery.

She sought out and passed the required exams and ultimately was hired by the US Navy as a fingerprinting instructor. She devised and sold a line of fingerprinting kits for law professionals that also appealed energetically to the general public, especially budding young boy and girl detectives. These kits appeared each December 25th in many a Christmas stocking. Her stories as told to Weir set off an explosion of inspiration for him. He already had the forthcoming book's dedication written:

> To Mary Holland: This is your book. It is you, woman detective in real life, who suggested Madelyn.
> It is the stories told me from your own notebook of men's knavery that suggested these exploits of Miss Mack.

But now here he was in Buffalo due to his past article on Fingy Conners written for *Human Life* Magazine which came on the heels of Will Irwin's "Fingy Conners" piece for *Collier's* weekly, now the subject of this lawsuit. Indeed, had Fingy seen the *Collier's* article beforehand, he never would have acquiesced to a meeting with Hugh Weir, so infuriated was Conners at being so aggressively branded a murderer and a scoundrel.

Weir's additional tie to Fingy Conners was his appearance as a stage actor in a non-speaking role in the Broadway play based on Fingy Conners, Edward Sheldon's "The Boss," where Fingy himself as an audience member had recognized him.

There were many things that had been omitted from Weir's *Human Life* article, such as the sworn stories told by those grieving families of unionizer laborers crippled and murdered by Fingy's thugs and hooligans. These roughs were imported to Buffalo by Conners from Chicago's infamous Chute and New York's storied Bowery to do his assassins' work.

Then there was that storied account of Fingy physically assaulting Buffalo's Catholic prelate, Bishop James E. Quigley, in front of a thousand striking workers at St. Brigid's Hall at which only Quigley's intercession saved Fingy from being torn limb from limb by the mob. Or that the same Bishop, no pacifist himself, and almost a full head taller than Conners, both an accomplished athlete as well as a West Point candidate in his youth, responded in kind by driving Fingy Conners right to the dirt with only one powerful hammerblow.

Authors Irwin and Weir were on amicable professional and personal terms, having written for many of the same periodicals. They had encountered one another in a tavern in New York's Algonquin Hotel a year after both their Conners articles had been published. There they divulged to one another harrowing details of what they had uncovered but dared not print, or better put, their publishers dared not print.

Now, having been subpoenaed to testify in the lawsuit trial that Conners had brought against *Collier's*, Weir and Irwin were together again, this time in Buffalo, anticipating revealing these withheld victims' testimonies. Neither could believe that Conners could be so stupid as to have his crimes aired so publicly, as the lawsuit had attracted national attention due to Conners' own misguided publicity efforts. But air them they would under an oath sworn to tell the truth, the whole truth and nothing but the truth, so help them God—every lurid, vile, homicidal detail.

❦❦

Hugh Weir strolled out the hotel lobby and halted on the sidewalk to gain his bearings. He had to squint to help clarify his poor vision. He was not feeling very well. For a moment he entertained the idea of reentering the hotel, enjoying a good meal, and retiring to his bed. Ultimately rejecting that, he headed toward Main Street.

The ruse of registering a decoy at the Iroquois Hotel had not worked. Buffalo Police Detectives Jordan and McGowan, who had secreted themselves in a shadowed nook of the Statler hotel lobby lurking, followed him outside stealthily at a distance. Conners had caught on to the hotel switcheroo thanks to a friendly agent at the Statler.

Weir was quite a walker. His doctors had advised this. Feeling a bit faint upon reaching Main Street, he felt in his pockets to make sure he'd brought his strychnine tablets, also prescribed by his doctor. He entered a candy store on Main Street near Genesee. The coppers tailing him followed and seated themselves at the soda fountain. Weir dawdled there a bit, seemingly confused. Then he ordered a glass of grape juice. When the juice was served, he took out his tin of medicine, placed a strychnine tablet in his mouth, and washed it down with the drink, whereupon Detectives Jordan and McGowan shot up from their stools and tackled Weir to the floor. Then they dragged him into a back room as he shouted for help.

"What was that yous just put in yer dirty mouth, you dope fiend!' shouted Jordan. Weir protested that he only took medicine, but the cops would have none of it, for Fingy's orders by way of Police Chief Regan had been made clear.

They dragged him off to the nearest police station and searched him. They found on his person six letters, including the letter requesting him to come to Buffalo to provide testimony in the trial of Conners vs. *Collier's* magazine, as well as his room key from the Statler. Despite having a room in Buffalo's finest hotel and half a week's wages in cash in his pocketbook, the police nonetheless charged him with vagrancy and threw him in a cell.

All night long he pleaded to call for his attorney and his friends, but his request was denied. In the morning he was dragged into court where the detectives lied barefaced, claiming they had found an assortment of drugs on Weir's person, and condemned him as a dope fiend, recommending to the judge that he be transported immediately to the infamous Auburn prison.

The Judge apparently doubted the policemen's story upon Weir telling him the reason he was in Buffalo in the first place. Judge Noonan, finding himself caught between an obvious setup and his own shameful allegiances to Fingy Conners, discharged Weir but ordered him out of Buffalo. This strategy, he calculated, would keep the innocent witness Weir out of jail, get him out of town before the trial, and shield Noonan from Fingy's inevitable wrath.

Fingy and Chief Regan thought they had successfully rid themselves of the primary witness against Conners in the trial. Despite Weir's poor health, he had proven himself a daring journalist, clever schemer and an adventurer of renown. He had attained a reputation as a cagey and tough character. He did not back down or allow Fingy's obvious malevolence to intimidate him. Upon his release he refused to leave the city. Rather he headed straight to a meeting with Will Irwin and the *Collier's* attorney. He related the story of his arrest, and as neither man was under any local spell pertaining to the power or threat of Fingy Conners, they unhesitatingly retaliated.

The following morning the *Buffalo Express* printed a statement made by Will Irwin followed by the arresting detectives' version of the same story.

INTIMATES IT WAS A JOB
Collier's Reporter's Version of Arrest of Hugh C. Weir.

Will Irwin writes a letter to The Express dealing with the arrest by the local police of Hugh C. Weir. Mr. Irwin wrote the article in Colliers' which W.J. Conners complains is libelous and on which he is suing. Mr. Irwin's letter follows.

Editor, Buffalo Express:
In this morning's issue of the Buffalo Express appears an article setting forth the alleged facts concerning the arrest of Hugh C. Weir, a magazine writer, for vagrancy. This article is false not only in many particulars, but in spirit. The facts are as follows.

Mr. Weir came here on Saturday from Ohio as a witness in the pending suit of Conners vs. Collier's. He reported to James W. Osborn, special counsel for Conners and went to live at the Hotel Statler. Mr Weir is a magazine writer of standing and has an income large enough to make a charge of vagrancy absurd.

He has been in very poor health for the last few years and has lost the sight of one eye and part of the sight of the other. By the prescription of his physician he takes (strychnine) as a heart stimulant.

During Monday evening Mr Weir ordered a glass of grape juice in a candy store or a drug store on Main St. With this drink he took a strychnine tablet. He was immediately arrested by two spy detectives who threw him into the back room of the store, knocked him down, and searched him. They confiscated several letters, including one asking him to testify in the Conners case, and took him to Precinct Three and locked him up. Mr. Weir showed his room key at the Statler and $70 in money to prove he was not a vagrant and asked to be able to communicate with friends and employ counsel. He repeated this request several times during the night and was each time refused. In the morning he was arraigned in the city court and charged with vagrancy. One or other of the detectives testified that they had seen him using "dope" and had found in his possession "several kinds of dope." The magistrate after hearing this testimony discharged Mr. Weir but advised him to leave Buffalo. It is not true as alleged in the Express that he left for Syracuse. He is here and living at the Hotel Statler. I believe it is not true that he or the magazine retracted an article of his against which acting Chief Taylor filed a suit for libel. And I am sure it is not true that he is a victim of any drug habit.

Mr. Weir's money and part of his property were restored by the police. The papers taken from him were not restored. When he demanded them he was told that they had "been lost."

Detectives' Statement

Detectives Jordan and McGowan who arrested Weir made this statement: "We stopped in a candy shop on Main Street on the right hand side going up between Broadway and Genesee streets after ten o'clock Monday night to get a drink of soda water, as neither of us drink intoxicants.

"We were seated at the counter when a man hurriedly entered, ordered some sort of a drink and swallowed it after placing some kind of pill in his mouth. As he threw back his head, a wig he was wearing became disarranged and almost fell off. He was nervous and shaking and we asked him what was wrong thinking he had taken some sort of poison. He said it was none of our business and tried to pass us to get to the door. One of us, McGowan, grabbed him by the arm and he made a smash at McGowan, cuffing him as he swung. Jordan said "He may have a gun. Search him." McGowan felt the outside of the man's pockets to find if he was armed. Weir resisted and as we were taking him from the store he slipped his overcoat and under coat and ran out toward Chippewa Street. We got him within a few feet and took him to the Pearl Street station. There he was searched as are all prisoners and locked up on the vagrancy charge. Half a dozen letters and about $4 as near as we can remember were taken from the prisoner. He was in a cell all night and did not ask for an attorney. If he had requested one the lawyer would have been called, as there is a standing order to that effect in all stations. In court on Tuesday morning before Judge Noonan said in discharging Weir. "I'll give you 24 hours to get out of this city. We have more than enough dope users here now." Weir, the police said, promised to get to Syracuse and as far as they learned he left Buffalo on Tuesday night. Last night Chief Regan sent a couple of detectives to all the leading hotels in the city including the Lafayette, Genesee, Iroquois, Statler etc. They reported Weir was not registered at any of them. Chief Regan says he will have Weir arrested if he is found about the streets. As for Irwin's intimation that Weir's charge against Inspector Taylor was not retracted, Inspector Taylor last night said "If Weir, Irwin or anybody else says that the attorneys representing the magazine in which that article against me appeared say that the case was not settled by a money transaction and a retraction, they are crazy and I can prove my statement at any time for any person."

Attorney Sears called Police Chief Michael Regan and promised him that he would be brought up in federal court the following morning on an obstruction of justice charge if he did not meet with them immediately. Regan did not argue, and not just because Fingy Conners had not succeeded in owning any of the federal judges. He canceled all appointments in order to accommodate Mr. Sears.

"I done all I could at that point for Fingy," Regan later told Detective Jim Sullivan afterward over beers at the Mutual Rowing Club's parlor, "but I sure as fuck weren't goin' to lose my job for that asshole."

CALLED ON BIG CHIEF
Collier's Representative Mr. Sears and Weir See Regan

Hugh C. Weir, the witness in the Collier-Conners libel suit who was grabbed by the police on Monday night accused of being a dope fiend and later requested to leave town by a city court judge, was taken to call on Chief Regan yesterday by Charles B. Sears of Rogers, Locke & Babcock, the New York attorneys for Collier's, and Will Irwin, according to a statement by the latter last night.

"We called Regan's attention to the statement he made in the Express," said Mr. Irwin, "that he had said Weir would be arrested if found on the street or if he stayed in Buffalo. We demonstrated to him that Weir had a right to be here and told him he intends to stay here. The Chief said he had not made the statement credited to him in the Express. He finally said Weir would not be molested by the police."

Chief Regan's side of the story could not be obtained last night.
—from the *Buffalo Express*

Will Irwin

Neither able to kill Weir nor drive him out of town, Fingy Conners was forced to reconsider his untenable position. It was without question now that Weir would testify, as would also Will Irwin. Fingy's brazenly engineered kidnapping of Weir attracted intense nationwide scrutiny, rather than just local investigation. Collier's lawyers were set to reveal details of Conners' previously unpublicized depraved criminality in public court with news reporters hanging on every word.

Fingy's attorney in the final minutes of the 11th hour offered to settle.

The details of the settlement were not made public. However, court records revealed that Fingy paid $50,000 to Collier's, $5,000 to Will Irwin for damages, and $5,000 to Weir for the crimes most recently ordered committed against him by the Buffalo Police Dept. Fingy was silent about the trial cancellation. Only tiny notices pertaining to it appeared, buried on inner pages of Buffalo newspapers. When it did not happen people naturally wondered why, but knew better than to probe very deeply.

It had been questioned if Conners was so incensed about the Will Irwin article in *Collier's*, why he waited seven years to sue. The reason was Collier's powerful publisher Peter Fenelon Collier despised Fingy almost as much as he hated Fingy's mentor, publisher William Randolph Hearst.

Collier, a fellow Irishman and an immigrant boasting a powerful rags-to-riches American Dream story, had friends whose importance, wealth and power eclipsed that of Fingy Conners. Conners wasn't about to tangle with a man holding so much damning information about him, but once Collier had died Fingy took the opportunity and swooped down on it.

Fingy Conners could not let well enough alone. Any sane person would count his blessings and shut up, hoping the whole thing would just go away. Not Conners. He openly boasted to all who would listen that he had "won." Soon after the settlement, with dust settling and all the principles back in their respective cities, Fingy claimed victory in the lawsuit. He lied that *Collier's* was ordered to pay him $100,000. This complete fabrication was echoed slapdash by newspapers across the land.

Mindful that if the *Collier's* attorneys became inflamed by his relentless lying he might end up right back in court again, only this time with Weir and Irwin as furiously vengeful witnesses against him and inciting another even more determined round with *Collier's* fed-up-to-here legal representatives, Fingy Conners grudgingly accepted his attorneys' advice and never mentioned the lawsuit, at least publicly, again.

His Lips Forgot The Taste Of Truth

The Mutual Rowing Club trophy cabinet.

Chewing The Fat

As preparations for child-killer Hickey's trial proceeded, much publicity was generated in competing newspapers with regard to the dueling alienists. With defense attorney Murphy bound and determined to have Hickey declared insane, he rummaged through the discards pile to find just the right "doctors" at the right price. The prosecution had no alternative but to hire its own alienists to counter Murphy's quacks' ludicrous exculpatory diagnoses of the killer.

It was loudly stated by those doctors on the defense side that no one in his right mind would do what Hickey had confessed to doing, ergo, he was insane and not responsible for his actions and should be found not guilty of the murder of Joey Joseph.

Such naked and incondonable excuse-fabricating infuriated Buffalo's citizenry.

At the Mutual Rowing Club boathouse parlor on one particular evening there was much heated conversation about the case as men gathered with a beer in one hand and a polishing cloth in the other as they participated in the twice-a-year ritual of brightening the scores of treasured trophies in the club's showcase.

No one supported a medical assessment of insanity. They agreed it was a red herring. All present had witnessed their fair share of evil acts of all stripes over the years, committed not just by common folk, but by higher officials as well. Police captains, judges and politicians had all committed terrible crimes against helpless victims. People died, officials' pocketbooks had been enriched, the eyes of justice conveniently averted, the public's attentions deflected elsewhere.

Ed Stanton, one of the club's oldest founding members, recollected to his mates that it was former First Ward Alderman Jack White who murdered the beloved Doc Green, the man who had personally brought quite a few of the club members into this world, including Ed himself.

"It was a terrible pill to swallow," he staunchly reminded them, "learnin' that the man who safely drew me out from me dear mother's belly into this existence was in turn removed from the same by that bastard Bostonian wot done so much damage to us in this ward durin' his long sorry tenure. And White was let off with no penalty at all 'cept fer a small fine! He was just let go, as if it was nothin' wot he done. Damn shame that was! An' not just because Doc Green took care of all of us, and our kids, but because no one should be allowed to get away with murderin' a good man."

Alderman JP Sullivan nodded in agreement sitting next to the club's trophy case, schuper in hand, not doing much polishing.

"Nobody was more set on getting rid of Jack White back then than me," sniffed JP, seizing the opportunity to promote himself.

JP had beaten Jack White when he initially ran against him for the office of First Ward Alderman in the 1889 election, but the vote was rigged to award White the victory regardless. This was an intentional scheme whose purpose was to use the powerful, grateful and now-indebted Jack White as a well-established manipulator in the Common Council to redraw Buffalo's ward lines the following year. This was done to the benefit of the vile Sheehan political machine. After that had been accomplished, White was done away with, and Sheehan brother John was put in White's former spot.

JP was rewarded with victory in the following year's election as the new alderman of the cunningly reconfigured 2nd Ward. It was something about which JP never went into in great detail since the feat was as unlawful as it was morally corrupt and he had played the pivotal role in its success.

"Them damn alienists," steamed JP's brother Jim, "are as crazy as the people they're claimin' to be helpin'."

Jim Sullivan as the founder and recognized elder statesman of the Mutual Rowing Club had practiced the art of persuasive lecture in his role as principal speaker at most of the club's more auspicious events. He was adept at presenting his ideas as cogently as a professor and as methodically as the trained police detective he was.

"What benefit," he continued, "to anyone except Hickey himself could possibly come of finding Hickey insane, and by default not responsible for his appalling crimes against innocent little children? I tell you, having spent as much time as I have talking to Hickey, that if he does go to the lunatic asylum, that slippery little weasel with his wily ways and well-practiced charm will have them fool asylum directors wrapped 'round his little finger in no time. He's tricked everybody so far, even by their own embarrassed admission. He's sure to convince them that he has recovered from his insanity and will be out walkin' the streets in a year or two, killin' children left and right once again—believe you me!

"To ignore the obvious truth that Hickey is evil and his actions are evil, and instead attribute these disgusting crimes to insanity goes against all that is human and good. It seems that his protectors have never even heard of the devil! Hickey might well be the devil himself in fact—the devil incarnate here on earth. Hickey is the ultimate example of a blackened soul, a withered heart, a roiling mud pot of a heinous mind. Hickey needs to pay mightily for it! Callin' evil by any other name erases the very meaning of the word entirely. Callin' evil 'insanity,' or a 'sickness,' is the coward's excuse that removes all responsibility from the evildoer. We must always question the true motives of these deplorable apologists! We inhabit a world wherein evil monsters live on our street, attend our church, loiter by our children's schools and playgrounds. These alienist doctors cannot tolerate the thought that deranged people pass by them unrecognized, since recognizing aberrant behaviors is the entire purpose of their profession in the first place. As a result they fall back on providin' them a convenient cover as a way to protect their own tenure.

"They advertise the wicked lie that men who don't realize the evil they are doing are somehow less dangerous than the ones who fully know! Well, let me tell you fellas somethin'. In all my years of policin' I encountered all types and been forced to deal with 'em. I got my own police knowledge that makes them doctors' knowledge look foolish by comparison. Them alienists know nothin' 'bout real people, neither good nor bad. It's us cops who deal with these bad apples day in and day out, who see the world as it really is, rather than the way we wish it was. We see the innocent and the guilty, the victims and the gangsters. Pretending that sheer evil is anything other than what it is, and workin' so hard as they do toward connivin' others into believing as they wish them to, well, that's just out-and-out razzle-dazzle!

"I always wished that them who defend the monsters would soon thereafter encounter their own monster and be made their victim, to teach 'em their lesson. But that's just wishful thinkin' on my part.

"Hickey has the type of smirkin' face that severely tempts otherwise decent men to ram their fist right through it. If I could get away with shootin' Hickey in his head, knowing what he done, picturin' in my mind the horror of my own son or my nephews bein' tortured at the hands of this freakish animal, I would be pleased to watch his brains explode out his shiny little bald skull. And he well knows it."

He didn't voice it as such, but all present knew Jim's escalating passion was related at least in part to his frustration, as unwarranted as it might have been, for Hickey slipping through his fingers ten years previous.

"Ye know, Jim, it ain't just them alienists that's fools," interjected Stanton, "it's that dirty attorney Dan Murphy that's doin' worse damage yet, tryin' his damnedest to find a way to free Hickey. Don't know how such a man with children of his own can sleep at night, much less live with hisself."

The alderman chimed in, "Murphy's near as corrupt a man as Hickey is, then. Like they always say, 'You are who you defend.'"

Jim had himself a bit of a chuckle, as it was his wife Hannah, JP's longtime adversary, who was so fond of reciting that particular saying.

"Oh, if I could only emulate our dear Grover Cleveland and take on the job of Hickey's executioner!" wished Jim.

A chorus of "What?" went up, as the evening gathering had swelled to twenty or more. After supper the neighborhood men habitually gravitated to the Mutuals' clubhouse. Even those who were not members were welcomed as long as they were in the company of a member and conducted themselves well.

The beer had loosened the crowd up a bit.

"What do you mean, 'executioner?'" JP asked.

"Oh, you remember now, dontcha, JP? When Cleveland was Sheriff, back when I was in the employ of Sam Clemens at his house up there on Delaware Avenue?"

"Nope. What *are* you talking about anyway, brother?"

"All right, don't tell me you never read it. Remember a month or two back I returned that copy of the *New York Times* to you with the long article I circled in red, the one written about Cleveland bein' the hangman, pullin' the pin on the trap door that sent the hoodlums danglin' at the end of a noose?"

"Oh, *that*. Uh, well, yeah, I have it put aside in the reading pile on my nightstand. I'm sure I'll get to it at some point."

"Wait!" Stanton said as others chorused the same. "What's this story yer talkin' about?"

"Well," began Jim, "way back in the early seventies...seventy-one, seventy-two, somewheres thereabouts...when we was kids, there were some terrible murders here. One was this fellow named Morrissey who long enjoyed a reputation as a bad man. He lived with his mother in a little house down on the towpath near Commercial Street. Morrissey come home drunk one night, and grabbin' a big bread knife from the table, stabbed his mother through the heart over some minor thing. She died instantly. Morrissey was convicted and set to hang, so me and Mike Regan naturally went down to the courthouse to witness the event. There weren't no Edisonia picture shows back then!" he laughed. "There must've been a thousand people millin' about, but they wouldn't allow no one to view the hangin'. They had the yard blocked off with big tarps so's nobody could see inside.

"Now back then, the state law was such that any person convicted of murder in the first degree must be hanged by the neck until dead, and the enforcement of that law was expressly and literally imposed upon the Sheriff of the county where the conviction was secured. That person in this instance was Grover Cleveland. When Cleveland was campaignin' for Mayor you may recall he visited old Halloran's Saloon to speak his piece, and me and you JP, we waited out on the stoop for him to arrive, remember?"

"Yep, I do remember that night," replied his brother.

"Before that though, when he was runnin' for Sheriff, Cleveland said that if he was elected that he fully intended to discharge the duties of the Office strictly according to the letter of the law, without fear or favor. He won that election handily because of that bold promise.

"For a decade previous to that there had been a Deputy Sheriff named Jacob Emerick on the job. Cleveland's predecessors had for many years followed the custom of tasking Emerick with any and all of their more loathsome duties, including public executions. So often had he officiated at hangings that publicly and in the newspapers Jacob Emerick came to be known as "Hangman Emerick." Although Emerick was a rugged fellow and not oversensitive, this nickname became a source of embarrassment to him and his family, and after a while as his kids grew older a feeling of shame and resentment about it began to grow within him.

"I recall being angered that as bad a fellow as Morrissey was, and as terrible was his crime, that somehow he managed to secure himself some worthwhile friends who until the end were trying to save him. All I could think of back then was our stepfather Peter Halloran stabbing our dear mother with a butcher knife when we were boys, and how she might well have died, and that Morrissey should well pay for his crime—and be right quick about it.

"Finally the day came, and Cleveland—I have to say how much I admired the man for doin' this—Cleveland announced publicly that he would personally perform his duty as executioner. His friends and family tried to talk him out of it, as he entertained higher political aspirations as we all know, but he would not budge an inch on the matter. He pointed to the letter of the law requiring the Sheriff to perform the duty and insisted that he had no moral right to impose upon a subordinate the more degrading tasks that attached to his elected Office. He felt an ethical obligation to at long last relieve from Emerick and his family as far as possible the onus of the wretched title he had been shackled with of 'Hangman.'

"Cleveland had said, 'Jake and his family have as much right to enjoy public respect as I have, and I am not ready to add to the weight that has already brought him close to public execration.'

"Thus it happened that Grover Cleveland, obscured by a screen, pulled the pin that dropped the gallows' trap upon which Morrissey in his final moments on earth stood. There are a few Buffalo men who yet live who can bear out the statement that this act of ending a man's life made Cleveland quite ill for some days afterward. He was not so indifferent a man as people have been lead to believe. The following year he again performed that same duty upon John Gaffney, the Canal Street shooter."

Silence followed the story, as many had not known these facts about the highly esteemed President of the United States and former Mayor of Buffalo.

"Gosh," "Gee willikers," and "Jesus Christ," were uttered in response.

"Well, now I know what I'll be readin' tonight before goin' to sleep," joked the Alderman.

His Lips Forgot The Taste Of Truth

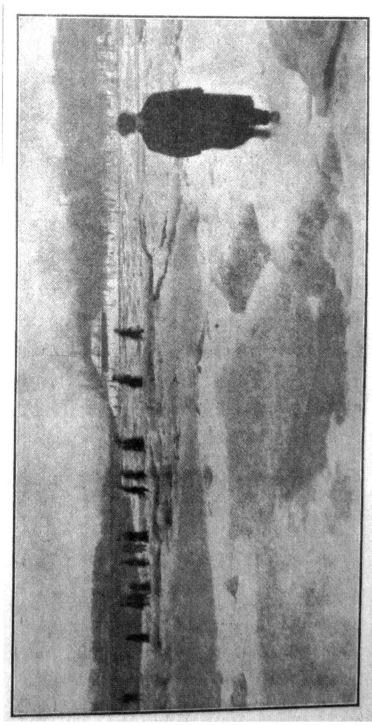

WHEN THE AMERICAN FALL RAN DRY: PEOPLE WALKING AROUND THE BRINK.

1909
THE DAY NIAGARA FALLS RAN DRY

Crraaack!

Alderman John P. Sullivan's ears pained brutally at the distant explosive sound. He gazed in horror out the office window over the endless white expanse of Lake Erie ice. It was a gray-bright day, the silvery sky so identical in hue to that of the frozen surface of Lake Erie that the horizon was completely lost. Sky blended with ice indistinctly, causing dizzying disorientation. There was no up or down, only an endless featureless void.

Again JP heard the dreaded shattering.

"God damned son of a bitch!" he uttered a little too loudly. He turned to make sure no one had overheard his cursing. He did have a reputation to uphold after all.

"I heard that, Pop," laughed son Thomas from just the other side of JP's office door.

"Don't you dare tell your mother," JP shot back.

"Say, Pop...that raise for me we've been talking about—this might be a good time..."

The alderman cut him off. "Yes, this might be a good time for me to begin cutting back on all the extraneous and redundant forces holding this business back from its rightful success!"

Nothing but silence was afterward heard from Thomas' side.

If JP had discerned no headache walking into the Sullivan Ice Co. office that morning, he certainly had one now. Fiscal tragedy was threatening minute-by-minute there at the vast ice storehouse on the beach situated along the Hamburg Turnpike.

An ice dam had begun to form at the mouth of the Niagara River two days previous, and still another downstream, right above the American Falls at the top of Goat Island. JP's stomach had been tied in knots ever since. Unless the dams were disrupted, broken apart somehow, the astonishing volume of water relentlessly flowing from the vast inland ocean formed by four of the five Great Lakes toward the mouth of the Niagara would begin to back up, raising the lake level currently contained under near ten inches of solid, beautiful, profitable intact ice.

The ultimate outcome of the nightmare unfolding at that very moment was the fracturing of the lake ice just as it had almost reached peak thickness for harvesting, making it virtually unharvestable. Shortly thereafter lakefront communities would most likely face flooding from the backup with the below-zero air temperatures immediately freezing the inundation into a treacherous imprisoning conglomeration until a thaw or some other welcome force of nature destroyed the dam.

Ice harvesting was the alderman's bread and butter. Presently, with little warning, that business was threatened. Splintered ice could not be cut. Shattered ice could not be safely ventured out upon by his crew of seventy men. Workers would have to be laid off. Families would suffer. The alderman's finances, always a challenge to untangle even under the most favorable of circumstances, would be plunged into indecipherable chaos.

And I just spent all that money on that gig lowering machine, he thought to himself. The apparatus had cost a pretty penny, having a state of the art 38 foot drop. Its purpose was to more efficiently remove ice from the ice house to the waiting wagons and rail cars below. It was portable so that it could be also used within the ice house itself to transfer product from one location or level to another.

Hundreds of ice fishermen were presently encamped all over uncounted square miles of frozen Lake Erie in the immediate area bridging Western New York and Southern Ontario. If rupturing took place, many could be trapped and lost with no alternative for making their way back to the safety of shore. JP could only imagine their panic if the solid surface supporting the fishermen's closet-sized wooden shacks, their sleighs pulled by beloved horses, their dear children brought along to get them out of their mothers' hair, their faithful dogs, shattered and flooded and separated. JP wasted no time in pushing the disturbing pictures from his imaginings.

He telephoned Gerhardt Lang, who had long pestered the alderman to allow the brewer to make permanent use of the huge, highly visible but blank facade of the icehouse to advertise his brewery. The alderman was hesitant to again deface his own business with advertisements for other businesses, having just the year before eradicated the last of the previous lot, but the looming loss of the ice crop called for desperate action.

❧❧❧

At that same moment JP's brother, Detective Jim Sullivan, was dispatched to N⁰ 202 Elk Street with his partner Jerry Lynch. An ambulance from the Fitch Hospital preceded them. Upon arrival they witnessed thirty-five year old Mrs. Katherine Cooley prostrated on the icy sidewalk, flat on her back with a two-foot long board nailed to her face.

It had been embedded there since the previous night. She could not speak since her jaw had been nailed shut.

Jim and Jerry followed the ambulance to the hospital where surgeons labored to remove the two nails, each about three inches long. Complicating the procedure, the nails were bent and rusted. She had been knocked unconscious by the blow and was afterward carried into the house by her children from her place in the snow out front of the family home.

Mrs. Kate O'Day of N.º 47 Moore Street had called on Mrs. Cooley the previous night and accused her of turning her stepson against her. In the row that followed, Mrs. O'Day picked up the board and with both hands propelling it delivered a brutal blow to the left side of Cooley's face, knocking her out cold. No reason was given for the ambulance not being summoned sooner. Come morning Cooley made her way outside her house with her face securely impaled to the heavy board but the pain and shock caused her to collapse, whereby an ambulance was finally summoned by someone undetermined.

The detectives returned to the scene to arrest Mrs. O'Day. She protested her innocence, but her own children verified that she had disappeared and not returned home the previous night. They had been terribly worried and had slept little.

❀❀❀❀

The alderman's namesake, Johnny Sullivan Jr., his youngest son, excitedly enlisted his best friend Jack Hartnett to skip school and ride the Yellow Car to Niagara Falls. The car was unusually jammed with excited thrill seekers of all sorts, all having heard the irresistible news: Niagara Falls had gone dry.

An immovable ice jam had formed just upriver from Prospect Point at the American Falls. A long-continued northeast wind held back the water and bared the Niagara River channel so that the ice had a chance to accumulate in the rapids and form a wall from the head of Goat Island to the mainland. A similar spectacle had been afforded recently only twice in local memory, in 1848 and again in 1903.

The Horseshoe Falls still flowed, but at a diminished volume due to the additional ice bridge that had also formed at the mouth of the river up at Buffalo. This obstructed flow threatened the electricity supply, for electricity production was created by and dependent upon the volume and power of the flowing water.

The American Falls on the other hand had been stopped almost completely, save for a few comparative driblets. Such a natural phenomenon was considered a once-or-twice-in-a-lifetime occurrence.

Upon arrival the boys headed hurriedly to Prospect Point to witness for themselves. They were astonished to see hundreds of people walking out along the rocky brink where normally vast volumes of water thundered mightily over the lip. Some weak rivulets were running still, but for the most part the American Falls had completely stopped. The boys peered over the brink to see massive accumulations of ice-covered rock at the base which normally would be obscured under vast quantities of crashing water and rising mists. The amassment attested to the destructive eroding power of centuries of falling water.

"Let's go!" Hartnett exclaimed.

"Better not, lads," advised a man who had overheard them. "That ice dam could collapse at any time, and if you're caught out there when it breaks, you'll never make it to safe ground in time, what with the treacherous footing."

Deaf to the warning, they descended the bank to join the crowds exploring the naked riverbed.

"Don't say I never warned yous!" came the man's final caution.

Their hiking destination was Goat Island, but one powerful rivulet could not be traversed, the slippery obstructive ice accumulation adjacent making such any such effort dangerous. They backtracked and walked upriver to Goat Island bridge, crossed the span, then walked toward the lookout at the brink. The riverbed was completely dry in that spot, so they climbed the rail and carefully made their way down the embankment out toward mid-stream where scores of people had gathered on the dry riverbed, some with Kodaks.

"Damn! How could I forget my Kodak?" cursed the alderman's son.

"Well," a nearby stranger said, "I'll be happy to snap one of you and your friend."

"Gosh Mister, that would be swell! That's some fancy camera you got there," Johnny marveled.

Arms around each other's shoulder, the volunteer had only just stepped backward so as to include the wide expanse of dry riverbed within the frame of his N⁰ 3 Folding Pocket Kodak Model G Camera with Rapid Rectilinear Lens when suddenly shouting rose up from those standing mid-stream.

"Run! Run! The dam's broke!" people screamed.

Panicked men struggled to pull along ladies whose long skirts and heavy woolen coats interfered in their speedy evacuation. Mothers grabbed children's hands, losing their grip and pulling their gloves clean off in their hysteria. People scrambled in whatever direction safety seemed most reachable, crying. The boys began to run, their path impeded by gargantuan beached ice floes tilting at wild angles, the floes having been deposited obstructively *in situ* when the water had receded.

The boys took off running and wildly slipping when suddenly they heard the man's shouts.

"Help! Help me boys!" cried the man with the fancy Kodak. He had gotten his foot caught up to his shin in the joining between two mammoth ice blocks. For an instant the boys didn't know what to do, as distant screams were now mingled with an ominous rushing sound.

"Help me please!" he begged, his body prone on the ice and twisted in an awkward and painful-looking position.

"We gotta help him!" Hartnett said.

Apprehensively peering upstream, the boys backtracked to the man.

"I can't move!" the man shouted.

The boys assessed his predicament as the rumble grew louder. Water was rushing toward them but they had no way of knowing how close it would come. It was not like a tidal wave, such as a giant wave of water extending from riverbank to riverbank, but rather was a piecemeal meandering flood tossing huge ice floes clear up in the air in the distance as it sought a pathway through which to reestablish its normal course.

Johnny said, "You grab that arm and I'll take this one, and let's twist him 'round onto his back."

"My God, you'll break me in half!" cried the Kodak man.

"No, Mister! We won't. We're just settin' you straight so we can pull your leg out!" Johnny said. The boys stood motionless waiting for instruction. The roar drew closer.

"Never mind! Go ahead, do it your way! Just get me out of here!"

And with that they twisted him back into position as he screamed, "Oh! My poor back!" The boys each grabbed an arm allowing him to pull himself up mostly on his own power. He was then able to extricate his leg with minimal fuss.

"Go!" he shouted. "Go! I'm all right now! Save yourselves!"

The boys ran, being among the last to vacate the flooding riverbed. From the higher vantage point they looked back to see the Kodak man very painfully limping toward safety, incrementally and unbalanced, slipping and sliding, his camera nowhere to be seen. With great difficulty he negotiated the slick wildly askew grounded ice floes piled high in his path of escape.

Gazing upstream and seeing they were not as yet in mortal peril, the boys backtracked to provide support to the man and help him to shore.

Shouts and commotions continued as more warnings sang out from those upstream witnessing the acceleratingly serious collapse of the ice dam. Luckily, the ice levee as yet still had not given way in its entirety as a single unit, but rather was breached in places, allowing the Niagara River to rush through here and there.

Everyone was thus able to reach safety without exception, the only casualties being the man's expensive Kodak, a few hats and gloves and a walking cane or two. Once on solid ground, everyone laughed nervously as to their close call, the boys being no exception.

"How can I ever thank you?" stuttered the man. "Boy, that was a close one!"

"Ain't no need, Mister," said Johnny. "Sorry we couldn't save your Kodak. Say, you don't look so good. Are you hurt?"

"Seems I twisted my back, that's all, I'm just having a little trouble breathing without shooting pains going up my spine."

"Oh no! We're sorry Mister! But we didn't know how else to..."

"No! Stop that now! You did good. Your did very, very good. I might be dead if not for you boys." He tried to straighten up, using the guardrail for support. " Say, are you fellas still in school as yet?" he asked.

"Yes sir," they answered in unison. "Ninth Grade."

"Well then here, take my calling card, won't you?" He gave each boy a card. "If you find yourselves in need of employment at some point, you both come and see me, and I'll do whatever I can to help you in return."

"Why, thanks, Mister!" Jack Hartnett said, briefly studying his card. "Hey Mister...you came all the way from Rochester just to see the dry Falls?"

"Yes I did, son."

Johnny chimed in, "You sure you're all right now?"

"Yes, yes boys, I'll just be resting here for a bit. Don't concern yourselves. Nothing's broken. Just a little sore, that's all. Just need to catch my breath," he said with a pained smile. "I'll be fine in a minute or two, thanks to you both." It was obvious he was in quite a bit of pain.

"Aw, it was nothin," Johnny smiled.

People had now rushed toward the rails at all points of vantage to watch transfixed as a growing volume of roiling water and mammoth ice floes launched skyward by the power of the unleashed river raced headlong for the brink. At first confined to just three or four powerful streams, within thirty minutes' time the volume expanded to a deafening roar of whitewater and somersaulting icebergs as the American Falls returned to its near-normal powerful force.

The boys stood with the injured man marveling at the unstoppable intensity of nature, hesitant to abandon him there.

"Imagine, Johnny—just a few minutes ago we was standin' out there in the middle where few others ever stood before us. That makes us pioneers of a sort, don't it?" asked Hartnett.

"More like trailblazers, Jack. I'd say. How many others 'cept you 'n' me can say they ever done *that*?"

The recovering Kodak man interjected, "I'd say 'heroes' is a more accurate and appropriate description of you two boys. That's what you both are, lads. *Heroes*. Your parents should be very proud of how they raised you."

❧❧❧

Upon arriving home safe and sound, Johnny never mentioned the day's events to anyone, neither to his parents nor to his siblings.

"Where on earth have you been, Johnny?" his mother scolded. "We been waiting! Supper's ready."

"Gimme a minute Ma. Gotta get these wet clothes off."

After prying his cold wet socks from his icy feet he opened his top drawer to retrieve a dry pair. Before dropping the man's calling card into the jumble of clean footwear he scanned it: George Eastman, Eastman Kodak Co., Rochester N.Y.

Then, with neither a second thought nor glimmer of recognition, he slammed the drawer shut where the card would lie dormant and overlooked until the day it changed his life forever.

THE FIRST WARD IV

BRIDGET BLACK

Despite the crafty old lady's having resided in the Erie County Poor House for far too many months at this point—if we're to consider the attendants' complaints—she managed to retain an undeniable measure of fighting pride about her.

She filched a quarter and a dime from the unattended purse of an especially despised custodian—not that she didn't hate each and every last one of them. She then mustered the strength to sneak out and haul her arthritic bones aboard a Main Street streetcar destined for the public library downtown. There with the help of a hesitant librarian, who nearly retched from the stink of the old woman, she discovered the name in the Buffalo Directory for which she had long searched, along with an address: "McGowan, Ruth, w., 68 South Street, Buffalo."

On her way back to catch the streetcar before her absence was detected, an automobile knocked Bridget Black down.

❦❦❦❦

Hannah Sullivan's friend Ruth was having a miserable time of it.

For two endless days her head had pounded viciously, relentlessly. The only activity she could manage was a soft moaning, for even the sound of her own voice was torture. When Hannah again arrived at her door to help attend to her, Ruth sent her away.

"There's nothing you can do for me Hannah. It hurts even to breathe. Please go. I need to just lie down quietly."

Hannah walked away dejectedly, worried about her trusted confidante, fearful about her friend's predilection.

Laudanum, Ruth claimed, was the only thing that had provided relief from her history of head injuries. The drug, a combination of morphine and opium, had ensnared her previously at least twice before that Hannah knew about. Each attempt to wrestle away from its enslaving clutches had required of Ruth superhuman determination and fortitude.

She told Hannah of a time years previous when in response to an advertisement in The Cosmopolitan she invested a small fortune in The Chinese Cure from The

Chinese Drug Co. It turned out to be a sham. But now she was critically ill and again desperate for deliverance from her severe torment. Any deliverance. This put her in a precarious position whereby anything at all which might provide relief at any monetary cost or physical risk was an option.

As Hannah made her way back down South Street toward home, her efforts to block out the screeching of the Buffalo Union Furnace's hoists loading product into a whaleback docked in the Union Slip, along with her dread that her friend might even die, insulated her within her thoughts. She did not notice the patrol wagon slowing as it passed her. Had she turned and looked behind her she would have seen the police stop in front of Ruth's cottage.

Ruth sat in her armchair facing away from the windows overlooking the Buffalo River, a wet towel over her eyes. The towering cement grain elevators across the way mercifully blocked out a good portion of the cruel late afternoon sun. She clutched the arms of the chair so hard her pink knuckles turned white. She rocked back and forth, eyes throbbing, trying to push out of her thoughts her longing for the vial of morphine she kept hidden in a Chinese vase on the floor next to her chair for just such an emergency as this.

As per a recent campaign by Chief Michael Regan, the Buffalo police had become more vigilant than ever regarding those who might use pain-alleviating drugs, despite their own doctor's prescribing them freely for medical purposes. The medical profession had made far greater strides in the pharmaceutical methods for controlling and relieving pain than it had in curing the illnesses that caused the torment in the first place. New laws had been passed as more and more suffering people sought temporary, or even in some of the more desperate cases, permanent relief from life's travails.

As Ruth sat there dwelling in the severity of her agony, a loud knock came at her door. She assumed Hannah had come back, and thus ignored it. The visitor was persistent. Each knock increased in volume, ricocheting cruelly inside her pounding skull. Suddenly, squinting tight against the blinding glare as she turned to look, a scowling face appeared at the glass.

It was a policeman.

Having spotted her, the officer hollered that she must open the door. Ruth required all her might to rise from her chair. She wobbled to the entrance. She cracked the door a few inches. The searing light stabbed her in the brain. She shielded her eyes with a trembling hand.

"Mrs. McGowan? Mrs. Ruth McGowan?"

"Yes? What do you want? Can't you see I'm ill?"

"Mrs. McGowan, may we enter?"

She struggled to gain her bearings.

"Officer, no. I have a terrible, terrible headache and I am feeling very sickly. Please go away."

"Mrs. McGowan, do you know a Bridget Black?"

The mere speaking of that vile name was enough to send her right to the floor. She held tight to the door latch in order to remain upright.

"Oh my. Why do you ask?"

"Do you know Bridget Black?" he repeated.

They've come to my door to tell me the monster's mercifully, thankfully dead, Ruth thought to herself.

"Yes, at one time I knew a certain Bridget Black, but I have not seen her for many, many years."

"Bridget Black is confined to a bed at the Sisters Hospital as we speak. She says you are her daughter."

Ruth remained silent, still defending her eyes from the searing glare. This was the last thing she needed, or expected, to hear.

"Please officer, I am very ill. Please leave me alone."

"Bridget Black is being released from the hospital but the doctors want her not to end up in the Erie County Poor House again. She says she is your mother. She told the doctors you would take her in."

"What? That's impossible! Can't you see? I can barely stand upright myself!" she cried.

"She is in a very bad way, ma'am. She will probably die soon."

"What is she ill with?"

"That we are not at liberty to say, for the sake of her dignity. The doctors will tell you all you need to know. Please contact them today."

He scribbled on a piece of paper and placed it in her hand.

Anxious to get rid of them she agreed she would, and abruptly closed the door. She raced for her chair lest she topple.

❧❧❧

The following day a letter arrived from the attorney, and with it escalated the awful throbbing as before. Pain notwithstanding, the letter's contents so rattled Ruth that she was propelled from her chair and down the street to Hannah's house. As Hannah cleaned the bathroom there came a rapid knock on the door. Zeke shot up and ran to the entrance barking. Hannah pulled him away by his collar and opened the door. Ruth stood there quivering.

"Hannah, they can't do this to me! They simply can't! You have to help me. Ask your Jim to help me!"

"What on earth Ruth?"

"Read this! It's from a lawyer! They're saying my mother's sick and I have to take her in! They say I have to take care of her and let her live in my house! They can't do that, can they? My mother living with me would be like the eight level of hell!"

Ruth gripped tightly to the door jamb trembling like a leaf.

"Ruth please, come inside and sit down before you fall down," Hannah urged.

※※※

Hannah Sullivan recalled the many stories from years gone by printed in the newspapers in which adult children were publicly shamed by the courts for not caring for the needs of their aged and sickly parents—even in some cases where the offspring had documented the parent's history of having been terribly cruel and neglectful towards them. Despite that, as a Good Catholic self-described, Hannah had nonetheless been stricken by these accounts of destitute elderly being abandoned by ungrateful families, wondering what kind of ingrates were some of these unfeeling sons and daughters.

Her views changed abruptly upon being informed by Ruth that she was being sued for support by the violent mother who had thrown her out onto the street to fend for herself while as yet a child. Her mother, a career prostitute, no longer able to make a living plying her chosen trade, was currently subsisting in the poor house.

Ruth, if she lost the suit, would have no other choice but to break into her life's savings. For decades she had painstakingly socked away money to meet the challenges and soften the blow of the inevitable maladies certain to present themselves in her later years. She had never wanted to be a burden to others. Soon after the attorney's letter arrived she was faced with the prospect of engaging the services of an advocate herself at significant expense, as much as she hated the entire lot of them, in order to defend against this parasitic threat to her future livelihood.

"These lawyers have become a necessary evil. They have cemented themselves into society so firmly that their expensive services will always be required," Ruth complained bitterly to Hannah.

It was being demanded of Ruth to appear before a judge to argue as to why she should not be made to support and nurse the barbarous and brutal mother who had with regularity beaten her senseless, who had encouraged paying men to have their dirty ways with her, who had banished her from her house while yet a young girl to live on the street, who had cared not one single particle for her own child.

"The sheer gall of that woman!" Ruth cried. "And those courts too, ruling that children who barely survived their parents' torture be compelled in their adulthood to diminish their own finances, not to mention peace in their own home, so as to care for those who did not so much as give a flying whit for them!"

Hannah listened sympathetically.

"Hannah, I can barely stand without vomiting from the pain," she groaned. "How in God's name am I going to appear in court in my condition? How can I possibly argue my case? I am in no circumstance to even feed myself properly!"

Widow Ruth had neither living husband nor children. Hannah had often worried about her friend's state of affairs and promised herself that she would always be there for Ruth in peace or upheaval. She offered an off-the-cuff proposal.

"What say you, rather than be compelled to take this monster into your home, sell your house and move in with my family? You can hide the money from the sale of the property, claim you lost it or perhaps got it stolen from you. Me and Jim can say you're penniless and that we took you in out of charity."

"Oh dear Hannah. Thank you. You are the sweetest thing...but allow me to first try and fight against this outrage. Surely many others as well have been caught in this vicious scheme supported by the courts. This absurdity must end. The same society that refused to interfere when parents horribly mistreated their children gladly takes up the cause of these same monstrous parents against the very children they defiled once the time arrives for the parents to face the consequences of their actions.

"They are defending and absolving the criminal while punishing the victim over and again—and that must stop! I was abandoned as a child by the neglectful authorities, which was unforgivable enough, but now these same minions of the devil want to torment me still and yet again, in both instances because these bureaucrats have failed miserably at their appointed job. How vile these miscreants are!"

※※※

That evening, frazzled over her friend's plight, Hannah swallowed her pride and went next door. There she sat across the desk from her brother-in-law the alderman in his little home office.

"JP, can I talk to you about something—the way I would talk to a priest in confession?"

"What is it now, Hannah?" he sighed, thumping his fingers impatiently on his green ink blotter.

"I mean I want to speak candidly with you about somethin' very, very private, about a friend who's in trouble, but you can't never tell nobody, 'cause she don't know I'm comin' to you."

"Hannah, have you yet to learn the importance of remaining faithful to your friends with respect to their privacy?" he stated scoldingly.

"JP, please do not lecture. Me and you got a long history of not gettin' along together, but nevertheless we're still family. And my friend, she's like family too. And when trouble comes to any one of us, as family we need to stick together. I am begging you to promise that what I am about to tell you will never go beyond this little office of yours. Blood is thicker than water, after all."

"And shit is thicker than blood, Hannah!" he shot back. "So exactly what is this latest shit you're up to now?"

JP felt he was being pushed into a corner by his adversarial in-law and didn't like it one bit. But Hannah had rarely come to him like this...really only once before, to tell him that his young Johnny was being abused by that priest, for which the alderman was admittedly grateful.

Stone-faced, she did not respond to his cruelty with justified anger as might well be expected, which caused the alderman to soften a bit.

"All right Hannah," he said reluctantly after a few moments' thought. "I've had a bad day. It's made me cross. I promise. Go ahead. Tell me what's upsetting you."

"Thank you, JP. Do you recall meeting my dear friend Ruth, who came to Thanksgiving dinner here at your home a while back?"

"The woman with all that disarranged copper hair? Yes."

"Ruth was raised in a house of ill repute down at the Ganson end of Michigan Street. Did you know that?"

"My God. No, I did not."

"Not only that, but her mother was a prostitute in that house, and was very, very cruel to her. She beat poor Ruth to within an inch of her life. She did the most terrible things to her. She had a habit of knockin' Ruth over the head with a heavy hairbrush, leavin' Ruth to this day with terrible headaches lastin' for days on end.

"A while back Ruth slipped on the ice in front of her house and banged her head on the sidewalk. At the hospital the doctors took X-rays. These films showed a terrible history of damage to her skull in the form of a spider's web of cracks that have since healed, dozens and dozens of them. The doctors were shocked when she told them what her mother done to her. They told her they were surprised she had managed to survive these beatings at all.

"When she was only fourteen Ruth was banished from that evil house, tossed out onto the streets like so much trash. She hasn't spoken to that awful woman since. But only recently she got a letter from an attorney sayin' she was bein' sued for support by her mother who's now sick and old, and Ruth is absolutely beside herself! If she weren't so sick herself these days she'd fully intend to fight this in court and expose her mother's cruelty. But considerin' the many articles I read in the newspapers in the past about cases where adult children who were on the outs from their parents were portrayed as ungrateful wretches for not supportin' them? I fear she would not only be publicly lambasted, but that the courts would rule against her, considering all them other historic examples.

"JP, this so-called mother of hers nearly killed her, and made her early life a livin' hell. She exposed her to the dregs of society and failed to protect her from those terrible men—some who you yourself still do business with to this very day."

JP flinched.

"And now the cruelest blow of all will be the publicity and the likelihood that she will once again be victimized by both her mother and the courts. Ruth is very sick herself right now and cannot even leave her house, let alone mount a proper legal defense in court! She may lose her savings and perhaps even her good reputation. She's got nobody to take care of her when she herself becomes old and sick, and now that awful old mother of hers is threatening to suck away what little money Ruth has managed to save. Can't you please do somethin' to help her?"

JP shrugged. "Hannah, what do you expect from me? What could I possibly do? Bribe a judge? No, I will not. Threaten or blackmail some lawyer? Impossible. Hire someone to kill the miserable old lady? Well—perhaps you might discuss such a possibility with your own brother."

Hannah was taken aback by the savage dig. Ignoring the almost insurmountable urge to respond in kind, she forged ahead.

"JP, you got a lot of political power, and famous friends and many favors owed. Ruth is an innocent victim who's got nobody and needs your help. She voted for you after all. You're always helpin' your other constituents! Why not her?"

"Well...let me think about it. I'll see if I can come up with something," he mumbled dismissively. He stood to signal the end of the conversation.

She knew right then he wasn't going to do anything. He could do favors for everybody else—get men jobs, get delinquent boys out of jail and good boys into the university, perform all sorts of good deeds all the live-long day for everybody and anybody in the First Ward. But his own sister-in-law apparently was a different story entirely. Decades of acrimony existed between the two.

"Now I have some important telephone calling to do if you don't mind."

He picked up the receiver on his telephone whose severed wire ended under the rug on which he stood. The unconnected phone was utilized to fake problem-solving conversations for the benefit of drop-in constituents he might want to be quickly rid of. Hannah knew as well as he did that telephone did not work, and he knew she knew.

She nodded with full understanding and left to walk back next door.

She opened the door to find Zeke whining behind it. He needed to relieve himself. She undid his leash from the hook on the door frame and connected it to his studded collar, then led him away from the house toward the river.

"Hallo there Mrs. Sullivan," called the young men on South Street in unison. They carried a 4-man racing scull hoisted over their heads from the boathouse and across South St. toward the little Mutuals dock.

"Hello lads," she responded with a wan wave, unsmiling. She stopped to watch them for a few moments as they settled the craft into the water and climbed in. Zeke pulled insistently. He needed to poop, and his favored area was in the weeds just over the Erie tracks. Hannah obeyed. She halted when he located his customary spot and stood there waiting the ceremony out.

"Oh, dear sweet Jesus Mary and Joseph, Zeke! Pee-yew! What on earth did you eat for Christ's sakes?"

As she stood there anxiously waiting for the sputtering dog to noisily finish his business she gazed back at the Mutuals' boathouse. JP's cruel remark about her brother came back to needle her.

Suddenly she had a brainstorm.

Quickly she led Zeke back to the house. She stooped to clean his feet, then lifted his tail to inspect that area before approving his entrance, and the two clambered up the stairway. She went right to the cheap little Larkin desk in the parlor, turned on the lamp and put pen to paper:

> Dear Mr. Conners,
>
> I have some information about my brother David J. Nugent that will be of utmost seriousness to you. I cannot divulge the concerning details in writing. I urge you to meet with me face to face very soon, before it's too late. Please have your secretary telephone me with a time and place, preferably away from your office for privacy reasons. I suggest we meet at Pet's when the last morning Mass is over.

Regards,
Hanna Nugent Sullivan

THE FIRST WARD IV

The Trial of J. Frank Hickey

Hannah was perturbed that her husband was not able to procure her tickets for that day's court proceedings. She and her circle of church friends had become obsessed with the trial of little Joey Joseph's confessed murderer. It was all they talked about. It was all *anyone* in the city talked about, for that matter. Even her sister-in-law Annie had recently made friendly overtures and engaged in discussions about the case, despite her having raked Hannah over the coals about her "unhealthy" interest in it only recently.

Hannah's friend Ruth McGowan, despite waging a battle against her own personal demons, was the most even-keeled of Hannah's confidantes on the subject, she succeeding in bringing Hannah back on track during her more emotional outbursts over the affair.

Meanwhile, Jim too was concerned about his wife. His Hannah had too much time on her hands these days, devouring the newspapers for bits and pieces for which to over-concern herself. Daughter Nellie had become distant and cold, refusing to talk to her mother about it at all, despite her willingness to chatter endlessly about it with her coworkers at the Larkin Building.

Jim was assigned to accompany Joey's father George Joseph, who that day was scheduled to testify at the trial without his aggrieved wife present to spare her the anguish of hearing the horrifying details. Jim decided for the sake of peace at home he would tell Hannah he was simply denied tickets for her and her friend Mary Sweeney. Each day previous to that Hannah had brought to court one member of her pedro club as a guest, and Mary had been anxiously awaiting her turn, except now that Mary's day had arrived there were no tickets waiting.

"Hannah, the fact is everyone involved in this trial is in the same boat as me, with wives and sisters and friends who all want the favor of a ticket. It's only a fluke that I got you all them tickets I already did. I had to make promises I'd rather not. Pure and simple, too many people are clamoring for too few tickets."

She didn't believe him of course. With very few exceptions he had always procured tickets for her to previous exciting trials. Why would this one be any different? She suspected Jim was stonewalling her intentionally.

The day previous, after the end of court session, as Hickey had been in the process of being removed back to his cell, Nezla Joseph waited in the corridor for the killer. Surprisingly she had expressed a demand to lay eyes on the confessed slayer of her little boy irregardless of her husband and Dr. Ross both protesting the wisdom of such an encounter. She had previously not even been able to summon the emotional strength to sit in the courtroom to observe the proceedings, but now puzzlingly it seemed she was ready to face her fears head on.

Detective Jim Sullivan, whose primary duty was to prevent the curious public from engaging the grieving couple, relayed her message to Lackawanna Police Chief Gilson. Gilson thought it an odd turn of events, since in each of his encounters with Nezla Joseph she had dependably exhibited all the fortitude of a newborn baby lamb, but he did not object to the meeting. At the end of that day's proceedings they all gathered in the lower corridor through which Hickey would be passing on his way to the tunnel that would take him back to his cell at Police Headquarters. As Hickey came into view, led handcuffed down the stairs by Deputy Sheriff Crane, Nezla stepped timidly forward, hand shaking, holding aloft a cabinet card with the image of her murdered child for Hickey to look at to remind him of the little boy he killed.

In her limited English she lashed out.

"You dirty bad man!" she screamed. "You killed my baby! You stoled my little boy! He never hurt nobody! Look at his sweet face! Why did you kill him? Why? Why?"

Without warning, in direct and unprecedented contrast to the collapsed wreck of a human she had always previously displayed herself to be, Nezla launched herself through the air at the killer, teeth gnashing. She was captured by her arms mid-leap by Detective Sullivan, who held her aloft kicking and screaming, she leaving a track of fingernail scratches across his face after freeing one arm.

Hickey responded with no more concern than if he had just avoided colliding with a low hanging beam or an open cupboard door, and continued on his way unfazed.

Nezla sobbed uncontrollably. "I'm sorry, I'm sorry, I'm sorry!" she whimpered.

"That's alright, Mrs. Joseph," soothed Detective Sullivan, holding a red-spotted handkerchief to his cheek. "I understand."

"I wasn't talking to *you*, idiot!" she shouted angrily. "Not you neither, dirty cop!" she screamed, spitting at Chief Gilson's feet.

"I apologize to my poor little Joey!" she wailed, shaking her fist at the policemen so hard that the object of her failed plan dislodged from her dress folds at that very moment and hit the floor with a clang. The officers looked down to see the nine

inch dagger that had fallen from her black funerary frock.
She sobbed uncontrollably over her failure to avenge her child.

THE FIRST WARD IV

Day Of Reckoning

On the final day of Hickey's speedy trial the circus that was the defense side's psychiatrists' testimony took place. The proceedings deteriorated to a showdown amongst these dueling alienists.

Each side had called two doctors to testify as to their findings upon their examination of the defendant. Deeming it useless to try and acquit the killer, defense attorney Murphy's goal was to arrange for him comfortable refuge at the lunatic asylum. There was far too much evidence against Hickey for any possibility of acquittal, including his confessions to various and sundry friends, strangers, news reporters and police officers of the crime for which he was now on trial.

Hickey showed no concern for his fate and even less interest in his own arraignment. He was strangely unfearful. His attitude throughout the proceedings was described as "nonchalant." He sat bored and yawning even to the last day of the trial, even as Joey Joseph's father testified through floods of tears erupting from all those present.

The previous afternoon Hickey had been nonplussed at being attacked by Joey's enraged mother in the courtroom corridor. He displayed no overt reaction as little Gordon Pitton, Joey's playmate and the last person to see the boy alive, pointed Hickey out as the man who had bought him and Joey candy, ordered Gordon's departure from them, and stole Joey away. He was unmoved by the testimony of alienists relative to his degeneracy, his so-called murder lust and his supposed mental and physical deformities. John Frank Hickey sat through the trial from its beginning straight through to its close without any display of emotion.

The alienists for the defense, Dr. Herman G. Matzinger and Dr. Edwin A. Bowerman, spouted wantonly the most preposterous and shameless opinions, little doubt revealing a few of their own personal psychological foibles in the process. Many of those present surely thought it queer the absurd lengths the alienists exceeded in order to try and convince the jurors to excuse Hickey from personal responsibility in the horrific murder of a helpless child.

Most vexing of all were the alienists' haughty, superior attitudes and their chilly detachment from the nightmarish act itself at the center of Hickey's trial, both traits so troublingly in agreement to those of the murderer himself.

One of attorney Murphy's choices, Dr. Matzinger of N° 99 Soldiers Place, took the stand and went to ridiculous lengths to blame a purplish scar on Hickey's head claimed, yet not proven, as having been inflicted as a boy by his father, as the cause of Hickey's insanity, so-called. His examination as recorded in his testimony also detected "signs of a broken nose." This was stated theatrically by the doctor on the witness stand as if such a common injury was of any significance whatsoever in this case.

To add to the long list of supposed deformities and deficits that this alienist called forth in his attempt to absolve Hickey of his grotesque behavior, Matzinger claimed Hickey also exhibited an abnormality in the formation of his back.

"I looked for physical marks of degeneration and found the body lines regular, but there was a queer formation on the man's back," he testified breathlessly. This was stated with an air of momentousness, as if he were announcing his discovery of a previously unknown planet in the solar system.

"Oh my," responded Mr. Murphy, his contrived facial expression contorted with equal parts awe and concern. "To what might you attribute this unusual condition you found in Hickey's back?"

"That is what is called a stigma, or sign of degeneration," the doctor declared absurdly.

"Would this formation of his back have much to do with his mental condition?" asked Murphy.

"In an indirect way," inveigled Matzinger.

Detective Sullivan scoffed aloud from his guard position at the door. *In an indirect way, indeed!* he mocked silently. The prosecution's two alienists rolled their eyes at their colleague's desperate experiment at deflecting from providing the obvious answer, which by all rights should have been a simple "no."

"Any other physical defects or peculiarities?" asked Murphy.

"Why, yes. I found numerous self-inflicted bite scars on the backsides of the upper right arm and left arm and on the legs about the knees on the inside."

This same ridiculous testimony came from both of the defense's alienists. Their baseless insistence was that the many scars that decorated the back of Hickey's upper arms and the backs of his thighs were self-inflicted bite marks. These were an irrefutable sign, in their opinion, of the accused's insanity. The problem with this theory, presented by the doctors as inarguable fact, was that Hickey possessed only one upper tooth in his head and was missing many of the lower. Additionally it would require the double-jointed dexterity of a sideshow contortionist to reach those areas with his mouth.

The prosecution attorney, District Attorney Dudley, upon Matzinger's insistence the scars were from bites self-inflicted, first questioned how the scars he was observing, which looked nothing like bite marks to his eye, were determined by the good doctor to positively be human bite marks.

The arrogant alienist sniffed that his professional opinion as to the nature of the scars might be challenged.

"How then, doctor, do you know that if the marks were indeed made from a bite, as you claim, that they were not made by his many admitted victims fighting back against Hickey's murderous attacks? Could you tell whether the mark on Hickey's arm was inflicted by his own teeth or by a bite, perhaps from the Josephs boy?"

"Not really."

"How old are the scars?"

"Several years old."

"Do you know for a fact whether or not his nose was ever indeed broken, Doctor?"

"I did not make an internal examination, if that's what you're asking." he replied.

"But just a minute ago you stated that in your opinion Hickey had suffered a broken nose."

"Well..."

Then perhaps it might have been a naturally formed nose?"

"Well," he fumbled, "then in that case that would be yet another stigma," claimed the self-satisfied alienist.

"If you knew his nose was broken would you say he did not know what he was doing?"

"No—my own nose was broken and I know what I am doing," said the doctor with a smile.

"And yet you just a minute ago testified as to the broken nose as if it had any significant relevancy to this case. How about the scars on his leg?"

"I have the same opinion about them as I have about those on his arms."

"Would it not have been rather unhandy for this toothless man to have inflicted bite marks to the back of his own upper legs himself?"

"Not in the least."

"Despite the fact he has no teeth?"

"He has enough to do the job."

"Wouldn't it have been handier for someone else to have done it than himself?"

"Not at all."

"How do you know they were not made by a dog or other animal?"

"They are clearly human, and most definitely inflicted by Mr. Hickey himself."

Murphy then invited Hickey to display the scars and back abnormality for the jurors. He made no protest; in fact he yawned and stretched throughout the exhibition to illustrate his boredom with the exercise, even as each juror was invited to trace with his own finger the blue colored indented scar on Hickey's forehead.

None of Murphy's theatricalities were protested by prosecutor Dudley, despite Hickey's attorney's inference that the head scar' was complicit in the murderer's so-called insanity. Frustrated by the stubborn stalemate between the two alienist teams, one of which claimed Hickey was sane and knew full well what he was doing during the act of murder, and the opposing team claiming Hickey was insane and therefore not responsible for his actions, Judge Brown called in his own doctor to break the stalemate.

Dr. B. Ross Nairn testified that he believed Hickey was sane at the time and knew exactly what he was doing was wrong.

Throughout the final day the story of the murder of Joey Joseph was told and retold as Hickey lay back in his chair eating sassafras root and gazing at lethargic flies walking upside down on the ceiling lights, unconcerned and disinterested—that is, until Gordon Pitton took the stand.

Looking younger than his eight years, Gordon sat in the front row on the prosecution side of the courtroom with his highly nervous mother. She had instructed her son, when she had first read the terrible news that Joey had gone missing, to keep his mouth shut lest becoming involved in the investigation upset the family's immediate plans to move to Detroit. To this day about that decision she felt quite justified, so her nerves were rather about the possibility that Gordon, despite being ordered by her not to mention this detail, might let the cat out of the bag. She did not want to face criticism or castigation for her decision, or worse, the possibility of criminal charges for obstruction. It mattered to the woman not one iota that perhaps at the time the information that Gordon might have supplied the police could have led more expeditiously to the discovery of Joey's remains and Hickey's identification and capture.

Judge Brown called Gordon to the stand.

As he rose to move forward, Mrs. Pitton locked her child in a cold stare and gave him a good hard pinch as a reminder.

Gordie yelped.

"Sorry darlin'," she sweetly chirped. "Don't be afraid, now. Just remember what Momma told yous. Everything'll be all right."

She bathed with false humility in the compassionate attentions those in the courtroom showered upon her as Gordon made his way up to the witness stand.

From behind, a well dressed woman gently touched her shoulder and whispered "How lucky that boy is to have a mother like you!'

Once seated, so tiny was Gordon that his eyes barely peeked over the witness stand rail.

Justice Brown asked, "Do you know what an oath is, Gordon?"

"Yes, sir," replied the boy in clear, steady tones.

"Do you know what the Bible is?"

"Yes, sir."

"Do you go to Sunday school?"

"Used to, but lately I have not been cuz there's no Sunday-school near our house."

"How old are you?"

"Eight years old, January 2nd," replied the lad as he confidently looked upwards into the reassuring eyes of Justice Brown.

"We will receive the statement without swearing the witness," announced the court.

"Where do you live, Gordon?" asked prosecutor Mr. Dudley.

"One-oh-seven-three and one-half West Avenue."

He testified that he had lived for nine months in Detroit and before that in Lackawanna.

"Do you know Mr. Hickey?"

"Yes sir."

"When did you see him last?"

"Last year ago," he responded.

"You may tell us about it," said Dudley.

"We was makin' mud bricks, Joe and me. We was playin' in the road near a bridge at Lackawanna the day Joe got lost, just me 'n' Joe, playin' with the bricks. They was makin' a bridge there. I think it was right after school, 'bout 4 o'clock. This man come along and asked if we wanted some candy. We said we did. Then he took us to a candy store and bought us some lemon suckers. He went into the store with us and asked us what we'd have."

"Hickey went inside the candy store with you and Joey?"

"Yes sir, he did."

Detective Sullivan, fuming in the doorway at the back of the courtroom, flashed on the candy store owner insisting that no man ever came in the store with the boys, that he did not in fact ever lay eyes on the man in question.

At Gordon's statement to the contrary, Lackawanna Detective Daley, who had questioned the store owner along with Sullivan, wheeled around in his seat upon hearing that information to lock eyes with Sullivan. They nodded to each other knowingly.

"Then he took Joe by the hand and went over the bridge and he told me to go home, for my mother wanted me."

There was a hush in the courtroom at this, for with the exception of his murderer, Gordon was the last person to speak to Joey.

"Have you seen Hickey since?" asked Dudley.

"Yes, over there," he said, pointing out the window toward the jail house.

"What happened over there, lad?"

"I was taken there to 'dentify' him," said the youngster. "There was four men there together but I knew only one of 'em—Mr. Hickey."

Hickey forced a friendly smile as the boy made his statement, but beneath the table his hands were tightly clenched and his fingers interlocked. He swallowed hard and sweated profusely. His defense attorney took notice and became alarmed that this change in behavior might be noted by the jurors.

Attorney Murphy thought better than to question Gordon.

The boy was dismissed from the stand. Immediately his mother moved forward to take his hand and lead him from the courtroom out onto the street where they boarded a streetcar.

"I done 'zackly what yous told me to, Ma," Gordon said as they situated themselves aboard the streetcar. "Didn't I?"

"Yes. Yer a good boy, Gordie," she smiled with a deep sigh of relief.

"Can I have my Hershey bar now?"

"Maybe later."

His Lips Forgot The Taste Of Truth

THE FIRST WARD IV

A Father's Agony

George Joseph, Father of Murdered Boy, Relates the Greatest Sorrow of His Life Through Blinding Tears and Trembling Lips—Pathetic in the Extreme Was This Man's Grief.

Shaking like a reed, overcome by grief through the terrible death his little son had met at the hands of a fiend incarnate, George Joseph, father of Joseph Joseph, the seven year old boy brutally assaulted and foully murdered by J. Frank Hickey, this morning told his pitiful story in criminal term of the supreme court, where Hickey is now on trial. With tears streaming down his cheeks his emotion frequently overbearing his courage to be brave under such heartrending circumstances, Mr. Joseph related how his little lad had mysteriously disappeared, how his wife and himself had simply sat down and wept the tears of sorrow that only parents can know and endure; how postal cards began to arrive from a hidden source, searing and burning their hearts by the uncertainty of the contents and the unspeakable references to the atrocity committed on the body of their child; and finally how he, assisted by Police Chief Gilson of Lackawanna found the decomposed remains of the child in the vault of a filthy outhouse at Lackawanna.

Imagine a father plucking frantically at the sickening filth-covered thigh bone of his darling boy—victim of a fiend's lustful desire and uncontrollable impulse to slay! Imagine the terrible grief and anguish which George Joseph must have suffered when the disintegrated remains of his son—a mere baby boy—were brought to view from an outhouse vault on the end of a long pike pole! Imagine the crushing burden that rested upon the soul of this parent as he took the witness stand in supreme court today and bared his bleeding heart to twelve men of his peers and a crowded courtroom of spectators many of whom were emotionally affected by the harrowing tale. Imagine this father facing there the man who confesses such a horrible crime in all its bestial degenerate details; the brute who snatched away a young life to gratify an inordinate passion of animal lust!

No wonder spectators wept. No wonder their hearts went out to grief stricken parents. And no wonder George Joseph broke down completely.

—*Buffalo Enquirer*, December 19, 1912

George Joseph was instantly recognizable when he entered the courtroom with Lackawanna Police Chief Gilson at his side due to his resemblance to no one else present.

Dark skinned, a stocky man of short stature with thick black hair and a large black moustache, the skin darker around the eyes betraying his having suffered many a sleepless night, to observers he appeared every inch a Syrian. He sat down in the front row, Gilson to his right. His fragile wife Nezla had been requested to stay away due to the difficult scene predicted to take place.

George Joseph was highly nervous about having to testify. English was not his first language. He worried about understanding and being understood. He was anxious to tell his story and to tell it well enough so that the jurors would fully comprehend the depth of his and his wife's agony, and sentence the monster to the electric chair awaiting at Auburn Prison, charged up in readiness to gift the parents their rightful retribution.

Mr. Joseph was called to the stand. As he approached he took care not to look at the killer, but once seated in the witness box, he locked eyes with Hickey. A test of wills ensued with his son's murderer, each staring down the other, until Mr. Joseph broke the stalemate and casually looked away.

In a voice quivering with emotion, George Joseph related his story.

"Please state your name," began Prosecutor Dudley.

"George Joseph."

"You are the father of little Joseph Joseph, whom the defendant is accused of killing, are you not?" asked Prosecutor Dudley.

"Yes, I am," answered George Joseph.

"When was the last time you saw the boy?"

"I saw him at noon on October 12, 1911."

"He went to school?"

"Yes."

"What school?"

"Number 6, I think."

"You never saw your son alive after that?"

"No sir."

Hickey never took his eyes off the witness. He covered his mouth a few times to stifle a yawn as if bored with the whole thing, and stretched.

Dudley produced the postcards that had been sent to Mr. Joseph by Hickey.

"You received this collection of postcards in the mail?"

"Yes."

"What did you do with them?"

"I read them myself."

"Then what?"

"I cried," he said as he began to sob. He pulled a handkerchief from his coat pocket and kept it at the ready.

"And after?"

"I went to my wife. I was crying. I could not believe the words. The words were cruel, and, and...I don't know the word in English." He paused to think. "Mock. The words mock. The words torture me. My wife read the postcards and she cry too. We cry together. I say, 'that's what I thought. That's what I thought happened to my son. The same thing like the words.' I always thought somebody killed him, somebody killed my little boy."

George broke down at that point, not only affecting the spectators emotionally, but Judge Brown as well. He was given time to recover.

"You went to the Chief afterward, to Ray Gilson, with the postcards?"

"At first I didn't know what to do, but finally I brought the postcards to the police."

"And what did Chief Gilson say?"

"He say me the postcards were hoax, a bad joke that cruel person was playing."

"Did he hand the postcards back to you then?"

"No, he took them."

"Tell the court if you will what you did on that Saturday when you found your boy."

"I was in my store. The mailman bring another postcard. It say my Joey buried in the outhouse across the street where we live. I got very sick when I read this message. I was afraid. I cannot explain but I was not able to move for few minutes. I was paralyzed. I could not believe it was true. I could not believe that my boy, missing so long, was there. So close to me and my Nezla. That Joey was there the whole time, so close to his house, to his sisters and brother so close. Finally I force myself to move from the store. I cross the street. I find the place, I look in the hole, but there was nothing. I not want believe my sweet beautiful little son be there in such disgusting place, in dirty water, and again I cry."

At that point he began to sob and wail. It was as if all the spectators and jurors and the judge had stopped breathing.

There was no sound in the room at all for some long moments. Even with all those many people gathered it was totally silent, until sniffling could be heard here and there. Tears moistened virtually every cheek.

George Joseph was in deep torment. Everyone in the room was caught up in the emotion of the man—everyone except Hickey.

The murderer just sat there, immobile, unperturbed, one elbow propped up on the chair arm, his chin resting in his hand, the other shoved deep into his coat pocket. He was silent and expressionless as he kept his eyes on George Joseph, just regarding him intently the entire time that he gave witness.

"I went to police with paper and Chief Gilson read. Ray and other police came with me to the place and police begin to tear down little house. A pole was there and Ray put the pole in the water to see how deep and very soon touch something. He raise the pole and..."

George Joseph's voice broke and he began to breathe erratically. He held up one hand as if to say "give me a few seconds to recompose myself," but failed to resume his testimony, rather crying all the while. Many spectators joined in with him.

It took some minutes but eventually he regained control of his emotions sufficiently to continue.

"...attached to pole hanging on end I see little leg...and a,..a...stocking...and a shoe on, and I know it. I know the shoe and stocking," he blubbered. "It was my boy's shoe. It was my little boy's leg. I shout 'It's my boy! It's my little Joseph! Oh my God it's my boy!' And then I be quiet because my wife and children live across the street and I did not want them hear me and know."

He braced himself in the witness box at that point with one hand on the bench and the other on the rail, his body bent over as if trying not to collapse. It was a pathetic scene. Tears continued to flow from the eyes of all the spectators, but not from the prisoner. Hickey continued to observe with stoical indifference the grieving torment suffered by the father of his victim until George Joseph disintegrated into incoherent sobs, at which time Hickey looked away, out the window.

"I try to take it. I try to take my boy's leg off the pole," he sobbed. "but Chief Ray say me 'Don't do that, George.'"

"Ray, he put Joey's leg—it looked kind of fresh like had been only just pulled out of the body. With it was a piece of Joe's hip. He put it on a newspaper. Then Ray dug around more. I couldn't do nothing at all.

"What then?"

"Then we found more bones. After a while I went to the place where the workmen collected them and saw a lot of bones scattered in the grass. Then we went to the saloon and telephoned Dr. Ross to ask him to come. And a priest too. To come so they would be there before my wife was told what we found."

Murphy interrupted, "I move that part be stricken out."

"It is so ordered," ruled Judge Brown.

"What did you do with the bones?" Dudley asked.

"Put them in a pail and sent them to undertaker White's place."

"Was there anything else to show that the remains were Joey's?"

"Yes. His skull was round and large. There was two front teeth missing."

"You mean Joey had two front teeth out?"

"Yes sir, baby teeth."

"That is all," concluded Dudley.

Defense attorney Murphy declined to question Mr. Joseph.

"No questions," said Mr. Murphy.

Mr. Joseph left the stand and returned to his seat, avoiding looking at Hickey as he passed, but Hickey's eyes followed Mr. Joseph's progress to his place. While a short pause ensued during a wait for the next witness there was not a sound in the court, the mood having been made funereal by the harrowing tale told by the victim's impassioned father.

Next, prosecutor Dudley asked to admit Hickey's confession to the crime into evidence. Attorney Murphy objected, but Judge Brown overruled. A reading was made.

The confession included various events in Hickey's early life as well as interesting details about his employment, but the section of the confession in reference to his murdering the little Kruck newsboy in New York City was left out as not being relevant to the crime being tried.

"The greatest remorse has come to me in the past six months," Hickey's statement read. "I have got on my knees and prayed to God to be brought to my senses—and then got right up and began drinking again. I was not always drunk when the urges came over me. A feeling of exultation would come over me when I was killing and yet my mind was there and I watched and felt a horror over what I was doing. I have actually prayed to God when I went out to kill that I might succeed in my goal to murder little boys. I killed the Joseph boy on October 12. I strangled him with my bare hands."

"Were you remorseful after this?" he was asked.

"Oh God yes. But not so much so until later, and then it was hell. You may think it strange but I could not help killing that boy. I could not help it. When I was killing that boy he was no more to me than a dog. On the day of the killing I drank until 2 o'clock in the afternoon. Then I went to the steel plant where I found my men working without me. I was their foreman and they needed me. I knew this and it made me feel bad. Jepson told me to go home because I was drunk. I left the steel plant to go home and that is when I met the Joseph boy. He was a little fellow and did not try to get away from me. I strangled him with my bare hands at 4 o'clock."

His Lips Forgot The Taste Of Truth

THE FIRST WARD IV

The Jury Deliberates

As the jury was led out to begin their deliberation Hickey yawned dramatically, stretching to whatever limits allowed by his many alleged physical deficits, scars, deformities and stigmas. He was taken away through the underground tunnel back to his cell, but not before posing for pictures with his keepers for the *Buffalo Enquirer* photographer at the tunnel entrance. Fingy Conners had arranged it with Chief Regan so he might get a photograph for the front page of the next edition.

"The only thing what worries me is my dinner may be already cold!" fretted Hickey to a deputy sheriff as he was being led toward his cage. "I feel I could do justice to a beef steak," was Hickey's first remark to jailer Fink when he emerged from the subterranean walkway. Dancing a jaunty routine of clog steps to his cell as if he had not a care in the world, the confessed murderer smiled and sat down to a table on which were beef steak, yellow pike, mashed potatoes, creamed tomatoes, bread and butter, apple pie and coffee.

"That sure looks good to me!" he exclaimed, and started to eat as half a dozen newspaper reporters lounged attentively just outside the lockup scrutinizing his every movement. After his meal he smoked a cigar as he read passages aloud from the Bible. Then, as had become their established habit, he and jailer Fink sang solemn religious hymns together.

"What do you think about going to Matteawan?" he was asked by a reporter when the singing ended.

"Oh, I think this trial here is just a preliminary step—and that later I will get another trial. It's all right to go to Matteawan, and maybe I'll get a chance to smoke some of them good cigarettes Harry Thaw has. I know quite a few people who are close friends to him. I know a man named Murphy there, too. I have had many a drink with a few of the boys who are there. Those were the good old days. Then I always had about $5,000 cash in my pockets."

As his cigar burned down Hickey looked up at the ceiling wistfully.

"Well, I wish it was all over. I *am* tired, I must say," he stated in the time-honored fashion of the unjustly persecuted.

After finishing his cigar he immediately curled up on his swinging bunk and went fast to sleep. The reporters who had accumulated outside his cell, taking Hickey's loud snoring as their cue, departed for their respective newspaper offices to file their stories.

That same day the City Courts had been busy with other equally essential and necessary business as well, such as the case of fifteen year old Herbert Rother, who had been arrested for vagrancy.

Rother had been found crying, missing a leg and lying helpless in the middle of Main Street the previous Sunday night. According to his story, which was verified in all details, Rother was making his way down Main Street with some difficulty during that evening's powerful wind storm when a gust blew him over, breaking the boy's artificial leg. He was unable to rise of his own power.

He had lost the limb several years earlier as a child of nine after falling into a threshing machine upon the boy's being rented out by his parents to perform physical labor for a neighboring farmer.

Rother, unable to walk, had to be carried into the courtroom. Probation officer William Galvin had located the boy's brother who said he would see to it to having the leg fixed. Judge George L. Hager found Rother "technically" guilty of vagrancy but suspended his sentence.

A taxi was called to take the helpless boy to the Erie County Poor House where he was ordered to remain until which time the broken artificial leg could be properly repaired.

His Lips Forgot The Taste Of Truth

District Attorney Wesley C. Dudley

The Verdict

From the very outset District Attorney Wesley C. Dudley had been publicly criticized for his timid and lackadaisical prosecutorial style in his case against child rapist and murderer J. Frank Hickey.

In his opening statement at Hickey's murder trial Dudley set off alarms among those most anxious to see the monster electrocuted, not the least of whom was Detective Jim Sullivan. He had been stationed at his post by the courtroom door to check tickets and ensure order. His partner Jerry Lynch was on watch as well a few yards away. Any patrolmen could have performed this task, but Sullivan and Lynch, having a special interest in the case for more than just one reason, had lobbied Chief Regan for the duty.

Sullivan was curious whether D.A. Dudley would act on any of his advice about dramatizing Hickey's sheer evilness as a counter argument against the defense's strategy of claiming insanity.

On the first day of trial D.A. Dudley reviewed the facts in his opening statement regarding the grand jury having found an indictment against J. Frank Hickey of murder first degree for the killing of Joseph Joseph at Lackawanna.

"I expect to prove that Joey Josephs, a boy six or seven years old, was strangled to death on that day and that on the same day Hickey was in Lackawanna where he had been working for Rogers, Brown & Company. I will show that Hickey met Joey and another little boy near a candy store on the Ridge road. He took the boys to the store and after buying them candy took Joey Josephs to a small house in the rear of a saloon. After abusing the boy he strangled him and buried his body."

Upon hearing Dudley's bizarrely condensed and sanitized version of the sequence of events and the prosecutor's unfathomable understating of the horrific known facts, Jim Sullivan could not believe his reddening ears.

He screamed silently within.

It's 'Joseph' you ignoramus, not Josephs with an "s". You can't even get the child's name right after all this time? Six or seven years old? That moron doesn't even know the age of the poor child? Took him to a 'small house'? A small house! What in God's name is this idiot sayin'? It weren't no Hansel and Gretel gingerbread cottage he took him to! It was a fuckin' stinking shit-filled outhouse where drunks puked and defecated! What's the intent of this here prosecutor anyways? And he states the boy was 'abused'? Kicking the boy might be called abuse! That little lad was raped—horribly, terrifyingly raped! Dudley's too timid to say the actual word? Joey had his little insides viciously ruptured and bloodied by a full-grown pervert! What the hell is this 'abused' bullshit all about anyways? Call it what it is! What's Dudley tryin' to do here, exonerate this fuckin' savage, or convict him? And then he claims Hickey 'buried his body'? He didn't fucking bury his body! He stomped that poor little fella through a shithole usin' his boot heels, breakin' the boy's bones to force him into a pool of stinkin' shit! How do we even know for sure that poor little Joey was even dead as Hickey crushed his little bones? He didn't 'bury' that poor child! Dudley's makin' it sound like Hickey provided little Joey with all the proper Forest Lawn solemnities!

His mind roiling, Sullivan recalled his arguments with Dudley outside Chief Regan's office. He relived in his mind Dudley's insulting him. It was taking all the will that Jim could muster not to fly up to the front of that courtroom and smash his fist through stinking chain-smoker Dudley's nicotine-ravaged teeth.

Instead he raged silently, heatedly at his station at the door trying not to imagine little Joey's terror and suffering.

His mind went back to his own childhood, when close to the same age as Joey was, he had been placed by his mother in the orphan asylum to endure the sadistic violations of those in charge there. How helpless and frightened he had been! This painful recollection then led to his reliving his seven year old son John's drowning eighteen years earlier, followed by cruel remembrances of the illnesses and lingering deaths of his other children, babies Daniel, Hanna and Katie.

He would give anything to have his dead children back with him, yet a mere few feet away sat a monster sucking noisily on gumdrops who delighted in murdering such innocents, and a timid prosecutor seemingly hell-bent on saving the killer from his rightfully deserved fate.

As Jim Sullivan continued tumbling down this emotional rabbit hole of his life's tragedies, his mind raced as furiously as his heart pounded. Perspiring and lightheaded, he was forced to take a couple quick sideways steps to catch his balance.

"Whoa! You okay there, Sully?" whispered Jerry Lynch, catching his partner by the elbow.

"Uh, yeah," Jim mumbled back. "Sorry. Shouldn't o' skipped out on breakfast."

Jim recalled coming home to Hannah a few days earlier when she recounted to him her latest meeting with her friend Ruth in which the two women speculated that Hickey's attorney's blind determination in saving the monster was infuriating. The attorney had been stating this intention in newspaper interviews before the trial began.

He had listened patiently as she ranted. Jim fully understood her anger and gently told her so. He reminded her, perhaps in too patronizing a fashion, that it was the defense attorney's job to defend the client as stridently as he might, even in such a horrific case as this.

But now, upon hearing Prosecutor Dudley mealy-mouth his opening statement to the point of befuddling and confounding the matter, Jim wondered if Hannah might not be onto something. It's one thing for a defense attorney to favor his client: that's his job. But this prosecutor was undoubtedly showing favors toward the accused as well.

Jim happened to be looking at Judge Brown's face as Dudley had uttered the phrase "buried his body' and seemed to detect a flinch in the judge's expression.

"What in God's name's goin' on here?" Sullivan had mumbled aloud that first day.

※※※※

In his final arguments, defense attorney Murphy claimed that J. Frank Hickey, as a degenerate, was not possessed of the soundness of mind to make him responsible for murdering Joey Joseph. He again detailed the various abnormal physical and mental anomalies of the accused to bolster his insanity defense.

"Look at the circumstances in this case," he intoned. 'A drunkard all his life, possessing characteristics of degeneracy at birth that honored medical men testifying here in this court swear they have never seen before. He exhibits a peculiar bridge formation in his mouth and finds pleasure in gnawing at his own flesh. Try biting your own leg when you get in the Jury room! Hickey has practiced this habit for years, for the scars are old.

"Why does not the Divine Providence refuse to allow such creatures to live among the beautiful? But that is solely for Deity to know and for mere mortals such as we to wonder.

"Hickey is a dangerous man to be at large," continued Murphy, "but should he be held responsible for this act? If Hickey had a 'murder lust,' as Dr. Putnam testified, he could not deliberate and premeditate on this murder, and therefore he is not guilty of murder, first degree.

"If you find him guilty of murder in the first degree it will be the first time in the history of this country that such a verdict has been found in such a case as this! Send him to the mad house instead. Do not enforce the law as you get it from the cracker barrel at the corner grocery store or from the curbstone on the street corner, but as you get it from the court. Do not send this man to the electric chair! Let the people say 'That awful Hickey trial has ended. It was a fair verdict, a just and fair Jury, an intelligent, honest and upright Jury.'"

While Murphy was making his case Hickey ate candy and looked dreamily at the slowly falling snow flakes outside the big courtroom windows. Even when Murphy's voice was raised to its most emotional apex, Hickey never turned his head from the window or changed his expression. In fact, he often smiled as if pleasuring some invisible delight.

Reveling in his ability to so easily wrap his adversary Prosecutor Dudley around his little finger, Murphy, after droning endlessly on as to the claimed deformities, physical and emotional, of his client, had the unmitigated gall to complain about Prosecutor Dudley's presentation.

"I think District Attorney Dudley was over-zealous in the performance of his duty," Murphy chastised haughtily. "The placing of the father of the murdered boy on the witness stand and requiring him to rehash the details of the finding of the body, causing the outburst of grief and his awful suffering, was completely unnecessary!

"Two questions to the father would have been enough to prove the identity of the body. Was this done to arouse the passion of this jury to forget their solemn oath and be swayed by sympathy?" attorney Murphy whined, disregarding his own numerous brazen exertions during the previous days to cast the child murderer in a sympathetic light.

Dudley sat there like a eunuch, accepting Murphy's chastisement.

"There is not a person who has ever heard of this case but has breathed a sigh of sympathy for the bereaved parents. There was no excuse for the manipulation of the emotions of those in this courtroom with this unnecessary testimony!"

Murphy's application of the double standard solely to his client's benefit was breathtaking in its outrageousness. Yet the non-objecting gelding, Prosecutor Dudley, remained cowed and impotent, passively allowing Murphy's hypocrisy to go unchallenged.

Far worse than failing to rebut or disaffirm, Dudley saw fit to actually atone.

In his role as both legal and moral representative for the dead boy, Prosecutor Dudley, rather than angrily and forcefully hitting back at charlatan Murphy's misleading and deflecting in his closing statement, dismayed all those present by apologizing.

He weakly justified something that required nothing of the sort—the impassioned words of the dead boy's tortured, loving, grieving father, the child's one and only advocate, the murdered child's sole voice in that courtroom.

Every deponent that Murphy had called to testify had been encouraged by the defense attorney to broadcast their outrageous theories and nonsensical conclusions at length and with impunity, eliciting no objection from Dudley whatsoever. Dudley never questioned the sheer impossibility of Hickey being able to gnaw the back of his own thigh, a feat most any acrobat would find impossible. It did not occur to Dudley to call in a dentist or perhaps two to examine the very suspicious so-called "bite" marks, instead allowing Murphy's alienist-fakirs' claims as such to go wholly undisputed.

Murphy in his summation had the sheer audacity to chastise the one solitary voice speaking for the hideously murdered child, that of his own father, relating actual indisputable, horrific, unfiltered facts.

"I wish I had not been obliged to put George Josephs on the witness stand," Dudley apologized remorsefully, "but I had to identify the body as that of little Joey Josephs.

"This is an atrocious crime, but when Hickey was arrested by Sheriff Tilton at Keswick Colony, did he act like an insane man? No—he was like any ordinary criminal trying to deny his guilt and profess his innocence.

"On the train going to the jail with Sheriff Tilton he tried to make himself a big fellow by telling how successful his son has been and how much be thought of him despite admitting he had abandoned his family when his son was but three years old. Hasn't he also tried to bolster up his case by telling of his fraternal relations?

"The phrase Hickey uses, 'uncontrollable impulses and obsessions'—where did Hickey get those words and expressions? Has he been studying up on these things for use in just such an emergency as this?

"On the train coming up to Buffalo he got remorseful and unnerved. There is no claim here that he was of sound mind. If he had a strong mind he would never have done this act. But are you going to say that men are not responsible for any crime they commit because of that? Was there ever a man in the world when he committed a crime who did not have an uncontrollable impulse?" An uncontrollable impulse is not a defense against murder in this state.

"Do not turn a deaf ear to reason, gentlemen. Do not be blinded by the theories of counsel, but take the facts as they exist naturally and honestly."

❧❧❧

Before retiring to the Jury room, an avalanche of requests were made by jurors to have the court statements and testimony read, reread and then reread yet again to the point where Detective Sullivan muttered out loud, "Have these old fools been sound asleep during the entire trial?"

Even Justice Brown himself was tested by this. He questioned the capability of these men who seemed so lost and unsure as to what they should have plainly heard and understood had they been paying proper attention.

Juror Foster, who took copious notes during the trial, said: "I'd like a repetition of your honor's charge, in relation to the question of upon whom the burden of proof rests in showing the insanity of the defendant."

Judge Brown responded, "I do not know that I used the burden in speaking of the proof in connection with that. The burden of proof is with the people to show the prisoner is responsible for his act and is sane."

"That is the principal difference of opinion among some of the Jury," said the foreman.

Another juror asked, "The prisoner having pleaded guilty to the crime, does it rest with the defendant to prove he is insane or with the people to prove he is sane?"

"The presumption is that everyone is sane," said the Justice, "but when a defendant pleads insanity then the people have the right to offer proof that he is sane. The term, 'burden of proof' is technical, meaning balancing up the proof. The final, ultimate solution of the question must be determined on all of the evidence that he is guilty, and on that point the burden of proof rests with the people."

Juror Winkler said: "I have one question. I would like to have you repeat that portion of the charge you gave up as to what you said about Hickey knowing what he was doing."

"I cannot go into those statements. The evidence covers that," said the increasingly exasperated judge.

Juror Foster then desired that the stenographer read that portion of Hickey's statement about the day of the murder when he did not work.

The stenographer read that part of the testimony.

"Will your honor have that read again?" asked Foster.

It was again read.

"Can we have that part of your charge read to us about the doctor's testimony?" asked another juror.

That was read by the stenographer.

"Would it be possible to let us have a copy of the record of testimony in the case?" asked Foster. "I have some of the statements written down, but some of the jurors don't agree with me about them."

The request was denied.

"I wish your honor would read again the vital points about the doctors' testimony," said yet another juror.

"I did not mean to convey to your minds any vital points in the testimony," said Justice Brown. "It was simply a gist of summing up of that testimony."

As the stenographer read the physicians' testimony and the court's comments upon the law governing the taking of such testimony, Hickey ate chocolate candy and smiled at familiar faces about the court room.

"Then will you please read the statement made by that little boy," said the same juror.

Gordon Pitton's statement was read, and Justice Brown's comments upon its validity were given.

Brown's chagrin with the jurors, most of them elderly and befuddled even by the most uncomplicated testimony, was on full view as he, drained and displeased, excused himself.

"Gentlemen," Judge Brown sighed deeply, "if I can be of further service to you I will be in the building for a while yet."

The jury retired to the jury room and thirty minutes later when no word was received from them, Judge Brown took his leave, longing for his supper, a cognac, and his easy chair. Murphy and Dudley too retired to their respective homes.

At midnight, George C. Winkler and Henry J. Hess, two of the jurors, left the jury room for a few minutes in the custody of a guard. Both went without collars and were wiping the sweat from their foreheads.

"It's a pretty hot place in there," said Hess.

"Don't you wish your were home?" he was asked.

"Any place I hang my hat is home," rejoined the Juror. "but there's hardly no room to hang my hat in there."

At forty minutes past midnight the jury was in the midst of a hot debate. That they entertained no hope of coming to an early agreement was apparent from the large amount of food and cigars which a deputy sheriff was detailed to get for them.

A glance through a window into the jury room showed the Jurors in a highly agitated state. The air was blue with smoke and the Jurors gesticulated vigorously.

❧❧❧

The verdict was a compromise. There had been thirteen ballots. On twelve the vote was nine for murder in the first degree and three for not guilty on account of insanity, which was the murderer's plea. The suggestion of a compromise came from a member of the majority. The jury was out twenty-six hours.

With only a twitching of the facial muscles Hickey sat unmoved by the verdict. He gnawed on peanut brittle during the ordeal in spite of the minimal presence of necessary teeth. His only words were that he desired to have the Rev. John W. Ross and Mother Ross present when sentence was pronounced upon him.

Mother Ross unfortunately was indisposed at the time due to her recent admittance to the New York Asylum for the Insane on Forest Ave. upon issuance of an emergency order sworn out by her deeply concerned son, the physician Dr. Wellington Ross.

Father Ross found himself suddenly called out of town for an indeterminate period and was unable to attend.

❄❄❄

When the verdict came down the people were appalled and disheartened. The *Courier's* headline blared "Justice Brown Shocked."

The jurors had not done their sworn duty, quickly buckling under as they freely admitted to the discomfort of the stifling little deliberation room in which heated arguments were pursued while deprived of sleep. No allowances had been made for an interruption in their deliberations for much needed rest. They were expected to deliberate nonstop until either a decision was reached or they collapsed from exhaustion.

Angry with the three jurors who refused to convict Hickey of first degree murder, Juror Henry J. Hess, a weighman living at 102 Bissell Street, was questioned by a reporter for the *Courier*.

"Whatever you do young man, put me right with the public, And especially with the people with whom I have lived all my life," said Hess when he was asked what he thought of the verdict. "I don't want to be classed with those who were not with the nine."

"How was it during the night?" the reporter asked.

"It was awful! We were divided against each other, nine to three, and we argued every minute. We never had a minute's sleep and of course some of the older men are nearly all in. It was a terrible strain but we nine tried to do our duty to ourselves and the people of this community. We tried to uphold the law.

"In truth I was compelled to compromise just to put Hickey in a dungeon where he belongs rather than in a sunny hospital from which he could be soon enough released to kill more children. We have all seen such a travesty before.

"A chill went through me when those so-called alienist doctors were on the witness stand. So cold, so removed, as if to say, 'oh Hickey's sick, he doesn't know right from wrong so let's put him in a hospital for a little while so he can get well.' Hogwash! A killer doesn't ever 'get well.' A killer of innocent children especially deserves death in the electric chair to rid this world of his kind, no matter what these so-called doctors and alienists testify as to the killers' state of responsibility."

In discharging the jurors, Judge Brown did not hold back his inference that they failed to do their sworn duty.

"Ordinarily," he said, teeth clenched, "it is quite the uniform practice to extend the thanks of the court to the jury for their care and consideration in reaching a conclusion. Your services have been onerous and troublesome. You have been out all night. It is extremely to be regretted that justice could not be done to this defendant. The public and the court do not feel satisfied with this result. For those of you who have earnestly endeavored to procure a different result the court desires to extend to you its most appropriate and sincere thanks for your efforts to render justice.

The city seethed with resentment toward the sanctimonious three who continued publicly arguing their supposed moral superiority after the fact. More than a few speculated whether these three enjoyed some commonality with Hickey that had informed their stand on the matter.

※※※

The day following the trial, Buffalo Detective Jim Sullivan and Lackawanna Detective Daley met as planned on Ridge Rd. in front of Tony Frank's candy store, directly across the street from the murdered boy's home.

Before entering they peered around as to who might be observing them, and when the coast was clear they turned the door handle. Their eyes immediately fell directly on a spot that should have been vacant: the proprietor had replaced the little penny gambling machine that he had been ordered to, and promised to, destroy.

As soon as he saw the officers enter, the Syrian froze. Daley turned and lowered the shade on the glass door after flipping the sign from *Open* to *Closed*. Sullivan heaved up the heavy gambling machine and catapulted it against the glass candy display case, which shattered into a thousand shards and collapsed loudly to the floor.

Tony Frank bolted.

He tried to run out the back, but his path was blocked by packing crates that the lazy proprietor had not quite gotten around to organizing. Daley tackled him. Sullivan grabbed Frank by his oily hair and raised him to his feet.

"You fuckin' Arabian piece of shit! Because of your lies, that little boy's killer almost got away with it! That murderin' fuck was standing right here on this very spot—and *you* could've identified him! So what's the story, Frank? What are yous really up to here in this store? You and that fuckin' Undertaker?" he screamed just an inch from the man's face.

"That poor child was one of your own people!" growled Daley as a number of Tony Frank's teeth began bouncing off the bloody planks.

It just so happened to be the final day of business for Tony Frank's Confections on Ridge Rd.

1913
BUSY DAY FOR THE ALDERMAN

On the same day that the newspapers announced Alderman JP Sullivan's victory over Fingy Conners in the fight concerning the location of the proposed Southside high school, the same news organs screamed about JP's steamrolling the Scajaquada Creek project through.

The people in the Scajaquada Creek district had been plagued by floods for many years. So long as the creek was left in its historic state, nothing even approaching an adequate sewer system was possible. In consequence, a great expanse of territory, otherwise highly desirable, remained undeveloped and largely uninhabited.

Those who lived in the territory could expect to be inundated at least once a year, while the unsanitary backflow from the sewers filled their cellars at all seasons.

This was especially urgent in the tony Delaware Park neighborhood. Alderman Sullivan had bought himself a centrally located property there in the name of an agent, as had some of his fellow aldermen, past and present, in anticipation of an upcoming flood abatement project that would make these properties skyrocket in desirability and value.

Some time previous the Department of Public Works prepared tentative plans for the abatement of the nuisance. It was proposed to sink an immense trunk sewer about 12 by 18 feet in dimensions extending along the general lines of the present creek, which would route the creek into that drain. This would end the floods and make possible the building of an efficient, sanitary sewer system.

The Legislature gave the city the right to issue bonds to pay for the work.

Just as soon as the matter reached this stage, the real estate speculators jumped into the situation with their scheme to run a boulevard atop the sewer. The fight over this land deal resulted in involving and delaying the legitimate and original flood abatement improvement plans for many months.

Former alderman Jacob Gangnagle called upon his friends in the Council to jam through his proposal that the city buy his parcel for $160,000, four times its assessed value. When that didn't happen, he tried again with a different parcel, for $86,000. Both parcels were located at Genesee Street and Grider, where he insisted the proposed trunk sewer should begin. His main opposition was Public Works Commissioner Colonel Francis G. Ward who smelled a rat. Colonel Ward declared emphatically that the construction of the drain must begin at the mouth of the creek west of Main Street and not at Genesee Street, where the real estate agents were trying to sell land to the city at fancy prices.

From the Buffalo Evening News:

Scajaquada Creek Steal Is Put Through By The Aldermen

Cunning and Audacious.

The manner in which the raid was railroaded through the aldermen yesterday was as interesting as a play. The deal was in capable hands. There are few things that Alderman John P. Sullivan, the dean of the lower house, can't put over single-handed when he gets his mind on the job.

For strategy, cunning, resourcefulness, he hasn't had his equal in the board of aldermen in a quarter of a century. It makes no difference to Sullivan whether the board is Democratic or Republican; he dominates just the same. There hasn't been a man in the lower house since the late Jack White left it that knows the aldermanic game as well as Sullivan knows it and who could play it with the deftness, audacity and success so characteristic of this long-headed politician and businessman.

And Alderman Sullivan was in charge yesterday and as deeply interested as he ever was in anything that had come up in the lower house for years. And at his aide was another past master, John J. Griffin, who has helped to wear out the carpets in the council chamber "Inside the rail" during the last 20 years and whose smiling face has, perhaps, become more familiar than that of any other man's at the little brass barred window in the city treasurer's office.

Bars Let Down.

It was evident early in yesterday's session of the board that the bars were down; that nothing was going to stop the raid. Most of the aldermen sat grim and silent in their chairs, never opening their mouths except to vote for the deal and against every effort to delay it.

The proven fact that in this case the real estate promoters in their haste had included in their offer land that the city actually already owns was airly waved aside.

The startling revelation that five parcels of land included in the "60-foot strip," as originally offered, had been omitted from the deal as resubmitted to the board was another hurdle that was lightly leaped. The report before the lower house to be acted upon stated that 25 parcels of land were to be bought for street and sewer purposes.

Sullivan at His Best

The fact that only 20 parcels, and not 25, were actually involved in the offer, made no difference. The discovery that the Erie Railroad and the Lackawanna Railroad, with their right of way, barred the possibility of a street without litigation and tremendously expensive grade crossing construction had no other effect than to make one alderman hesitate.

Sullivan was eloquent and at his best.

Alderman Haffa threw a bomb into the chamber by announcing that detectives from the William J. Burns detective agency had been in the city investigating this Scajaquada Creek deal.

Makes Open Threat.

"Remember, gentlemen," shouted Alderman Sullivan, "there are but three more meetings before this board dies and if this is not acted on now, many a good man here will never have another opportunity to vote for it."

When not speaking, Sullivan was slipping around from member to member on his side of the house or whispering to Griffin, who either beckoned to him from his station at a sidewall or sent the sergeant-at-arms after him.

Alderman Haffa characterized the deal as the "rawest" he had ever known and "an outrageous attempted raid on the public," but Alderman Sullivan only laughed at him.

Fine Roguery, Says Holloway.

While it was generally understood that the "frame-up" was complete in the board of aldermen and could not be broken, the speed with which the steal was put through the lower house created something of a sensation nevertheless.

"I was astounded," said Councilman Holloway who was an interested spectator of the proceedings. "This sort of thing takes a fellow's breath away. It is a bold deal and I have to take my hat off to those who have had the audacity to put it through in broad daylight. I hope the Mayor will be firm and veto this transaction."

"It is the finest piece of roguery that I have ever encountered." That is the way Councilman Frank T. Coppins characterized the raid.

His Lips Forgot The Taste Of Truth

The Markeen Hotel dining room and stairway up to the Foyer and Music Room.

February 15, 1914
The Incident At The Markeen Hotel

New York District Attorney Charles S. Whitman was closing in fast.

He was anxious to entangle in his net some agent of the Inner Ring of the graft conspiracy so as to ensure his victory in his current campaign for the office of Governor of New York State.

On February 4th the *New York Times* named Fingy Conners as the chief person of interest on Whitman's list.

Whitman subpoenaed transcripts of Conners' bank accounts, as well as those of the ex-boss of Erie County, William H. Fitzpatrick. The graft conspiracy was so loyally organized however that despite the intense pressure being put on the many suspected conspirators, not a single informant had stepped forward. Whitman was becoming convinced he'd never break Fingy, Fitz, or any of the other big names. But once he'd set his sights on former Buffalo alderman and current Treasurer of New York State John J. Kennedy, he knew he had the bait to hook the big fish.

An hour after returning to their residence at the Markeen Hotel from Sunday Mass at Blessed Sacrament Chapel, Kize Kennedy excused himself.

"I'll be back in a few minutes, darling Ottilie," he said as he kissed his wife warmly on the cheek. "I'm just going down to the lobby for a short meeting with an associate."

This was stated by him cheerily, almost as if nothing at all were awry.

Before going out the door he made it a point to say goodbye to his grown children, son William and daughter Jennie, which to Mrs. Kennedy upon reflection after the fact seemed telling.

He'd been acting queerly for two weeks, ever since ladder-climbing D.A. Whitman had targeted him. Whitman had deposed Kennedy in Albany two weeks earlier. Acutely sensitive to criticism historically, Kennedy was severely unnerved by the ninety minute interview, and ever since, deeply depressed. Now he'd been served yet again with a fresh subpoena to appear before Whitman the following morning in New York City. Inside his breast pocket was his sleeper car rail ticket for the midnight train.

Kennedy shut the door of the elegant apartment behind him, entered the lift, and descended to the lobby. There he encountered Fingy Conners awaiting him.

"Let's go somewheres we kin talk private," murmured Conners, more a command than a suggestion.

"The Foyer," Kennedy responded.

They evaluated those who might be within earshot before seating themselves on facing divans where they commenced their muted conversation.

"Yous shoulda fuckin' come t' me first, Kennedy. Before any o' this. Before meetin' with that clown Whitman in the first place—as soon as yous got that first subpoena!" scolded Fingy Conners. "Yous saw wot my attorneys done for Nugent, keepin' him out of the penitentiary an' all. I woulda had 'em do likewise fer yer benefit as well."

"Whitman was out to get me, Fingy!" Kennedy was close to tears. "He made me believe otherwise. Said it'd be a piece of cake. I thought if I went to you about it, it'd make me look all the more suspicious in his eyes causing him to throw the same suspicion onto you. So I thought it best I handle it myself and keep you and the others out of it, to throw him off your scent. If only I could do it over I'd..."

"Well yous can't," interrupted Fingy. "I made the mistake o' thinkin' yous was a lot smarter than this. Me 'n' Murphy ain't about to go down wich yous—just so's ye know."

The two old friends since their boyhood seafaring days sat examining each other intensely on the entresol level overlooking the Markeen Hotel's elegant dining room. New York State Treasurer Kennedy remained motionless while accepting his chastisement from Fingy, head hung, sweating bullets.

It was the day after Valentine's Day.

Kennedy and his family had lived in the hotel residence for nearly a year. As Fingy lectured him brutally, he stared out vacant-eyed at the huge antler chandeliers that hung from the ornately painted vaulted ceiling of the dining room. The clatter of dishes and silverware being set out beneath their warm glow helped cloak the men's hushed conversation. The staff was readying the venue for Sunday dinner which would be followed by a post-Valentine's dance. Kennedy, despite his severe mood, had promised his daughter he would accompany her there. She was caught up in the new Tango fad and delighted in every opportunity to show off her recently acquired skills.

"I know you'll be doin' right by us, Kennedy. You 'n' me mighta had some differences here 'n' there along the way, but one thing I knowed fer sure—I could always trust yous to do the right thing in the end."

※※※

Fast friends since toddlers, born a few months apart, Conners and Kennedy had gone off to work on the Lakes together at age 13 aboard the steamer *Niagara* as steward's assistants and cabin boys. Their teen years were spent sailing the Great Lakes together and forging a close association borne of their shared childhoods of misery, deprivation and shame.

As young adults they returned once more to the First Ward. Kennedy's no-good father being dead, he reconciled with and went to work for his uncle James Kennedy, the principal grain contractor on the docks in Buffalo's waterfront 19th Ward. The elder Kennedy had sixty men working for him at the time. He owned two local saloons and held an interest in three more.

At the same time Kennedy went to work *for* his family Fingy went to work *on* his family.

After the interesting sequence of rapid deaths Fingy ended up in possession of his parents' and sister's insurances and modest estates, his late father's Mariners Home saloon, and his regretfully-surviving nine-year-old niece Minnie Hayes,

Kennedy, despite realizing the toll that Fingy's distressing absence of humanity was taking on him personally, nonetheless recognized advantages to maintaining their alliance, both financially and politically.

Back in 1884, a year after Fingy Conners' loss to his rival in their contest for the office of Alderman of Buffalo's First Ward, Kennedy successfully ran for Alderman of the 19th. Freshly mindful of the charmless Conners' mistakes, Kennedy had put his handsome good looks, his naturally kind demeanor and conviviality, and his contractor-uncle's many connections to work in winning the aldermanic seat that he would occupy continuously for the next twenty-six years.

Their relationship began to unravel once Conners looked beyond the lines of his own First Ward domain to hungrily set his avaricious sights on what Kennedy had achieved in the 19th. It took Conners' loss in that 1883 election to make him realize that he did not have to win political office in order to exercise power. All he had to do was to make himself invaluable to those who sought political office. Thus his new role as "kingmaker" was born.

Fingy claimed in more recent years that John J. Kennedy's ultimate financial success came about due to Kennedy's imitating Fingy in establishing waterfront saloons and entering into the labor contracting business. Fingy Conners did nothing to dissuade people from their repetitions of his empty tale.

But as Kennedy was the nephew of a grain contractor who had thoroughly schooled him in the ins and outs of business, it was in fact Fingy who learned from the Kennedys about the labor contracting business, about awarding priority employment to men willing to spend a shameful portion of their children's bread and milk money in their saloons. But no one could deny that Conners had exponentially expanded upon what he'd learned from James Kennedy's modest labor contracting techniques into something cruelly unique and wide-ranging. That "something" ended up making Fingy millions.

Whatever the preferred story, ultimately Kennedy's success in his labor contracting pursuits would be limited by his being morally repulsed by the idea of inflicting cruelty and domination over his downtrodden neighbors—a compulsion Conners fully embraced, celebrated and advanced unmercifully.

Once Fingy sensed this particular weakness in his longtime friend, he moved in to abscond with the Kennedys' pioneering ideas, and then ultimately, a good portion of their contracting business.

Kennedy, as his political career and contracting business advanced, and his own appetites for wealth increased, established a fashionable eating and drinking establishment located downtown at Pearl and Eagle Streets, called the Hotel Vega. This was of a decidedly higher class than others surrounding, and too within walking distance of city hall. It boasted quality food and top-notch adornments and comforts which through his able promotion attracted a gathering of politicians from both parties. Deals could be struck amid elegant surroundings away from the scrutiny of those self-appointed guardians of the public welfare at city hall, such as perennial do-gooder, and Buffalo's electorate-thwarted savior, Charlie Feldman.

About the Hotel Vega Kennedy was familiarly called "Kize." It was short for Kaiser, signifying to his followers that he literally was the king of his realm. Kize was universally liked. Men opposed to him politically were proud to class him as their friend.

If anything unsavory was told to Kennedy about anybody, and he was asked for a comment, he pretended not to hear. He could legitimately do this since he was deaf in one ear. Men trusted him and readily took their confidences to him. He never once repeated anyone's secret. John J. Kennedy was loyal to a fault.

When Fingy Conners switched allegiance from the Republican to the Democratic party following his defining aldermanic 1883 loss, he invaded the district of his childhood friend Kennedy seeking a constituency from which to build up leadership for himself. This was an egregious betrayal in Kennedy's eyes, as it would be in anyone's.

Fingy Conners was all about bulldozing over any and all those in his path, and although relatively rich in dodgy alliances, Conners was to remain dirt poor in genuine friendships throughout his entire lifetime—those claiming closeness to him doing so for advantageous reasons. The epitome of hubris, Fingy carried out his poaching right under Kennedy's nose at Kize's own Pearl Street establishment. It was the sort of brazen tactic which Conners utilized throughout his life. To say that Fingy Conners had gall would be to woefully understate matters.

Things began to get sticky in 1910 when Kennedy wrapped up twenty-six years as a Democratic alderman, the longest-serving in Buffalo history, after winning the election for New York State Treasurer as a Tammany-backed candidate. He had been thrice-elected president of Buffalo's Common Council and acted numerous times as pro tem mayor of the city when those newly-enriched elected leaders departed their native environs to pursue extended follies to Europe and other parts.

The Democrat Kennedy, like his friend and fellow Democratic Alderman JP Sullivan, had a cunning for working both sides of the aisle at the city hall, even when the Republicans held power. Kennedy knew how to work with the machine leaders of the opposing party for mutual benefit. He well understood the political value of franchises and favors to corporations and was singularly adept at extracting full political value from them. This and the wheeling and dealing transpiring at his Hotel Vega kept him solidly within the clique that controlled things.

During his reign Kennedy was continually a target of the civic reformers who correctly accused him of being a tool of corporations seeking facilitations and privileges, but they could do little to impede him. The people loved him for his establishing playgrounds, public swimming pools and free Sunday concerts in the parks. So popular was he that, like Alderman JP Sullivan, he had little need for spending election funds on campaign pinbacks, ribbons, pencils, or other superfluous paraphernalia employed by rivals. Both Kennedy and Sullivan were automatically reelected, their opponents bewildered by their severe but entirely predictable drubbing at the polls.

As State Treasurer, Kennedy, like most men in politics, felt he was long past due his justly deserved rewards, and construed things to his financial advantage. Primary among these was his suggestion to banks wishing to become depositories for New York State's funds to do their bonding business with the United States Fidelity and Guaranty Company of Baltimore, Maryland. Before Kennedy was elected as New York State Treasurer, he was Vice President of USFG and served as its chief agent in Buffalo. USFG was an arm of Tammany Hall, and Tammany men were numerous among USFG's board of directors. Upon his election to State Treasurer, Kennedy's twenty-one-year-old son William, a Cornell graduate that same year, inherited his conflict-of-interest post.

Publicly, Kennedy denied any favoritism. He had always been a clever sleuth who believed he had skillfully obscured his activities with the help of his numerous allies. But allies are only such so long as they themselves feel unthreatened. These allies most assuredly felt imperiled upon Kennedy's being contacted by ambitious and unrelenting New York District Attorney Charles Whitman. In the soulless Whitman's conducting of a John Doe graft inquiry, State Treasurer John J. Kennedy was the panicking seal and Whitman the tightly circling killer whale.

On January 29, 1914 Kennedy at the request of Whitman had appeared before the Grand Jury of New York County. He signed a waiver of immunity and was examined at great length over a ninety minute time period. The wily Whitman knew things he never should have been privy to. Someone had squealed. Someone cunning enough to stay out of Whitman's clutches. Someone who would throw his own mother under a streetcar in order to save his own skin.

The humiliating deposition fiercely rattled Kennedy.

Kennedy had been summoned along with other members of the State Canal Board largely as a result of contractors having submitted bids complaining bitterly that members of the Canal Board had hit them up for "political contributions." Revelations were made regarding the alleged attempt of Canal Board member James E. Gaffney to extract from Contractor James C. Stewart five percent of a three million dollar Barge Canal contract which Stewart expected to receive from the Canal Board. Stewart did not agree to pay the percentage and he did not get the contract.

Contractor Stewart came forward and swore that he had been "held up" by Gaffney for the sum of $150,000. Gaffney was best friend of Tammany Leader Charles Murphy and agent of both Murphy and Fingy Conners. Kennedy was one of the members of the Canal Board who voted not to award the contract to Steward despite Steward being the lowest bidder. Instead half the contract went to a firm with strong Tammany affiliations, P. McGovern & Co., at a price 20% above the canal engineers' own estimate.

To finish him off, Whitman humiliatingly grilled Kennedy as to his fitness for the office of State Treasurer to which he had been elected and presently occupied.

There were several prominent bankers on the Grand Jury. They did not hesitate to question the witness sharply as to fiscal matters. Their questions pertaining to things financial were so basic that even the lowliest bank clerk would naturally have a ready answer at his tongue's end.

Not so Kennedy.

Whitman's queries related to the size and importance of banks in New York City and to the methods of transacting banking business. State Treasurer Kennedy admitted that he did not know the name of the largest bank in the city.

The State Treasurer in fact could not name even one of the five leading banks. New York State's own elected Treasurer did not know how much interest the State was getting on its funds as compared with New York City.

Tempers exploded, especially among those wearing pin-striped suits.

Those members of the Grand Jury who were prominent in the banking world were completely blindsided by Kennedy's preposterous revelations pertaining to his complete lack of even the most basic knowledge pertaining to finance.

Their bafflement and incredulity swelled to bursting until their acrimony toward

Kennedy detonated.

"We voters have been hoodwinked!" shouted one.

"How is it possible such a fraud can occupy this crucial office?" demanded another.

"This imperils the very foundations of our nation's economy!" screamed a Wall Street executive.

Abruptly they realized that the very stability of the banking industry could no longer be taken for granted, and with that bombshell they were shaken to their core.

Kennedy appeared as if he might collapse. All color drained from his face. Dry mouthed, his hands shook to the point he could not lift his glass of water to drink without spilling.

One of the bankers was so infuriated as to call Kennedy "a thoroughly incompetent and undignified gangster," and demanded his resignation from State Office right then and there. He added that he would "discharge any of his own office boys who had displayed as little understanding of banking" as had New York State's own elected Treasurer.

So traumatized was Kennedy by his exposition as both fraud and ignoramus that the fear of a public hearing under which he would face even greater scrutiny became unbearable, not to mention the grilling bound to come about concerning his very deep associations, financial and otherwise, with Fingy Conners and Tammany.

Kennedy privately told his friends afterward that if compelled to take the stand he would never again submit to examination in the public investigation. This declaration was relayed back to Whitman, who smiled with delicious satisfaction upon hearing it. The Machiavellian D.A. deduced that Kennedy's declaration of alarm could be of significant advantage to him, making Kennedy a valuable asset if compelled to testify.

Whitman reasoned that the panicked Kennedy might willingly reveal the inner workings of the Democratic machine if Whitman spared him the ordeal of a public examination. Such revelations would entail outing his friends and associates, most productively—and fearfully—of all, William J. "Fingy" Conners.

As a result on February 11 another subpoena was served upon Kennedy personally in Albany. It demanded his appearance once more before the Grand Jury on February 16. In this February 16 meeting the manner in which Kennedy handled $150,000,000 of State monies during his administration as State Treasurer was to be closely examined.

Piled atop that, fellows of the State Canal Board of which Kennedy himself was a member were to appear as well to establish what was known about the Board's declining a contract to James C. Stewart after Stewart had declined a request to make a sizable political contribution, specifically to Charles F. Murphy, leader of

Tammany Hall, and Fingy Conners' involvement in that.

Unnerved, Kize Kennedy had visited his old friend JP Sullivan just the day before, which was Valentine's Day. He showed up on JP's doorstep on Hamburg Street unannounced during supper. Annie had reached an agreement years earlier that JP would never interrupt the family meal for business, and ninety-nine percent of the time JP complied, but this unusual visit required he break that promise.

He led Kize into his little home office in opposition to his wife's scowl and closed over the door. Sullivan was not involved in the financial scheme. Kennedy thus viewed him as a neutral party from whom he might receive unbiased counsel. JP listened intently to the convoluted particulars, impressed with its audacity in theory, but alarmed for Kennedy. JP deduced that Kennedy was being set up as a patsy by Fingy and his friends.

"Now you listen to me, Kize, and listen good. You were not meant for these kinds of shenanigans. You are too sensitive and too loyal. These others are stone-hearted, coldblooded creatures. If you do not give D.A. Whitman what he wants, he will send you to prison. I am sure of that. You could not survive there, a man of your temperament and nature, in a prison with killers and thugs."

Kize answered, "But if I turn on the others, I fear what might happen to me."

"And I fear what will happen to you in prison. There you will surely and in short order suffer an 'accident' or some-such to keep you from ever revealing what you know. You will be assassinated because those men know you will be desperate to get out once you are in there. They cannot allow you to remain a possible witness. You were promoted as a candidate for State Treasurer for only one reason—to do their bidding. Yes, you profited too, but they get the lion's share. Now you've done that. But their scheme is threatened presently and you are the reason. You must testify. You must save yourself by telling what you know."

"But they'll kill me outside of prison as easily as inside!"

"Not nearly so easily, no. I wish I could assure you that you would be safe, but I cannot. You will accomplish nothing for yourself if you go to prison, but you will have better luck at saving your skin outside prison than inside. In prison you will be trapped and crimes against you will go unwitnessed, but walking free you can more readily avoid solitary situations. I hate to be so blunt, Kize, but you are in danger no matter what you do. And that being the case, wouldn't you rather take the chance of being free than imprisoned? If I were you, I'd rather be looking over my shoulder as a free man than looking over my shoulder in the shower room at Auburn Prison."

"But you don't get it JP. If I snitch it won't be just me they'll come after. My wife and children will pay the price for my decision, perhaps with their own lives. Perhaps, I daresay, considering the primary player, in an arson fire.

His Lips Forgot The Taste Of Truth

❧❧❧

Fingy stood up, signaling to Kennedy their meeting was over. The savory smells coming from the Markeen Hotel kitchen were making his stomach growl.

Kennedy mused, "How is it that we're punished so severely for speaking the truth yet rewarded handsomely for our worst deceptions?"

Fingy scoffed, "People can live with their lies, Kennedy, it's their truths that destroy 'em."

Fingy gathered his things and prepared to leave. "Happy belated Valentine's Day, Kize," he said, patting him on the shoulder.

The older and sicker he got, Fingy had cultivated a repulsion for shaking hands. Grasping the crook of his cane tightly with his right hand in such situations successfully discouraged the practice. The pat on Kennedy's shoulder with his thumbless left was meant to suffice, the gesture ending with Fingy dropping something weighty into Kennedy's suit pocket. Conners turned to leave, then stopped to momentarily wheel around again to face his old friend.

"Yous heard about Dr. Park?" inquired Fingy.

"What? No. What about him?"

"Dropped dead—two hours ago at his home. Thought yous already heard. Tsk-tsk," he said, shaking his head mournfully. "Goes t' show yous just never know when it's yer own number wot's come up."

Dr. Roswell Park had led the team of physicians who attended to President William McKinley in his valiant struggle for life after being shot at Buffalo's Pan American Exposition back in 1901. Park in fact had not all that long ago brought Mrs. Kennedy out of a dark malaise and restored her to robust health, a blessing for which Kize Kennedy expressed eternal gratitude. In thanksgiving he had cried in Dr. Park's arms.

To his friends Kennedy was known to be the most sensitive of men. "As sensitive as a little girl," is a statement that had been made about him in intimate circles time without number.

Fingy exited, leaving Kennedy standing there alone awash in old fears and fresh terror amid the clatter of fine bone china. JP Sullivan's advice haunted him. But Kennedy didn't just have his own safety to worry about. Who knew what actions the gang might be capable of with millions of dollars and Federal Prison at stake? The State Treasurer hesitated only momentarily before quickly descending the limestone escalier to the grand dining room.

"Is there a lavatory somewhere here?" he asked a worker.

"Yes sir," was the reply, taking notice that Kennedy wobbled a bit, pale and sweating, "but it's closed for cleaning right now. There's another one downstairs you can use," said the server, pointing to the narrow carpeted staircase. "It's not fancy, but you'll..."

Kennedy briskly followed his direction. At the bottom of the stairs he entered a small windowless tiled room having just one toilet and one large square pedestal sink with water-spotted nickel fixtures and a towel rod freshly resupplied. He closed over and locked the door. He looked up to notice the transom over the door tilted open. He looked around for a window pole with which to shut it, but none was to be found in the toilet's narrow utility closet. However, he noted inside were stacked half a dozen rolls of brown toilet paper, a box of matches, two bars of Pears' soap and a glass bottle of a green deodorizing chemical having a pull-up wick.

He turned to the mirror and paused to admire himself. Staring back was a still-handsome specimen of a man with a full head of luxurious salt and pepper hair and an elegant moustache to match. He sighed deeply. He removed a small tin of wax from his coat pocket and smoothed his moustache with its contents, upturning the ends. He then undid his diamond tie pin and dropped it into his breast pocket. He took his necktie and tucked it into the same pocket to keep it from getting wet. Then he bent over the sink in rehearsal. Satisfied, he splashed his face with water, then dried it on the white hand towel.

A fastidiously neat, well dressed man, Kennedy wished not to leave a mess.

Ascertaining that he might manage to keep his navy serge suit unsullied, he reached into his pocket to retrieve Fingy Conners' final gift.

He opened the blade.

The razor handle was white mother-of-pearl. The blade itself was ornately carved in script reading "1901 Pan American Exposition Buffalo N.Y." It glinted in the bright electric light of the hanging lamp.

He did not pause or ponder.

He bent forward looking intently into the mirror as he positioned the blade below his left ear. In one skillful swoop he pressed it deep into his flesh, surgically severing his internal and external jugular and carotid as he drew the blade clear across his own throat to the base of the right ear. Examining his progress in the looking glass all the while, his right carotid gaped wide open. More fascinated than horrified, he watched as the flesh separated and the interior workings of a human cervix were exposed like some ghastly mocking crimson smile awash in a torrent of blood, blood that spurted against the mirror and gushed down onto the white shirt he had taken pains, obviously fruitless, to protect. He had envisioned he would collapse over the sink and the blood would flow cleanly into the drain, sparing those who ultimately found him from a sticky coagulated mess.

But that's not the way it happened.

Choking, he tightly grasped the sides of the sink with both hands to keep himself righted. He felt himself losing consciousness. With each beat of his fading heart erupted an explosion of blood outward from each artery like some grisly fountain in a horror novel. Blood splashed against the mirror and poured down his front like tomato juice from a spilt pitcher. He gurgled and gasped in a futile attempt to draw fresh breath. He remained upright for a few seconds until it dawned on him that the effort to remain vertical wasn't worth the energy required. He collapsed to the perpendicular, relieved. The hexagonal white tile floor collided violently with his cheekbone, cracking it. The guilty razor clattered to the side of his head just inches from its spurting handiwork. The final beats of Kize Kennedy's tortured organ gushed what little remained of his life's flow out the severed conduits into an impressively gruesome puddle of crimson.

As the metallic smell of iron offended his nose, he closed his eyes.

❧❧❧

Mrs. Kennedy was becoming alarmed. Her husband had been gone an hour, and it was almost time to begin getting ready for the dance.

"William, will you go check on your father, please? I'm beginning to get worried," she asked, her voice trembling a little.

Will, concerned as well, grabbed his coat and quickly exited the apartment. He raced down the stairs rather than await the elevator car. He scanned all the faces passing and going. He approached two men, one of whom resembled his father from the back. He put his hand on the man's shoulder, who then turned. It wasn't him.

"Sorry. I thought..."

They both smiled weakly. William moved on.

He looked around the lobby and asked some hotel staff if they had seen his father. One recalled him going into the mezzanine area but stopped short of revealing that he had been accompanied by the infamous Fingy Conners. Finding the seating area there unoccupied, William descended the escalier to the dining room where a waiter told him he had recently directed Mr. Kennedy to a basement lavatory.

William flew down the stairs with the concerned waiter at his heels and pushed against the secured door.

"Here, allow me," said the waiter as he produced a ring of keys. He opened the obstructed door to a nightmarish apparition, one that would fail ever to abandon either man's memory even as they drew their own final breaths.

Will shouted for a doctor, who upon arrival, estimated that Kennedy had been dead already ten minutes.

"If only I'd come looking for him sooner," William blubbered to the physician. As he uttered the final syllable of that mournful regret, primeval shrieks rang forth. The Kennedy women, mother and daughter, in pursuit of father and son, ended their search here, standing in the doorway, shattered for all time by the horrific spectacle.

❧❧❧

District Attorney Whitman made no secret of having his heart set on the office of Governor of New York at any cost.

He had sought out high profile cases guaranteed to win for him front page ink in the newspapers. He had been confident that the Kennedy affair was the skyrocket that would propel him into the state's highest office.

Faced with the public's emotional backlash in response to his aggressive tactics against Kennedy, coupled with their shock and grief over the sympathetic and much-loved politician's suicide, Whitman scrambled to distance himself from blame. He claimed he had no personal beef against Kennedy and that his subpoena was simply an innocent gesture for the purpose of verifying a few known facts.

In reality, as all who knew him would attest, Whitman, possessing both a face and disposition not unlike that of a cruelly tortured farm animal, had been preparing a mortifying all out, take-down, career-destroying assault on Kennedy in order to further make a name for himself. Election Day wasn't too far off.

It was said by Kize Kennedy's attorney Michael P. Dirnberger Jr. that a flash of temporary insanity induced by worry over his impending appearance before a New York Grand Jury had been the cause of his suicide.

Interviewed by the *Buffalo Express*, Fingy Conners stated courtesy of the newspaper's grammar-corrected prose that he had known Kennedy for almost fifty years and was "mystified completely" as to the cause which prompted him to end his own life.

"Mr. Kennedy must have been worried in connection with the Stewart contracts about which much has been said, for he probably got orders from Charley Murphy of Tammany not to award the contract to Stewart. He was a man who would not lie or double cross a friend. Another thing that worried Kennedy was the trial of Dude Walters, who was accused of murdering a man in a brawl at his Buffalo saloon. Kennedy led a straight life, hadn't been drinking for ten years, did not need any money particularly, and was strictly honest. The last man I would have picked as a possible suicide would have been Kennedy."

The funeral service at Blessed Sacrament Chapel did not include a High Mass, as Kennedy's suicide precluded that Catholic service. The ceremony lasted less than a half hour. The pallbearers included Alderman John P. Sullivan, Buffalo Mayor Louis Fuhrmann, and former Chicago Mayor John P. Hopkins.

Among the more than 50 honorary pall bearers were Congressman Dan Driscoll, Buffalo Evening News proprietor E.H. Butler, and Fingy Conners, trying his utmost to appear bereft.

Kennedy was buried in the family plot at Holy Cross Cemetery.

✤✿✿✤

Fingy and Murphy lunched together at the Ten Eyck Hotel in Albany a week after Kennedy's funeral.

"You coulda saved him, Fingy."

"Nah."

"We coulda headed this thing off together, you and me. That Whitman's a dolt, and now we got to find a way to get rid of him now too. We shoulda gone after him earlier, then Kennedy'd still be around."

"Best fer me 'n' yous he ain't around. He was soft. Couldn't take the pressure. He'd've given away all the names. We'd all be in hot water right about now. So let's us figger how to do away with Whitman goin' forward. What I know about men is this: the more right-minded they make themselves out to be in public, the more dirt they're hidin' in private. So let me get my detective lads to diggin' some up."

"Don't get too cocky," warned Murphy. "Whitman put away Becker for murdering Rosenthal at Big Tim Sullivan's hotel in New York, and he woulda gotten Big Tim hisself too had fat old Sully'd lived long enough. A murder conviction against a New York City police lieutenant that Tammany controls? That's unprecedented. Let's not underestimate that Whitman guy."

"Yeah, but he didn't get Big Tim, now did he? And it's best for us that Big Tim Sullivan's dead 'n' gone as well. Count yer blessin's, Charlie."

President William McKinley in Buffalo with his fellow Civil War veterans at the 1897 GAR Reunion.

Fingy And The Presidents

It was one part humiliation and another part anger at being rebuffed by the President, or more correctly, the President's secretary, that riled Fingy Conners. Conners was President Wilson's strongest booster, and had nothing but good things to say about the man. How communications or facts may have gotten crossed no one could explain. Conners nonetheless labored under the impression that he had an appointment to meet with the President at the White House that day.

As owner of the *Buffalo Courier* newspaper, Conners had run stories concerning his upcoming travels, chief among them was his boasting a meeting at the White House with President Woodrow Wilson. Indeed when Conners arrived at the White House for that meeting, he waited hours only to be told it was impossible for him to obtain an audience.

He left with his tail between his legs, searching for a way to save face.

Reports of the incident got around Washington, amusing some people who claimed it was nothing less than an intentional rebuff, according to a piece published in the Troy (N.Y.) *Times*.

Conners, a master of distraction, concocted an inaccurate reminiscence to feed to his friends at the *Troy Times* to disseminate on his behalf.

He told about when, back in 1897 leading up to the Buffalo GAR reunion, the noted reunion of Civil War soldiers, he visited then-President McKinley in the White House. Then too he had an appointment, and similarly he was told upon his arrival by McKinley's secretary John Addison Porter that President McKinley would not be able to see him.

Weeks previous to Conners' arrival he wired his Washington DC correspondent directing him to make arrangements for a meeting with McKinley about a purely private matter. By custom, McKinley held semi-weekly public receptions in the East Room of the White House, and Conners' correspondent attended one of these. Waiting for the crowd to dissipate at reception's end he approached McKinley and explained Conners' desires.

"It will give me the greatest pleasure to see Mr. Conners," the *Troy Times* reported McKinley as saying, "and I will be glad to have him here next Tuesday afternoon at 5 o'clock."

But Mr. President," Conners' correspondent reminded him, "Tuesday is Cabinet Day."

"Makes no difference," replied McKinley, "the Cabinet session will have ended by 5 o'clock and if you will be kind enough to send up and tell Mr. Porter and also Major Loeffler that I have made this engagement I shall be greatly obliged."

Porter responded to Conners' correspondent that an appointment had been entered in the book.

When Conners arrived at the White House the day of his appointment he announced himself to President McKinley's secretary. Porter was well acquainted with Conners' history and felt it inappropriate that the President of the United States meet with such a person. Porter asked Conners to take a seat while he excused himself with the pretense of announcing to the President Conners' arrival, which in actuality he did not do. Upon returning he told Conners, "The President is about to take his afternoon drive and I am sorry to say that he will not be able to see you today."

Conners being Conners, he lost his temper and commenced in the use of the bad parts of his vocabulary, loudly. Just as he was about to depart in high dudgeon, Major Loeffler entered the room and announced, "Mr. Porter, the President expects Mr. Conners of Buffalo, and if he is here he would like to see him at once."

The *Troy Times* continues the tale in a supportive story printed 17 years after the supposed fact:

> Without further word, Mr. Conners walked toward the President's room with his head turned so that his glance struck Porter from across his left shoulder, and that glance he gave the President's Secretary said enough to have chilled the marrow of a cast-iron mule. The President greeted him cordially and said:
>
> "Mr. Conners, what can I do for you?"
>
> "Well, Mr. President," replied the Chief of newspapers and the grain trade of the Lakes, "I learnt that you are coming to Buffalo to the Grand Army Reunion. The *Enquirer* is my yacht and she is the finest on the lakes, and I want you to honor me by taking a trip in her from Buffalo to Cleveland after the reunion."
>
> "I regret very much, Mr. Conners," said the President, and his tone carried regret with it, "that I have made an engagement to run from Buffalo to Cleveland with Senator Hanna on his yacht. Otherwise I should have been delighted to have accepted your very kind invitation."
>
> Mr. Conners' face fell, but instantly the President dissipated the gloom by saying, "But, Mr. Conners, if you would consent to take me for a

run, say, fifty miles, up the lake and back, it would give me extreme pleasure to accept your courtesy."

Mr. Conners slapped the President on the back and said, "You bet your boots I will do it, and will give you the time of your life, Mr. President."

And history says he did.

In fact history said no such thing. It did not happen that way.

Editors of other newspapers outside the boundaries of Buffalo, and even some within, were known to fall all over themselves at times to do Conners' bidding, as is human nature among its weaker members easily led. It appeared that the *Troy Times* was the only journal reporting this particular McKinley story, seventeen years after the fact. No previous published account, not even in any of Conners' own newspapers, supports this particular tale of the supposed White House meeting.

The *Courier* allowed the *Troy Times* to do Conners' face-saving following President Wilson's slight by printing their piece recalling the McKinley meeting on its editorial page.

In truth, when McKinley arrived in Buffalo for the GAR, it was Senator Hanna's yacht *Comanche* that ran McKinley up the lake, as was reported in Conners' own Buffalo Courier newspaper, not the yacht *Enquirer*.

Fingy Conners was entertaining members of the Chicago organization, the Columbia Post. Members boarded the *Enquirer* awaiting them in the Coit Slip and "as she shot out into the harbor with flags and banner flying and her canon answering the salutes of the steamers in the harbor, the yacht Comanche was seen waiting near the head of the breakwater."

On board the *Comanche* was President McKinley who had accepted the offer of an escort by Conners' *Enquirer* up the lake for a few miles.

As the *Enquirer* pulled up alongside McKinley's craft, Conners' brass canon rolled out the Presidential salute of twenty-one guns to which the President bowed his thanks and waved his hat while the *Enquirer's* guests from the Columbia Post cheered. For ten miles the two yachts kept along at easy speed with the parties saluting and cheering.

Pulling ahead on the way back it was seen from the *Enquirer* that the *Comanche* had halted ahead dead in the water and a rescue boat was being lowered. Full speed ahead, the *Enquirer* raced up believing someone had fallen overboard, horribly enough, possibly the President.

As Conners pulled up, Senator Hanna laughed and shouted, "we thought we could hurry you back with that boat stunt! By the way, Mr. Conners, there's a man on this craft who says he rather wishes he was on that one."

"If there is anybody there who wants this boat, he can have her," replied Conners according to the report printed in his *Courier*.

"We wouldn't rob you of your beautiful boat, Mr. Conners," said President McKinley, "We just enticed you back to wish you a goodbye."

❧❧❧

Less than a year later, according to the New York Times, Senator Hanna sold his $48,000 yacht to the US Government for $115,000, joining Fingy Conners and many other wealthy Americans in unloading their aging luxury craft in an enrichment scheme hatched with the cooperation of corrupt Naval officers tasked with the purchasing of essential water craft for the Spanish American war effort.

Most of the craft were purchased after the Spanish fleet had already been rendered impotent, and were therefore entirely unnecessary.

Senator James Hamilton Lewis of Washington State inserted in the Congressional Record a speech claiming that "Assistant Naval Secretary (Theodore) Roosevelt rebelled against this infamy, but was hushed. It is publicly known that this was one of the things that forced him to leave the Navy Department."

Newspaper magnate William Randolph Hearst was the sole yacht-owner among a dozen or more millionaires who made a no-strings donation of his luxury yacht to the US war effort.

All others profited handsomely.

Ironically, John R. Hazel, the attorney Fingy Conners engaged to act as mediary in the crooked yacht transaction, in which he ordered Hazel to get $100,000 for the rusting boat, was the very same John R. Hazel who would administer the Oath of Office to President Theodore Roosevelt in Buffalo at the Wilcox Mansion after President McKinley's assassination in 1901.

His Lips Forgot The Taste Of Truth

THE FIRST WARD IV

TELL IT TO THE JUDGE

Hannah Sullivan sat nervously in a pew at the back of the church near the confessional. Only three or four people were present, scattered about the cavernous space, praying, lost in their own dilemmas.

The door opened and Fingy entered alone. He stood there for a minute, his eyes adjusting to the dimmed interior of Our Lady Of Perpetual Help Church. Finally he spotted her. She raised her hand in greeting. He approached.

"Wot's this all about Hannah?" he whispered gruffly. "Wot did Dave do now? It better be good. I got important people t' see!"

"All right," she said, clearing her throat and preparing her say.

"Do you recall when you came to JP's house on Thanksgiving Day when we were all there havin' dinner?"

It was not his finest moment, that.

"Wot of it?" he growled.

"My friend Ruth was there, remember?"

"Who?"

"She has bright orange frizzy hair. No one forgets that hair."

At that he realized instantly that something bad was in the works.

"Wot's it got to do with Davey?" he snarled.

"Ruth is set to appear in Court, to testify under oath. That means there'll be a public record."

Hannah went on to recount the story of Ruth's cruel childhood rape at the house of ill repute where she lived with her mother.

Fingy was boiling. His ruddy face turned as crimson as the votive candle glass flickering at the feet of the statue of St. Theresa a few yards away. He was being had, and was ready to bolt.

"Are *yous* tryin' t' bleed *me?*" he challenged incredulously, voice raised. The praying stopped as worshipers turned to look.

"I'm not doin' nothin' here except tryin' to help you, Jim," she whispered hoarsely. "It's the Court that's threatenin' you, and I'm here as your nephew's only sister just to help save you, to warn you beforehand—so's you can put a stop to it. That's all."

"You old fu....*yous* tricked me here!"

"It's the only way of knockin' some sense into that thick head of yours, Jim Conners! You must've took too many kicks to the noggin durin' all them pug years of yours. You ain't bein' rational. You're in trouble and I came here to help you and this is all the thanks I get, you hollerin' at me in church in front of God and all? You and me, we're family now—that's got to mean *somethin.*'"

"I ain't family wit' yous or nobody lessen I say it's so!"

"Ruth's bein' drug into the Court by her whore mother," she vehemently whispered. "She's suin' Ruth for support—and after all the cruelty she put onto that poor girl! Ruth's got to convince the judge why she shouldn't be forced to take that woman in, and that means tellin' in detail all them awful things she done to her. That means *every, single, thing.*"

Fingy was set to explode.

Hannah mistakenly expected she'd have him right where she wanted. But now she was becoming unnerved and trembling a bit. She began to stammer a little.

"The judge's heard m-many cases like this already, and he always rules, uh, the adult children got a-a obligation to take in their offensive parent, regardless! She can't possibly live under the same roof with that horrible monster! After all that awful woman done to her—she went and turned Ruth out onto the cold streets when she was still a baby!"

"Wot do you expect me to do Hannah? Of all people yous should know better'n t' shake *me* down? Huh?" he growled threateningly.

"I expect you to do the right thing for yourself and for the person who's life you scarred forever! That's what!"

"Watch yer mouth, woman!" he hissed.

"You go to that judge, Jim, and you tell him! Tell him just like you told him so many times before and told all them other judges before him what outcome you expect from the case, and that way Ruth won't have to stand up in public and tell all the details of her sufferin.'"

"Y'ain't gettin' away wit' blackmailin' me, girl!"

The angrier Fingy Conners got the more deeply he reverted to the crude diction of his youth spent on the streets.

"Call it what you might! You well know what happened to that girl! And now you got to do somethin' so's it don't become the public record! Talk to the judge! Have him dismiss this before it ever gets to court. People who ruin the lives of children must not be rewarded!"

Fingy took that last statement personally. He stood up and glared down upon her angrily.

"Yous shoulda never o' stuck yer four eyes 'n' big nose into this, Hannah Sullivan," he growled threateningly. He then turned and stormed out, cursing.

His Lips Forgot The Taste Of Truth

Fingy Conners' second wife, Mary Jordan Conners

Yesterday's Debutante

From the *Buffalo Evening News*, December 22, 1914:

Mrs. William J. Conners' reception from 5 to 7 o'clock yesterday afternoon, to present her daughter, Miss Alice Jordan Conners, was a very brilliant affair and during the two hours the house was thronged with guests, including several out of town friends.

The house, which is one of the very beautiful residences of Buffalo, was a study in red from top to bottom, three entire floors being wrought out in a scheme of Christmas decoration, which had a rare background in the walls and ceiling frescoes and decorations and in the draperies and oriental furnishings.

As the guests came down the broad stairway into the reception hall they passed through a pergola of Southern smilax on the landing, relieved with bright crimson of poinsettia, ruscus and thistle bloom. The newel posts were topped with great bunches of poinsettia, ruscus and heather and doorways and windows were draped with smilax, red thistles, poinsettias and ruscus.

An orchestra played a very delightful program of popular music, stationed in an alcove back of the reception hall, entirely screened by palms and evergreens. The side and front verandas were enclosed and floors were covered and walls hung with very gorgeous rugs and Oriental tapestries, soft lamps in crimson shading and palms gave a charming effect and made them inviting resting places.

The debutante's flowers were something out of the ordinary and quite filled the music room, baskets of every conceivable shape and kind, French bouquets, garlands and loose bunches of roses, violets, orchids, lilies of the valley and roses galore. They were massed on the piano, on cabinets and mantel.

Mrs. Conners received with the debutante in the large living room, standing before the mantel, which was banked to the ceiling with American Beauty roses. Receiving with them were their house guests, Miss Ethel Campbell of Philadelphia and Miss Mareta Black of Elgin,

Ill. Mrs. Conners wore a handsome toliet of pink with tunic of appliqué lace, and bodice and girdle of the pastel shades. Miss Conners wore a lovely frock of opalescent spangled Chantilly lace, veiled with white tulle and she carried one of her gift bouquets, made up of orchids and lillies of the valley.

Miss Campbell wore cerise satin, combined with pearl trimmings and net and carried pink roses and lillies of the valley tied with pink ribbon. Miss Black was lovely in a gown of iridescent embroidery over white net and chiffon with a cape effect of rose velvet. She carried Sunset roses and lillies of the valley tied with yellow. Assisting were a group of friends of the hostess and the debutante.

Refreshments were served in the dining room and the conservatory adjoining. The table was centered with a shower of Scott Key roses, with small white baskets filled with lillies of the valley, suspending from the rose shower. Tall white candles in silver candlesticks standing in flower cups, corresponding in tone to the crimson roses of the centerpiece, illuminated the table and confections and the room decorations carried out the general plan of ornamentation.

The reception was followed by a dinner of 120 covers and later by a charming dance in the ballroom on the third floor. The stage where the musicians sat was very elaborately decorated with palms and the reds and greens used throughout the house. The ballroom itself was particularly attractive. From the center of the ceiling suspended a great ball of ruscus and heather, and from it to the corners were festooned garlands of ground pine.

His Lips Forgot The Taste Of Truth

THE FIRST WARD IV

1915:
THE YEAR EVERYTHING CHANGED

As the speedboat accelerated, Fingy cried "Faster, faster!"

"But Commodore! We ain't acquainted with this part of the lake!" shouted one of the two mechanics accompanying him. They wore their cork lifesaving jackets, which Conners had refused.

"That's an order! Faster!"

Barely had the exhortation left his lips when Fingy Conners experienced himself flying through midair.

This'll surely be the end o' me, he thought in flight.

He landed hard, the wind knocked out of him, but he was somehow able to tread water. The mechanics landed nearby, one of whom was bleeding from the forehead.

Richard Croker, former Tammany boss, had witnessed the whole thing unfolding from the veranda of his spectacular home facing Lake Worth. The February Florida sunshine was glorious. Croker, who had become a millionaire off bribes from New York saloons, whorehouses and gambling dens, had been enjoying his retirement with his Seminole Indian wife, Ketaw Kaluntuchy, sipping an iced tea laced with whiskey. His attention had been drawn by the high pitched whine of the speedboat engine racing offshore.

Fingy's boat had hit a barely submerged log and broken apart. It sank partially atop a submerged sandbar. Luckily for him he was thrown clear of the debris. As he struggled to stay afloat the mechanics made their way to his side. "This way, Commodore," they said as each took an arm, pushing debris out of their path with their free hand. Fingy finally felt his toes touch bottom. He was on a sandbar. It was low tide. The three made their way to its apex where they stood knee deep getting their bearings. There they caught their breath and composed themselves for a few minutes.

The town of Lake Worth was tiny and sparsely populated having only recently been founded, and Croker was the only witness who might provide aid. He shouted and beckoned to them across the still waters to come his way. After a few minutes of discussion the trio decided to try and swim to shore. They set out from there, the men with the life jackets having to support either side of the rotund millionaire who had refused the lifesaving apparel offered to keep him afloat. They hopscotched from sandbar to sandbar, which had in fact more accurately the consistency of mudflats, swimming, wading, walking and squishing until after twenty five minutes they reached the shore where Croker stood waiting to greet them wearing his wife's wide brimmed straw sun hat.

"You all right Conners?" the old man asked.

"Yeah, fine, fine, Croker" he answered. "Nice bonnet. Ain't never seen yous look so fetchin' before."

"Come up on the veranda and take a load off, all o' yous. Come on."

Mrs. Croker, unhappy about the mud they were tracking up onto her porch, offered spiked ice tea to the survivors, but they much preferred straight whiskey. After proposing to take them back from whence they came in his boat, Croker rustled up some clothes for the men. Fingy, being many sizes larger than Croker, was fairly busting out of his borrowed outfit when he was later seen climbing up onto the Royal Poinciana Hotel Dock. Otherwise he was none the worse for wear.

The dangerous incident had Palm Beach all abuzz for a week.

※※※

Hannah was more than upset. Her plea to Fingy Conners on her friend Ruth's behalf had not just been ignored, but firmly stomped upon. She thought she'd had him, but master con Conners couldn't himself be conned. Fingy did go to the judge hearing the case of Ruth McGowan, not to nix the whole thing, but to warn him about the kinds of lies that the "teetering on the edge of madness" McGowan and her female rabble-rousing friends were prepared to tell.

"They'll say anything not to have to take in that poor old lady. The taxpayers shouldn't have to foot the bill for the Poorhouse when the woman's got a daughter with money!" he blustered.

Hannah was afraid to tell her husband, to admit she tried to get one over on Fingy Conners, if even for honorable reasons. He might explode, or he might laugh, or perhaps condemn her as foolhardy. She could think of no other way to save Ruth from the misery that would inevitably be hers should her vicious old mother be allowed to take up residence in her tranquil little South Street cottage.

Fingy reminded the judge that they shared a common virtuous trait, the strongly-held belief that it was one's moral obligation to take in family members incapable of caring for themselves. Fingy recast himself as a hero, recounting to the judge his time-worn tale of rescuing his little niece Minnie, whom he claimed he barely knew at the time, from an orphan's fate after her mother and grandparents had mysteriously died.

When Ruth finally appeared before the judge he had already made up his mind.

He did not allow Ruth to plead her case based on her "unprovable" stories of what she claimed happened to her as a child by her mother's hand. He did not allow Hannah to speak in support of her friend. He shamed Ruth and berated her publicly, she standing there a frail version of her former self due to the flare up of her old head injuries. Even her own well-compensated attorney failed her, objecting to virtually nothing.

Her mother did not show up to court. It was claimed she was too ill to attend. Ultimately the judge ruled Ruth must take her mother into her home and care for her.

Ruth was beyond consolation.

She departed the courthouse weak, sickly and in tears, Hannah supporting her sturdily by the elbow. The attorney, no longer in the presence of the intimidating judge, told Ruth not to worry. He claimed that he could fix things to her advantage yet.

"Really Mr. Hansen?" she responded hopefully. "Oh, thank you!"

He was lying so as to continue billing her for his services.

The Erie County Poorhouse was eager to get rid of the cantankerous old wretch. Bridget Black made everyone's lives there—the matrons, the overseer and the other inmates—miserable. It was true that less care had been undertaken in her transfer than might have been afforded some other inmate considered a more agreeable sort. But it was also true that for once she wasn't peppering her handlers with a hail of nasty invectives as was her behavior typically due to her diminished physical condition. The two men carrying the cot on which the patient lay let slip her bed almost into the gutter while lifting her onto the ambulance.

One of the long-suffering attendants chuckled "Oi, the gutter! How befittin' the likes o' her! Right where she belongs!"

As the ambulance rolled up in front of her cottage, Ruth's head throbbed with an excruciatingly familiar pounding. She had cleared a space at the rear of the house, off the kitchen, a room that used to be a small porch but had been enclosed against the elements in recent years. This would be her mother's space in the tiny bungalow.

The attendants walked to the rear of the vehicle and opened the door. The old lady's stench was overpowering.

"God damn!" one sputtered, grimacing as they grabbed hold of the cot's frame rails and lifted the woman out roughly. "A dead pig don't even smell this bad!"

Uncharacteristically and for once, Bridget Black did not protest their carelessness, not because she had won her case, not because she'd had the last laugh against her long-suffering daughter, not because she was finally freed from the draconian confines of the Erie County Poorhouse, but because she was, indeed, dead.

No one had noticed.

They carried her up the steps to the porch where Ruth, in a morose state of defeat and resignation, opened the door. She barely glanced at the old lady, so disheartened and traumatized was she by the Court's decision, so debilitating was her head's incessant pounding. She pulled a lace handkerchief from her bodice and held it to her nose against the stink, then led the attendants to the tiny rear room.

"Here?" one of them asked. "This here ain't no bigger than a broom closet."

Ruth responded, "Perhaps you can find more suitable accommodations at your own home? You're welcome to her."

The attendant sneered in response as the two lowered the cot into its designated place, then exited hastily without uttering so much as a goodbye. Closing the entry behind them, Ruth sank into her settee, fingers pressed forcefully to her temples trying to massage away the pounding. There and then she gratefully welcomed sleep.

❦❦❦

Hannah wasn't able to be present when Bridget Black was delivered to Ruth's unwelcoming portal. She awaited in her deep loneliness a promised visit from Junior and his new wife Mary Ellen. She hadn't seen her son in weeks despite his living with his wife's family mere blocks away on Mackinaw Street. The loss of Junior's company had hit her unexpectedly hard, coming as it did on the heels of her brother-in-law the alderman's family sneaking away to a better life like brigands in the night, followed by the loss of her protector Zeke.

The house at N° 16 Hamburg had never felt lonelier or more stilled.

Just the week previous with the temperature unseasonably well above freezing, she had gone into the backyard to hang laundry. There under the line, where as a puppy he delighted in tearing fluttering sheets from their anchoring clothespins, lay old Zeke, dead.

"Oh Zeke!" she sobbed, dropping to her knees.

He lay on his side, tongue lying flat against the earth pressed beneath his snout, eyes closed, lips already retracted, teeth bared. She'd put him out after his breakfast and had been too preoccupied to notice he did not come scratching at the back door asking to be let back inside as usual. He apparently had been dead for hours.

Hannah looked around for someone to tell, but no one but she was at home. She looked up hopelessly at the curtainless windows of the alderman's abandoned house next door. She wrapped her thin arms around Zeke and hugged him there for some long minutes, petting him as she always had, brushing dirt off his coat, telling him she loved him, bidding him farewell. Not knowing what else to do she took up a shovel and started digging at the corner of the back fence. The fence helped form one wall of a corridor walkway between the backyards of the Hamburg Street houses and the length of the extensive brick facade of the Mutual Rowing Club building. As she dug she heard voices coming from the walkway on the other side and recognized them as belonging to the neighbor Bresnahan twins.

"Is that you, John Bresnahan?" she called.

A green eye peeked through the gap in the boards.

"Hallo there, Mrs. Sullivan, Yes, it's me.

"Aye, it's me too," called his twin, Anna.

"Oh, sorry to bother you both, but can I pay you John to help me dig a hole? My poor Zeke's just died," she said, voice breaking.

"Oh my goodness no he didn't, did he? Poor thing. Why surely I will help. I'll go right away and fetch me shovel."

Brother and sister returned minutes later with shovels and together the sweaty trio managed to have gotten down almost three feet by hour's end. They wrapped old Zeke in a damp sheet originally intended for earlier hanging on the clothesline. They gently laid him to rest. John stood in the hole as his sister and Hannah placed Zeke in his arms. He lowered the beloved dog to the bottom, then climbed out. It was only then as they began covering him with dirt that the choking tears began to flood from Hannah's bespectacled eyes.

She thanked the Bresnahan twins profusely once the sorry job was completed upon their adamant refusal of payment. She entered the house and placed a call to her husband at work.

"Do you want me to come home, Hannah?" he sniffled through his weeping.

"No honey, I just needed to hear your voice," she responded.

After hanging up the Detective worried if he should go home anyway.

She slowly climbed the stairs and took to her bed, her tears generously watering the bare mattress, its intended sheet now three feet under.

"What else might ye be yet plannin' on goin' wrong for me hereabouts, God?" she blubbered. "I can only stand just so much."

❦❦❦❦

The work whistle screaming from the Buffalo Union Furnace shocked Hannah out of her recollections. As she lay there awaiting Junior's arrival, the Regulator's brass pendulum ticked away noisily, the chime ringing every half hour to remind her of how forsaken the house felt now with Zeke gone, Junior absent, Ruth embroiled in her own problems, and the alderman's family having moved on to the perfect green lawns and breezy verandas of bucolic Central Park. The silence inside only amplified the racket outside; the blaring of ships' horns, the Furnace's incessant cacophony, the spine-piercing screeching of its behemoth hoists swaying dangerously high above just outside her window.

Her eyes rested on the little shrine erected two decades previous that held cabinet card images of her dead children. She regarded each of the four one by one, resulting in a gloom overtaking her not unlike a varnishing of molasses, dark and sticky and suffocating. As she tallied her losses she never felt lonelier in her life.

It was clear by now that Junior wasn't coming, yet again, nor did he call to explain. He didn't have to really. His wife had successfully isolated him from his family in favor of her own.

The exchange of vows had taken place the previous year at Our Lady of Perpetual Help Church in front of two sets of parents, one happy and relieved, the other decidedly not.

In their late thirtieth year Jim Sullivan Jr. and Mary Ellen Diggins were united in a marriage ceremony that many of their philosophical friends believed a union of convenience if not sheer resignation. Mary Ellen had no other suitors and Jim felt somewhat committed and duty-bound, the couple having commiserated socially for more than half their lives. It was rumored the two had made a pact sometime during the previous decade: if neither had married by the time they were thirty, they would marry each other.

Their original plan had called for the newlyweds to live with Detective Jim and Hannah Sullivan, their big empty house at N⁰ 16 Hamburg St. allowing the couple plenty of room and privacy. Agreed to before the wedding, Mary Ellen abruptly made it clear once the ceremony was solemnized that she was unwilling to reside there. After two nights she abandoned her new husband in a strategic plan to get her own way. She fled back to her father's nearby house on Mackinaw Street. Junior was bereft.

"You go get her—drag her back home by the hair if you got to!" ordered his angry father. "Nip this in the bud, Junior, or you can expect that girl's tantrums and string-pulling manipulations to become a permanent feature of your married life."

The capricious new bride had acted just as the detective suspected she would. The spoiled brat was bound and determined to get her own way.

Junior reluctantly did as told. The Diggins girl returned to N⁰ 16 Hamburg stone-faced, completely shunning everyone in the house including her new husband as she proceeded to solidify her scheme.

In their bed that same night before they slept she outlined her arguments for living in the crowded Diggins house as opposed to the empty Sullivan house and as always, Junior quickly buckled under to her demands so as to "keep the peace."

Junior's parents had nudged him toward a couple of neutral solutions, including finding a house to rent away from both families. Junior was intent on buying a house removed from the confines and filthy industry of the First Ward in one of the handsome new real estate developments in South Buffalo which at this point was growing by leaps and bounds. But the only way to attain that goal was to live with one family or the other while the required down payment could be accumulated. Within a day of Junior dragging Mary Ellen Diggins back into his childhood home, she had steered him back into hers.

The wedding reception had been held in the church parlor because Mary Ellen Diggins was concerned about neighbor busybodies traipsing though her family's house, snooping. Her father Dennis agreed to this but for additional reasons. He had done well by taking advantage of the insurance windfall from the careless railway death of his brother Patrick, buying the large handsome Diggins home on Mackinaw Street and three other properties close by. He wanted the neighbors to know that the former grain scooper and employee of Fingy Conners had made something of himself by being able to afford to rent the church hall. Dennis Diggins was excited too about the joining of the two families, as the famous Alderman John P. Sullivan would be an honored wedding guest.

It was at the church parlor reception that the alderman had first confided to his detective brother that he was seriously looking at houses in the prosperous Central Park section.

"Yer plannin' on movin' away? After all your life livin' in our mother's house?" Jim was surprised.

"No disrespect to Ma, but you know as well as I do what a shithole neighborhood we live in. After all these years I owe it to myself and my family—clean air, green trees, and the smell of fresh cut grass and flowers instead of oil and sulphur and rotting fish—and a little peace and quiet for chrissakes! I always told you that the first chance I had to move away to a quiet clean neighborhood I was going to jump on it. I owe Buffalo's voters a card of thanks actually, for providing me the push. Now that they've voted in the new commission form of government, my job is over and done here in the First Ward, and I'm getting my family out."

"Well, don't tell Hannah about it just yet, JP. Losin' Junior is havin' a depressing effect on her. If she finds out Annie and all her nephews and nieces are leavin' too, it might well just put her into her sick bed."

Hannah did find out, that very hour in fact, when Annie told her.

"But how can that be, Annie?" Hannah argued. "The alderman of the ward has to reside in the very ward he represents. It's the law."

"Oh Hannah," she deflected, "We're not leaving right away! No. But with the new city charter the Board of Alderman will be no more and JP will be free to live wherever we want. We talked about this before, you and me."

"Yes, but I thought you were only daydreamin'. Your whole family lives here in the Ward, Annie. Your mother and your sisters, all the Driscoll and Saulter cousins. They're all here. What are they goin' to think? What'll they ever do without you?"

Annie just looked at her pittyingly, knowing Hannah was of the sort who'd never leave the First Ward, even if she inherited a million dollars.

"Well let's us just enjoy the here and now Hannah. It's still a long ways off yet."

※※※

Unable to fall asleep with her thoughts boiling, Hannah got up to make coffee. As she lingered at the kitchen table still entangled in her musings over these events, Hannah startled to a loud rapping on the door. No familiar comforting protective barking came from her Zeke in response, causing her to feel newly vulnerable. She cautiously approached the entry as the rapping grew more urgent. Through the lace curtain she saw Ruth standing there. Hannah opened the door to find her friend in an agitated state unlike anything seen previous.

"Hannah! Oh my God! She's dead! My mother is dead! She's dead!"

"My goodness gracious, Ruth! What...what happened?"

Gasping for air, Ruth cried "I don't know! They brought her to my door before lunch and put her in her room. I...I was beside myself with a headache and I thought she was sleeping, so I just let her be. I fell asleep on the divan. But when I woke up I thought it strange she had not made a sound, so I went to check on her. She looked horrible. She wasn't breathing and she was gray and ice cold!"

All right Ruth, please come in. Sit down. I'll call Jim. He'll know what to do."

"Hannah! What if they think I killed her? I didn't even look in on her because I was so sick. What if they say she died because I neglected her?"

Hannah was distracted trying to make a telephone connection and only half listening. Finally she was put through to Jim at Police Headquarters.

"Jim, can you come right home now, please?"

"Hannah, what's wrong? Is it Zeke?"

"Jim...well, no...they, the people from the Poorhouse...they brought Ruth's mother in an ambulance to Ruth's house just a short while ago, and now she's dead!"

"Already? My goodness, that friend of yours sure don't waste no time gettin' the job done right, now does she?"

Hannah couldn't help but laugh. "Jim! Don't joke," she scold-whispered even though Ruth was standing right there. "This is serious! Ruth is near collapse. We don't know what to do!"

"All right. I'll leave here right after I call the coroner. You and her just go 'n' wait on Ruth's front porch for me to get there."

"All right. Hurry!"

Coroner Danser pulled up in the department's shiny new motorized Ford truck with two attendants and approached the steps where Jim, Hannah and Ruth awaited. The word CORONER emblazoned in white on the black truck quickly attracted a crowd.

"Detective Sullivan, Mrs. Sullivan," Danser tipped his hat in respectful greeting. "Where's the body?"

Jim led him and the morgue attendants inside to the little back room while the women remained out on the porch. Neighbors approached to question them.

"Go away!" Ruth scolded.

Danser pulled down the blanket in which Bridget Black was tightly wrapped almost like a mummy. She was in full rigor mortis. Stiff as a board.

Once he had completed his preliminaries he returned to the porch.

"Mrs. McGowan, is it?"

"Yes sir."

'What happened, ma'am?"

"Oh my! Well...the ambulance from the Poorhouse arrived with her about eleven o'clock this morning. They brought her into the house and installed her in the back room. To me she seemed to be sleeping. She smelled terrible, so I closed over the door. I was suffering a terrible headache and the smell was making my stomach turn so I went into the parlor and quickly fell asleep there. When I awoke about three o'clock it was silent and it dawned on me she had not called or made any sound. I looked in on her and she was just as you found her. I touched her and she was ice cold, so I ran to Detective Sullivan's house because I didn't know what else to do. I have no idea at all what happened to her, Mr. Danser!"

"Well Mrs. McGowan, you may rest easy. It wasn't your fault. That woman has been dead well over twelve hours or perhaps even longer. Today's chill has delayed her dissipation. That odor is the aroma of decomposition. It looks like the attendants at the Poorhouse never bothered to see if she was still alive before delivering her to you and that is detestable indeed. I promise I will get to the bottom of this! Such incompetence is unacceptable and frankly very, very unusual. Please calm yourself. You had nothing to do with this, and I cannot apologize enough on behalf of the Poorhouse staff! What a terrible thing to visit upon you."

Ruth was so relieved to know that she would not be held accountable for the death, nor would she be responsible for caring for her childhood torturer, that she didn't care about anything else, even the lingering odor. She was free now.

Once the coroner departed with the body Jim returned to work at Headquarters and the looky-loos were shooed away. Hannah stood with Ruth at her front doorway. Ruth, the dedicated agnostic, hugged Hannah warmly as she giddily rejoiced, "God really does answer our prayers after all, doesn't He?"

They hugged goodbye with promises to speak the next morning.

As Hannah walked back home down South Street, an automobile pulled up next to her, its horn honking. She looked over to see that the driver was her brother.

"David! Oh my goodness!"

David J. Nugent hopped out of the car and embraced her.

"What are you doin' in Buffalo?" she asked.

"Uh, just here on a little business, Sis. Say, I need to talk to you. Hop in. I'll drive you home."

Her life-long habitual reflex to spare her brother discomfiture activated. She decided to keep the many troubling events of that day to herself. They made pleasant talk as they climbed the stairs at No. 16. Hannah put the pot on and they sat at the kitchen table waiting for it to boil.

"Hannah, I got a favor to ask yous."

"What is it Davey?"

"I been seein' a nice lady here in Buffalo. Name's May. Turns out, I love her."

"What...w-what? Oh David! No, I don't...Oh my God! What about Minnie and the children? My nieces and nephews! Your marriage? What on earth are you thinkin'?"

"I'm thinkin' about bein' happy for once in my life, Hannah! I never realized how miserable I was 'til I met May."

"Miserable? Why David, you got *everything*! Money, position, a beautiful family, a handsome house in a lovely neighborhood..."

"I don't love Minnie no more, Hannah!" he interrupted. "An' she don't love me no more neither. It's just that simple. We ain't really been husband and wife for a long time now. May opened my eyes again. I feel just like I did when I was young."

"David, you're married with a big family. Nobody expects things to remain the same durin' the passin' of the years. Look at me and Jim for example. I must..."

"Well *I* do!" he again interrupted. "*I* deserve to be happy, don't I? And May makes me happier than Minnie ever did. You know full well I never married Minnie 'cause I was in love with her. I married her because Fingy pressured me into it. I done what was expected of me. For *him*. I gave her children and a good life, but what did I get out of it? Nothin' but misery!"

"Misery? You're surely exaggerating! You live an envious life there in Milwaukee. You got a life out there most men here in the First Ward would kill for..."

He again cut off her arguments.

"Hannah, she's going to have my baby. *May*...is going to have my baby."

"Dear God, Dave! When?"

"In a couple o' months."

"Well...wha...what do you plan on doing?" she asked, shocked and mystified. "I don't understand." Hannah was clearly blindsided.

"I want you to help her, you and Jim. Let her come live here with you, and when her time comes I'll take the train from Milwaukee and we can call a midwife."

"Here? I...Jim would never allow that, you know that as well as I do! You're just not thinkin' straight, Dave. What then? What happens after the baby comes?"

"She'll put it in the orphanage of course. What else *can* we do?"

❧❧❧

"Are you *insane*, Dave?" May Lynch exploded.

"I had to give up my secretary position with Mr. Conners and now you want me to give up my baby too? I gave up more than enough for you already, David Nugent. Now it's your turn! How dare you treat this like this is my problem solely! You made this baby, and you're going to take care of him—and me!"

"But sweetheart, what can I do? I'm married! I already got a family! No. You'll have the baby and you'll give it away. That's that," he ordered.

May Lynch seethed. She'd devoted the past four years to this man, giving up chances to be with other suitors. He always promised her that he'd take care of her. He had even mused about leaving his family so as to be with her instead, to start over again with her in Buffalo.

David stalked out angrily, slamming the door behind him.

May's first instinct was to panic. What if he stops sending her money to force her hand? What if she never sees him again? She couldn't bear that. But she was also not about to allow him to abandon her in her greatest time of need, and so she picked up the telephone.

"Connect me to Mr. Conners at the Buffalo Courier," she asked the operator.

THE FIRST WARD IV

Chief Regan's Priorities

Alderman Sullivan sat at his home office desk opening Saturday's mail. A note arrived with an attached news article. The note said.

> Alderman Crook:
> This illuminating news piece from the Washington paper appeared nowhere in any Buffalo papers, and don't we all know why? You are all alike, your kind. You are all no better than dirt.
> We'll all be finished and done with you and your crooked friends soon enough. Praise be Buffalo voters for ending the likes of you and others who think your job is to tell the rest of us how to live our lives whilst picking our pockets. You should have been ousted twenty years ago or more.
> Good riddance!
> (signed)
> - An Independent Citizen

JP scoffed, then unfolded the news article and began reading. It had been cut from the *Washington Herald:*

WOMEN'S DRESS HALTS CHIEFS
Hot Fight Rages In Police Convention When Subject Is Brought Up.

Grand Rapids, June 17 — The international Association of Chiefs of Police held a session which was three-fourths peaceful today. It was peaceful while the chiefs discussed the "drug traffic," the necessity for police aeroplanes, and the social evil. It was war-like only when the chiefs ventured to talk about women and women's clothes. William A. Pinkerton of Chicago "bolted" the convention as soon as the topic was mentioned.

"It's too silly to talk about." he muttered as he strode away. "This is not a convention of modistes!"

All the chiefs agreed that there are two sides of the problem of "segregation." They all agreed that the "aero-bandit" will be next in criminal evolution, necessitating aero-police. And they agreed that something drastic must be done about the sale of habit-forming drugs.

"But the important matter before this convention," impressively said Chief Michael Regan of Buffalo, "is the matter of women's clothes. It is a crying shame and a horrible disgrace and an intolerable outrage the way they are dressing. We ought to —"

"Ought to leave them alone," interrupted Chief Downey of Detroit. "What do we want to bother about women's clothes for? Let 'em wear what they want to. In my opinion the women never looked prettier than they do the way they dress now. They'll never get styles too extreme to suit me."

Chief Gleason of Chicago agreed with Downey of Detroit.

Segregation came in for a heated discussion. Chief Young of St. Louis who recently put the red light district in his city out of business said that since the abolishment of the segregated district his department was unable to control vice and that crime was on the increase. He declared that segregation was the only way to control the social evil.

Chief Regan of Buffalo took exception to Chief Young's statement.

"We have put the red light district in Buffalo out of commission and we are regulating the social evil better than ever before. Some say that vice can only be controlled in large cities through segregation. This is not true. We are controlling it better in Buffalo now than ever before."

JP recalled the Chief's recent fuming over the way his daughter was dressing. Regan's daughter Nellie was a free-thinking married woman who had rebuked her father strongly for interfering so brazenly in her personal affairs—and her marriage—and told him as much.

"If you continue on this way, Father, I will have no other choice but forbid you from seeing your only grandchild," she warned.

Her successful blackmailing infuriated him.

It was obvious that Regan's Grand Rapids' prioritizing of the bizarre proposal that the nation's police should take charge of determining how American women dressed themselves had its source in his inability to take charge of his own independent daughter. JP knew well the feeling of public ridicule regarding his own past blundering, and thought of the matter little after sharing the news clipping with his brother Jim.

Jim knew otherwise: Regan's unhinging was more in response to his rumored impending firing, in large part due to other preposterous public propositions and excessive overstepping not unlike those documented in Grand Rapids.

Fingy Conners still figured strongly in Regan's leadership and the city's other newspapers were no longer turning such a blind eye to their alliance. Front page stories told of the many recent failings of Chief Regan, his arrangements with saloons to overlook violations for a 40% cut, and his reported payoffs by gambling concerns. Had the Chief not been so blinded by his own hubris, he might have smelled his impending extinction a little more strongly in the air.

The *Buffalo Evening News* accused the city's Police Commissioners of dereliction of duty, allowing Regan to do as he wished with no oversight, as had in recent times been clearly documented. These examples demonstrated no interest in the traditional ways in which previous commissioners forged relationships and communications channels with Captains and even members of the rank and file. These days, the one and only person the commissioners ever consulted was Chief Regan. As the *News* stated:

> It is up to them to believe what he says, and when he says there is no gambling, no excise violation and no thieves in the city, they believe him.

It was the Chief's close friend Alderman JP Sullivan in his quest to protect him who schooled Regan as to what was what. That is how the Chief came to the decision to retire, not out of any sense of morality or duty, but because it was the most financially advantageous thing for him to do.

❧❧❧

Fingy was so angry on the long distance call that he could barely keep hold of the telephone. He jammed the ear piece tight to his ear.

"Great Lakes Transit, Milwaukee. This is Dave Nugent speaking."

"Just who the fuck do ye think yous are?" roared Fingy.

David Nugent froze in fear.

"Uh...Boss. Whaddya mean?"

"You know damn well what I mean! You made a baby with May Lynch? While yer married to my niece? Are you fuckin' insane, Nugent?"

Fingy had never called Dave solely by his family name before.

"I...uh...we couldn't help it, Boss. It just happened! I never meant things to go like this! She refused to have an operation! She..."

"What about my niece, you blockhead? And them kids o' yers! Them are me own grandnieces and nephews!"

"May's gonna surrender the baby when it comes! Nobody needs t' know. I got it all figgered out!"

"Oh, yous got it all fuckin' figgered out now, do yous, genius? May just called me! She ain't givin' no baby o' hers t' no orphanage, you idiot. She's keepin' it! Ye know I was wonderin' how strange it was when she just up 'n' quit her job with me all of a sudden. I suspected it might be somethin' like this, but I never thought it'd be *you*, Dave Nugent, that you of all people'd be so ungrateful and stupid to lay a problem like this at my doorstep! I gave yous all thatcha got. It all come from me. Every bit of it. I looked out fer yous ever since you was a boy. I gave away my only niece to yous in a church in front of God 'n' everybody—bringin' yous into the family officially so ye'd always be taken care of! I spent a fortune to get you off the hook for shootin' them polaks on the Mather. When I toldja t' go teach them there polaks a lesson I wasn't meanin' t' fuckin' kill 'em, you moron! So then I went 'n' set you up real good in Milwaukee runnin' my business there so's t' keep yous outa reach of the law an' outa Auburn Prison. An' you got rich doin' it! An' now you shit on me by fuckin' May Lynch an' knockin' her up and puttin' my Minnie and yer own kids down in the dirt, an' makin' me look the fool in the meanwhile?"

Dave right then had an epiphany.

He stopped trembling. It seemed Fingy was more concerned about how this made him look than anything else, about the social standing he'd fought so hard and for so long to attain. He was afraid of what people would think, not just about Minnie, but about himself, for allowing such a scandalous situation to go unchallenged right under his nose. Dave realized Fingy was most upset that others might interpret the situation as Dave having put one over on Fingy. But punishing Dave would mean by association also punishing his niece and grandnephews and grandnieces as well.

As red-faced Fingy stopped to take a breath Dave nonchalantly said, "Well, Boss...what's done is done."

That wasn't quite the reaction Fingy had anticipated. He fully expected apologies and groveling, but instead received a dismissal.

"What the hell do yous mean, wot's done is done? Wot're yous plannin' on doin' about it, Dave Nugent?"

"What *can* I do, Boss? May's havin' my baby. She refuses to give it up. Yer worried about how it looks fer all involved. Seems to me the only thing that will make things right fer everybody is fer me to take in May's baby and have Minnie raise it."

His Lips Forgot The Taste Of Truth

Fingy Conners' yacht, the *Mary Alice*.

Aboard The Mary Alice

Fingy Conners was jubilant, at least for the moment, as his glorious yacht, the *Mary Alice*, named for his eldest daughter, knifed through Lake Michigan's rough blue waters northward from Chicago. He was in the company of friends whom he had invited aboard at Buffalo to set sail for Water Carnival in the Windy City. There the *Mary Alice* had won the $500 Edward Morris prize for the best decorated boat in the Venetian Night Parade for its colorful electrical display.

In Chicago he had offloaded his guests. Now it was on to Milwaukee to deliver the news.

Minnie Nugent, Fingy's niece, had excitedly informed her children, mostly grown now, of their granduncle's impending arrival and his invitation for the whole family to join him aboard the *Mary Alice* for a Lake Michigan excursion.

The older boys recalled the last time they had spent time with him, at their little cousin David's Confirmation party in Buffalo. Uncle Fingy had barely acknowledged them back then, and too, his domineering behavior at that soirée had not instilled within them much confidence as to the goodness of the man.

Still, Fingy was both their mother's blood uncle and their father's employer. He had made their comfortable life in Milwaukee possible—and they had never been on a millionaire's yacht before. It would be fair to say despite some reservations that they were indeed excited about the prospect.

All eyes were awed by the sight of the imposing *Mary Alice* docked at Milwaukee harbor. She was 174 feet in length with a beam of near 19 feet and a top speed of 20 knots. With a prominent smokestack midships flanked by two towering sail masts strung with colored electric lights, her streamlined hull epitomized the latest in modern elegance, speed and luxury. Photographers from the local Milwaukee newspapers set up their tripods on the dock to record the ship's arrival.

The Commodore, as Fingy insisted he be addressed while in command of his imposing craft, awaited at the head of the gangplank as the entire family pulled up, sardined into their cramped automobile.

"Welcome, welcome, he bellowed jovially. "Ready t' set sail?"

The group's eyes wide as saucers, neither David J. Nugent nor his wife Minnie had ever been invited aboard previously. A steward standing by Fingy's side poured champagne for the adults and Coca Cola for the offspring, despite the three older boys being age 25, 24, and 23 respectively.

Fingy led them on a tour, their being most impressed by the parlor-like staterooms belowdecks with their polished beams, oriental carpets and canopied featherbeds.

As they oohed and aahed the ship set sail, passing the lighthouse at the end of the concrete pier and heading north toward Port Washington. It was a beautiful Wisconsin day. Lunch was served on deck; grilled Lake Michigan pike, asparagus with new potatoes, chocolate cake for dessert and endless glasses of iced tea.

After lunch Fingy invited his niece Minnie to take a stroll alone with him to the elegant bow. He had something to say. As was his usual way he wasted no time on niceties.

"Minnie, me and yous got the same problem—an' its name is Dave Nugent."

She was taken aback. "What do you mean, Uncle Jim?"

"Well, I seen yous two together in recent times, and yous hardly look at each other no more. It's pretty clear things ain't right between yous."

Minnie began to cry. "Oh, dear Uncle...if you only knew the half of it!"

"You can tell me Minnie, after everything wot you an' me've been through together in this life. I'm listenin', sweetheart."

She gathered her courage.

"Oh my goodness. How can I even say it? There's somebody else! He hasn't touched me since, since...I don't even remember since when, Uncle! It's been so long. I'm so terribly lonesome anymore. I wanted us to have one more baby before we got too old, but he won't even hear of it," she sobbed. "He said he's over and done with babies."

Fingy pulled out his handkerchief and placed it delicately in her hand. She dabbed her tears not at all suspecting what was coming.

"Well, yous still gotcher other kids, anyways. Are ye wantin' a divorce, Minnie?"

"Oh Uncle! You know that's impossible! We're Catholic! I confronted him about her but he refuses to talk about it. I begged him to go with me to see Father Callahan so we can fix whatever's wrong, but he only just gets more and more angry. I've gotten afraid of him, Uncle. He's gotten so unreasonable. It's as if he hates me! I done everything I can think of to please him. He just keeps pushin' me away. And these days he treats the boys worse'n even his workers! They can't do nothin' right no more so's far as he's concerned, and yet they bend over backwards tryin' to please him at every turn. It breaks my heart so to see it."

Fingy peered out toward the endless blue horizon, then cleared his throat.

"Well...looks like I got some bad news fer yous, Minnie."

Her mouth fell open.

"What?"

"I had Dave followed when I suspected he was steppin' out on yous. I had my detectives snoop around t' see what he's up to," Fingy lied, "an' they found out some things."

"What kind of things, Uncle?"

"Minnie, here. Sit down."

Without question she sat on a deck chair and looked expectantly into her uncle's squinty eyes.

"Minnie, turns out he does have somebody else, in Buffalo. You were right. And that lady's just about ready to birth Dave's baby."

Minnie gasped audibly and appeared as if she might pass out.

"*A baby?* Oh my God, oh my God, oh my God..."

"There's somethin' I gotta ask yous."

"No! I can't take no more, Uncle! Please!" she cried.

"Lissen. This lady he's been seein'. She worked for me at the Transit office. She ain't married. She can't keep no baby. Right now she's livin' in a boardinghouse out there in West Seneca outa sight. Nobody knows the pickle she's in, 'n' I wanna keep it that way."

"That's not my concern! I'm your family!" she exploded.

"I want you to take the baby an' raise it like it was yer own," he stated matter-of-factly, as if it were a perfectly logical solution.

Minnie was flabbergasted.

'*What?* You can't possibly be serious! What in God's name are you thinkin'? You expect me to raise David's bastard child after...after he wouldn't even hear of me havin' *a baby of my own?*" She spat out the word *bastard* as if it were a poison insect. "Raise his dirty baby by some...some...*whore!* In my very own house alongside my own sweet children as if it was one of my own? Is that how little you think of me, Uncle? No! I will not!"

"Minnie! That baby is your children's own blood brother or sister," he bellowed angrily. "Yous can't deprive them of their rightful kin!"

She had become hysterical.

"No! I said no! How could you ask such a thing of me? *We* are your family! *Me!* Me and your nephews and nieces! *Not* David! He's nothing to you except your, your..."

"Minnie stop right there!"

"...murderer! I know all about what he done for you, Uncle. He still brags about killin' people! Everybody back in the ward knows what he done!"

She was shouting now, and her sons all the way back in the aft section with their father stood to see what might be the matter.

"Sit yerselfs back down, yous! Mind yer own business," commanded their father as he peered expectantly toward the bow.

"Minnie, yous got no other choice," Fingy growled. "This is Dave's flesh 'n' blood. Don't be small, now, girl. Don't punish a defenseless little baby fer what David alone done t' yous. It ain't Christian. Yer better'n that!"

"Uncle! You're rippin' my family apart! How do you think the boys will react to such a thing? They ain't dumb little kids no more!"

"You'll tell yer boys it's the right thing to do, that it's yer idea, 'n' it's wot a good charitable Catholic woman does. You'll be teachin' yer boys a lesson about charity, like in the Bible. Teachin' 'em to be better people than their father."

"They wouldn't believe a single word of it! You don't even know my sons—and all their father's put my poor boys through…beatin' them black'n'blue for the least little thing! Makin' 'em feel like they're nothin'! Ridiculin' them in front of all them other stupid lowlife men, them…them *white trash nobodies* he's got workin' for him down there on the docks, them laughin' at my beautiful boys! But they sure do know their father—inside *and* out! You bet they do! And so do you! This will be the final straw for them. And for me too."

"I want May to come here before she has the baby," he said flatly, as if deaf to her words. "so nobody in Buffalo will know. I want yous t' do that fer me."

"Do *what*?"

"Make sure she's comfortable. Help take care o' her."

"Jesus Mary and Joseph, Uncle! Have you not heard a word I just said? I may not be able to prevent that whore from goin' wherever *else* she might, but she is not going to step one foot inside my house!"

"Don't argue wit' me!" Fingy Conners suddenly and quite characteristically erupted in entitled crimson rage. "I didn't go 'n' put *you* in the orphanage when yer Ma was killt like I shoulda, now did I? No! I didn't! I was only twenty-three when I took yous in! Twenty-three! I wasn't ready to be a father to no nine year old little brat—but I done it anyhows, because it was the right thing to do! The Catholic thing to do! Now you need to do your part, Minnie. It's your turn!"

"*My* part? *My* turn? My part is my children! My part is my marriage! My part is my own family! I done my part. I took my turn—over an' over an' over again—puttin' up with David Nugent and his shenanigans all these years! I will sooner take David's pistol and shoot him and his whore both through the head while they're asleep than allow that trollop to set foot in my family's house! After all, I did learn a thing or two about the ways to solve a bothersome problem while growin' up in that house of yours, Uncle! I am finished an' done talkin' to you about this! You should be ashamed of yourself!"

Minnie turned on her heels, determined to no longer be a shill, neither to her husband nor to her bombastic uncle. It crossed her mind briefly to just throw herself overboard, but instantly realized that might be exactly what the two conspirators were counting on. No. She was going to hold her ground.

The resentment over her husband's hubris in the matter of his mistress and bastard child was one thing, but the fermenting outrage of his three eldest sons, all having toiled throughout their young lives struggling to become the exact opposite kind of man their father aggressively chose to be, was quite another.

The remainder of the voyage was fractured. Resentment so charged the air like an electric current that one could almost smell the sparks. Minnie shut down completely, isolating herself from all the others. Without warning the memory of her mother burning to death before her very eyes as a nine year old little girl haunted her, as it did whenever her uncle Fingy behaved toward her in an overbearing manner.

Minnie's memories of that nightmarish event were fragmented and unclear. She pictured herself being tossed out the window by her mother into the waiting arms of panicked neighbors gathered below as the house became fully engulfed, her wounded uncle Dennis Hurley immediately following her. She relived the neighbors screaming hysterically for her heroic mother Julia to follow, only to watch in horror as Julia lingered too long, desperately trying to fit her beloved sewing machine through the too-small window in order to save it. Minnie pictured the nightmarish surrendering form of her dear mother disappearing into the flames as the house collapsed beneath her feet.

Julia had married well in Michael Hayes. Her husband, the father of Minnie, had preceded Julia in death by three years. The Hayes family was well-to-do, and Julia was willed a comfortable inheritance. When she died in the fire, Julia's will named her parents as beneficiaries tasked with raising her daughter Minnie, with no financial provision made for her struggling ne'er-do-well brother Fingy.

The suspicious origin of the fire that killed Julia and nearly killed Minnie and Fingy's stepbrother Dennis Hurley was never legally established. Neither were the deaths of Julia and Fingy's father and stepmother very shortly thereafter. The inheritance of the estates of all the dead went not to Minnie, not to her other two uncles, but entirely to Uncle Fingy alone. As she grew to adulthood Minnie had often wondered how the norms of inheritance could have been so misconfigured as to allow her Uncle Fingy to so richly and solely benefit.

As Minnie paced the deck raging under her breath, Fingy busied himself as proud Commodore of the *Mary Alice*, while David J. Nugent brooded and fumed at the rail as if it were he who had been the one debauched.

As her sons tried to rally to their mother's side they were ordered away by their father. The boys had no idea what had transpired but as always they knew their despotic father was at the forefront. While their mother remained secluded up near the bow, the boys retreated further aft where among themselves they stealthily discussed what might have occurred whilst keeping one wary eye on their father and the other on the Commodore.

Once the *Mary Alice* had dropped anchor and tied up back in Milwaukee, the family disembarked in somber silence and obediently entered the automobile.

"I gotta stop at the office," David said.

The auto drove to the end of 6th Street at river's edge where he ordered David Jr. to come inside with him. All three sons worked there but the younger two were ordered to remain in the vehicle.

After his brother and father disappeared, Michael Nugent turned to his mother and said, "Momma, what happened? What on earth is goin' on?"

Minnie could only hang her head. The obedient wife did not respond at first. Then she said, "Michael, where is the revolver your father gave you for your 21st birthday?" Then she looked out the window at a ship slowly churning its way up the Menomonee so the children could not see her tears.

"What are we doin' here, Dad?" asked David Jr., once inside.

"Sit down," his father ordered. "I need yous t' tell yer brothers somethin', so listen up. That mother o' yers finally drove me t' do somethin' I ain't exactly proud o'— but what's done is done. There's this lady in Buffalo I was seein' and now she tells me she's havin' a baby, an' it's mine. Yer granduncle decided that it won't look good t' have this lady bein' seen out 'n' about back in Buffalo so he wants her to come here. She's gonna be livin' with us. So you need t' tell yer brothers so they can be on their best behavior."

David Jr. wasn't so shocked by the news of the mistress or the baby as he was floored that Fingy and his father had conspired so brutally to disrupt the family's lives as to scheme the fallen woman move in with them. To expect everyone to accept such an egregious act of disrespect toward their mother and betrayal of the entire family was pushing the limits of previous intolerable acts on their father's part to an even more unendurable extreme.

After ten minutes the two Davids returned and the auto departed for the family home.

All three eldest sons worked in their father's labor contracting business, their compliance informed by equal parts blood, money, and fear. Since their young teens each had been groomed dutifully for a position in granduncle Fingy's stevedore enterprise. They worked at the company after school and during summer vacation and no other possibility was entertained by their father as to any alternative.

The phenomenon newly recognized by alienists of those domineered and tyrannized remaining tied with their abuser despite awareness of their being victimized was exampled in this case to an uncommon degree. The boys had often talked about breaking free of their father's domination to pursue college or a career borne of their own interests and talents, but that's as far as it ever went—just talk, as a means to vent the resentments and frustrations at their remaining shackled.

Although they were all grown men now, whenever faced with the threat of unleashing their father's rage, they predictably reverted to the coping ways and methods of the tortured young boys of their vulnerable youth.

THE FIRST WARD IV

Czar Michael Regan

Buffalo Police Chief Michael Regan was completely out of control.

Angry, illogical, lying publicly and absurdly, alternately threatening and carrying out threats, he had divided the Buffalo Police Department like no predecessor ever had before him.

Terrible crimes went unsolved due entirely to his lack of interest and failed leadership. A dangerous known highwayman terrorized the city for ten days, shooting and robbing citizens with little effort made to apprehend him despite the newspapers' screaming headlines.

Regan had shut out Buffalo's news reporters from obtaining what every citizen had a right to know. As a prisoner was being searched at a Headquarters desk, the reporters present questioned the desk sergeant for details. Regan turned his back on the reporters and in a voice that could be heard even on the second floor of the building said to the desk sergeant, Edward Armbruster, "Don't give any of them reporters nothin'. Remember, sergeant, nothin'. Don't give 'em nothin'.'"

Regan then took command of the prisoner who had been arrested after grabbing $400 out of the hands of his victim. Patrolman Shook had made the arrest, but Regan placed the crook into the hands of one of his favorited detectives, who then got credit for the arrest. Deprived of his rightful commendation for apprehending the crook, Patrolman Shook was left shaken and angry, since advancements were awarded within the Buffalo Police Department based on performance. Shook's being cheated out of acknowledgment after chasing down and capturing the criminal at his own peril was viewed quite naturally by him as both shameful and unfair.

Among the detective-sergeants—the department's elite squad—Regan had favorites while ignoring others entirely.

"Among the twenty men attached to the detective bureau, Chief Regan does not even pass the time of day to five of them," wrote the *Buffalo Evening News*. "Oblivious to his own advanced years, he has many times said the members of the bureau were a lot of 'old women and they ought to be thrown out of office.' This was said not only in the presence of news reporters, but in the presence of local businessmen."

Although childhood friend Detective-Sergeant Jim Sullivan was among those favored by Regan, he was nonetheless disturbed by the Chief's more recent outbursts and inexplicable animosity toward the unfavored portion of the squad whom Sullivan admired and respected. Sullivan's suspicions were piqued further upon discerning parallels between the escalation of aggressively audacious self-serving tactics newly exhibited by his soon-to-be-retiring alderman brother JP and those of the Chief. When he brought the subject up as they enjoyed a beer in the Mutual Rowing Club's parlor, JP dismissed his concerns.

"Don't worry 'bout it, brother. Mike's just trying to figure a few things out."

"Alright," Jim responded, "but exactly what is it that *you* are tryin' to figure out, JP?"

Regan had taken half the detectives off crime solving and had them doing little other than investigating letters that people wrote to the B.P.D. looking for missing relatives or property. Regan had stripped nearly every power formerly invested in these out of favor detective-sergeants, launching the city into a full-scale crime wave. He allowed the unfavored only to do what he said in regard to their actual police business. If there were any favors to be handed out, no matter how hard an out-of-favor detective-sergeant had worked on a case, one of Regan's favorites was called in and the credit given to him.

This system newly injected into the department took the heart out of the detective-sergeants. What formerly had been, and still should have been, the most important office in the Buffalo Police Dept. became little better than a letter investigating bureau.

Upon the acceleration of his authoritarian actions the *News* headed a crusade to rid Buffalo of Regan, headlining "A Crisis In Police Misrule."

Every Captain in the department had rebelled against Regan's policies except for one, and every rebel, thirteen out of fourteen, was immediately and *en masse* transferred out of their former precinct to punish them for daring to revolt in solidarity against a system that, as the *News* put it, "tied them hand and foot when it came to the performance of their duties that common decency directs."

In an address the following day to the members of the men's club of the First Presbyterian Church of Dunkirk, Regan said there was absolutely no reason for his being attacked because he alone was responsible for the fact that "there is no crime in Buffalo."

The preposterous claim made jaws drop. Questions regarding Regan's state of mind rippled through the city.

"There may be a few burglaries once in a while," he claimed, "but no women are attacked or assaulted."

Aghast, the *Buffalo Evening News* produced the public records from just the previous week to disprove Regan's lies. It listed:

Murders: 4
Burglaries: 64
Hold-ups (six were women) : 11
Rapes: 2
Swindles: 6
Pickpocket Jobs: 12
Fake solicitors: 5
Robberies by dope fiends: 4

Among the burglaries Regan says were "few" and "once in a while," some of these had been committed in the homes of the city's wealthiest citizens and thus reported prominently in the newspapers. These prosperous victims were astounded to learn Regan's claim that these crimes never occurred. The loot from the reported period was valued at over $7000 according to police records, and only 25% had been recovered, much of that from pawnshops by Detective Sergeant Sullivan, head of the pawnshop detail.

The *News* also accused Regan of having inflated the figures of recovered property regardless of the actual value of the stolen goods so as to enhance his department's reputation. It was pointed out that inflating the value of recovered property stolen during a period in which no crime was taking place in the city was quite a neat trick. During the period that Regan claimed was crime-free, eleven armed holdups took place, six of these against women, two of whom were also raped.

Regan blamed the *Buffalo Evening News*' having obtained these records on the police Captains and on those detective sergeants that had fallen from his favor, when municipal law made it clear that these records were public records to which the general public and the newspapers had every right to inspect. Regan claimed to be above the rule of law, blaming and punishing his own men for undermining his dictatorial commands.

The *News* reiterated in each story pertaining to this crisis:

> In justice to the police captains, detective-sergeants and desk sergeants who will undoubtedly be blamed for the giving out of this story, the NEWS wishes to announce for Superintendent Regan's benefit that the records listed above are in the NEWS office now and they are duplicates of Superintendent Regan's own records and they were collected by a NEWS reporter without the assistance of any member of the police department.

Regan's erratic and bombastic behavior could well be tied to Alderman John

P. Sullivan. Regan had acted this way because at long last he could. It was JP who informed Regan about something that no one in any official capacity had forewarned the Chief.

Sullivan revealed to Regan that if he tendered his resignation as Police Superintendent any time after January 1, 1916, the commencement of the new commission form of government having been set to rule from that date forward, Regan's pension would amount to $850 a year. However, if he quit before then, his pension would amount to $2250 a year, almost three times as much, the amount the present form of government had stipulated for retiring Superintendents.

With nothing to lose and everything to gain by retiring, Regan felt free in the final months of 1915 to let loose his years of petty resentments and perceived slights on anyone and everyone who irritated him in any way whatsoever.

His many public statements that stirred the citizens' ire and were unprecedented for the historically even-keeled Chief became a revelation of who he genuinely was and how he honestly felt about things, rather than the controlled public face he had meticulously cultivated for so long previously.

After being allowed to run free for ten days the highwayman terrorizing the city was finally arrested. As the highwayman's most recent shooting victim fought for his life, Regan concluded it was a good time to take a vacation, and off he went.

His Lips Forgot The Taste Of Truth

THE FIRST WARD IV

Black Eyes All Around

With two black eyes swollen near shut, Minnie tiptoed her way into May Lynch's room. The baby stirred in her bassinet next to May's bed. Minnie had gone into the bathroom to cock the trigger so as not to alert anyone before the act could be carried out. Her two eldest, David Jr. and Michael, were still hospitalized. William was home recovering in his own bed.

It was 3 a.m.

Minnie wanted David and May and the baby all dead. She was sure her sons would help cover it up once the deed was accomplished, but she dared not alert her boys beforehand for fear of their talking her out of it.

It had been a cold and calculated plan until something Minnie never anticipated happened: she found herself falling in love with the baby.

❦❦❦

May had let out a scream and a grunt at exactly five minutes before ten in the morning as her water broke, gushing out onto the Nugent's kitchen linoleum.

Mixed with the water was a copious amount of blood. For Minnie it was a dream come true. It appeared to her troubled mind that May might die in childbirth along with the baby, and thankfully no one was at home to interfere in the execution of such a blessing—only she and the whore.

As was her habit when others had been at home, Minnie completely ignored May as if invisible. She did nothing to care for her and the result of that was beatings at the hand of her husband who had assigned her as both handmaiden and midwife to his mistress. Minnie was determined she would be neither.

David made the mistake of punching Minnie in front of them when all three eldest boys were at home. Finally, at long last, they ganged up and wrestled their father to the floor. David Jr. put him in a choke hold and held on for dear life, cutting off oxygen and blood flow to the brain, as the other two pummeled him until the old man passed out.

When he finally came to, his three grown sons hovered over him. David Jr. pressed his revolver to the old man's head and said, "If you ever lay a hand on our mother ever again, we will kill you."

As May cried in fear, Minnie chuckled.

"The baby's comin'!" cried May to deafened ears. "Call the ambulance!"

Minnie ignored her, hoping for a quick end. She knew it might still be hours before the baby finally came and nervously looked at the clock to calculate. The two youngest would be home by four. That gave her six hours.

"Shut up, whore," warned Minnie.

"Minnie, you can't do this to me no more! Please! The baby's comin'! The baby's comin' right now!" May cried as she doubled over in pain. Holding onto the edge of the kitchen table, she squatted and immediately the baby dropped to the floor with a wet thump, much to Minnie's shock.

Minnie stood silent and motionless. She noticed there was practically no blood, not the blessed crimson gushing she'd hoped for that might signal May's imminent demise. May scrambled, slipping on the wet floor, trying to get away from the stilled baby in horror and repulsion.

"Help me Minnie! I'm gonna bleed to death!" May cried.

Minnie remained a passive observer.

May had never birthed a child before. She had neither natural instincts nor any idea at all about what to do. It hadn't occurred to a princess like her that she might perhaps read a book on the subject, so assured was she by her paramour that his wife would tend to her every need. He'd been mistaken.

The baby made no sound. It didn't move. It was a girl.

Minnie gazed at the glazed bluish form and thought to herself, *I always wanted another girl.*

The baby looked just like her very own kids when they were born. She was always disappointed that they resembled more their father than her, even the girls. The baby looked especially like Dollie. As the lifeless infant lay there, May whimpering concern only in regard to her own well-being, paying no mind at all to the dead baby, Minnie's instincts kicked in. She couldn't allow this child who could easily be mistaken for one of her own, die.

She picked the baby up, turned her over so her chest rested on her palm, pivoted her forward, head down, and firmly rapped the baby's back. It made a choking sound, mouth open, as if trying to breathe. Minnie reached a finger into the baby's mouth and pulled out a glob of mucous from her throat, then hung her upside down by the feet to rap on her little back until another glob was expelled and the baby began to wail.

May sat on the floor, legs spread eagle, dumbly not knowing what to do or say. When the baby came to life and her transparent skin turned from blue to pink, May did not rejoice. She did not cheer, "Thank you, oh thank you" to Minnie as any normal mother would upon seeing her dead baby come to life entirely due to the heroic exertions of an intervening savior.

At that moment Minnie realized that May wanted her baby dead even more than she herself had.

❧❦❧

As Minnie stood over her sleeping rival ruminating, the heavy revolver cramping her hand, trembling at the prospect of what she was about to do, May awoke with a start. She was momentarily stunned silent during her perceived final moments of life until she at last screamed.

Into the bedroom rushed David J. Nugent.

Seeing his wife pointing a revolver at his mistress, he tackled her to the floor. But she held tight to the pistol, refusing to let go until it discharged by his ear. He instantly recoiled, releasing her, believing he had been shot. The baby screamed, the new mother shrieked, and poor William limped in from his recovery bed despite his shattered ankle.

David checked himself and determined he had not been hit after all, even as Minnie kept the revolver pointed at his head. The gas had been let out of him. He couldn't hear a thing. People around him seemed to be speaking, the only clue being their moving lips. In all his years as an enforcer for Fingy Conners, and all the men he had shot, shot at, bricked, piped, drowned, stuffed into barrels, beaten to within an inch of their lives in concert with his gang, Nugent had never actually come this close to dying himself.

This awakening was a revelation.

He raised himself from the floor, Minnie following his every motion with both hands cradling the gun, her finger pressed to the trigger poised to fire again in response to any wrong move on his part. He did not speak. He did not holler, warn, heckle, menace or otherwise respond in any way that could be interpreted as typical of his usual threatening manner. His foremost thought at that moment was self preservation.

The three youngest, Molly, Dollie and George, lingered outside the door in the hallway crying.

Dollie called out, "Mommie!"

Minnie responded loudly, "The three of yous! Back to bed, now!" and they obeyed. William was in no condition to respond physically, neither to help nor hinder, so he stood there propped against the closet door for balance. He just watched, hoping his mother would put a bullet into his father's head quickly. He would vouch for her, testifying that it was purely self defense. His word and her black eyes would be proof enough for the police.

"May—get yer ass outa that bed." David ordered.

Virtually paralyzed with fear and traumatized by how close she had come to death, May struggled to do as told.

"Get some clothes on," David told her. "We're leavin'."

May got up and reached for the baby.

"Get your dirty whore hands off that baby," warned Minnie. "You just leave her where she is."

Minnie never lowered the gun. As the two lovers left she followed at a distance, silently pointing the revolver, finger on the trigger, ready to end the two sinners, until the auto pulled away from the house and disappeared around the corner.

"Jesus Christ! What do we do now, Ma?" exclaimed William as Minnie comforted the baby.

"I don't know Billy," she answered. "We'll see, though, won't we?"

❦

Two days after the adult sons of David J. Nugent had wrestled and strangled their father into unconsciousness for beating their mother black and blue, they were at the stevedore office, all working.

None were on speaking terms with their father then, nor he with them. They just carried on with their work as dependably and efficiently as always. They were secure in their belief that they, as a trio of levelheaded mature adult men, had changed their father's mind about how he was allowed to treat their mother, as well as themselves, from that fateful day forward.

David J. Nugent glanced out the window at the gathering of dockworkers by the shed. A steamship was being nudged upriver by two tugs, all three ships' horns and whistles screaming their exertion. He unhooked his hat and silently exited without a word, the boys relieved to have him gone.

As he got into his automobile, Nugent signaled to the gang, the leader nodding in response, and stepped on the gas. As he turned up 6th Street, the twenty or so stevedores entered the office and pounced, dragging the boss's three sons out the door and behind the office where clubs, fists and various pugilist dirty methods were applied to their flesh and bones.

The three lay motionless as the ambulance arrived with the police. Only William had been capable of speech.

"Our father had his dock gang attack and beat us," William cried to the disinterested police officers who were chuckling.

Nugent's order to the stevedore gang and the peacekeepers had been simple: try and see to it that none of his boys actually died.

His Lips Forgot The Taste Of Truth

Alderman Sullivan's new home in Central Park,
330 Depew St.

Moving Day

Alderman John P. Sullivan's final year in office, 1915, was fraught with wily schemes hatched in conspiracy with his corrupt pals at the city hall, schemes engineered to wring every last penny from land deals and the legislative body members' associations with the corporations.

With no penalty feasible for his moving out of the Ward he represented considering the transformed political reality, he had done so before the end of his term. The beautiful three-story house was of pink and green serpentine stone with a grand semi-circular front veranda situated at No. 330 Depew Street in the city's Twentieth Ward.

The actual moving day had been filled with emotion for Hannah. 1915 had been a year of loss for her.

The houses at Nº 12 and 16 Hamburg St. had originally been purchased by her savvy mother-in-law Mary Halloran after the Civil War. Hannah had married Mary Halloran's son Jim Sullivan in 1883 and the side-by-side houses had always been occupied by family and their boarders. Hannah had certainly had her share of problems and run-ins with Jim's brother JP through the years while at the same time maintaining a solid if at times tempestuous relationship with JP's wife Annie. The women were united by marriage, but also by their resentment toward their husbands, two brothers who did not value them as they might have. They grew to become highly dependent upon one another, at times indivisibly so.

Many others who could afford it had moved out of the First Ward for better circumstances offered by the tempting new housing developments sprouting up along the bucolic elm-lined streets of South Buffalo built largely by Fingy Conners and his business partner in this particular enterprise, building contractor and Democratic Boss William Fitzpatrick from Seneca Street.

It was an unspoken understanding that few of these expatriates, once they had escaped, would ever return to the mean streets of the First Ward, even to visit. To do so would entail transversing a forbidding industrial wasteland of steel plants, chemical factories and the filth and smells and piles of waste expectorated by like industries through which the main conduit Elk Street ran. This dismal gritty industrial no-man's land served as both depressing reminder and psychological barrier; that once having escaped the demoralizing conditions in the bordering First Ward, few wished to ever cross over again.

Annie had extended an invitation to Hannah to tour the new home in the Twentieth Ward only once, soon after they had moved in. Hannah had visited the Central Park neighborhood only on one occasion previously, in 1899. Then, the alderman had rented a house there for six months to escape violent threats against him and his family by rabid strikers during the infamous grain scoopers strike. Hannah remembered it being like a dream, that visit to Central Park at Christmastime 1899, it embodying the opposite in every way her existence in the First Ward.

Annie like so many other former First Warders wished to forget the past once and for all, to leave it all behind once having moved on to greener and cleaner pastures. She was welcoming to all her siblings and other relatives, but except to attend otherwise inescapable wakes and funerals, she never again voluntarily set foot back in the First Ward.

It had been a daunting task to pack up a lifetime of memories and acquisitions. The Alderman had occupied N⁰ 12 Hamburg Street since the day of his marriage. All eleven of his children were born in that house. Three little ones had died there.

As for the Alderman's wife Annie, she couldn't get out fast enough.

She'd always feared she'd die before ever escaping. From the Alderman's earliest days in office she had become enamored with the trappings of being an important politician's wife. While sister-in-law Hannah next door struggled to make ends meet, she had enjoyed dinners in fancy restaurants, a house servant, and the lovely new frocks required for making the proper impression at social gatherings. When after each such gay event she returned to the gray forlorn house across the street from the bedlam of the Buffalo Union Furnace, the endless ship traffic and blaring horns and whistles, the screeching of metal against metal at all hours, she felt herself undeservedly brought down.

Her pleas to at least move to a quieter section of the First Ward were resisted by her husband who had schemed to locate the voting booth for the 6th district just steps from his front door where he might keep a paternal eye on the operations of the voting on election day.

Hannah offered to help Annie in the move, volunteering her youngest, David, to assist.

There was much hullabaloo as the remaining seven offspring still living at home gathered up their memories, possessions and clothing, at times arguing over who exactly had the right to lay claim to what.

Annie sighed deeply as she crouched her ample form down to explore the hidden recesses of low cupboards and the dining room sideboard, the far reaches of which she hadn't explored in years. There were things crammed into corners she had completely forgotten she owned. The most common phrase uttered by one and all was "I always *wondered* where that went!" upon rediscovering a neglected something or other.

JP enlisted two of his Sullivan Ice Co. trucks from his small fleet to haul the inventory to the new Depew Avenue house which was fully twice as large, and more, as the Hamburg Street house. The move required multiple trips back and forth between the First and the Twentieth wards.

JP was especially proud of his little Pierce Arrow fleet of trucks and boasted of them in an article he arranged to have printed about the Sullivan Ice Co. in the latest issue of *Ice and Refrigeration* magazine. In it they ran a wonderful photo of the three vehicles lined up in the loading bay along with his praises as to their modernity and convenience. He purchased fifty copies to send to all the local newspapers, to friends, and to the top clients of his few remaining competitors. He felt his dream of becoming the sole supplier of ice in the city, of buying out all his rivals and cornering the market so as to raise prices coming closer to fruition.

The previous year the same magazine ran a full eight pages devoted to Sullivan Ice's new 50 ton electrically driven raw water ice making plant. Being able to actually create ice, rather than wait out mother nature's temperamental moods, opened new markets for clean ice which previously relied entirely on the winter ice harvest from Sullivan's spring-fed Crystal Lake located in nearby Freedom N.Y. Summertime clamorings could finally be fully met. Pure bacteria-free ice-on-demand meant a boom for, among other businesses, ice cream parlors and soda fountains. The number of these had doubled in the city with the introduction of year-round clean product.

What JP failed to see, right in front of his eyes, was the increasing development of electric refrigeration. As progress went, home-sized units could well be foreseen in the not-too-distant future, rather than just the current industrial versions, meaning homemakers might soon no longer have a need for commercially-supplied ice to keep food from spoiling.

Workers from the ice plant along with the two trucks made what might have been an arduous move from the First Ward to the Twentieth a breeze. What surprised everyone, even the alderman, was how quickly everyone adapted to the new house, as if they had always lived there. There was little ceremony upon leaving the old home, as the move was intended to be secret, seeing as it was technically illegal in the sense that JP was still the alderman of the First Ward. But with just months to go until the end of his term, and having recently suffered foreboding night dreams, just like those of his wife, of his own death shortly before ever being able to enjoy the new house, he threw caution to the wind.

They chose a school day to be as stealthy in the move as possible, yet the ruckus attracted quite a few neighbors anyway, miffed that the Sullivans were sneaking away without so much as a proper goodbye or a farewell party after 45 years.

Everyone said they were sorry to see them go, and they meant it. Having their alderman living practically right next door had served every one of them quite well at some point or other, but besides that, the alderman and his family were all genuinely well regarded.

As the final aldermanic year wound down, the various politicians were making their disparate preparations to move on. JP's good friend and colleague Supervisor James Mead of the Eleventh Ward had resigned his office the previous year so as to run for State Assembly. In his place to complete his term as Supervisor was appointed one-armed Edward Moylan. Moylan had been a Lehigh Valley Railroad detective, then foreman, for many years. He had lost his appendage to an accident in Canada while constructing a roller coaster at Crystal Beach Amusement Park in Southern Ontario at the turn of the century.

He had in fact been hospitalized for this mishap and placed in the very same room as Alderman Sullivan when JP had also been hospitalized. It was during this hospitalization that they first became acquainted.

A rabble-rousing politician of the unapologetically corrupt school, Moylan had ascended to become Democratic General Committeeman of the Eleventh Ward. In 1912 Moylan and his cohorts had brazenly tried to steal a local election in which Albert J. Rhine had been elected to replace Moylan as General Committeeman.

Taking his place at Buffalo city hall at the end of 1914 to fill Mead's seat, Moylan was ecstatic over his new powerful political role. He enthusiastically tried to resurrect his relationship with Alderman Sullivan, recalling to him their being roommates in the hospital together, but Sullivan remained distant and business-like having no memory of this due to the heavy sedative laudanum he'd been administered.

All his years of hard work for the Party was finally paying off, Moylan joyfully maintained. However, his euphoria was to be short-lived. As the changeover to the Commission form of city government upon the close of 1915 drew closer, it was decided by the Party not to run Moylan as their chosen candidate in the coming election.

This news had a devastating effect.

With his wife Nora and unmarried children present in the house on Lovejoy Street, Moylan retired to his bedroom around 10 p.m. on the night of October 26th with a pistol in his one remaining hand. It was reported on the front page of the

Buffalo Evening News the following afternoon that his son Edward Jr. had found him that morning at 8 a.m. when he went in to wake him. The pistol yet remained in Moylan's hand while a bullet hole breached his skull. No one in the house, it was testified, had heard the shot.

People reading the account in the newspapers couldn't help but wonder, *Where did his wife sleep that night?*

❧❧❧❧

It had nevertheless been an open secret in the First Ward that the Alderman's family had vacated their homestead of forty five years, with word eventually getting around to the wrong ears. The abandoned house lay vacant until one day on an inspection visit JP inadvertently walked in on individuals stripping the house of its fixtures.

As always he spun the story for the *Buffalo Express* to his dramatic advantage, exaggerating the peril of the situation for effect. Young neighborhood boys were dismantling some plumbing when he had walked in on them. Embarrassed, they immediately panicked and fled. They recognized the alderman and he recognized them, but he had no desire to punish them, for he remembered when he was a boy that he was no angel himself, and even so, the victims of his own boyhood pranks never did seek reprovement against him.

His account to the newspaper reporter was that the perpetrators were dangerous hoodlums who brandished pistols and threatened his life, causing him to wisely flee. The headline of his creative news account made the soon to be ex-Alderman smile:

Owner of the House, Facing the Revolver,
Acted as Discreet Hero.
IT WAS SULLIVAN.

The Alderman's solution to the house's vulnerability was to have his eldest son Thomas, co-manager of the Sullivan Ice Co., move into it with his wife Mae and their firstborn, daughter Marion.

Come January 1, 1916, legally freed of his elected obligation, JP announced to the newspapers his purchase of the home at N°. 330 Depew Ave.

The family, now mostly grown to adulthood, were thrilled with their new socially upscale life. The endless years of living amid the industrial chaos of riverfront lower Hamburg Street was at long last history. Only his eldest, Thomas, had married; the rest of the brood moved into the new house continuing to provide the alderman the historic family hustle and bustle so important to him. The older children,

Thomas and Daniel, Mazie and Jennie, were all employed in the family business at the new Sullivan Ice Works on Broadway with its modern Arctic sanitary artificial ice-making apparatus.

With war raging in Europe, JP feared for his sons, and the future of his company, despite the solemn promises of Woodrow Wilson to keep America out of it. JP knew of Wilson's ways and methods as Governor of New Jersey and harbored deep doubts about the President's sincerity in this regard.

His Lips Forgot The Taste Of Truth

Honorary Banquet
tendered to
Hon. John P. Sullivan
upon the completion of
Twenty-five years service
as Member of the Board of Aldermen
by the People of the First Ward
Saturday evening, December eighteenth
Nineteen hundred fifteen
Hotel Iroquois

The End Of An Era

After a quarter century in the Board Of Aldermen, his final year serving a third term as its President, John P. Sullivan was done. The citizens of Buffalo, a few decades too late some might say, decided after having been robbed blind for half a century that the city needed to abolish the existing form of government altogether, and the Board of Aldermen in particular, and start over.

"Good riddance," they said, "and John P. is the reason."

It had been Sullivan's dominance that ultimately turned the populace in favor of a complete overhaul, not just of their politicians, but of the form of governance itself.

No one epitomized the rot and dysfunction of Buffalo's bureaucracy more vividly than Sullivan while curiously at the same time collecting so many admirers. The love/hate relationship with Sullivan was embraced by voters, other politicians and even the city's newspapers. They hated his politics but loved his humanity.

No place else in the city was as unconcerned about political affiliation as was Buffalo's First Ward. It had always been that way, during the entire quarter century of John P.'s tenure as First Ward alderman, and for the entire quarter century preceding that during Alderman Jack White's similar lengthy and corrupt reign. Republican or Democrat didn't matter, not to the candidates nor to the voters: for over a half century the two political parties may just as well have been one and the same.

❧❧

At first JP's neighbors planned a little get-together at the Alderman's house on Hamburg Street with the intention of citizens dropping by throughout the day to thank him—or perhaps otherwise—for his twenty-five years. Once word spread however it became clear that the house could never hold such a throng. Anyway, the family had already moved out and the house was empty of furniture.

Grander plans were hatched for a large celebration at the Hotel Iroquois.

A committee of thirty-nine members was formed to plan the grand shindy. Four hundred guests bought tickets. JP was in his glory, and wasted no time working on his farewell speech. Although none-too-secretly bitter at losing the long drawn-out battle against a new form of city government whose purpose was to do away with him, he was of the mindset that what's done is done, and ruled out any reference in his remarks to his disappointment. The banquet was planned as a purely joyful affair.

The thirty-nine men on the planning committee ranged from a Supreme Court Judge to a career street thug, the judge being Herbert Bissel and the thug being Dick Nugent, first cousin to Hannah Sullivan and her brother David J. Nugent, and Fingy Conners' most eager toadie.

Tickets to the fancy banquet were offered to any and all wishing to attend. Luminaries were polled and they fell all over themselves bidding for a speaker's role. Indeed, more speakers applied than could be accommodated.

One of those who did not respond to the announcement of the occasion was Fingy Conners. The day before the banquet there was still no word from him.

JP and brother Jim Sullivan threw a little pre-celebration at the Mutual Rowing Club boathouse for the fellows on Friday night. Remarkably, skinflint JP actually sprung for a keg on his own dime. There was much back-slapping, free-flowing Beck's, and a good share of off-color jokes.

Jim said, "JP, I ran into Lawley today."

Lawley was head of JP's banquet committee.

Jim continued, "Ain't seen him this excited since he managed to marry off that homely daughter of his, poor thing."

"Which one?"

"Whaddya mean, 'which one'? He's only got the one."

"No, I mean, which one is the 'poor thing' you're referring to? Him or her?"

"Well...both of 'em—now that I think of it."

They laughed.

"He's got everything under control and runnin' smooth," Jim stated.

"Lawley's a fine friend indeed," JP nodded.

"You sore about Fingy smokin' you?" Jim asked.

"Nah, he didn't smoke me. He just didn't say he was comin', that's all. It'd be just like him to just show up. You know him, above it all and better than the rest of us. And you know how much he loves making an entrance. He'll be there."

"Well it ain't important anyway, JP. And it shouldn't be to you. All them other men are your *true* friends—and *their* attendance is all what really matters."

"You're right," JP said out loud.

But inside he thought differently. Quite a number of men with whom he had fought against in bloody battle had bought tickets. Men who had denigrated him publicly. Men who made no secret they were no friend of John P.

But what these same men did demonstrate was their respect, and a certain flavor of admiration, despite their differences. That made JP smile, proud that they thought this way about him regardless of their past political squabbles. It was something that he had always been very jealous of in his late friend John J. "Kize" Kennedy. Men who were against Kennedy politically were proud to call Kennedy a friend. Growing up, JP had striven to be like him. And now it seemed that, in some important ways, he had achieved that.

"It's going to be a bit empty not having Kize there," JP said after his minute of introspection. "You know something, Jim? There's a certain phrase that's always dusted off at people's funerals and in their obituaries. It's that curious expression, "estimable qualities." These are spoken of broadly and generally, with no elaboration, meaning it's seldom detailed exactly what these 'estimable qualities' of the deceased are. It seems no matter how familiar or not the speaker or writer happens to be with the deceased, they use that same catch-all in place of having to provide actual examples of such. But that phrase truly did apply to Kize. So many estimable qualities that lovely lad had that I never found in nobody else since. So very many."

He took a long triple gulp of his beer.

"Sure do miss him." JP said, choking up.

"Amen," agreed Jim.

❧❧❧

Hannah Sullivan couldn't even recall the last time she'd attended such a fancy affair, if ever. Jim wanted Nellie to take her mother to the department stores to buy a special dress.

"You're a fine seamstress, Hannah, but wouldn't you like to make a day of it, tryin' on some new fancy dresses for the occasion?"

"You know I don't like wastin' money Jim. Mary Sweeney has some lovely material and we been talkin' about tryin' a new style for me."

"Well, suit yourself Hannah, but this here's a fancy banquet with fancy people."

"My cousin Dick isn't exactly fancy people," she scoffed.

"I don't give a damn if Dick Nugent shows up in nothin' but his boxin' trunks, Hannah. He's not what I'm talkin' about. I want you to feel as pretty as you are. We ain't exactly broke, you know. I can afford to buy you a silk dress and a trip to the hairdresser's for this shindy."

"My goodness! I don't know..."

Nellie overheard the conversation from the next room.

"We'll go downtown tomorrow Ma, just me and you. We can have lunch at Hengerer's Tea Room. It'll be fun!"

❧❧❧

After finding nothing suitable at Adam, Meldrum & Anderson's, Nellie said to her mother, "Let's go try Flint & Kent."

"Flint & Kent? Oh no, that place costs too dear!"

"Come on, Mother! We'll just go in and have a look. They might have something nice on sale."

"But them sales ladies are all so snooty. They look at me like...like..."

"Like you're from the First Ward?" Nellie completed her mother's thought.

They both busted a gut at that truth.

"To heck with them. Our money's as good as anybody's!" Nellie encouraged.

Flint & Kent had a certain scent about it. As they walked in the door Nellie told her mother it was the smell of money. Hannah thought it more like a citrus perfume. They passed by the little memorial. Nellie looked at it askance.

"That thing is still up? Tush!" she sniffed, dismissing it.

"What thing?"

"That memorial there—to that Kent fellow. I mean, the Titanic's been sunk over three years now!"

Edward Austin Kent had designed the beautiful Flint & Kent store with its central sky-lit atrium and Tiffany stained glass.

"Was he related to the store owners, do you think, Nellie?"

"I don't know Ma. Oh, look! There's Aunt Annie. And cousin Jean...oh no. And *the others*," she snarked.

Sure enough the Alderman's wife and daughters were there shopping as well, most likely for their banquet frocks.

"Look, Ma. She's gained back all that weight, and then some."

Annie had always been fat, but due to an illness she'd suffered a few years earlier, she'd lost a lot of heft. People failed to recognize her back then, as her face was so different. Hannah had been taken aback as to how pretty she was, almost like when she had first married JP. Thinking she was being encouraging, Hannah had told her as much, but Annie took some offense.

"She's lookin' just like her old self again," Nellie chastised abrasively. "And I do mean '*old*.'"

"Nellie! Stop!"

"Hallo, hallo," sang Annie when she spotted them. Immediately Annie's daughters nearly butted heads in their haste to warn each other about their abrasive cousin Nellie's presence. They put on their best smiles anyway and approached.

Nellie had always resented her cousins for all they had which she had not, but now more than ever, their having recently moved up in the world to Central Park. Regardless, the Alderman's brood were polite.

"Your hair looks lovely, Nellie," said cousin Jean.

"Yes," her sisters agreed.

Nellie smiled insincerely.

"Mama I'm hungry," whined Mildred, Annie's youngest.

The cousins hadn't seen each other in months, not since the alderman's clan had moved away. But even previous to that, the once-close relatives had grown up and gone their own ways in recent years, and had fraternized little.

"Mildred, those curls! I'm so jealous!" Hannah said. "I saw your photograph in the newspaper. I cut it out and put it in my scrapbook. You looked so pretty and so grown up!"

"Really Aunt Hannah? Oh thank you!" Mildred bubbled.

Mildred had pulled the cord to unveil the tablets that her father had lobbied his cronies in the Common Council to purchase. The tablets commemorated their service to the city. It was intended to be a memorial in light of the Board of Aldermen soon to no longer exist. The tablets were affixed to the wall of city hall in the Common Council chambers, and the Alderman chose his little Mildred to do the unveiling honors at the public ceremony.

The *Buffalo Evening News* in commemoration of the auspicious event editorialized:

> It is the sole Sullivan hand-tooled resolution at which the public could afford to laugh. It cost the taxpayer nothing unless it be the defacement of a few feet of mural space in the City hall to remind the citizens of a group of men whose only claim to recognition is a number of measures, like the "Island deal," calculated to filch the public purse for individual gain.

JP had called in all the newspapers to record the event. Photographs were made by all, and Mildred got to be famous for a couple of days. It went to her head and the other kids in the neighborhood let her know about it. Predictably, the Alderman was roundly mocked for the self-serving plaque, some wishfully referring to it as "John P.'s tombstone."

The Alderman's Mazie sized up her cousin as they stood there in Ladies' Silks. Mazie did not suffer fools gladly.

"Are you hoping to find a frock for the banquet, Aunt Hannah? We've been looking everywhere," Mazie said.

"We just walked in the door, Mazie. Did you find nothing that you like here?"

"Oh yes, but then we went to Hengerer's to see what they had, and now we're back here to make up our minds."

"I'd be surprised if they got anything to fit a flat rail like you, Mazie," Nellie quipped. "You really should be eating something once in a while. You look ill."

Hannah stiffened at the inevitable.

"Well, what about you, Nellie? I'm surprised you don't take better advantage of what they picture in the Larkin Soap catalog, especially considering they give you a nice discount for working there."

"Tush! You well know Larkin don't sell no fancy dresses, you bird-brain!" Nellie ridiculed. "Just about everything else, *but!*"

"Who said anything about dresses, silly?" Mazie shot back. "I meant the soap!" Her sisters roared.

"All right you two, now stop it this minute!" chastised Annie. "Hannah, we'll see you all Saturday night at the Iroquois. I'll arrange for you to be at our table."

"Why, thank you Annie. That'd be really lovely of you," smiled Hannah. "Bye!"

Annie mirrored Hannah's smile and turned, dragging her daughters away by their coat sleeves as they giggled uncontrollably.

Hannah angrily turned on her daughter once they were out of earshot.

"Nellie! What on earth has come over you recently? No wonder you got no friends no more! Why do you have to be so mean?"

※※※

The banquet room at the Iroquois Hotel was abuzz with the nearly 400 celebrants who'd come to honor John P. Sullivan.

City and State movers and shakers rubbed elbows with First Ward grain scoopers. Judges made small talk with criminals who'd had their share of appearances before the bench in court. The Mayor joked with his electoral adversaries.

Each guest was presented a bronze medallion commemorating the Alderman's 25 years, his image embossed in bas relief, a red ribbon attached for looping around wearers' necks—the only criticism being the ribbons should have been green.

Hannah, Jim, and their three offspring were seated at a table adjacent to the Alderman's family, Annie apologizing for the fact her brood took up an entire table and then some.

"You look lovely, Hannah!" Annie enthused, and her daughters all agreed brightly. Hannah had visited the hairdressers, she had found a silk frock that proved very becoming to her, and Nellie helped her apply a bit of lip color and rouge. Hannah otherwise never wore the stuff. Nellie only nodded to her cousins in acknowledgment before parking her hind end in the seat and burying her head in the programme's menu page.

The alderman's Mazie said a little too loudly and a bit too testily that cousin Nellie's face was just begging for the back of her hand, at which time the elbows of both her mother and her brother Daniel collided with her ribs from either side.

"Ouch!" Mazie cried, looking at Daniel accusingly.

"Not here!" Daniel scolded. "Have it out later if you will, but not here. Not now."

Mazie quieted.

Just then three unmarried girls approached the table to fawn over and flirt with Daniel. He was considered the most eligible bachelor in the entire First Ward for his tall handsome looks, his athletic build, and his prestigious position—being still only in his mid-twenties—as manager at the Sullivan Ice Company. His mother Annie in recent times had grown quite perturbed at the forwardness of the various young girls, and even some brazen married women, wherever they went who made themselves quite obvious. For them, Daniel was like a magnet.

"What is it with girls nowadays!" Annie cried in disgust, "throwing themselves so blatantly at men!"

"They're not throwing themselves blatantly at *men*, Mother," corrected Mazie dryly. "They're throwing themselves blatantly at *Daniel*—there's a *difference*," she giggled. In response all the sisters laughed uproariously, Daniel blushed a bit, and Annie was left puzzled by the entire thing.

"How fancy!" said Hannah excitedly, picking up her toast card to inspect it. Her name was written there in fancy calligraphy atop the silver-embossed initials JPS.

Unsurprisingly, Junior's sour wife Mary Ellen had claimed to be too ill to attend. She was not enjoying her first pregnancy. No one missed her, regardless. She had often expressed her distaste for the Alderman.

"Sorry to hear that, Junior," his father responded insincerely. Then he whispered in Hannah's ear, cocking his head toward their daughter Nellie, "We sure don't need *two* sourpusses sittin' at this table this evenin' to put the damper on things—one is more than enough."

The room crackled with excitement. At precisely 8 o'clock just as the last of the guests were seated, the curtains at one end of the room were parted and escorted by six of his closest friends, John P. Sullivan entered to standing cheers and song. Dinner was immediately served: Cream of Tomato soup, Erie Whitefish, Mushrooms and Crayfish in a puff pastry, Roast Squab, asparagus.

At 10 o'clock the speeches got underway. 21 men were seated at the toastmaster's table. It promised to be a very long night.

Regrets were read first, from former Lt. Governor Billy Sheehan and Buffalo-born former Chicago Mayor John P. Hopkins, both begging off due to prior commitments.

Fingy Conners was not present, nor did he send his regrets.

Mayor Fuhrmann gave an egotistical speech in praise of himself. Supreme Court Judge Bissel regretted that as one of the bishops of the legal profession he was forbidden involvement in political doings. Bissel confessed he could not "restrain a strong feeling of longing, a strong desire again to become a belligerent down in the First Ward where things are lively."

Council-elect John F. Malone, who would be replacing Sullivan in the new city government, praised John P.'s undying devotion to his family and the "manly men and beautiful women" his children had become. At this remark, Annie looked around the family table, proudly beaming while some other agreeing lustful eyes in the room affixed to Daniel.

It was close to one o'clock in the morning when John P. finally got his turn at the dais. He praised others, his cohorts and adversaries alike. He grew emotional upon his remembrances of his departed colleagues, naming them and honoring each, one by one, to great applause. He reminded the gathered of the many great men the First Ward had produced: Lieutenant Governor of New York Blue-eyed Billy Sheehan, Alderman Jack White, and Police Chief Michael Regan, each in reality more criminal than the next, yet saintly in JP's estimation. The Chief's loyal apologist stated that Regan was a man "much abused by public criticism."

Wrapping up, Sullivan reserved a special tribute for the absent Fingy Conners.

"As all are aware, William J. Conners has left an indelible mark upon Buffalo, and on the First Ward in particular. He and I have found ourselves adversaries as often as we have been allies, but in the end his strength and the courage of his convictions have been an inspiration to me, and his charitable works, usually gone unlauded, have benefited hundreds of families in need. Mr. Conners, although he could not be with us tonight due to pressing business concerns in his beloved Florida, telephoned long distance to express his congratulations, and assure me he is with us here in spirit."

Jim and Hannah traded cognizant glances at that last remark, both knowing full well that Conners had shunned the occasion—and the honoree in particular.

Jim chastised his brother silently: *Still bendin' over backwards tryin' to win that little prick's favor, even after all these years, huh JP?*

It was more than that really. JP felt a powerful need to save face, as all would interpret Fingy Conners' absence and his neglect to send his regrets as an intentional public snub.

"I may not have official connection with the government of Buffalo henceforth," JP concluded, "but nevertheless my interest in her future will not lapse, nor shall I be found wanting in the work necessary to her wholesome development.

"For myself though, I'm through, retired, or whatever you wish to call it, and am well content to sit back. And though the passing has no heart burnings, an occasion such as this makes it all the pleasanter."

It was well after 2 o'clock by the time the last well-wisher walked out the door. Annie and kids had all left with JP's blessing as the schmoozing promised to go on endlessly, despite JP's inching himself ever closer toward the exit.

Junior volunteered to take his mother Hannah and his siblings home so his father could linger with JP.

As they walked toward their automobiles, the only machines left parked on Main Street at that hour, Jim said, "I don't get it, JP. That was your big opportunity. That was the perfect time, in front of the news reporters and the perfect gathering of notables, all there to honor you, all excited for you, to announce your candidacy for Congress. We talked about this! What the hell happened in there?"

※≈≈≈≈

Buffalo Evening News Editorial, December 20, 1915:

Piping A Pilot Over-side

Saturday evening's testimonial dinner to retiring Alderman John P. Sullivan was distinctly unique, as the affairs of a great city go.

Four hundred men of our citizenship—the most and the least of it—gathered about the banquet board to pay him homage. There were judges and jack-snipers there, heralds and henchmen, leaders and laggards—men who could buy a thousand tickets to such a function and men who had to skimp and conserve to purchase one.

We do not recall a finer testimonial to the many sides of an individual.

A certain type of man will wonder at this outpouring of sentiment in favor of a man who, more than any other, made our city's recent political revolution necessary.

Such a man is unhealthy in his deduction, and needs a change of glasses. His vision will then improve until he can see in Saturday evening's gathering a splendid tribute to the personality of a man, rather than to his political standards.

The NEWS has no illusions about John P. Sullivan. His political methods we abhor. We shall be as ready in the future as we have been in the past to dispute his political schedule unless that schedule is planned to better form. Mr. Sullivan knows this and we choose this time to say he has always been a fair enemy and a splendid loser—qualities that have made great generals.

And we share the general admiration of John P. Sullivan's personality and quality of friendship. In a fairly long and more than commonly active span we have met many men conspicuous among their fellows for one merit or another. Well among the first of these, in our recollection, is John P. Sullivan, whose unconquerable sense of humor, whose willingness to help those in distress, whose good companionship, friendship and loyalty to his legion place him far out of the zone of the commonplace.

But there is a place for him when he can come back with new standards and a new understanding of city welfare and requirements. There is always need of men of John Sullivan's energy, foresight, powers of leadership and general qualifications when these qualities are well directed.

Considering solely the political aspect, the passing of the aldermanic president creates an irresistible impulse to dip the "Jolly Roger," call the whole cutlassed, turbaned crew to starboard, and pipe him over the side—The greatest of them all!

But there is another phase—a kindlier phase that prompts a kindlier sentiment—a genuine desire to share the goodbyes of his better friends and join them in a hearty "Goodbye John! Take care o' yourself!"

His Lips Forgot The Taste Of Truth

THE FIRST WARD IV

The Friendly Sons Of St. Patrick

Woodrow Wilson's 1916 Presidential reelection campaign was built solidly on the promise to the American people that he would not provide American boys as cannon fodder to protect England, but those behind the scenes knew that America could not keep out of it.

The world could not collapse around it and leave the United States happily unaffected economically or emotionally, not the least reason being that neighbor Canada had been in the war since mid-1914. By 1916, 20,000 heroic Canadian boys had already died, a fact that Buffalonians, living right on the border with Canada and many having Canadian kin, could not ignore.

The spirit of the Fenian movement, whose principal aim was Ireland's freedom and independence from Britain, had never died out. The Fenian invasion of Canada in 1866 as a method to force the issue of Irish independence from Britain may have been the penultimate North American event in Fenian history, but it was not the last. For decades afterward, Canadians from time to time became fearful of a repeat occurrence.

"Me Patrick's pot on you" was at that time the familiar salutation with which Irishmen all over the world on St. Patrick's Day greeted their countrymen.

In 1866 the largest St. Patrick's Day picnic ever held in Buffalo took place at Clinton Forest, a grove located on Clinton Avenue, Black Rock, with over 20,000 people being in attendance.

In 1887, 21 years later, an equally large picnic was held at the same park at which a sham battle was fought between the Rochester and Buffalo companies of the Irish Army under General Spear. This event was so extensively advertised that the Canadian government became alarmed through a belief that this was simply a ruse to make another attack on Canada, and sent the tug *Robb* to the mouth of the Niagara River and marched a large force of Canadian troops on the other side. It is needless to say the Canadians had no trouble from them at that particular time.

Former Alderman Sullivan had always been a champion of an independent Ireland, and as the European war drums grew louder, so did he. He knew that once Wilson was reelected, the President's message would quickly begin to change as he oiled up the American people to prepare them for the inevitable.

It turned out that John P. Sullivan missed his political life as leader in city government more than he'd expected. He remained at the helm of the Democratic Party of Erie County, but the challenges and adventure which that post offered paled in comparison to the ritual of day-to-day wheeling and dealing in the city's combative Common Council.

His Congressional aspirations were still only such at this time, due to his experiencing doubts about his having the heart to reignite his engine politically. So until he could make up his mind, as a way to energize his post-aldermanic life, he took on a new passion: Irish Independence.

The Friendly Sons of St. Patrick selected the veteran master of ceremonies John P. Sullivan as toastmaster to preside over the organization's annual dinner at the Iroquois Hotel on March 17, 1916, together with his wife's maternal cousin Daniel A. Driscoll, former Congressman representing Western New York in Washington D.C.

Driscoll at first did not wish to attend as he was still depressed from his loss in the most recent Congressional election. His anticlimactic return to the Driscoll family undertaking business did little to lighten his darkened mood. In fact his Congressional term had only just ended a mere two weeks previous to the St. Patrick's banquet. The wounds were still raw.

But buoyed by Sullivan's enthusiasm for his historic passion regarding Irish autonomy, Driscoll stepped onto the dais to forewarn the members about the expected change in policy by President Wilson once he claimed victory in the upcoming election in November. Driscoll and the other members in attendance who had enjoyed a background in politics were united in their belief that Wilson's continued vigorous promise to keep the US out of the war had been merely a ploy to get himself reelected.

As guest of honor of the banquet, Driscoll drew upon his insider knowledge of the Nation's Capital to predict what was to come. Together with JP, Driscoll rallied the members to unite in their demand that no American boys of Irish descent be provided to the British cause to fight on behalf of that wicked kingdom that as yet still held the Motherland in shackles.

"It befuddles me to this day," railed John P. Sullivan, "after so many years on this earth, to understand how and why the United States steadfastly stands at the ready as ally to a country that has visited such untold suffering and evil upon the entirety of mankind, Great Britain.

"Why, only 14 years ago, back in 1902, England signed an alliance with the wily Japanese that was against our interests and our nation's very security, the Japanese being a people who are not exactly friendly to the United States. Six years previous to that, a crisis in Anglo-American relations very nearly led to the United States once again going to war for a third time against England. This was precipitated by the Venezuelan Boundary Dispute in which our own Grover Cleveland declared to Britain and to the world that the United States would henceforth forbid the establishment of any European colonies in the Western Hemisphere."

Driscoll lectured on. "We cannot trust England. Never could, never will. Thus, as the probability of war in Europe with the principal goal being the defense of Ireland's historic enemy, every American son of Ireland must rise up and demand, before even a single American soldier is committed to England's cause, the immediate and unconditional granting of independence by Great Britain to our beloved Ireland! There can be no negotiation on this matter, gentlemen! If England wants to survive against the Germans to live another day, then it will first release the chains under which it has imprisoned Ireland for the last 800 years!"

The cheers that rose up shook the hotel building so profoundly that guests unfamiliar with the gathering were put to a fright. Sullivan promised the assembled that he and Driscoll would begin setting their demands in motion the very next morning.

The following day Driscoll postponed their meeting due to feeling ill, so alternately JP met with Fingy Conners at his office at the *Courier* to tie up loose strings regarding their latest business deal. The former Sullivan Ice building at N? 119 Chicago Street and all the ghosts that went with it were being sold to Conners.

The block and tackle mechanism within the three story brick structure was its main attraction. The edifice had been built by proprietors Loomis and Bush of the Buffalo Mantel Works during Civil War times for the manufacture of slate goods: sinks, grates, floor tiles and especially mantels painted to look like marble. The block and tackle was part of the original structure utilized for moving the cumbersome creations. When Sullivan Ice bought it, that apparatus had its uses in hoisting heavy pallets of ice blocks, and if sold to him, Fingy Conners would utilize it for moving and storage of heavy printing presses and other equipment removed from his Courier newspaper operation, or so he claimed.

Throughout the years every building that the alderman had occupied, either as a home or as a business, had burned to the ground, except for this one. The first Sullivan ice house on Columbia Street burned in the 1880s. His Hamburg Turnpike ice warehouse on the beach near Tifft Farm and its replacements burned completely three times. His house on Hamburg St., his brother's house next door, and the original wooden Mutual Rowing Club house located directly behind those two family homes, burned to the ground along with his Toronto icehouse—all within 18 months of each other. And the stables behind 119 Chicago caught fire, killing fifteen hardworking horses and destroying all but one of the Sullivan Ice delivery wagons. The Buffalo Fire Dept. structure on Chicago Street was located mere yards away, and the firemen had arrived very quickly. Despite throwing blankets over the horses' heads and trying to force them out of their stalls, all but two of the equines were too terrified to move. Despite the firefighters' heroic efforts and threats of bodily injury under the hooves of panicking steeds, almost the entire herd burned to death, leaving their grieving drivers bereft, and the alderman with no way to transport his product.

In truth JP was beyond relieved to abandon the First Ward and leave such historical wreckage behind. He himself had come close to death there due to illness on four separate occasions. He was a survivor, but at a cost only he could fully tally.

※※※※

"The quizzical thing about the war," reflected JP sometime later, "was how immediately before, in March, a polling of voters reported four out of five Americans were vehemently opposed to entering the imbroglio. This opposition was not always expressed quietly. In public demonstrations people shouted their disapproval passionately, and some were not at all hesitant to reveal their violent discontent."

Not least among those loud denouncers was former alderman John P. Sullivan, former congressman Daniel A. Driscoll, and the majority of members of the Friendly Sons of St. Patrick.

However, within hours of war being declared on April 7, 1917, the very same people began waving American flags and pledging their loyalty and support to President Wilson as thousands of young men flocked to recruitment offices to sign up for military service. Those who had only in days previous voiced their vehement opposition, who had proposed holding out for Irish independence before approving of a war declaration, found themselves overwhelmed by an upswell of patriotic fervor that caused others to challenge the protesters' loyalty and obscured their pledged objective.

Sullivan and Driscoll were equally perplexed at this one hundred eighty degree reversal in the pronouncements of their Irish neighbors and friends, especially coming on the heels of the disastrous Easter uprising in Dublin the year previous.

"Just consider the irony of it, JP," said Driscoll over a whiskey at the Buffalo Club. "Britain was in a fight for its very existence against Germany, with no United States troops and few munitions to rely upon, their island completely encircled by German U boats, supply ships laden with food and munitions destined for the desperate British people being sunk right and left by the enemy, people being forced to endure the rationing of food and all basic supplies, fighting for their very lives! And yet amid this insurmountable threat of total annihilation of their own people, their country, their Crown, thought it imperative and crucial and a priority to commit precious troops, borrowed money, and scarce military hardware to declare war against the Irish whom they have held prisoner for centuries rather than grant them their independence, even though thousands of Irish lads had joined the British in battle against the German enemy! It's insane!

"How did so many Americans who had previously been incontrovertibly against the war, even after the Germans had sunk the *Lusitania* resulting in the loss of so many American civilian lives, and who were discovered systematically patrolling the United States eastern seaboard with their U boats, reverse so fully and with such breathtaking speed their sentiment once Congress had made its declaration of war?

"For the life of me, I will never understand people," undertaker-by-trade Driscoll lamented. "Perhaps that fact helps explain my preference for the dead."

FINGY RAILS AGAINST WOMEN SUFFRAGE

Little in the world, even a world currently embroiled in a horrifying war, rankled Fingy Conners more egregiously than women demanding the right to vote. The mere thought of females with children in tow awaiting their turn at the polling places enraged him.

How could he control elections as he so brutally had done with his gangs of hired Canal Street pugilists and savage street fighters if the election premises were no longer exclusively male? Perhaps at one time he may have entertained the idea that a woman who insinuated herself into men's important work deserved whatever knocks came her way, but this was no longer the primitive nineteenth century in Buffalo's ruthless First Ward.

"Wimmin gettin' the vote'll cut men's power in two!" he ranted and fumed, correctly.

Women smiled with vindication at his expressed terror over their undisguised intentions, at the thought that they were now on the cusp of claiming what they should have had all along: the right to vote.

"The appalling truth is that Negro men have had the right to vote for fifty years now, but white women have not!" was just one of the many electrically-charged justifications some suffragettes made. "Men who have been allowed by male judges, male police, and male politicians to escape the law, especially in regards to crimes and injustices committed against women and children, will no longer be allowed to do so once women get the vote," was another.

Five more sound arguments were provided by William Jennings Bryan in his address to members of the Ellicott Club in Buffalo on October 18.

"First," Bryan began, "man trusts woman as his wife. Why not trust her as a voter?

"Second — The husband trusts his wife as his partner in the finances of the family. Why not trust her as his partner in politics?

"Third — the father trusts the mother with the care of the body, mind and soul of his child. Why not trust her with the ballot?

"Fourth — Most of the men who vote never go beyond the eighth grade and thus in the graded schools gain all the knowledge of the science of government that they will ever gain from books. Nearly all the teachers in the graded schools are women.

If women know enough about government to teach the men all they know about this subject, don't they know enough to vote?

"Fifth — They used to say that women ought not to vote because they did not go to war. But the war itself has demolished this argument. Women have taken the places of men who have gone off to war. They keep the factories running, the farms producing, the troops supplied, the country in existence. The war has caused England and Russia to declare for women's suffrage. Why should the United States be behind Great Britain and Russia in recognizing women's right to the ballot and the county's need of women's vote?"

Across town at the Buffalo Club, another luncheon was honoring a notable, albeit one not so accomplished a speechmaker as Bryan—Fingy Conners. His editors had crafted a speech derived from the previous day's editorial in Fingy's *Enquirer* newspaper and practiced it with him so as to avoid the man's penchant for speaking extemporaneously his unsorted thoughts in longshoreman's diction. Providing guidance to Fingy Conners was always an exercise in tippy-toeing on eggshells, but much to their satisfaction, Fingy was amenable to their counsel and he stuck to his script in making his argument against women's suffrage.

"Public opinion," Fingy began, "will largely be in agreement with Senator Myers of Montana that the proceedings of the militant suffragists picketing the White House have been outrageous, scandalous and treasonable. He is right in presuming that the American people are disgusted with the doings of these featherheads!

"Why, just yesterday the Senator introduced a bill in Congress prohibiting the practices of these misguided women who have caused disorder and harmed the very cause they were intended to promote. Unfortunately the President has not signified approval of the Senator's legislation. He has been patient to a fault and in my opinion too considerate to the picketers, pardoning several who had been given jail sentences for their unpatriotic activities. As we well know, both sexes and all races and classes of humanity include a percentage of foolish persons. Our President has greater and graver matters to occupy his mind than the ill-conceived suffrage amendment to the federal Constitution and the antics of unbalanced females making fools of themselves.

"The average male voter with the inclination toward granting the ballot to women communes with himself to the effect that women who picket the President's residence are the type that will force themselves into leadership of women in politics. From that horrifying prospect the average male voter applies his prayers and will apply his vote for deliverance!"

At the same moment Bryan wrapped up his speech at the Ellicott Club.

"The strongest argument in favor of women's suffrage," Bryan said, "is the right of a mother to have a voice in shaping the environment that shall surround her child. Her life trembles in the balance as she gives birth to the child, and for years the child is the object of her constant care. She expends upon it all her nervous force and energy. She endows it with the wealth of her love and finds her joy in dreaming what the child will be and do.

"It is unjust to deny her the right to protect her home when wicked men set traps and lay snares for her and her child. As long as the ballot is given to only men, some of whom conspire to entrap defenseless women and children, it is not fair to tie the mother's hands while she struggles to guard her home and family."

And as if speaking directly about Fingy Conners, William Jennings Bryan concluded, "Every man who profits by vice and makes money out of sin is an enemy of women's suffrage. The man who opposes women's suffrage raises the suspicion that he has some political plan which he cannot defend before the bar of conscience."

Those reading Fingy's words took issue with his opining that the suffragettes' demonstrations at the White House were "treasonable." A letter-writer in the Buffalo Express said "Conners would do well to acquaint himself with something called the United States Constitution's Bill of Rights, which guarantees the rights of these women to demonstrate and speak out. Indeed, his falsely calling their rightful actions "treasonable" is in itself treasonable, so let the punishment for treason fall on Fingy Conners."

Fingy Conners' editorial in the *Enquirer* energized the *New York Call:*

Why We Support Women Suffrage

Perhaps it is not altogether ladylike and sweetly feminine to picket the White House and publicly display banners reflecting on the alleged autocratic character of President Wilson. It may not be the best way. We are not sure that it is not, but we don't know. Yet curiously enough whenever this feeling of doubt comes over us somebody always comes along and says something which swings us clean over to the side of the women again. And thus:

"The women responsible for the picketing antics have made it quite useless to take the coming vote on suffrage in New York state. Woman suffrage will be beaten far worse than at the last trial and for no other reason than the exhibition staged day by day at the White House gates.

"The average male voter with the inclination toward granting the ballot to women communes with himself to the effect that women who picket the president's residence are the type that will force themselves into leadership of women in politics. From that horrifying prospect the average male voter applies his prayers and will apply his vote for deliverance."

And when we read that and consider the source it comes from, for the time being at any rate, it swings us clean over into the suffrage camp, and leaves us prepared to endorse almost anything the women may do in their campaign. Picketing the White House seems perfectly all right—yea, even the essence of morality, refinement and good taste.

For before our eyes, when we read the above, arises the vision of the Buffalo waterfront in the good old days of eye gouging, biting, stabbing and shooting; of bloody strikes and lockouts; of "tough" bosses and equally tough longshore gangs; of slugging and blackjacking; of barrel houses and rum doggeries; of putrid petty political graft; and amid it all a bull-necked, fat-jowled brute with a maimed hand—a finger missing, probably "chawed off" in a scrap—holding regal sway—the toughest of the tough.

And we recognize that hand in the above diatribe against the suffragists. "Fingy" Conners, "editor and proprietor" of the Buffalo Enquirer, from which the editorial quotation above given is reprinted!

And when "Fingy" shudders with horror over the prospect that these women are the "type that will force themselves into leadership of women in politics," we know that his giant intellect is recalling the old days of the Buffalo waterfront and that he doubtfully regards future competition. So he, like the "average male voter" he claims to know so well is reduced to "prayers."

Prayers! Prayers by "Fingy" Conners!

Good Lord, deliver us!

Prayers! On the Buffalo waterfront!

What is the world—this man's world—coming to?

'Twas not thus in the old days. Labor—interspersed with man-killing—was then prayer. Why can't "Fingy" get the remnants of the old waterfront gang of sluggers together and go down to the White House gate and clear the jades out? Wouldn't the "average male voter" pray for his success and bless his efforts?

Perhaps he would. But we are not the "average." We're probably below it. Therefore this decides us that our place is with women suffrage; and whenever we falter we will fervently pray that "Fingy" comes to the rescue to guide and strengthen our tottering steps.

—October 17, 1917

❦❦❦

Outside the White House, Fingy Conners met with reporters.

"What's this about your booming Hearst for Governor of New York?" he was asked. "What about Governor Whitman?"

"Whitman ain't got no chance! He's on the wrong side of Prohibition. And it'll be my friend President Wilson for re-election," Conners continued. "They can't beat him. They can't talk against him. You know what would happen to a man who dared get out right now and criticize him or any of our boys 'over there.' Mr. Hearst always gets what he wants. He always wins."

"How about the campaign of 1906? He didn't win then," Conners was challenged.

"Well, that was different. This is war time."

"What did you meet with the President about?" asked another.

"I brung the President a crate of Irish potatoes from my farm in Florida. They're the best that can be had. Nothin' beats Florida soil. He said he was very happy to receive them."

"What about the potato blight?" questioned another reporter.

"It's true that the potato blight has cut American crop production 25% in the states that produce potatoes, but my superior methods have so far been successful in keeping the blight away from my Florida farm."

"Is that all you talked to the President about? Potatoes?"

"Additionally I felt the need to advise Mr. Wilson about the stevedore problem, and how essential the right man be in charge of them stevedore units over there in France. There's nobody better'n me for the job. I don't need no title or no commission. I just want to do my patriotic duty to this country that gave me so much."

From the *New York Herald;*

W.J. Conners Will Aid Army In France

Herald Bureau,
No. 1.502 H Street, N.W.,
Washington, D.C.

William J. Conners of Buffalo, formerly Democratic State Chairman of New York and credited with laying the foundation for his great fortune by being able to handle the roughest stevedores who ever trimmed cargo on the great lakes, will be the American Director of Docks in France, and as such the commander of the three regiments of stevedores which the War Dept. has just organized.

Of course Mr. Conners' friends can see nothing less than the rank of brigadier general for him, although it may be he will be one of those $1 a year civilian employees of the government, like Herbert Hoover, Frank A. Vanderlip and Howard Coffin.

American transports landing in France have been greatly delayed at piers there because of inefficient stevedore work. The War Dept. organized the three regiments of stevedores and then cast about for the most capable "boss stevedore" and Mr. Conners was selected, despite his millions of wealth. He says he can upload the largest ship ever made in twenty-four hours. "It is a matter of handling the men," he says.

His Lips Forgot The Taste Of Truth

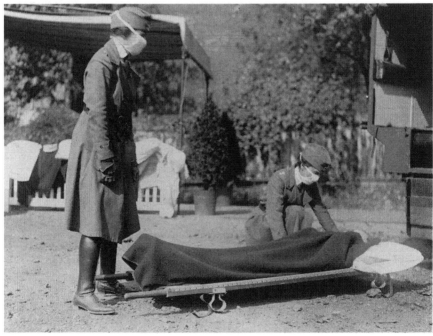

Heroic Red Cross Ambulance "Girls"

1918

THE WORLDWIDE INFLUENZA PANDEMIC

Former Alderman JP Sullivan and former Congressman Dan Driscoll's maneuvering to rally Americans against the British war cause without England first vacating its hold on Ireland was a failure. About this they were quite bitter, especially as the time arrived to supply to the government their own flesh and blood.

"I'll be fucked up the ass on the stage at Shea's Theater in front of an audience of nuns before I'll lose any of my boys to Britain's rescuing!" JP seethed. In solidarity the two cousins conspired with their friends in high places to ensure none of their sons were shipped overseas.

JP's two eldest, Thomas and Daniel, together ran the Sullivan Ice Company. He depended on them indispensably for his family's livelihood. Both sons were married, but only Thomas had a child. Daniel's medical problems in seeking a deferment included hearing loss as a result of his rescuing his older brother from the freezing waters of Lake Erie when they were teenagers and a chronic knee injury stemming from a recent motorcycle accident.

JP's other sons, James P. and John P., were not married. They claimed no deferments, but the former alderman through his connections successfully kept them out of harm's way. Son James P. had been a second year student at the Massachusetts Institute of Technology when he took his leave to join the Army. Son John P. joined the Navy; he was stationed at Great Lakes Training Camp when the shocking news came. There was no time to make it home.

On September 20th reports were made of an influenza epidemic raging at the military facility at Niagara-On-The-Lake, just across the border. Dr. Franklin C. Gram was Buffalo's Acting Health Commissioner, appointed the previous April when Health Commissioner Dr. Francis Fronczak was commissioned in the Army. Gram asked that the city's physicians report any and all cases of influenza they encountered.

On October 7, as cases in the city mushroomed, a special sub-committee was formed to head an anti-influenza campaign which declared that a sweeping closure order might soon be necessary. Committee men who were owners of the larger stores, saloons, and theaters in the city vehemently opposed the directive on that day, even as influenza cases had doubled with each setting of the sun, and hundreds had already died.

On October 10th, 700 new cases of flu were reported. Buffalo Mayor Buck, acting under emergency order, closed all schools, churches, movie houses and theaters, ice cream parlors and soda shops, pool halls, saloons, five-and-ten stores, and barred all indoor gatherings and meetings of any sort effective 5:00 a.m. the following morning.

It was hoped these provisions would bring the epidemic under control and forestall the need to extend the order to include commercial businesses, factories and industrial plants. Brewers and saloon owners protested the order angrily, as did the Christian Science churches, the only religious denomination that dared.

The public was strongly urged to wear masks as a precaution against contagion. Red Cross workers went into high gear fabricating these items for distribution. The Christian Scientists resisted these preventative measures.

They declared ludicrously that God would prevent their becoming ill—even as their members dropped like flies. Then they admitted contrarily that regardless of the fact that God wasn't preventing their members from becoming sick, He would most certainly cure them, but for that miracle to happen, their churches needed to remain open.

Their leader Burton H. Wade scoffed at the idea of wearing face masks supplied by the Red Cross in public as a preventative, saying only if it became law would Christian Scientists do so, and derided the health department's posters on walls all over the city for their frightening people.

He stated "How absurd is it to put out daring posters throughout the city to convince people that they have influenza while at the same time one of the primary injunctions of the poster is that the reader must not worry! If the board of health doesn't want people to worry why go to so much trouble to frighten worry into their minds?"

Elevators were shut down, much to the chagrin of hotel operators. Public telephones were off limits and businesses were urged to disinfect their telephones multiple times throughout the day. Sporting teams were banned from engaging in activities although many ignored that directive. Shared drinking cups and roller towels in public restrooms were removed.

An ongoing streetcar strike was credited with preventing an even greater spread of the pandemic. With churches, schools and businesses closed and streetcars not running, the city took on an eerie stillness. People were forced to stay home and become reacquainted with their families.

On the day that the Mayor's closure order took effect, 1700 new flu cases and

53 deaths were reported. Hospitals were overwhelmed and in desperate need of medical personnel. Retired doctors and nurses were beseeched to come forward to once more make available their crucial services. Motorists were urged to give a lift to any white armband-wearing female they saw walking, as this signified these women were nurses. The Central High School downtown was converted from classrooms to hospital wards housing 1,000 beds. In all, 22,000 cases and 1800 deaths were reported in Buffalo in the month of October 1918 alone.

The great influenza pandemic, known by such names as the Spanish Flu and The Three Day Fever was sweeping around the world killing far more people than the war itself. Panic took hold as the rumor was spread that the Germans had developed a biological weapon they had inserted into Bayer aspirin. A severe worker shortage diminished government services and industrial production. 25% or more of police officers, sanitation workers, nurses, doctors and firefighters failed to report for duty. Transportation, food supply, and communication networks were equally in peril. Homes with inhabitants suffering from flu symptoms were put under quarantine with no one allowed in or out. This meant food and other necessities were in many cases unavailable to occupants.

Physicians were required to report new cases to the health department, but due to the hardship and inconvenience suffered by quarantined families, some did not. Because of the fear of being placed under quarantine many sufferers waited until the second or third day of their illness to seek treatment, which was by then too late for them in many cases, once pneumonia was allowed to take hold.

It was said that by the 5th day of illness, the typical influenza patient was either dead or well on his way to convalescence. The fight against the Spanish Flu permeated every aspect of life, even working into children's skip-rope songs:

> I had a little bird
> And its name was Enza
> I opened the window
> And in-flew-Enza.

Oddly, the epidemic proved deadliest among those who should have been best equipped to fight against it, people in their prime between the ages of 20 and 40. Not to be spared was the 28-year-old matinee-idol-handsome towering Sullivan son and brother Daniel, newly married. He took ill on Columbus Day, October 12, 1918 at his home on Vandalia Street, literally a stone's throw from the Hamburg Street house he had been born in.

By the time Daniel took sick, Buffalo was in very deep crisis. The pandemic hit so quickly and so fiercely and was so unprecedented in scope that pandemonium ensued. No plan had ever been drawn up for such a possibility. No municipal body had been created or tasked with managing a mass illness, and city fathers, themselves dealing with sick and dying family members, could not cope. Providers of essential civic and medical services died or were taken sick themselves, including priests and ministers, gravediggers, morticians and casket builders. Bodies remained at home as family members who did not already own cemetery plots searched high and low for some dignified spot in which to inter their decomposing loved ones.

The day previous to Daniel falling ill, the health department at 3:30 p.m. virtually ceased to function. Reports of new influenza cases so swamped the telephone exchange that it became inoperable. By 11 p.m. the new cases from only that one day, October 11, tallied 1237, amounting to almost one new case every minute, with over 55 deaths reported, including Sullivan neighbor Alice Bennett, daughter of Mutual Rowing Club member Maurice Bennett from N⁰ 50 Hamburg St.

Helen McQueen of 150 O'Connell St., Estelle Quinn of 143 O'Connell St., George Masterson of 100 Vincennes St., Bridget McClellan of 92 Tennessee St., and Albert Murphy of 41 Arkansas St. were just some of the Sullivan neighbors a mere stone's throw away counted among the dead on that day, October 11.

Price gouging was the order of the day with costs of coffins doubling or tripling and morticians' services, if even obtainable, out of reach for even some middle class citizens. Available burial plots were snatched up in a buying panic at inflated prices, leaving many with nowhere to bury their beloved family members. Corpses remained unburied as families searched for unobtainables—a willing, available and affordable undertaker, a proper casket, and someone to dig the hole.

The system of body disposal was stymied and thus the hastily put in place rules demanding the immediate burial of the dead within 24 hours had to be by necessity overlooked. This lead to municipal and hospital morgues becoming backed up, overwhelmed as to their capacity.

Buffalo Health Commissioner Dr. Gram, when told that there were not sufficient caskets in Buffalo to bury the dead within the required 24 hours, tasked the Department of Health and Sanitation to begin building coffins to be sold at cost to families that could afford them, and given away to the poor for free.

Undertakers were enraged to encounter the municipal government competing with them in their own business during this boom time. Dr. Gram, who compared the undertakers' questionable business practices to those of the Standard Oil trust, stated "I was never so serious in anything in my life than in the determination that there should be burials without excessive cost. We can make trimmings and iron handles look like oxidized and provide a stained pine cloth-lined coffin no one need be ashamed of. The undertakers don't want the health department to compete with them. They don't want anyone to know just how cheaply people can be buried. A proper funeral should be had for no more than $25."

With the digging of graves curtailed or halted, cemeteries stacked caskets inside work sheds, outdoors under tarps, or even within the cemetery office itself. As terrible as this state of affairs was on the surface, the deleterious effect such a disruption of norms as they pertained to the customs of death and dying was profound.

The Red Cross Girls Motor Corps were lauded as heroines for their organization of an ambulance service. The young ladies drove ambulances and their own private motor cars from long before dawn until far into the night tending to the sick, carrying patients on stretchers from their homes into the ambulances, and then into the hospitals, and often tucking them into bed there.

Daniel's death came so quickly and so surprisingly that the alderman had to scramble. The Driscolls were sick and their undertaking services had been suspended. No unoccupied gravediggers could be found. Catholic priests prioritized tending to the dying and performing last rites over eulogizing the already dead. No priest was available for Daniel's funeral. Half of JP's girl children were ill. His other sons were away serving their country. Only Thomas the eldest was healthy and available. Luckily there was the family plot at Holy Cross cemetery. A handful of men, including JP's brother Jim, Jim's son Junior, and a couple of neighbors not yet infected, gathered at the cemetery with shovels for the arduous task of digging a six foot hole. Junior defied his wife's orders not to participate.

"You got six month old baby David to think about," she lectured, "and your four year old son Jimmy! You can't be bringing home the influenza!"

Junior defied her to do his part for his admired cousin.

To everyone's relief a health department-built coffin was obtained at the last minute. No one wanted Daniel laid bare in the ground wrapped only in a shroud.

Daniel Sullivan had been the day-to-day Supervisor at the Sullivan Ice Company. He, like many other citizens, placed financial and other non-health-related issues at the forefront, and he, like many others, continued to go to work after falling ill, feeling it was his duty to his employees and as breadwinner in his household.

His recent bride Catherine worried. Two Sullivan Ice employees had already died and many more were ill. She tried to dissuade him from going in to work.

"But we're desperately short-handed with so many out sick!" was his response.

Because of his athletic background and impressive physical stature his argument in favor of his decision was not vehemently challenged. It was thought he was too strong and healthy to fall ill.

On October 15 he was rushed to Sisters Hospital with severe pneumonia. He died within hours. The brief funeral was held right there in the hospital room, bedside. Only immediate family were allowed to attend. Daniel's body was afterward taken posthaste to Holy Cross cemetery just as the health department had mandated regarding the handling of flu victims in order to minimize the risk of public contagion. Because funereal gatherings were forbidden during the pandemic, Daniel was deprived a proper customary wake and funeral from his home and church to commemorate his life. He was nonetheless remembered as a beloved husband, son and brother. It was added that until his motorcycle accident, he had been a celebrated member of the World Champion Buffalo Germans basketball team, which it was noted, held the record of one hundred and eleven consecutive wins.

During the height of the pandemic, the Spanish Flu sickened 25 million Americans, one quarter of the nation's population, and killed 550,000. One in four human beings on earth were infected with the flu virus as well. Up to 50 million died worldwide.

As the Sullivan family stood around the box suspended above their hastily-dug hole at Holy Cross cemetery, they regarded how under normal circumstances there would be 200 or more mourners honoring the life of Daniel J.H. Sullivan instead of just his wife, parents and siblings. And under normal circumstances too they would be dressed in their Sunday best rather than in muddy shirtsleeves, and sweating.

The group took hold of the ropes and lowered the casket into the ground, struggling mightily to keep the heavy box level. JP stood by his sobbing wife's side after leading the priestless little group in a final prayer. He hesitated for some long moments, shovel in hand, palms blistered.

Finally through his tears JP said, "We're gonna have to cover you over now, my dear Danny Boy. I'm sorry. I don't want to leave you here cold and all alone in this decrepit box. We love you and miss you. But we'll be seeing you again soon, my lovely son. All of us. I promise."

And with that, each member took turns filling in the grave—wife, mother, sisters, brother, father, cousin. In the end all felt proud and satisfied by their contribution, realizing that digging the grave with their own hands, lowering their beloved into it, and taking turns covering him up had instilled within them a therapeutic effect that eased somewhat their deep feelings of grief.

JP, in reliving the remembrance of that gathering in later times, realized how the undertakers' profession had so cunningly usurped the roles of family members in the funeral process without anyone realizing it or protesting, inserting themselves into the most deeply personal of rituals where strangers rightly did not belong, thereby stealing away the final act of intimacy with the deceased from those who would come to mourn the loss most significantly.

Daniel J.H. Sullivan at the Sullivan Ice. Co. Office.

Detective-Sergeant Jim Sullivan, Buffalo Police Dept.

Resignation

Optimistically, Detective Sergeant Jim Sullivan had planned to retire on the 40th anniversary of his joining the Buffalo Police Department. But the natural infirmities associated with the advancing of the years, coupled with decades of physical abuse suffered while carrying out his appointed duties as a police officer, including a broken nose four times over, compelled him to reconsider.

He had in fact contemplated retiring from the Department numerous times in the past only to doggedly continue pursuing that which rewarded him his life's purpose. Regardless, the unmistakable signs were now demanding his full attention and thus he began making preparations. It was time to go. It was time to plan for the future, for the next chapter in his life. Chief among these new plans was his recommitment to the activities and objectives of the Mutual Rowing Club, the athletic organization he'd founded back in 1881.

In 1911 Police Chief Mike Regan had put Jim fully in charge of the Department's pawnshop detail. Jim's job was to track down, recover and return to the proper owner stolen goods. At that point many pawnshops were little better than clearing houses for thieves and shoplifters and a source of bargains for citizens who didn't trouble themselves as to the origins of shady goods.

Ultimately, as crime victims became more aggrieved over the schemes of the city's Shylocks, the authorities were compelled to step in and better control the business. This included the confiscation of suspect goods, of which the monies loaned by the pawnbrokers to those pawning said merchandise would never be recovered by them.

Jim Sullivan had made more friends than enemies in the pawnshop trade. Perhaps possibly he may have been persuaded once or twice by the offer of some especially attractive knick-knack to overlook a discrepancy or two so that the shop owner might remain in business.

Alternately, at times he may have stepped in when victims and citizen do-gooders became overly aggressive by declaring the entirety of a given shop's inventory ill-gotten, when in fact many a citizen in dire financial straits had been saved by the pawn brokers' willingness to loan them crucial funds while holding precious family treasures they fully intended to recover at a later time.

For these and other various reasons, accommodations and favors over the years, the modest Sullivan home at № 16 Hamburg Street filled up with beautiful items.

Daughter Nellie, who was a private music tutor in the First Ward on Saturday afternoons and on some evenings after her workday ended at Larkin Soap, became the delighted owner of some beautiful instruments: a Hungarian violin, a Spanish guitar, a cello, a banjo. Nellie's instrument of choice was the piano, but she gladly accepted those others with the full intention of learning how to play them someday, and also because they were lovely.

Waterford crystal, a collection of petite sterling silver lidded boxes, a French mantel clock, various examples of arts and crafts furniture, a brass coal settle from an old sailing ship embossed with its portrait, Japanese vases, American Indian pottery, a pair of Indian moccasins with exquisite beading, some lovely plein air oil paintings, modest gold jewelry and more accumulated in the house over the many years, all to Hannah's great irritation and guilt.

Despite Jim's claims to the contrary, these items she was convinced were the result of thievery in one form or another. She had asked for Father Lynch's guidance in this vexing matter during her Saturday confessions, these divulgements becoming more frequent as her aging body accelerated its betrayal of her. Father Lynch assured Hannah that in his opinion the goods were gifts from grateful store owners who appreciated the fair and even-handed treatment they received at the behest of respected pawnshop detective Jim Sullivan. But despite her reverence for the priest, the goods' presence nevertheless gnawed at her and tortured her by their mere residing in her home. Hannah Sullivan was never the type to be seduced by pretty knickknacks, favoring the purely utilitarian and practical. Crystal and pottery and artworks and such only collected dust and grime that compelled her constant attention, thereby only exacerbating her already resented housekeeping workload.

"Washin' the pots and scrubbin' the floors are necessary tasks to keepin' any home nice, but dustin' the curlicues of fancy goods I don't even want is an aggravation and a waste of my time. I've gone from carin' for little children in my younger days to carin' for useless old objects in my elder years," she'd complained to her friend Ruth. "I've come to dread Saturdays. How much more simple my life would be without all this jumble underfoot!"

Tellingly, she never said any such thing to the husband who continued proffering these gifts as a demonstration of his love.

With each new addition he brought home she had smiled and said "Thank you, it's grand!" never revealing to him her suspicions of the sins associated with the objects' origin or the drudgery she felt being made a slave to their upkeep.

Much to Hannah's relief Jim resigned from the pawnshop detail in November 1919 in order to assume responsibilities as office man at the Detective Bureau. Hopefully this meant there would be a cessation to the unappreciated gifts. At the same time Jim was winding down his police workload he decided to run for the presidency of the Mutual Rowing Club in that organization's upcoming election.

As founder he had been the club's first president for the initial two years of its existence but had not sought the responsibility any time thereafter. The club had most recently lost three celebrated members, one due to the war and two due to the influenza outbreak. Also, public enthusiasm for the club's activities and the sport of rowing in particular had in recent times waned. General interest had in fact diminished similarly a time or two previous during the club's nearly 40-year history, at which intervals Jim stepped in to reinvigorate his beloved organization. He had saved the club before and he was convinced he could save it again, especially now with retirement on the horizon and child-rearing responsibilities well behind him.

Before even being fully conscious he was doing so Jim had in fact begun considering other new ideas as well, such as how to best fill his time upon his retirement. Throwing himself headlong into leading the Mutuals and bringing the club back to its former glory promised to occupy his time substantially. He welcomed such a diversion. No one else wanted the job really. Once he let it be known to the membership that he was in the running for president, no one stepped up to oppose him.

Officially he was to take office January 1st, but in fact had been the de facto leader from the day he announced his intentions. Since November he had involved himself in planning the annual January Old Timers' Ball. In a club that was known to schedule a major social event monthly, the Old Timers' Ball was the most festive occasion of the entire year. At that November meeting he suggested assembling a chairman, chairman's assistants, and a floor committee, and nominated some names. Then he walked around the corner to his home to take a nap.

Lying on the divan he revealed to Hannah that he had made the decision to retire June first. She listened attentively to his justifications despite none being necessary. Jim had been a member of the police department since 1883. He had discussed with her his idea that his upcoming 40th anniversary in 1923 would be a good year to give up his badge, but began to think better of it when the previous September he had been in a William Street pawnshop as two gunmen entered and robbed the place. He had not revealed this incident to her before, just as he had hidden so many previous, so as not to worry her.

It was obvious the robbers were on dope. His hackles went up as they waved their pistols recklessly in his face. Being in plain clothes they did not realize Jim was a cop, and not having his pistol with him he wasn't about to flash his badge. For the umpteenth time he was forced to consider how close he had again come to dying, and decided right there on the spot that if he expected to have any quality retirement at all, the time to hang it up was nigh. It couldn't wait another three years.

Hannah replied, "Why even wait until June, then? What's the point? What's wrong with now? *Right* now? We always wanted to see California together, to cross the country on the train, to see the Arizona desert. It's time, Jim. The kids are all grown and out of the house. We're not gettin' no younger. My knees aren't gettin' no stronger. While I still can walk, I *want* to walk—to walk around California and New York City and Montreal and God knows where else. You promised."

He nodded in capitulation, knowing she was right. She didn't accuse him of stalling, but he recognized that his target dates were unnecessarily off in the future for no practical reason. While they were both still able it was only judicious, after devoting his life to the department, to say his farewells and seek some adventure for himself and his wife in their later years while they were both still spry enough to be able to enjoy the journey.

"Hannah, you know somethin'? You're right," Jim agreed. "I don't know why I keep puttin' it off. Let's go. Let's go to California this summer."

"Why wait for summer? It's summer in Los Angeles right now," she argued.

"Well...okay, yeah. All right, we'll see. Why don't you go ahead and start lookin' into it? I'm sure I can get us a special fare on the train out there. I hear Santa Barbara is beautiful, and they say in San Francisco these days you'd never know there'd ever been a earthquake at all."

"Oh my goodness! Really? I'm so excited!" Hannah rejoiced. "I got brochures!"

She went to the little Larkin desk in the corner of the parlor and opened the drawer. She took out a half dozen descriptive leaflets and waved them at Jim.

"I know them all practically by heart. Here, take a look."

Jim sat up, put on his spectacles, and began looking them over.

Almost daily thereafter a new brochure arrived in the mail. Hannah had gone downtown to the library and checked out a guidebook to California and another to Yosemite. She recalled to Jim an exhibition she and Junior had attended ten years earlier when a tour on the Orpheum circuit stopped in Buffalo exhibiting the natural color Autochrome photographic plates of the photographers Clifton and McGinnis. These had imprinted on her mind vividly. This true-color photographic process, the first made commercially available to the picture-taking public, had been invented by the French Lumière brothers in 1903.

Stunning color life-like photographs of California projected on a huge screen had quickened Hannah's heart, the very existence of such an idyllic place where winter was unknown consuming her thoughts. It seemed impossible. The slides included landscapes of Santa Barbara, the California missions, the springtime hillsides of Eagle Rock and Glendale carpeted in purple lupine amid a sea of brilliant orange California poppies. She longed to see these sights with her own eyes on the arm of her husband.

They concluded that Lent would provide the ideal opportunity to go away, what with all club activities suspended in deference to the Holy season. Fortuitously this too would coincide with the blooming season for the lupine and the California poppy. It had long been Hannah's dream to witness this natural marvel for herself. In the meantime, Jim began initiating the process of his retirement from the Buffalo Police Dept.

At the February 8th meeting of the Mutuals, newly elected President Jim Sullivan thought it appropriate to give a talk titled "Preparedness." He chastised members for using the winter months as an excuse to become lazy and pointed out that the kegs in the club's parlor were attracting members' dedication more faithfully than was the club's rowing machine. At that meeting he appointed a committee to oversee the two remaining socials and the Mardi Gras masked ball scheduled to take place prior to the discontinuance of all such gayety for the duration of Lent, after which he and Hannah would leave for their dream vacation to California.

Jim Jr. showed up at that February 8th meeting after first visiting his mother around the corner with her grandsons in tow, Little Jim age 5 and David, 20 months. Both were bundled head to toe in handsome wool snowsuits, the boys' cheeks flushed from the cold. She told her son about their California plans, now finalized. His smile disguised the fact that to visit California was an ardent dream of his wife's as well, and how jealous she might be upon hearing that her in-laws would soon be taking the trip that was her fondest desire.

Junior apologized to his father again for not attending the Old Timer's Ball the previous month due to his wife's again "not feeling well." Junior no longer elaborated empty excuses for his wife, and Hannah no longer asked. Junior's wife had cut her in-laws out of her life almost entirely. Once she had successfully bullied Junior to take up residence at her father's home, nevermore did she visit the house at N⁰ 16 Hamburg. Neither did she welcome her in-laws to the nearby Mackinaw Street residence of her father. The only way Hannah and Jim could see their own grandchildren was for Junior to appear with them as he had on this day, wifeless, at the Hamburg Street house.

Detective Sullivan did nothing to soften his recriminations regarding Junior's continued kowtowing to his wife's whims and commands.

"I warned you about that girl, Junior," he said, pausing to cough, "didn't I? She's keepin' you from us, away from yer mother an' me, an' your brother and sister. You know as well as me she's got a bad habit of shuttin' out people she don't approve of, people who threaten her. She's a fearful girl with no confidence at all in herself, Junior. She pushes away anybody who perturbs her in any way, anybody she thinks might keep her from gettin' what she wants or might want to take what she's already got. You should be able to see that plain enough, Junior. Watch out—or soon enough you'll find yourself havin' no family or friends left."

※※※

The following morning Jim awoke not feeling at all well. Hannah encouraged him to stay home from work, but he insisted on going into the office. His final day with the police department was set for the last day of February. He had a lot of loose ends to tie up, including details of the big retirement party being planned in his honor.

Then, an hour before his normal return time, he plodded slowly up the stairs, weak and hacking and wheezing with a bad cold. Hannah put him straight to bed with the hot water bottle and applied a camphor patch to his chest. She fed him spoonfuls of Venos cough cure. The following day the doctor was called, and upon his worsening the day after that, the doctor arrived again as well. He prescribed Owbridges lung tonic.

Hannah's concern was turning to fright. The brochures sitting on the desk mocked her for believing her long-held California dream might be coming true.

※※※

As Jim lay in bed battling against his latest illness, he began taking stock of his life.

He recalled pivotal events, so many of them unpleasant. He thought of each one of his dead children. Danny. Katie. Hannah. Johnny. He had visions of the four, all older than the day they died, waiting excitedly by the gates of heaven for him to finally reunite with them.

He recalled his days as a boy working for Sam Clemens, and found pleasure in recollecting things Sam had said to him, guidance provided him, and about things which he under the *nom de plume* Mark Twain had later written and lectured.

His mind rested on something that Sam had said, perhaps to a reporter. Sam was asked if he were afraid of death. Sam answered without a second's hesitation, "I do not fear death. I had been dead for billions and billions of years before I was born, and had not suffered the slightest inconvenience from it."

Of all the thought-provoking utterances that had sprung from Sam's delightful brain, none had challenged Jim's intellect more thoroughly than this.

He recalled as a boy the delight taken by nuns and priests in terrifying him and his playmates with the concept of eternity, of burning in hell or purgatory until the end of time, eons and eons into the never-ending future, and the horror he felt contemplating such a mind-boggling concept.

That is, until Sam's brilliant countermand brought him peace.

Sam had challenged people to consider just where they might have been before they were conceived, and how they felt during those billions of years waiting to be born. During all that time were they anxious, fearful, terrified, miserable?

No, they were not.

Jim had never even thought of such a thing previously, never even considered it, but once Sam proposed it he found himself lost in the possibilities. Indeed, where *had* he been during those countless centuries spent in waiting? More importantly, how did he feel? And the comforting answer was that he had no idea. No idea whatsoever where he had been, or whether he existed or not at that point. Most importantly, he did not suffer mentally or physically while waiting to be born, and thus he concluded comfortingly that he would not suffer mentally or physically once he was dead.

The Church had never offered any explanation of where any of us were before our conception. What was to hinder people from insisting on their own memory of what transpired prior to their life on earth? If someone had claimed to recall it, what could anyone else say to deny the past experience of some other person insisting to have a memory of it, or opinion about it, except to project their own fears and doubts?

Jim thought it comical that it had never occurred to him before Sam's proclamation. That he had more or less accepted the Church's unabashed glee in torturing its youngest followers with deeply disturbing precepts and pronouncements regarding the afterlife. These included the eternal fires of hell, or babies being born into this world with their little souls already sullied by an Original Sin they themselves never committed, and thus would be kept from their heavenly reward if not baptized.

He roiled at how cruel a God the Church was promoting in declaring such dire consequences, and in doing so what was revealed about the sentient stability of those officers within the Church who derived such twisted satisfaction in their spreading such bleak and apocalyptic prophesy.

Indeed it seemed that the main goal of the Church was to minimize as much as possible any true joy or independence that human beings might experience during their one and only life on this earth.

In the haze of mounting fever Jim recollected the anguish of his mother Mary McGrady as her final illness advanced and she herself struggled with the Church's dire warnings of hell and purgatory. She had fretted to the point of self-torture about what lay in store for her as her last days played out. Her misery as she lay dying, Jim believed, stemmed not so much from the actual physical illness she suffered, but rather the deplorable mental torment inflicted by her unquestioning acceptance of Church dogma.

In these twilight days Jim Sullivan was once again made aware of just how deeply indebted to Sam Clemens he was, the man's words, his viewpoints, his encouragement and counsel. Sam Clemens had been the lighthouse of his youth—and now he was proving to be the friendly beacon of his final hours.

I enjoyed a peaceful unconscious nonexistence during the countless eons before I was conceived, and I will enjoy a peaceful unconscious nonexistence during the countless eons following my death, Jim concluded peacefully.

❦

On Valentine's Day Jim was transported to Deaconess Hospital by ambulance, suffering from severe pneumonia.

Junior left work to oversee his father's care. He and his mother and siblings Nellie and David hovered bedside at the hospital as Jim wheezed heavily. The doctor advised them to prepare for the worst.

Hannah was beside herself.

"This can't be happening!" she cried to Ruth, who had just then arrived to comfort her. "We were only now setting out on our dream trip to California at long last! He's retiring in less than two weeks, for God's sake!"

Jim's brother JP arrived without Annie, who herself was ill.

The family was anguished witnessing husband, father, and brother struggle to breathe. Finally, fighting valiantly against drowning in his own phlegm, Jim Sullivan's heart gave out from the strain of it all.

The family lingered thereafter for an hour, kissing him, holding him, saying goodbye. Hannah was absolutely bereft. All their future plans, years in the planning and dreaming, up in smoke. She couldn't even pray, so dispossessed was she.

"He wanted to die in his own bed, as do I! Not in this terrible antiseptic institution!" she blurted from out of nowhere.

Before leaving the hospital Junior filled out the death certificate and instructed that his father's body be released to the Driscoll Funeral Home. He knew Dan Driscoll would take good care of him.

❦

Dan Driscoll's assistant undertakers Robert Sinclair, age 36, and Edward Rogers, age 28, arrived at the hospital a few hours later to collect the body. While at the Driscoll Mortuary, during the process of embalming, the attendants conspired to remove the diamond ring from Jim's finger and substitute a paste version.

When Jim's body was returned to the family home for the wake, Junior removed the ring and put it on his own finger. Upon noticing the stone was loose he took it to the jeweler who had sold the ring to his father. The jeweler informed Junior that the ring, although similar, was not the ring he had sold to his father. The original had been substituted with one having a stone of cut glass. The police were notified.

At first the police thought the crime had taken place at the hospital, but ultimately the two funeral home attendants confessed and were arrested, and none too gently. They had earned the wrath of the entire Buffalo Police Department by their choice of victim: a revered fellow peacekeeper, and the most vulnerable example of one, a dead man. Their bail was set at $1000, an excessive figure that reflected the outrage of the members of the force.

Somehow that amount was quickly raised, and the men were released from jail on bond. Junior's wife Mary Ellen was beside herself with righteous indignation, especially misplaced for someone who had never tried to disguise her dislike for the victim of the crime—not that she'd ever set envious eyes on that ring, of course.

"They're allowin' them criminals out of jail until their trial?" she harrumphed officiously, "So they can just go out and steal again? Well, if it was up to me they'd be sent to the Penitentiary and given nothing but bread and water!"

❦❦❦

The Hamburg St. house was jammed with those who had come to pay their last respects. Hannah and Junior especially took note of the many people who arrived unexpectedly, people they hadn't seen in years, or even decades. Priests and nuns, a whole battalion of police patrolmen, detectives and captains, old and dear friends, former teachers, distant neighbors they hardly knew, complete strangers who shared grateful stories of Jim's kindnesses to them, pawnshop owners, every single member of the Mutual Rowing Club past and present, their wives and older children, the Mayor.

Hannah's brother David J. Nugent came in from Milwaukee, not with his wife and their children, but rather with the four year old daughter he had fathered illegitimately with his Buffalo mistress. This daughter he was raising alongside his other children, those birthed by his wife Minnie in Wisconsin.

Hannah had not expected such a brazen mockery of his primary family as she prepared a bed for her brother and niece in her home shortly before his impending arrival. David stopped by Hamburg Street with little Patricia after deboarding at the train station to inform his sister he'd be staying elsewhere with his mistress and their daughter if she needed to get hold of him.

Hannah had never met the little girl before. She appeared quite precocious and spoiled and chubby. She clutched tightly to a little brown paper bag filled with penny candy from which she ate continually. In Hannah's opinion the girl looked nothing like David nor any other family member. She pondered if perhaps the girl was not her brother's after all, if David might have been hoodwinked by a conniving woman looking to be rescued from the aftermath of her whoring ways. Even in her grief Hannah was stunned by her brother's narcissism and detachment, but said nothing of it.

David Nugent spent just one hour at the wake, thankfully arriving with neither mistress nor love child in tow. Fingy Conners arrived and spent some minutes huddled with his trusted henchman discussing business in hushed tones. Still fuming over Hannah's long-ago attempt at deceiving him, Fingy uttered but a few sparse words of condolence to the widow. Now that Jim Sullivan was dead and gone there'd be no occasion whatsoever that Fingy Conners need tolerate the woman's presence—or so he thought.

Ruth McGowan was present when Fingy arrived, and no longer a slave to drugs, boldly stared him down, consumed with imaginings of herself stabbing him over and over and over again. He did not seem to notice her.

It was apparent that Jim Sullivan had touched many lives. There were quite a few heartwarming and funny stories recounted about him, many unfamiliar to the family's ears. Although quiet and reserved by nature, Jim had loved telling others various reminisces of his exploits, and these in turn were repeated to the family.

The entirety of the alderman's brood attended. For some of JP's children it was their first time back in the First Ward since they had moved away almost five years previous.

Junior arrived with his spoiled bride Mary Ellen, who, had she not attended to pay her final respects, Hannah in her anger and grief had planned to march over to Mackinaw Street to slap across the face.

Retired police chief and Jim's childhood friend Mike Regan arrived, the now-private citizen insensitively bragging about his new private detective agency and his fine office in the Ellicott Square building, and inappropriately using the occasion to announce his political plans to run for the office of Sheriff of Erie County.

In its own way the wake was an uplifting occasion as it reunited many people who had lost touch. As might be predicted they departed the event promising to get together again and to renew their old friendships, but as might also be predicted, they would never carry though with those vows.

The morning of the funeral the pallbearers arrived at the house to perform their solemn duty. The detail consisted entirely of Jim Sullivan's fellow detectives with Police Chief Ryan at the lead. Jim was eulogized warmly by Father Lynch at the funeral Mass, and afterward, accompanied by forty motors following the hearse with traffic cops halting cartage and auto traffic all the way down South Park Ave. to Holy Cross Cemetery. James E. Sullivan was interred next to the final resting place that held the remains of his and Hannah's four predeceased babies.

After the funeral a reception was held at the family home, which was the third house from the Buffalo River. As friends and neighbors comforted her and partook of refreshments, Hannah's mind wandered elsewhere. Mrs. Manahar from a few doors down, trying to make conversation during a lull, admired a fine Japanese vase Jim had once brought home.

"Take it," Hannah offered, "it's yours."

"Oh my, no! I couldn't Hannah. I didn't mean..."

"No, Mrs. Manahar," she interrupted firmly, "I insist."

"I...I just can't," Mrs. Manahar replied, sensing Hannah's great upset. She knew it was the grief talking. Empty-handed, she soon enough bid Hannah her goodbyes after offering any assistance for whatever reason Hannah might need in the coming weeks.

As the afternoon wore on, Hannah grew quieter and more morose. Looking around she realized that only those she trusted most were still present—her church ladies and Ruth. She suddenly stood and asked Ruth if she might help her move a beautiful tapestry upholstered walnut footstool upon which Mary Sweeney's tired swollen feet rested.

"Oh!" exclaimed Sweeney as Hannah mindlessly pulled it out from under her. The piece was more unwieldy than it was heavy. Dutifully Ruth took her end, and following Hannah's silent lead, helped carry it down the stairs toward the street.

Only then did Ruth ask Hannah, "Where are we taking it, dear?"

"This way," Hannah answered coolly as they passed through the open gate and headed in the direction of the river.

As they approached the riverbank the increasingly troubled Ruth again asked, "Where did you say we're going with this, Hannah?" Ruth knew that grief did strange things to people and tried her best to accommodate.

Once they'd crossed South Street to the river side of that thoroughfare, Hannah put her end down next to the rail and rested a moment, catching her breath. She observed that the river still had quite a bit of free-floating ice due to the thaw that had been taking place all week. Ruth watched her closely, not knowing what to make of her friend's queer behavior.

Suddenly Hannah raised her foot as if to step up onto the stool. Ruth panicked. "No!" she exclaimed as she took ahold of Hannah's elbow and dragged her away from the rail. "I won't let you do it!"

"Do what?"

"Jump. I won't let you jump!"

"Oh God, Ruth! I wasn't gonna jump. I was just scratchin' my ankle," Hannah chuckled as she took up her end once again and stood waiting. Ruth paused a moment before following her lead. Hannah hoisted her end atop the rail and rested it there.

"What in God's name are you *doing*, Hannah?" Ruth said, no longer trying to disguise her alarm.

"We're gettin' rid of it, Ruth. It's plunder, plain and simple! I won't be havin' this loot in my house no more. Jim's gone now, so this has to go too."

"But Hannah, it's a lovely thing. Jim brought it home for you. A gift to the wife he loved. You're just upset right now. Wait a while why don't you? Give it time. You can't just chuck it into the river! Why, donate it to Pets' rummage sale if you must, but don't throw it away!"

"God don't want this tainted stuff in his holy church, Ruth! Somebody stole it. It's ill-gotten goods."

"Hannah you don't know that for certain. The pawnshops are full of things people bought and paid for that later on they needed to borrow money against."

"Then why was it still in the pawnshop all them years later?" Hannah questioned. "I'll tell you why, Ruth. Because it didn't belong to the family that pawned it, that's why. It was pawned by the thief who swiped it!"

And with that Hannah pitched it into the cold black water.

"There!"

Immediately and with a determined stride she headed back toward the house.

"You comin' Ruth?" she called over her shoulder to her befuddled friend.

Ruth followed, noticing all the ladies standing in the window who had just witnessed the act with mouths agape.

Walking inside, Hannah began gathering stashed items from their various hiding places and placing these on the dining room table: Crystal. Nellie's violin. The Japanese vase. Ivory scrimshaw. Miniature oil paintings in gutta percha frames. Austrian porcelain figurines. The works.

The ladies watched curiously in silence. As Hannah systematically emptied the shelves and the mantel and the sideboard and the end tables of objects, she handed the items to those attending her to pile atop the dining table. When finished, she stood over that which she had convinced herself was pillage, items that made her blood boil every time she was forced to take the feather duster to them, and made a little speech.

"You all know how much I loved my husband. But he was not a perfect man. This example sittin' right here tells the story. Jim was in charge of the pawnshops detail and I know for a fact that sometimes for whatever reason he averted his eyes to certain things and the men he did this favor for rewarded him with some pretty things.

"I know some are beautiful and some are valuable but they are the takin's of thieves, and in the end, they're dirty. I been livin' with these here spoils for years now and they been eatin' away at my Catholic soul ever since. I know I got to get right with God if I expect to enter the gates of heaven, and I got to make sure nobody profits from this loot lest I anger Him. So I got to dispose of it in the dirty river where dirty pickins are deserved to be disposed. If any of yous want to help me, I'll be grateful. But I won't be holdin' it against nobody who don't."

And with that, each and every member of the group took hold of a remarkable keepsake and followed Hannah outside and over to the river rail. One by one, as perplexed onlookers gaped and cars beeped their horns, in went the crystal, the musical instruments, the paintings, the silver, and any and all other pawnshop mementos that had been presented to her over the years by her loving but recently dead husband.

It was a curious parade, the likes of which in the First Ward was unprecedented in anyone's memory.

After the dining table had been cleared of its sinful burden, Hannah set about opening cabinet doors and closets to retrieve items she had long hidden away so as not to be offended by the guilty sight of them.

Chief among these was a sterling silver menorah. *What was that man thinking?* she wondered as she shook her perplexed head at the Jewish candelabra. For a solid hour the procession of ladies costumed in mourning black moved back and forth between the Sullivan house and the riverside railing. Neighbors gathered to bear silent witness.

Crystal facets refracted the weak winter sun's rays as a Waterford candy bowl, a bud vase and a salt cellar sailed through the air to their watery end. A periwinkle-blue Roseville urn stunningly decorated with yellow sunflowers landed intact on a slushy ice floe failing to submerge. It just rested there undamaged on its lethargic journey downstream taunting Lizzie Hartnett, whose heart broke upon launching from her reluctant hand the splendid piece she had long coveted.

"Hello, God," Hannah prayed at river's edge, "I know your only son was born a Jew and I hope you won't be holdin' this here against me," she said before letting the menorah fly.

One by one a treasure trove of valuable *objects d'art* that would have brightened the lives of others, earned money for the church, or quickened the hearts of collectors, sank beneath the surface of the Buffalo River. The heavier items embedded themselves deep into the black muck at the bottom, waiting there perhaps for some future dredging operation to resurrect—all that is, except for the lovely little ballerina music box that Mary Sweeney had secreted in the folds of her mourning dress. She had looked around to ensure that here were no witnesses before dropping the object into a dirty snowbank accidentally-on-purpose in order to divert from the act of her picking up a sooty snowball along with it and chucking that icy orb into the river in its stead. No one was close enough to witness her clever sleight-of-hand.

But for now, at least in Hannah's mind, the collection of guilty treasures was gone, once and for all.

"Good riddance!" she sighed as the last piece made a sharp report sounding like *plunk!* as it hit the surface and disappeared. It did not escape her at this moment of finality that 26 years earlier in this exact spot as she stood shrieking at the kitchen window she had witnessed her seven year old son Johnny sink beneath the same waters, destined to never resurface alive.

Junior heard the astonishing account of what had transpired at his mother's house straight from the lips of Mary Sweeney that very afternoon after she stopped to knock on the front door as she passed the Diggins' house on Mackinaw Street.

Hearing her story, at first Junior worried for his mother's sanity. But upon Sweeney's describing Hannah's reasonings for the odd ritual he nodded agreeably and said yes, he understood.

Mary then confidentially whispered into Junior's ear that Hannah, after tossing a gold trinket into the drink, had recalled to her that Junior's wife Mary Ellen had admired quite a few of those pawnshop things, as in friendlier times Mary Ellen had mentioned this to her. Junior couldn't help but deduce from this that at least in part his mother had gained some satisfaction in the disposing of those coveted treasures rather than allow her contemptuous daughter-in-law to inherit them someday.

After saying her piece Mary Sweeney continued on her way. Having made it far enough down the street to feel it safe to retrieve it from her pocket to admire, the soft chiming of the miniature orchestrina she'd rescued inspired a dance in her step.

Junior had gone back inside where he put on his hat and coat and wrapped a wool muffler around his neck.

"Where you goin'?" asked his wife curiously.

"Confession," he answered, and immediately set out for the police station to drop the charges against the two men who had stolen his father's diamond.

-The story continues in Volume 5-

MORE BOOKS BY RICHARD SULLIVAN

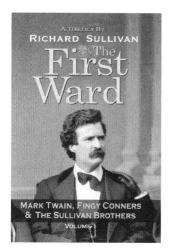

The First Ward

"...engrossing. The First Ward is vividly cinematic." — LA Weekly

"...engrossing saga..." — Publishers Weekly

"Sullivan has found a clever way of taking what we know and building a story around it. Samuel Clemens is brought to life with real believability... wonderfully involving." —Buffalo Spree magazine.

Based on real people and historical events, the immigrant Irish of Buffalo's First Ward and their offspring struggle to claim their share of the American Dream via less than honorable ways. Murder, disease, violence and terrible injustice were part and parcel of everyone's lives in the struggle to survive in hopes of achieving success whether it be on the straight and narrow, or not.

The First Ward II: Fingy Conners & The New Century

The saga of megalomaniac William J. Conners continues as he pursues further millions via backroom deals and illegal alliances. Based on actual historical events and the real people who drove them, **The First Ward II** documents the rivalry between dock-walloper turned millionaire Fingy Conners and two brothers who emerged from the Buffalo Orphan Asylum to claim political power, Alderman John P. Sullivan and Detective Sergeant James E. Sullivan. Their lives intersect with the giants of their day; heavyweight champion of the World, cousin John L. Sullivan, humorist Mark Twain, US Presidents William McKinley and Teddy Roosevelt, and publisher William Randolph Hearst. Additionally, the murder of Edwin Burdick grips the nation's attention and Detective Sullivan finds himself in the thick of it.

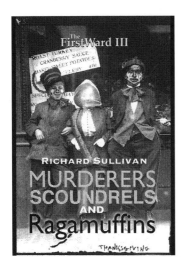

The First Ward III *Murderers, Scoundrels and Ragamuffins*

The abduction and murder of a little girl changes the freedoms that parents up until then allowed their children. The city is in an uproar as a Chinese laundryman is accused of the crime. Anti-Chinese sentiment explodes, affecting immigrants as far away as Toronto.

Buffalo's Old Home Week celebration is wildly successful, effectively doubling the city's population during the long celebration during which it is claimed by the police that crime was non-existent.

The railroads commandeer the city's streets, laying over 150 miles of illegal track within Buffalo city limits, bringing chaos and death.

Alderman Sullivan's son is the victim of sexual abuse. When President Taft comes to town, Detective Jim Sullivan zealously guards his charge. Famous cousin John L. Sullivan, heavyweight champion of the world, arrives in town and joins the fun at the Mutual Rowing Club's Calico Ball.

The Murphy clan seeks revenge for Fingy Conners' hired thugs murdering one of their own. Fingy Conners' only son meets tragedy. Fingy establishes a charity fund for the families of firemen killed in a terrible blaze, then schemes to keep all the money for himself. Fingy becomes Chairman of the Democratic Party of New York State. Collier's Magazine outs Fingy Conners as a murderer.

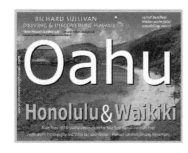

Driving & Discovering Hawaii: Oahu
Winner, Travel Journalism Award For "**Best Hawaii Guidebook**" by **American Airlines** and the **Hawaii Visitors and Conventions Bureau**. Named *"Best Hawaii Guidebook"* by the Los Angeles Times, the Chicago Sun-Times, the San Diego Union-Tribune, the Orange County Register, the San Jose Mercury, and The Oregonian. Read the **RAVE REVIEWS** on AMAZON.com

Los Angeles Times:
"I'd be surprised if there is a hidden byway or corner of beach or town that Sullivan has not revealed here --even on the leeward side of the island, which remains relatively unknown to visitors."

Chicago Sun Times:
"A must read is Richard Sullivan's Driving & Discovering Oahu, the best guidebook on the market."

San Diego Union-Tribune:
"Visitors contemplating a driving trip around Oahu will greatly enhance the journey by packing along a guidebook, Driving & Discovering Oahu, by Richard Sullivan... The text is fresh and insightful and the photo tips are of tremendous value to anyone wondering where to stop for the best views in unfamiliar territory."

Orange County Register (CA):
"...the best guidebook on the market."

Driving & Discovering Maui and Molokai
Another beautiful guidebook from award-winning author and photographer Richard Sullivan. Each photo is numbered and its exact location pinpointed on an adjacent map, making this Maui and Molokai guidebook your best bet for unforgettable sightseeing and great restaurants, as well as for vacation photography and video.

"A picture is worth a thousand words... which is why the 300+ beautiful photos in Driving & Discovering Maui and Molokai guidebook make this the best available, and a real bonanza for photographers searching for their best island shots. Nobody puts the "guide" in guidebook like Richard Sullivan"
-photonet.com

Driving & Discovering Hawaii: Oahu Spectacular Beaches

Oahu Spectacular! Beaches is loaded with links to Google Maps for each beach:
— Google StreetView images for each beach as it will be viewed from the highway from both directions so you can easily recognize it from the road **(many Oahu beaches have no signage)**.
— Daily updated wind, wave, tide, and general conditions of each beach.
— 360 degree view of the beach where available.
— Satellite view of the area does double duty by also showing the exact spot the photographer stood to take the photo.
— Hawaii's Greatest Driving Adventures Map to the island's beaches with detailed notes on each.
— Each Beach Page provides a beautiful photo as well as icons depicting the **attractions and amenities** available there (swimming, surfing, restrooms, food trucks, etc.). GPS coordinates help you find your way. Everything you need to choose, find and determine current conditions at your desired beach destination is just a click away! Don't go to Hawaii without it!

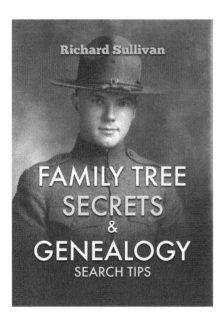

Family Tree Secrets & Genealogy Search Tips

Richard Sullivan uncovered such an avalanche of information on his previously-unknown ancestors that he has turned their saga into the historical novel trilogy, The First Ward. Garnered from the author's own personal experience in researching over two hundred family members he shares his knowledge here with those who are tracing their family genealogy.

Sullivan suggests traditional as well as non-traditional modes and areas of research and provides tips to avoid repetition and frustration that will result in a broader research net being cast. The author provides links **(LIVE links in the eBook version!)** and includes a wealth of clever sources, as well as tips and tricks to apply when using online search engines to maximize both the researcher's time and discoveries. His narrative clearly explains how he connected the dots, demonstrating how he utilized one find to lead to another, and then another.

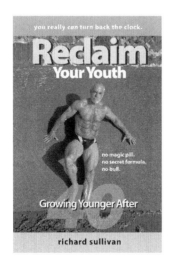

Reclaim Your Youth: Growing Younger After 40

Science reminds us that the more robust our muscle mass, the faster we burn fat and the stronger and more agile we are. The elderly don't fall down because they're old. They fall because their leg muscles have atrophied to such a degree they can no longer hold them upright. Increased muscle mass is your guarantee that you'll still be walking—and running—when your contemporaries may be using walkers.

Looking great *below* the neck is just as important as from the neck up. **Reclaim Your Youth** isn't about magic pills or the Secrets of the Hollywood Stars, because these things don't exist.

It's all about eating more nutritionally and less recreationally, and challenging your muscles so as to reverse their decline.

Made in the USA
Middletown, DE
03 November 2019